DRIVEN TO IT

DRIVEN TO IT

An Autobiography

JEAN OVERTON FULLER

MICHAEL RUSSELL

First published in Great Britain 2007
by Michael Russell (Publishing) Ltd
Wilby Hall, Wilby, Norwich NR16 2JP

Typeset in Sabon by Waveney Typesetters
Wymondham, Norfolk
Printed and bound in Great Britain
by Biddles Ltd, King's Lynn, Norfolk

FOR TIM
WHO DROVE ME TO IT

Contents

One

My father was a soldier, a captain in the Indian Army. He was shot in the afternoon of 4 November 1914, four months before I was born, in an ill-judged attack on Tanga in German East Africa. His original regiment was the 88th Carnatics, which he loved, but by some rearrangement he was now in the 63rd Palincottahs. He had confidence in their colonel, but thought it unfortunate they were placed under the command of a general who had never seen active service. This over-confident general had given the Germans forty-eight hours' notice of his intent to attack Tanga, expecting them to leave. Instead they spent the forty-eight hours bringing into Tanga practically every gun in East Africa. It was a massacre. The white officers, conspicuous amongst the dark faces of their men, were quickly picked off. With his dying breath my father said to the sepoy at his side, 'Memsahib ko mera salaam do', which meant in the language of his men, 'Give my salaams, my respects, my love, to my wife.' My mother had a letter telling her this from a Mrs Dallas, in India, to whom the sepoy had reported my father's last words As for the action in which my father died the only printed reference to it I have come across is one of four and a half lines terminating: 'Tanga stands as a fruitful lesson on how not to start a colonial campaign.'*

Just after the end of the war Mother took me to the zoo. It was not my first visit to that place of wonderment but this time we achieved the lion house. As we were coming out I saw three unusually tall men, with brown faces, wearing turbans. They were looking at us, and Mother was looking at them.

They hesitated, then – in apparent recognition – they came right up, and said, 'Memsahib!'

She asked them, 'Are you here for the celebrations?'

Yes, they were brought to take part in the procession.

'And you thought to see the zoo at the same time?'

Yes. They were speaking of Captain Fuller Sahib and I knew they meant my father. They were telling her a lot of things and I wished I

* *The First World War*, Cyril Falls (Longmans, 1960) p. 82.

[1]

could have understood them. I did gather they had not been with him when he was killed. It was after their paths had been parted. But they had been told all about it and were very saddened. They kept looking down at me with the most eager curiosity, and asked if this was the daughter of Captain Fuller Sahib.

Mother confirmed that I was.

Then they all bent very low before me, so low that I could see the whites of their eyes, saying, 'Salaam! Salaam! Salaam!'

After we had parted from them Mother said they were from my father's *old* regiment. Sepoys. She had never actually spoken to them before, but they were men she had seen my father drill on the parade-ground at Fort William, Calcutta. 'Then my eyes dropped to their shoulders and I saw the Carnatic flash. I'm glad you've seen the type of man your father commanded. Glad they salaamed you. To get their heads lower than yours, it had to be a very low salaam.'

During those early years we moved about, Mother and I – Dulwich, Surbiton, Bournemouth, Kew, back to Bournemouth, then Farnham, where we stayed at the Bush Hotel. Then Mother told me we were moving again, to Beckenham, where we would have a house of our own, 'with electric light'. This was to be 13 Manor Road. I asked if Gilby would come too.

Gilby was Mother's father, Colonel Smith. He had retired on his sixtieth birthday, 14 February 1918, and returned from Salonika to take up the post of Commandant of the Royal Military Hospital at Aldershot. It was to join him we had moved to Farnham, where we could all stay together. I had been told to call him 'Grandfather', but then Mother said he didn't want to be called Grandfather any more because it made him feel old. I was to think of another name for him. As he was the biggest, strongest man I had ever known, I thought to call him after the biggest, strongest dog I had ever known, which was a Great Dane called Gilby. He seemed to find this compliment acceptable. He came at first for only two days at a time, but then to stay altogether.

My transfer from a cot to a proper bed in what had been prepared as my nursery, the front first floor bedroom, coincided with the engagement of Miss Letheren to be my nursery governess. She was white-haired and wore gold-rimmed glasses. I knew Mother thought she was a bit simple, but I liked her. Her room was in the attic. Mother's room looked over the garden and Gilby's had the worst view, merely of the side of the next house.

I was allowed into Gilby's study for him to read to me for half an hour every evening. He familiarised me with Coleman's *British Butterflies* (1860) and introduced me to more formidable work, Kirby's *Lepidoptera: Butterflies*, daunting in that it only gave the names in Latin. He introduced me to Maunders's *Treasury of Natural History*, bound in leather with gilt tool – all these books I still have – and showed me the pictures in *Livingstone's Travels*. He also read Kipling's *Just So* stories, then from *Treasure Island* and said I should imagine myself to be Jim Hawkins hidden in the apple barrel listening to the pirates plotting how they should slit our throats. This was so exciting that I was sorry when Miss Letheren came to collect me and put me in the bath before putting me in bed; so Gilby handed the book over to Miss Letheren to continue reading aloud to me. She did her best but could not bring out the words 'lousy swab' with the vibrance he did.

Arthur Overton (Gilby's first cousin) was at that time a student at the Royal Academy and Mother at the Beckenham School of Art, and when he called they always used to show each other the drawings they had been making. One day Mother made some mention of the nude model. Poor Miss Letheren gasped, 'Are they people? I thought they were statues. They had no clothes on.'

Mother taught me to observe the effects of light on colour, the way it came in and shone upon objects, and the shadows which helped make objects, such as an orange, look round and three-dimensional, not just flat disks. And she warned me to note the yellowing effect of electric light. It was yellow, so that shining upon mauve, it took the colour out of it, turning it brownish, because yellow was its complementary, cancelling it out. Blue was all right, but was turned greenish, red all right but turned towards the orange; all yellows, of course, very yellow. This was important to remember when choosing curtains or evening dress.

I did a lot of drawing, mainly of horses, starting always from the topmost points of their ears and working downwards to end with the hoofs. Working on the floor, I did it with the ears towards me, the hoofs away. Some people called this upside down, but Mother said that in India she had noticed sometimes that their servants held a picture upside down to look at it and she wondered if that was not the natural way for the eye to focus.

Later, after she had taken me up to London to the Natural History Museum in South Kensington and I had stood amazed before the endless skeleton of the diplodocus and walked its length, I drew a diplodocus, fleshed out, with a grey thick skin like that of a hippopotamus; he stretched the whole length of the longest sheet of paper I could find, but his head bent down to his nest, wherein was a little one, and just the head and beginning of the neck of the other parent. I knew by now that to make a baby needed both a father and a mother, but Mother, viewing my picture, said that snakes and lizards, like birds, laid eggs, but unlike birds did not stay to hatch them out and feed them, and she rather fancied diplodocuses went like snakes and lizards rather than like birds. But I did not alter them. My diplodocuses were good parents and were obviously bringing their baby twigs to eat, and the nest in which it was standing up was round like a bird's.

Mother began collecting my drawings and paintings and sending to a Mr Ablet in connection with a scheme for fostering 'The Art of Childhood'. Every so often he would send back a red book into which he had pasted what he judged the best of them and made his comments on them. The diplodocus family went in.

Gilby had always enjoyed taking me out. Now that my legs were stronger, he took me into the woods of the Foxgrove Golf Club (of which he and Mother were members), and from there to the pond. Here he said we could play Robinson Crusoe; there was an island we could be marooned on. He picked me up but accidentally pitched me into the water. He knew Mother wouldn't be pleased.

So then we went there not to play Robinson Crusoe but to fish. We could find no fish but, bending to put his hand in the water Gilby brought up what looked like little bits of sodden twig. 'Ah, I thought so. Caddis worms!' These tiny creatures with legs either made their homes in twigs or pulled bits of grit around themselves to make the case for their bodies. We collected some of each kind, putting them into our jam-jar, also some water-boatmen, that scudded about upside down, and some beautiful, curled, ramshorn snails. We took them all home. On my next birthday I woke to find them transferred into a magnificent aquarium accompanied by two goldfish which Gilby had bought for me. There was water weed to keep the water fresh and feed the snails. What he wanted to find was newts. Newts weren't rare, he said, there were always newts in the canal at Horncastle (where he had grown up). 'This must be a barren area.' But we found frog-spawn, toad-spawn and a grown-up toad. I had it in my hand when Miss Letheren told me 'Put that dirty toad down!' I was surprised, because he was a clean toad, but obediently put him down on the table. Then she exclaimed, 'Not on the tablecloth!' It had been laid for lunch. I loved my toad.

Caterpillars were a further joy. Gilby told me to define an insect as a creature, evolving through four forms, ova, larva, pupa and imago, or egg, caterpillar, chrysalis and perfect insect, having six legs, compound eyes and, in the perfect state, wings. Spiders were obviously not insects, as they had eight legs, and none of the other required characteristics. Neither were centipedes or millipedes; all these were myriapoda, 'many leggers'. He said snails and slugs were called gastropods, because they walked on their stomachs – which were in fact composed of an infinite number of legs too small to see. 'If you draw your finger up their underneaths, you can feel all the little legs crawling.' But caterpillars he found me, I don't know where, and brought them home. They were creamy white, with black and gold markings along the sides. He said they were those of the magpie moth, *abraxas*. He brought in with them a sprig of the bush he had found them on, euonymus, and set it in a jar of water to keep it fresh, and he bought me a caterpillar-cage in which to rear them. I noticed that they had two legs at the back, by which they would hold on whilst drawing their bodies up into a loop. They were 'loopers' he said, and the pair at the back were not true legs but pro-legs. The true legs were the six at the front. I kept them on the table by my bedside in the nursery, so that I could watch them last thing at night and first thing in the morning. After some weeks they began to grow sleepy, ceasing to eat or move; then they somehow shrugged themselves into cases they were exuding around themselves, and looked as though they were dead. As there was now nothing more to watch, they were removed to a table on the landing. Weeks passed, and then one night Miss Letheren woke me, saying, 'Your grandfather says I'm to get you up. One of your chrysalises is hatching.' Something hastily thrown around me, I hastened to the landing. Mother, in a dressing-gown, emerging from her bedroom, had obviously been similarly summoned. Gilby, glowing with pride, bid us all watch. The chrysalis was wriggling. At the top, where it had taken the shape of an insect's head, an opening appeared, and then a head. Then legs ... but where were the wings? Horrified, I thought my moth had been born deformed, but he assured me that the wings were there, would uncrumple, unfurl, grow, and that it might take an hour. We watched it climb to a twig from which it could hang upside down, and indeed there were the wings, uncrumpled, unfurled, creamy white, with the black markings and the gold stripe transferred from the sides of the caterpillar to the borders of the wings. By what means, what magic, had this transference been made? (After I was grown up, I wrote a poem about this, which was printed in *Outposts*.) For me, it had the impact of spiritual reassurance.

Miss Letheren said to me one day, 'I know your mother doesn't want you to be taught religion, but I don't think she could object to my teaching you the Lord's Prayer.' And she taught me to say, 'Our Father, which art in Heaven ...' I was not sure what it meant, but she said I could add to it 'a prayer from your heart': '"Please God bless Mummy and Gilby and Mr Overton", if you think you should pray for him, "and Miss Letheren", if you would like to pray for me, "and all whom I love and make me a good girl."' This I did, though to be doing something hidden from Mother made me feel naughty, so I told her. She asked what prayers I had been taught. Again I told her. She supposed it wouldn't do any harm, but didn't look pleased. I still pray for all whom I love, to this day.

Mother did not only paint, she played the piano a lot and sometimes Cousin Arthur would do so with her. I did not altogether welcome this as it was something in which I could not join and I had to be quiet. On one occasion they said they were going to play a duet and they sat down side by side on the piano stool. In order not to disturb them I stood on a chair by the window to catch flies for my toad. Unfortunately I overbalanced and came down on our beautiful brass table, scattering all the brass animals on it and the silver spirit kettle. More unfortunately, the brass table upturned on its rim so that I came down astride it and cut myself between my legs. Mother had to take me to the bathroom to wash and dress the wound. It put me off music for years, and even today the word 'duets' has an ill sound.

Other visitors we had were Colonel Ventris from Dulwich (I think only at the beginning of our stay in Manor Road), Mr Gawthorn, who made a portrait of Mother that was 'accepted not hung' at the Royal Academy, and Mr Neale who was starting an airline from Paris to India. Gilby put his entire gratuity, received on retirement from the Army, into it. Mother advised him to put in only a part but he put in the lot. Mr Neale came with Mother and me when she formed part of a sketching group that went together to a small place called Wisant, near Wimereux in France. It was my first journey on the sea, by paddle steamer. Going through my box of coloured chalks, I noticed there was one I hardly ever used and wondered if I should give it to Mr Neale. Miss Letheren said that was not a nice approach. A present should be of my best chalk not my worst. I hadn't thought of it that way and didn't give him anything.

Mr Neale's airline to India never got off the ground, and Mr Neale vanished, as did Gilby's gratuity. Unwilling to think ill of a man he had thought all right, Gilby said he was sure Neale's intentions had been honest, and always hoped he would turn up some day, returning the money. Mother was sorry for a different reason. The return on the investment of the sum had been promised to her.

Gilby, although so interested in small creatures, hunted. I did not like this, nor did Mother. One morning when I joined her as I always did for her early morning cup of tea, which the maid brought to her in bed, she said I should not go down to breakfast because of something that had happened to Gilby. He had been out otter hunting and on his way home must, he thought, have gone to sleep at the wheel, for the next thing he knew he was lying on the road, face downwards, trapped by the overturned car. He thought it must catch fire and supposed he was going to be burned to death. But then he heard another car approaching and yelled with all his might. Suddenly there were three men lifting the car off him and carrying him into their own. They were three Russians, refugees from the Revolution, they said. He thought, landed without papers, but would keep that thought to himself. He directed them to 13 Manor Road and they deposited him at the door. He asked them in but they made off. The first Mother knew of what had happened was when he knocked on her bedroom door, opened it and said, 'Don't be frightened' – so she knew there was something to be frightened of – before he put on the light. He apologised for disturbing her and asked her to pick a piece of wood out of his ear. She said I should not go down to breakfast as he would look too awful. But I said I wanted to, and went.

When I entered the dining-room he had *The Times* raised so as to cover his face. He asked, 'Has your Mother told you I don't look pretty?'

'Yes.'

He lowered his paper. His head was so swollen that it was round as a pumpkin and his face was purple, excepting where there was the contrasting yellow of the iodine. I hoped he was not going to look like that always.

While Florrie brought in the tea he raised the paper again.

Mother had always poured out the tea, but the chair from which she did the honours was now vacant. I asked, 'Would you like me to pour out?'

It surprised me how heavy the teapot was but I managed.

He then paid me the only compliment I ever had from him. 'You'd have made a good soldier. You've got a good stomach.'

An inspector called one day and said it had come to his attention there was a child in the house of over five years old who was not attending school.

Mother said I had a nursery governess who was giving me reading and other lessons; she herself, being an artist, was teaching me art, and her father was teaching me natural history; it was a subject upon which Colonel Smith had considerable authority. At the sound of 'Colonel' the inspector shrank a bit. He left but Mother felt sure that he would come back. Miss Letheren must be stern about teaching me to read and all of them must stop reading aloud to me, as I must learn to do it for myself.

Gilby was not keen on 'burdening young brains' with formal lessons, at set times; there was time for that later. He was not anti-education, however. Mother recalled that when she was a child he had called at the local girls' school and asked what subjects were on the curriculum. Seeing that neither Latin nor Euclid were, he called at the boys' school and found that there both were included. So he arranged for Mother to go to the boys' school, the only girl amongst the boys.

It was, however, now decided I should attend the kindergarten of The Hall, from 9.30 until 11 – not from 9 as Mother did not think it necessary I should attend morning prayers.

Nevertheless, as she anticipated I was likely to hear something about Jesus Christ, she had better say something herself. Miss Letheren had read me the legends about Jason and the Argonauts, and the Golden Fleece in Charles Kingsley's book. These stories were what we called legends. Nobody knew whether they were true or not. There might have been such a person, but it sounded as though some of his adventures had been added to from the imagination. It was like that with stories about Jesus Christ. She said there were some things nobody understood. When she was a child, she had asked Gilby, 'Who made the world?' He said, 'God.' She then asked, 'Who made God?' He said, 'I don't know.' Nor had he let himself be further drawn, either then or thereafter. It was something nobody knew.

I asked her what she thought. She said it wouldn't be right for her to tell me what she thought as I might then feel I ought to think the same. When I pressed her, she said, 'I think there might be something.'

I wanted something to fix on. My eyes wandered round the room and came to rest on the gold brooch with which she had fastened her bed-jacket. It showed a snake climbing a rod. I asked, 'Is that God?'

'No, dear,' she answered hastily, 'that's an RAMC badge.'

Looking back, it seems to me remarkable that out of all the articles in the room I should have picked out a symbol of the deity immanent.

One Sunday morning when Gilby and I were coming out of the Foxgrove woods with the jam-jars in which we brought back our finds, we encountered a stream of people coming the other way. Gilby said, 'Ooh, look at all the good people coming out of church. They'll see we haven't been. We're the heathen.' I remembered his words but as I did not know what a church was, still less a heathen, the joke rather passed me by.

In the wood, he pointed to the way all the trees strove upwards to the light, and said, 'Survival of the fittest.' The phrase came again in Mother's exposition of the evolution of species. She said, 'Some people don't like to think we came from monkeys, but I think how clever of us.'

Here she was, without knowing it, misrepresenting Darwin. In her exposition it was through constantly trying to do better that we evolved, whereas what he meant by survival of the fittest was those whose shape and colouring best fitted in with their surroundings were the survivors. She had improved on it.

It was while we were talking about the 'black spot' in *Treasure Island* that Gilby told me he had once dealt with an outbreak of plague all by himself. It must have been when he was in Sierra Leone. It would have been no use talking to the black people about 'germs' because they had not been taught about them, so he told them the sickness was brought by devils, and these devils hopped not only from one victim to another but on to everything the stricken had touched, and the only thing to kill these devils was fire. They got the idea and cooperated perfectly, a team of sanitary inspectors could not have done better: they burned down their houses, their whole village, heroically. He kept himself apart until he was sure he was not carrying the sickness – he thought it was the energy given him by the emergency that enabled him not to succumb – but when he returned to the coast he had to explain why he had been up-country for so long. In his report he referred only to 'blackwater fever' – a common ailment that worried nobody. 'If I had said "plague" there would have been panic all along the coast, people rushing for the boats.' That was what was called 'a white lie'. Usually lies were bad and to be avoided.

[9]

Mother told me my father did believe in God. 'I don't know whether in Jesus Christ. I never asked him.' But in God. He was a Mason (I did not know what that was). As a matter of fact, he had an inclination toward the Mohammedan religion. The men he commanded were Mohammedans, and he thought they drew their manly qualities from their religion. But in one of his last letters, written when he expected to be going into action soon, he said that he had gone into a church and prayed for her and 'Baby'. For he knew I was on the way, and expected me to be a girl.

As the time for my beginning school drew near, Mother told me I must not be shy. If I saw another little girl standing alone, it might be she, too, was shy and I should go up to her, take the initiative in speaking to her. She illustrated her advice with a story.

While my father was in command of Fort William, Calcutta, the Dalai Lama visited India with some of his suite. He asked permission for them to see over a British fort, and Fort William was the one chosen by the British. There must have been some mistake about the time, for my father was out on the parade ground when suddenly someone Mother took to be the exalted personage and his two flanking aides were shown straight into her drawing-room. Nonplussed, she motioned them to sit on the sofa, and they sat on it, all three in a row, looking at her. They spoke no English and she spoke no Tibetan, so, just sitting looking back at them, she didn't know what to do, afraid of doing the wrong thing. Then it occurred to her, that if this was the first time she had had to receive three such persons as themselves, it was, for them, probably the first time they had found themselves in the drawing-room of an English lady. They didn't know what to do either, as they were frightened of doing the wrong thing. Emboldened by this thought, she perked up, took charge of the situation. She said 'Captain Fuller Sahib' and made walking movements with her fingers to indicate that he had walked out through the door (pointing to it), but, this time broadly smiling, said, 'Captain Fuller Sahib' for the second time, making this time walking movements with her fingers back from the direction of the door into the room. They understood perfectly. He had walked out but would walk in. They rose, bowed and retreated backwards from her presence. When they reached the head of the stairwell, she foresaw an accident if they attempted to go backwards down the stairs, so she turned her back on them, so that they might turn and look where they were going.

When they returned later, it was my father who took charge of them, showed them over the fort and explained everything, He didn't speak Tibetan either, but spoke Hindustani – one of the very few British officers who did. It was in his own time and at his own expense he had taken lessons, but he found that it made a better relationship with his men, being able to talk to them in their own language.

Later in the day, after they had gone, an emissary came to the fort bearing a gift. It was a prayer-wheel, and the gold-bordered visiting card that came with it read: 'Kusho Horkang Dzaza'. Mother always thought it was the Dalai Lama himself whom she had received, but when I was grown up and thought to verify this point by writing to the present one, telling this story and asking who Kusho Horkang Dzaza was, a reply I received from his secretary said Kusho Horkang Dzaza was at that time (1913) Prime Minister of Tibet. But in our family it was always referred to as 'the Dalai Lama's prayer-wheel', and Mother kept it in the cabinet together with my father's medals and Gilby's decorations and medals. She took it out for me and showed how the top could be taken off to reveal within the hollowed ivory strips of paper covered with writing in Tibetan characters.

Gilby drove me to school in the mornings and Miss Letheren called for me after the mid-morning break, during which I was supposed to get to know the other children. But they were all talking about 'gee-gees' and I did not know what gee-gees were, so they thought me very ignorant.

When I got home I asked Mother, 'What are gee-gees?' 'Horses,' she said. Some people called horses 'gee-gees' when talking to children. I had never been talked to in baby language, only in grown-up language.

It was like that with everything. Wishing to catch one of the teachers' attention to ask something, I said 'I say', and was told not to be impertinent. Yet I was sure I had heard Cousin Arthur attracting Mother's attention with this opening phrase, and she his. When I asked Mother what I should say, she was at a loss, then ventured, 'Probably you are meant to put your hand up and say, "Please Miss ..."' The phrases we used in our home were not necessarily right elsewhere.

It started with a chance remark I made to Miss Letheren, that the word 'butter' was not butter coloured. The sound 'u' in that word was more the colour of the buds of palm, a light greenish grey. To match the colour of butter, the word should be pronounced 'batter' for the lighter yellow, or perhaps 'barter' for the stronger yellow of buttercup, daffodils or the word 'father', which was the strongest yellow of all.

She must have told Mother, for later, at table, Gilby was saying it shouldn't be laughed at; there was a man called Galton (I registered this in my memory as an orange name, deep orange almost disappearing into brown) had written a book about it. He hadn't got a copy of it here but was pretty sure it alluded to the same phenomenon.

Mother asked if I could draw them.

I sat down to draw the sound of the names of the days of the week, giving to the round first syllables little grey tails, representing the 'dy' (day) of the second syllable. But here I ran into a problem. I had put Monday and Sunday down as, respectively, crimson and orange (very light orange), but these had the sound of the 'u' heard in 'butter', which was light greeny grey. Did the neighbouring 'm' and 'n's give to Monday and Sunday the different tint? Wednesday was a bricky pink, Thursday dark green-grey, Friday light bright yellow and Saturday even lighter yellow or just white. As I could not draw white on white paper I put a black line round it, and to all I gave their little tails. Then I drew the names of the month. Again, I gave them tails for their obscure second syllables, but July, since the dark sound was in the 'u' at the beginning, I shaded the left hand of a circle and outlined in black a long white tail for the 'y' making a grey tip.

I was six years old when I did the drawings of the coloured sounds. In the spring of 1922, when I was turned seven, a collection of my drawings including these was hung in the Royal Drawing Society's annual exhibition at the Guildhall in London. Mother took me up for it, and it seemed my coloured sounds had aroused disproportional interest. I was led into a smaller room where several men gathered round me, asking me questions. One of them made a whistling noise and asked what colour it was and I said 'Silver.' He then made a low groaning noise or roaring sound and I said 'Brown.' He then went to a piano and played the notes at the bottom and asked what colour they were. I said dark brown, almost greyish at the bottom. As he played them going upwards, I said more chestnut brown, golden brown; in the middle of the piano, golden; then as he went on upwards, paler gold, white, with at the very top where they began to get faint, an almost blue or violet tinge on the white. Though I did not know it, I was giving my first press conference.

There were reports in newspapers. The first to appear was that in the *Daily Mail* of 3 April 1922, under the heading:

MONDAY RED
CHILD ARTIST'S COLOURS
FOR THE DAYS

... Her name is Jean Fuller ...

This little girl sees colours in noises, too, Mr T. R. Ablet, the Art Director of the Royal Drawing Society, told a *Daily Mail* reporter:

'I made one sound near her and she said "silver". I made another and she said "dark brown".'

There was also a piece in the local *Beckenham Journal*:

DAYS OF VARYING HUE
BECKENHAM CHILD ARTIST'S
COLOURS FOR THE DAYS

... Her name is Jean Fuller and she lives at 13 Manor Road ...

Later, this was followed by one on the Children's Page of the *Daily Mirror* of 7 June:

WHAT COLOUR IS WEDNESDAY?

It was the one in the local paper that brought me torment. Everyone at school had read it, and the teasing, the ragging I endured was really upsetting. Even Miss Letheren was moved to say to me seriously, 'You see with your eyes and hear with your ears.'

I did not answer back but did not feel this was correct, or only partly so. As I put it to myself, there were the colours one saw with one's eyes, which had to be open in order to see, and the colours one saw inside one's head, which were just the same whether one's eyes were open or shut. It made no difference. They really did have more to do with the ear. Miss Letheren conceded one could see in one's mind's eye, but that was not the same as hearing the colours of the sounds in the word; and there were the many other things that one saw with one's eyes shut, not sounds but pictures of things of every kind, people, animals, objects, always in extremely brilliant colours and swift motion. What were they? They were not dreams for I saw them when awake. Why and how did they come? I was learning the elements of prudence and did not ask whether other people saw them in case they did not and the question led to more trouble.

One day when Miss Letheren came to collect me from school she said we must stand still for the two minutes' silence. I had not heard of

[13]

this before but she said it was because this was Armistice Day and I noticed there were poppy sellers in the streets and people wearing poppies. When I got home, Mother said she always liked to spend the silence alone and try to make contact with my father and ask him how to bring up their child.

Before, when I had asked if we should not come alive again after we were dead, and meet him, she had said no. Now it seemed she did believe after all that he was still alive. She was trying to speak to him again, 'on the chance'.

I cannot put a date to the day Mother told me Gilby was going to be married again. When he and Renée Compton had first met it was in China; she was the wife of a Major Compton and he was married to my grandmother. But since they had both lost their spouses (my grandmother had died of a sudden chill turning to pneumonia on their return from India) they had decided to marry and would live in Versailles, where Gilby had commanded the main Allied hospital in France in 1914. Mother said – a number of times – 'We mustn't be jealous.' I shouldn't feel we would be losing him. He would come over from Versailles as he used to do from Aldershot when we were at Farnham. We were going to London and would live in a hotel.

It must have been for the last of my birthdays in Beckenham that Gilby gave me two mice, one black and white, one brown and white, in a cage. He said their names were Robin and Rowena. They had a family. Mother feared Robin would attack their children, but his concern was only to wash them. There never was a better father.

For the summer holiday of 1923 Mother rented a country cottage at Seward's End, near Saffron Walden in Essex. It was there I learned to ride. In a field adjoining the one which went with the cottage, a horse was grazing, and Mother hired him for me. A saddle and bridle were procured from somewhere, I learned to groom him, and then, seated astride him, there I was in stout white long-legged bloomers bumping up and down. I don't think he was really a riding horse, he had been in blinkers, pulling something, but unexpectedly liberated began to recover in spirit. He found he could canter, and I lost my balance and fell off and his hoofs went over me. Mother, who had learned to ride in India, said the great thing after a fall was to remount at once. If one let time intervene, one could find it difficult to recover one's nerve.

The butterflies at Seward's End abounded. Peacocks, red admirals and tortoiseshells I had first seen at Bournemouth round the buddleia, but here all kinds of butterflies gathered round our tea-table. So did the wasps. When I saw that they liked the sweet things, I set a special wasp-table for them, with fancy biscuits, and would sit watching while they sucked up the sugar-icing from the tops of the biscuits, leaving them bare.

After the first fortnight Arthur Overton came to join us, with his new car. It was a Renault and had a self-starter. Gilby's Ford, which had been recovered after the accident and returned to service, had to be wound up by a handle in the front, after which he had very nimbly to get out of its way before it ran him down and get back into the car before it gathered too much speed. I felt that this new sophistication rather took away the excitement. But they took me out in it, and from it I remember seeing my first kingfisher.

There was an afternoon when Mother and Arthur had gone out by themselves and I was alone with the wasps. I found that if, using the tail of a tiny toy snail, I pressed one lightly to the window-pane, it extruded its sting; and if one then held the sting down, it flew off, leaving its sting behind. In this way, I removed the stings from a number, thinking only to render them pets harmless to other people. When Mother and Arthur returned, I opened my two hands to them, both crawling with wasps. They gasped. 'It's all right,' I said, 'I've taken their stings out.'

'But how? How?'

There is a sad end to this story. Towards evening my wasps began to look unwell. Indeed sickly. They were dying. I was most upset.

Some time after that, when I was with Mother in the village shop, I saw something horrible: a glass dome beneath which wasps were drowning. It was a wasp-trap. Beer enticed them in, and then they could not get out. I found the way to put my hand in, and the wasps used it as a raft, climbing up my fingers on to the back of my hand and so on to my arm and away. After this I went every day with Mother to the shop, to continue my rescue work. I always thought it was unnoticed, but one day I caught Mother and the woman who ran the shop watching, motionless, with fascinated horror. I was stung only once, and maintained it was not by one of the wasps I had rescued.

I cannot actually remember saying goodbye to Gilby, but it comes to me with a *frisson* that it was he who tucked us into our horse-drawn cab when we left Beckenham, as he had done long ago when we left Farnham. There was a lot of deciding to do about what he was to have shipped to France, where Renée felt more at home, and what was to go into storage here, in case Mother should ever feel like creating a home again. Gilby had bought the house and was selling it.

I remember that as we pulled away from 13 Manor Road I felt very bleakly that it was the end of a way of life.

Two

I was to attend Kensington High School. When we arrived in London the term had already started. It may have been only for a fortnight or so, and Mother did not think it would matter; but it did. All the other girls had got started and knew what they were doing, and I was lost amongst practices I did not understand. On the first morning they all got up in turn and recited what I took to be a poem, so when my turn came I rose and repeated the words:

Jay
Too ah
Eel ah
Ella ...

The last I took to be a girl's name, but understood nothing else. Back at the hotel for lunch, I told Mother about it. She divined I must have attended a French lesson.

More serious was netball. In the break the girls were all running about passing a ball from one to another. I did not know the object of this game, which way I was supposed to run, or why.

The hotel we were staying at was the Grenville, in Emperor's Gate. Mother and I shared a room (instead of having one each as in Beckenham) on the top floor. I got up as soon as the maid called us at 7.30 and went down to the businessmen's breakfast at 8. Mother stayed upstairs until the 9 o'clock breakfast. I was trusted now to walk to the school, where I arrived at 9 and remained until 12.30. I did not go back in the afternoon as some girls did, to do their homework. Lunch at the Grenville was at 1. I would get in just in time to join Mother at our table for two. At 2 Miss Kirk would come for me (we had said goodbye to loved Miss Letheren). Miss Kirk would take me off Mother's hands during the afternoon. We would go for walks or to the Natural History Museum. Gallery by gallery, I drew pictures of the exhibits and invited Mother to give them marks. My homework I usually did in the hotel lounge, around teatime, ignoring the conversation of the other guests. At 6.30 Miss Kirk would give me my bath, and change me from my daytime clothes into something more silky, in which (Miss Kirk departing) I would rejoin Mother for dinner at 7. At 8, bed – to start with; this was gradually deferred until 8.30, then 9.

Miss Kirk succeeded Miss Letheren in taking down at my dictation my endless poems and stories. A few of these were preserved by Mother but there must have been reams more. I don't think there was much merit in them, they were probably heavily derivative from the books I had been reading, a combination of natural history books and stories about animals.

Gilby sent me – as from Versailles but via W. H. Smith in Kensington – books by Ernest Thompson Seton and Charles G. D. Roberts with their stories about wild animals, and my greatest treasure – *The Adventures of a Lion Family, and Other Studies of Wild Life in East Africa,* by A. A. Pienaar, translated from the Afrikaans by B. and E. D. Lewis with an Introduction by Sir Percy Fitzpatrick KCMG (Longmans Green, 1923). Not really written for children, this one, God how it made one hate the hunters who lay in wait, night after night, for their 'big game' to come down to the water-hole. The lions were given names, Maahaar, Kraagmanetjie – 'old Kraagmanetjie will never rise again'. But the appended story of a rhino and a hippo, bereaved as calves who walked everywhere together – 'The Two Friends' – moved me even more deeply. They kept together for years, until the spear of a native hunter killed the hippo. The earth thundered as the rhino charged to avenge his friend. Then he stood up, for a very long long time, by the body of his dead friend. At last he turned 'on his lonely way far over the deserted plain'. I could never reach this point in the story without the profoundest of sadness. I have still read nothing that has moved me, been loved by me, more than these stories of the lion family and the rhino and hippo.

In return for the beautiful books he sent me, I sent Gilby letters illustrated with my own drawings, carefully addressing the envelopes to:

Colonel Frederick Smith, DSO, CB, CMG
4, rue de Grenelle
Versailles
Seine-et-Oise
FRANCE

On one I drew snails, stretching all the way up the right hand margin and round the top, extended in most acrobatic attitudes, their protruding eye-stalks waving all around. This he particularly appreciated.

He and Renée had been married at the British Consulate in Paris, without guests – and I think I met her on the first occasion when she came over (without him, I don't know why). She was pathetically anxious to be liked by his children and grandchildren, but there was a mistake when she called on my doctor uncle, Hector. The receptionist mistook her for a patient and she was put in the waiting-room with his patients. The mistake, though apologised for when discovered, caused lasting offence. Whether Mother met her and tried to help make it up I am not sure. It was a long time before we saw Gilby again.

Of his first visit I can remember only that he and I walked by ourselves into Kensington Gardens and along the Flower Walk, and that when we reached the Albert Memorial he said that when he was young everyone admired that, now everyone despised it. Could I tell him why?

Pressed for an artistic judgement, I felt challenged but inadequate. I had never really thought about it before and had no strong feeling about it either way. I said it had lots of gilt curly bits all over and I thought people nowadays preferred things less ornamented. Also, I observed, the base of the pyramid and the groups of figures at the four corners were in plain white stone, whereas the whole of the structure above was in gilt and in colours, not really in keeping with the style below. It was two different things, one on top of the other.

With this tentative explanation he seemed perfectly satisfied. He said he felt most of the people who used to speak of it with admiration when he was young did not know why they admired it and most of those who today despised it did not know why they did so either. It was just a matter of fashion, the 'done' thing to do.

We took a turn round the Fairy Glen and returned to the hotel.

Gilby then sent me a marvellous microscope, beneath which I could see that the powder on a butterfly's wings was, as stated in Coleman's book, made up of minute scales.

I had also discovered that next door to the South Kensington underground station there was a shop which sold, impaled upon pins for collection, butterflies of many species. More exciting, it sold the live chrysalides of South American silk moths, for hatching out. I bought one for a *scropia*. And it hatched. The moth which emerged was a huge thing, bigger than my hand, on which it would sit. It had on the back of its head a sort of fur, of a chestnut brown colour – which was the main colour in the wings – and I stroked it. But I could not induce it to eat, though I offered it honey, flowers with nectar and every delicacy.

[19]

At the shop they said that the *scropia* did not eat, which seemed to me very strange. It laid a quantity of eggs, and then died.

I continued my drawings at the Natural History Museum and one of the attendants suggested to me that I should sign the artists' register. I accepted this advice seriously, and thereafter signed when I went in.

Still wondering why the dinosaurs had died out, I suggested – to the hotel lounge – that it was because they, or some part of them had grown too big. The mammoth's tusks were too big and so were the diplodocuses' necks. If we died out, perhaps it would be because our brains had grown too big. Alternatively (and I can remember haranguing the hotel lounge with this thesis) we had to turn into angels. As minerals evolved into plants, plants into animals and animals into humans, so humans must evolve into the next thing up, the next kingdom. Looking back it strikes me as curious that this, which I enunciated as a child, was not so very different from what I believe today.

It can only have been shortly after we arrived that, coming down very punctually for breakfast, I found myself the sole occupant of the dining-room. The businessmen were late and I did not see the waitresses. On the mantelpiece was a clock under a glass dome which allowed one to see the pendulum swing. The hands stood at eight, and the thought came to me, 'It is eight o'clock on the eighth of October and I am eight years old', and with this thought came a vision of a spiral, forming itself in white light and ascending. I knew that all the rungs of it were decades counting from this moment and that each time the light came round to the nearest point on the next rung, a decade would have passed, and I asked myself, when I became a grown-up girl of eighteen would I still be me? And beyond that, when I became twenty-eight, thirty-eight, forty-eight, extending the eights *ad infinitum*, would I be able, still, to recognise myself as me, me as I stood now in the dining-room of that hotel, looking at that clock? Me, concerned with my toad, Tubby, and the cabbage-white butterflies I had hatched from the chrysalides made by the caterpillars I had filched from the tub of nasturtiums in Kynance Mews, and which unfurled their proboscises to suck up plum-juice I had squeezed for them between my thumb and its nail? I must try to tie a knot in this moment to preserve it.

I discovered there was in Derry & Toms, in Kensington High Street, a zoological department, and it was there I persuaded Mother to buy me a slow-worm. I called him 'Fragilis' because I had read in *British Reptiles and Amphibians* that if seized they could break their tails off and leave them in the hands of their attacker, slipping away without them. However he never played this trick on me. I wound him round my wrist and wore him as a bracelet – causing a stir amongst the other guests in the hotel lounge because they thought the legless lizard was a snake.

One day when there was to be a nature lesson I took him to the school and showed him to the nature mistress. She was so delighted that she put aside the lesson she had intended to give and gave one on slow-worms instead. After this, my stock went up.

Mother had taken a room ('the studio') just south of the Cromwell Road, in which she had installed the piano and a few bits of our furniture from storage to sit on. Although there was a piano in the lounge of the Grenville, she needed to practise some four or five hours a day if she was to take the AMusTCL that she was working for. She gave a party there on my behalf for some of the girls from school I got on with. She handed out crumpets for her guests to toast in front of the small gas fire.

It was also at Derry & Toms that I acquired Pip, the canary, and Chota Sahib, the avadavat – a tiny crimson South Asian bird. These were not bought as companions for each other, but something had happened to their respective partners. The canary, which turned out to be a hen, never sang but would chirrup.

My stickleback I had fished from the Thames at Richmond. He became so tame that whenever Mother or I approached the aquarium he would swim to the part of it nearest to us, trying to reach us through the glass.

Towards the end of our holiday at Seward's End we had made contact with the Pallett family from a neighbouring farm. One daughter, Cecily, took me out in the afternoons. The following Easter Mother arranged for me to stay on the Palletts' farm during the two weeks she would be motor-cycling through Wales with cousin Arthur. Ivy Todd Farm, near Ashford, was primitive, with an outside lavatory and only candles for lights; but it had a glorious foal, called Manna after the Derby winner. He was only a carthorse foal but he would jump up and put his hoofs on one's shoulders. I walked about with Cecily's younger sister, Ida, and saw the cows milked. My old horse, Tom, whom I had had at Seward's End, had been hired for me again. Though I had ridden on more elegant horses in the Row, where I had been having riding lessons with Mr and Mrs Carter, I felt quite differently about Tom, that he was my horse, who knew me. I wanted Mother to buy him for me, but she said we had no place to put him in Kensington and he could always be hired for me again when I went to the farm at Easter. But I hated the thought of his being returned to blinkers, and his coat, which I so carefully brushed clean, filling up with dust again. The two weeks he spent with me each Easter must have been the sole bright spots in his life. I still think of him. One day I rode him all the way into Ashford. I wrote this to Mother and then wished I hadn't when a telegram arrived: DO NOT RIDE TO ASHFORD OR ON MAIN ROAD.

Ida taught me how to turn a somersault over a clothes-line suspended between two trees in the orchard, and how to climb the trees. And when Mother and Arthur came to collect me, we were waving to them from the roof of the farm. Mother was alarmed and made me promise never to climb on to roofs.

For the summer holidays we would go further away. The first was to Hunstanton, where the cliffs were in layers of different colours, and the second to Llanfairfechan, in North Wales, whence I admired and partially climbed Penmaenmawr, and we made an excursion to Snowdon. On the way down, the cable-car went off the rails near the precipice. The third was to Felixstowe where amber and cornelian were to be found on the beach and I caught some red admiral butterflies and put them in a cage, but then felt that for the sake of having them closer, I had denied them space in which to fly. I said, 'I think my red admirals would be happier if I let them go', and opened the door of the cage so that they could all fly away.

Back in Kensington I made a school-friend, Peggy Pyecroft. She had stick-insects. They had been given her by her father. He was the curator of one of the departments at the Natural History Museum, so I was thrilled to be asked to tea there, behind the scenes. It was only bones he had to do with.

But one morning he telephoned to Mother inviting us to come over and see 'the sight of a lifetime'. Only there briefly and not on show to the public.

He might have said, 'the smell of a lifetime', for that was what it was, when we hurried along. It was the head of a sperm whale, which had been washed up somewhere on the coast.

Mother talked to him about my love of animals and interest in the Museum and – thinking forward to when I grew up – asked if there would be any possibility of my getting some kind of job on the staff; but he was discouraging about my chances.

It must have been some time in 1924 that Mother and Colonel

Ventris met again, I think through some chance. He told her he was now married. She must absolutely come to tea and meet Dora, whose father was a Polish count – and she must bring Jean to meet Michael. They met several times before I was to be taken along. Mother had gathered Ted and Dora were both pupil patients of Karl Jung, and before we set out told me I must be very careful not to touch Michael. Michael was never to be touched. It was so that he should grow up without complexes. And so we set off, to tea with them in their London flat. Mother always called Colonel Ventris Ted. In India, everyone had called him Ted. But Dora said she was trying to change this. One of his middle names was Vereker. That was so much more elegant, 'a nice name', why didn't he use it, and ask other people to use it instead of Ted?

I knew I was expected to talk to Michael, but the trouble was he was only two, whereas I was nine. Moreover, he was entirely engrossed in building some construction, house or palace, with toy bricks, trying out different layouts for the floors. He hardly looked up from this at any time. A withdrawn child.

On another day, Colonel Ventris, by himself, met us for morning coffee. He told Mother Jung said their trouble was that he had an Oedipus Complex and she an Electra Complex ... I don't know why all this was explained in front of me. I think it was because they supposed I was too young to understand. In fact I took in a lot and in the same way I could have told you the difference between butterflies and moths – butterflies' antennae always end in knobs, moths' antennae never end in knobs but are sometimes plumed at the sides – I could have told you that an Oedipus Complex was what a man had who was secretly in love with his mother and wanted to kill his father, an Electra Complex what a woman had who had secretly loved her father and wanted to kill her mother. Dora's father was the most ghastly tyrant, who used to hit her, and Jung told Colonel Ventris that what she really wanted of him was a replacement of that dreadful father. But he couldn't possibly hit Dora; and though his consideration for her feelings plainly irritated her, he didn't know what to do. Jung said it was because he secretly wanted Dora to replace his mother that he inclined, instead of bossing Dora, to let Dora boss him, which irritated her even more. Each wanted the other to be boss and neither was capable of bossing. Being analysed was the most painful process possible to imagine. All very complicated.

Once on a Sunday afternoon – I think just to take me off Mother's hands so that she could do something else – Colonel Ventris called at the Grenville for me and took me, by myself, to the zoo in Regent's Park. As we went through the turnstiles I noticed he did not have to pay. Every member of the staff knew him and greeted him cordially as we went on through the various animal houses. He seemed to know the history of every animal. If one had been sick, he inquired what remedies had been given and what was the animal's response. When we went through the big cat house, he went through the bars to touch the tiger, but the keeper asked him not to. However apparently tame, tigers could have your arm off in a trice. The Colonel Ventris I saw that day was in his proper element. When I mentioned to Mother, after our return, that he had not been required to pay, she said, 'He's a Fellow of the Zoological Society.'

It had begun to worry me that Tubby, my toad, was not looking well. Perhaps hotel life did not suit him. I could have released him on the farm but not in Kensington. And so I thought of offering him to the Zoo. I had a letter back saying they did not usually accept pets, but in fact they did not possess a common toad. So I might bring him. Mother took the occasion to ask Miss Proctor there whether there were other posts such as hers which I might get there when I grew up. Miss Proctor said the posts were few and hard to obtain. But she took in Tubby. I received from the Zoological Society an elegant letter of thanks:

The Zoological Society of London
Regent's Park, London NW8
21st November 1926

To Miss Jean Fuller
Grenville Hotel
Grenville Place, S. Kensington
SW7

Madam,
I am directed to return you the thanks of the Zoological Society for your kind gift of the undermentioned animal which has arrived safely and makes a welcome addition to our Collection.

Your obedient servant
P. CHALMERS MITCHELL
Secretary

1 Common Toad

and at the end of the month I received a printed document listing all their additions to the collection during November 1925. The list, which included many exotic species, ended:

1 Common toad (*Buffo vulgaris*), habitat Europe, presented by Miss Jean Fuller.

I went to see him sometimes in his new home. He shared his cage with a natterjack toad but had his own label, printed in gold letters on black: 'Common Toad, *Buffo Vulgaris*, presented by Miss Jean Fuller.'

I wondered if he could recognise me through the glass.

I seem to have passed over my tenth birthday; but indeed it *was* rather passed over. Mother had promised to take me out to dinner at some place more interesting than the Grenville, but at the last moment told me Arthur wanted to take her out. 'The seventh of March is his birthday, too,' she reminded me, and I must know what a fuss he made if he didn't get what he wanted. She knew that I was 'sensible'. It seemed to me a poor reward for being sensible; though to justify the epithet I abstained from complaining.

All the same there was an evening out that was glorious. *Treasure Island* was being performed as a play. Mother had booked seats for us but then I caught a chill. However, despite my having run a temperature she decided to wrap me up in rugs and take me, by taxi, all the same. It was Arthur Boucher's production and he was Long John Silver. At the end, when the orchestra remained silent, there were shouts of 'Play "God Save the King"'. There was no sound. Arthur Boucher was a Socialist.

Cousin Arthur certainly wasn't, but now in the General Strike he was shifting sides of beef onto a wharf somewhere down in the docks. Mother said she had never seen him looking so well; it was because he had something to do. Meanwhile food was being brought into Hyde Park and piled up, guarded by tanks, the buses were manned by young men with aristocratic accents who did not know the fares.

Mother also took me to a concert in which colours were seen on a cinema screen whilst music was played. She was keen to know if what was shown was what I saw. Not really, though I enjoyed them as being beautiful.

And then there was a film of Conan Doyle's *The Lost World*, of which I had the book. I can still remember the names of Pat Malone and Professor Challenger. To see the monsters fleshed out and brought alive was thrilling.

Mother said I was pale; London did not suit me. I felt all right; perhaps I was feigning indisposition too realistically to avoid scolding for having forgotten to do my school homework. But Mother said the bracing airs of Brighton had always invigorated me when we went there for a weekend, and that we should go to live there. I would finish the autumn term at Kensington High School and then we would move. At the end of the term, some of the girls in my form called with two gifts they had clubbed together to buy for me: an orange-tip butterfly and a brimstone butterfly, both mounted on pads of cotton-wool within frames. They must have come from that shop by South Kensington underground station. The colours are still bright. I have them still.

Then, shortly before Christmas 1926, we moved from Kensington to Brighton.

It was when we stopped at a hotel on a brief trip to Hastings, in Arthur's car, that Mother asked me if I would mind if she married him. He had asked her but she felt she had to consider how it would affect me, whether I would mind. I said he was very much with us as it was so I couldn't see that it would make much difference. No, I wouldn't mind. But nothing seemed to happen.

Anyway, we spent Christmas 1926 in the Portland Hotel, Regency Square, Brighton. During the early days of the new year I found on the beach a sea-bird with so much oil over him that he was unable to move his wings. He was a big bird, bigger than the usual gull, but I carried him back to the hotel and asked for Lux with which to wash him. A young man came to help Mother and me at the wash-basin. Even with the warm water and the Lux and whatever else we put on him, it took a long time, but eventually we discovered he was a black bird with a white front and blunt, powerful bill. As he recovered power to move he repaid our ministrations by doing his best to bite us, and we had to be careful. Somebody produced a fish, which was dropped down his throat. My book on birds was brought downstairs, and after flirting with the idea of his being a great northern diver, washed down from Greenland, or a guillemot (wrong type of beak), we decided he was a razorbill. At last we got him free and clean and I carried him, with something to protect me from his terrible beak, down to the beach, where I let him go. I thought he would fly into the sea at once, but he just stood where he was for a long, long time.

My new school, in Montpelier Road, was another of the Girls'

Public Day School Trust group, again paid for by the Indian Army Officers' Family Fund. (They would have paid for me to go to Roedean but I did not want to go to boarding school.) Starting in the second instead of the first term of the year set me back a bit: in history, the form was in another period, in geography in another continent, so that what I had done in the autumn term in Kensington did not help towards grasping where we were supposed to be in the new set-up.

Then one morning, as I came home for lunch, Mother asked me into her room, her face so long I knew there was something terrible to be divulged. She had found a lump in her left breast. She was to be on the operation table within hours, she had made her will, in which she named Uncle Hector and Arthur as my guardians, and left me to choose with which of them I should live. For the present I was to stay with Arthur in the furnished service flat he had taken at the top of Regency Square.

During the terrible days she was away, he was tender and solicitous. When she came back, however, he was tetchy with me, taking against a jam-jar lined with blotting-paper, between which and the glass were beans, sprouted as I had been taught at school. I liked them but they were horrible to him as evidences of 'emergent life', and I behaved badly, bringing them needlessly into his presence, for which I was reprimanded by Mother.

She had now received a report that what had been removed from her was a benign tumour, not cancerous; but the surgeon had cut through the big muscles at the top of her arm. When she asked him if she would be able to play the piano again, he replied, with unconscious cruelty, she could probably 'strum'. That wouldn't do. If she couldn't manage the challenging chords, she would abandon the piano altogether. In fact I had not seen it since it was put into store when we left Kensington but she had probably thought of taking another studio in Brighton.

Arthur and she decided to take a holiday. I was returned to the Portland Hotel, with a woman to look after me. Their idea was to make a motoring tour of Devon and Cornwall, and Mother sent back postcards. I had meanwhile discovered on the road into Hove a pet-shop, in which was a hedgehog. When I wrote to Mother asking permission to buy it, she objected that it would not make a suitable pet and said no. I beseeched and she gave way. Unfortunately it was full of fleas and, though it slept throughout the day, at night it ravaged my bedroom in unending search for non-existent snails. It was an unsuitable pet, and I carried it back to the shop. My tortoise, Loveable, who ate lettuce from my hand, was much to be preferred.

Mother and Arthur reached Devonshire, but stuck in a village called Modbury. They stayed there so long that I became restive. I was bored in the hotel by myself and felt left behind. I wrote that if they were going to stay longer in Modbury I would like to come and join them. Mother said not until the summer holidays, I must spend the summer term at school. I did not want to finish the rest of the summer term by myself in that hotel, and finally she gave way, on condition that I brought with me all the books for that school year. I could come by train; it meant changing at Portsmouth, but – she had inquired of the railway people – I would only have to get out and walk from one platform to another.

My overseer bought my ticket and put me aboard the train at Brighton, and I sat clutching the books in one hand and, in the other, the cage containing Pip and Chota Sahib, covered over with the cloth used to prevent their being disturbed at night by the switching on of electric light. It was, indeed, a simple change at Portsmouth, and at Plymouth both Mother and Arthur were on the platform to meet me.

We were staying at the Modbury Inn, in the High Street. We had a private sitting-room-cum-dining-room on the ground floor, and over dinner, when I used the word 'awfully' Arthur said, 'Shilling!' Mother explained it was a game they were playing: they fined each other a shilling each time they inadvertently used words such as 'awfully', 'frightfully', 'dreadfully' when they really meant 'very'. I joined with zest, but I remember it struck me that the 'very' could in most cases be dispensed with as well, leaving the adjective to do its own work.

Mother and Arthur did not go out a lot. Arthur either stood at the bar or sat at his easel, where he was composing in pencil something vast. I had not dared approach, but unexpectedly he asked me what camel's feet were like. Not hoofs were they? Honoured at being consulted, I informed him they had separate toes; the foot was rather broad and flat so as to avoid sinking into soft sand. 'Like this?' he asked, inviting me to look at his picture.

I said his camel did not look very well.

He said it wasn't meant to. It was dying of thirst in the desert. He invited me to look at all the scenes into which the whole was divided, and asked, 'What do you think of my picture?'

Everything seemed to depict some savagery or misfortune. There was one person in an operating theatre undergoing surgery. I said, 'It looks like something out of Dante's "Inferno".' It wasn't something I had read, but it was the right answer.

'It's meant to look something like that,' he said.

Mother told me he had been very much upset by her having had to undergo that operation, and had come to feel that if there was an intelligent power behind the universe it was malign.

I worked at my arithmetic, always my worst subject, and Mother explained to me vulgar fractions, which is probably why it was about the only arithmetical procedure I ever understood.

And we did make one expedition; it was to see a solar eclipse. Mother and Arthur said there would not be another such in their lifetime, though there might be in mine if I lived to be very old. It was very early in the morning, so that we had to get up before dawn to drive to the top of a hill. Our smoked glass was needless for the mist was so thick we saw nothing at all.

In the end, Mother told Arthur she and I were moving on to Plymouth, and left him in Modbury. In Plymouth we saw one of our new battleships in the harbour and thought it was either the *Rodney* or the *Hood*. We were in a small hotel in the nicer part and walked and sat on the Hoe. We had with us a book, *Name This Flower*, translated from the French of Gaston Bonnier, Professor of Botany at the Sorbonne, organised on an unusual plan, starting with numbered questions – plant with flowers or without flowers, herbaceous or not herbaceous, flower composite or not composite, leaves alternate or paired? It certainly made me very observant of details. I also found a copy of *The Scarlet Pimpernel* by Baroness Orczy. I was thrilled by this, and devastated when for a moment I thought his wife might betray him. I also took watercolour paints and a pad into the Aquarium and made paintings of the fishes, then into the bird museum where I started with the jay and went on to others. By boat, we made an excursion to the Eddystone Lighthouse. We also made an excursion to Tintagel, where Mother was so taken aback by the spectacle of the height it was almost as if she was ill. She would not let me go up it. She had an extraordinary, adverse reaction to anything ancient British which might have had druidic associations.

I think her idea in choosing Plymouth was that it was not too far away if Arthur should decide to catch up with us. He didn't and in the autumn we returned to Brighton, in time for the new term at my school.

Mother now noticed an advertisement for Miss Halsey's School of

Elocution and Drama, near the Old Steyne, and thought it would be nice for me to attend it on Saturday mornings. The class consisted of perhaps half a dozen girls; we would get up in turn and recite some poem or scene from Shakespeare. We were, in fact, being prepared to enter for the Incorporated London Academy of Music examinations which were held twice a year, with a judge coming down from London to the school. I was entered automatically for Grade III, in which I scraped a pass.

I went in for subsequent examinations, mounting the grades, in July and November of each year. I enjoyed the poetry and it was fun.

Then a blow fell. Mother found a lump in the other breast. This time I was sent to Uncle Hector and Auntie Maud during the days she was in hospital. They had a house in Southall called Strome Ferry. It was here I got to know my cousin Peggy, slightly younger than me and taking lessons in ballet dancing, at which she was reputed markedly gifted. She introduced me to the idea of dancing a story. Her brothers, Redmond and Ian, were much younger, but Peggy and some older girls took me on a walk by the river, and it was here I saw some boys mistreating a frog. I rushed in amongst them and seized the frog from them. I was afraid they would pursue me and hit me, but they didn't, and I walked on with Peggy and the others holding the frog. One of its hind legs had been hacked off and I did not know how it would fend for itself if I just returned it to the river, so I took it back to the house. Mother had told me I should fit in with the ways of the household and above all be no trouble, but I felt she could not have foreseen an emergency such as this. The frog was obviously unable to pursue food for itself yet must be fed. So I asked Uncle Hector to catch some flies for it against his window and bring them, and he did.

When it was time for me to go home, Auntie Maud accompanied me to Victoria Station and put me in the train, saying, 'Have you got your ticket safe?' I had my ticket in one hand and the frog in the other.

I found Mother in Norfolk Square, where a furnished flat had been taken for her for her convalescence. Again the report said 'a benign tumour', but the shock had been great.

Where was I to release the frog? None of the squares along the Brighton front were safe for him. I opened a map and saw that in Portslade there was a marsh. I had never been to Portslade, but recalled there was a bus with PORTSLADE written across the front over the windscreen, so that must be its terminus. I worked out that I had what I thought would be sufficient to cover the fare and, with my bag in one hand and the frog in the other – and without having said anything to Mother – I said to the conductor, 'Portslade, please.' I had a map with me, and with its aid was able to find my way from the stop to the marsh. And there I set the frog down, and with a somewhat bleak feeling watched him hop lop-sidedly away.

Mother now moved to furnished rooms in Medina Villas, Hove, where Arthur, who had come immediately on learning she was to have another operation, had taken rooms too. A Miss Jones was engaged to take me out in the afternoons.

I was to be Mustard-seed in Miss Halsey's production of *A Midsummer Night's Dream*, and bought the play to read. We were also doing *Iphigenia in Tauris* and though only in the chorus I enjoyed intoning Gilbert Murray's translation of Euripides. For the performance, at St Augustine's Hall on 1 September 1928, Mother made me a classical-looking white robe and did up my hair in the ancient Greek style. I was thrilled.

There was now an extra course at Miss Halsey's, in classical Greek dancing as re-choreographed by Margaret Morris from study of the attitudes depicted on ancient Greek vases. Mother made me a short tunic in emerald green. Some of the gymnastic exercises put in to make us supple were the same that form part of Indian yoga.

We had by now moved back into Brighton, to a hotel called Ravensworth, kept by a couple called Kemp. Their daughter Phyllis came up to our rooms offering to take down at dictation the book I was writing about the birds in St Anne's Well Gardens. Their dog, Bonzo, a bull terrier, also attached himself to us.

The two connections, with Phyllis and Bonzo, continued after our move to 68 Brunswick Place, where Mother had taken a flat and I saw re-emerge from storage the brass table and other furniture I had loved – augmented now, for Arthur had given Mother the furniture he had inherited from his mother. That is how I come to have the Japanese Samurai painted on silk with brilliant colours in a medium no one has been able to identify; and of course, the Chinese whatnot.

Looking at our books, now arranged on the shelves, I noticed they included a complete Shakespeare. The idea came to me that I should read all his plays. I took it down from the shelf and opened it at random, at *Othello*. I began reading the first scene, then wondered if I ought to have permission to read this, and went into the kitchen where Mother – she said she didn't like cooking but cooked well – was with Arthur, and asked, 'Is it all right for me to read *Othello*?'

She looked at him interrogatively. He said, 'Oh yes. Be thankful it's Shakespeare.' He said I could read anything of Shakespeare, 'Except *Titus Andronicus*.' That was nasty. And, he added, '*All's Well that Ends Well* and *Measure for Measure* could well be postponed.'

Mother said *Othello* was a wretched story all about jealousy but I could read it if I wanted to.

I had probably heard of *Romeo and Juliet*, which was why I read that next. I was smitten with the idea of playing Juliet, and asked Phyllis if she would read the part of Romeo in the balcony scene, so that I could respond by making Juliet's speeches. The idea grew up that we should make a performance of this at the hotel. Use of the sideboard was granted us for the balcony. Some curtains rigged up were drawn back to reveal Phyllis below and me standing on it. The dining-room tables had been got out of the way and all the hotel guests were seated on chairs. The Shakespeare was followed by some rubbish composed by me, my adaptation of a Rudolph Valentino film, *The Son of the Sheikh*.

This performance, which was in April 1929, was followed by a second, on 8 November, consisting of a play by Phyllis, *The Chinese Ruby*, a recitation by me of W. H. Davies's 'The Kingfisher' and Leigh Hunt's 'Abou Ben Adhem', a dance by Phyllis and a play adapted by me from Mason's material about the Roman occupation of Britain, *Under Bignor Hill*. We had programmes typed for both performances.

At Easter 1929 we went to Lugano. Arthur had gone there and wanted us to join him. On the day we were to have left Brighton I had run a temperature. Mother was concerned, but as our tickets were booked decided to risk the travelling. By the time we reached Victoria, my temperature was higher, but we went on. I cannot remember the boat or where we landed, but it was during the night we travelled through the tunnel in Switzerland. In our carriage were two loud-voiced men from the north of England who had drunk too much. I thought Mother looked distressed, A reason why she was not looking forward to this holiday was that Arthur had written to her that he had met a man there whose beliefs concerning the Creator (if any) were the same as his – meaning that He was malign – and he wanted her to meet this person.

When we arrived, in the early daylight, he was on the platform to meet us, and so was this new friend. We were taken in a taxi not to our hotel but to a restaurant in which we were all served with breakfast.

Mother protested that they must get me to the hotel as I was ill and ought to be in bed, but it was difficult to break away.

At last we were in the hotel and I was in bed, where I stayed for several days (I don't know what was the cause of my fever). Then Mother said Arthur had taken a dislike to Lugano and wanted us to leave with him straightaway for Paris. She had told him it was impossible because I was still in bed and could not be moved again. We had come here because he wanted us here and if now he wanted to go somewhere else it would have to be without us.

When, after perhaps three days in bed, I got up, he was gone from our lives.

The beauty of Lugano was a wonder to me, the shapes of the mountains descending to the lakes graceful and grand. We made boat trips up and down the lake, and day trips to Lake Como (which meant crossing the border into Italy) and Maggiore. We saw Holbein's painting of Henry VIII, and we sat in cafés. Mother said in a way it was a relief to be able to sit down at a table without having to wonder whether Arthur would ask her to change places with him because, where he was seated, he was facing someone with an ugly face. He could not stand anything that was ugly.

After a fortnight in Lugano we went to Paris. Gilby came to find us in our hotel, near the Madeleine, and then we went to Versailles to see him at home with Renée.

She was white-haired, elegant, anxious to make us feel at ease. I noticed in the flat several of the items of furniture that had been in our home in Beckenham: in particular the Tibetan leather trunk. Renée told us how she had worked to remove the tarnish from the silver lock. (Her pains were not appreciated by Mother who confided to me afterwards that she had always left the silver unpolished as she thought it looked better black, more in keeping with the ancient leather.)

Versailles had, for Gilby, special associations. In 1914 he had been appointed to the command of a military hospital in France. He had an officer to take him round by car to look at premises he might like to commandeer for setting it up in. He must have exhausted this man by turning down, for one reason or another, every grand mansion offered. One was perfect in itself but overlooked a field full of cows. Gilby asked if the cows could be moved. The farmer had nowhere else to put them, and they were his livelihood. In that case, Gilby had said, the building was 'not suitable'. Cows meant cow-flies, and they would settle on patients too. The windows would always have to be kept shut and the lack of proper fresh air would impede the patients' recovery. So again they set off, looking at yet more buildings and he felt his guide must be getting very weary. The daylight was beginning to fade when they passed the Grand Trianon Hotel and he said, 'Stop the car, I'll look at that.' The building was suitable in every way. He commandeered it. Guests and staff had to come out, as well as the hotel furniture. Officers turned furniture removers, sleeves rolled up, were helping carry out the grand piano. And then the beds and hospital equipment were unloaded from the vans that had been following around behind them all day, and carried in. And not a whit too soon. As dusk fell the first convoys of wounded began arriving from the front, by train and by road, needing instant treatment.

Gilby made no distinction between Allied and German patients. In his view, a man with only one leg was neither an Allied soldier nor a German soldier; he was a man with only one leg. Though visitors sometimes expressed surprise, the patients took this in good part and would lean from their beds to say, 'Hullo, Jerry!' and be answered, 'Ullow, Tommy!' Gilby said soldiers at the front did not hate each other in the way that people at home did. On one occasion he was told there was a German in a dreadful state about something. He went to find what was the matter. The German was complaining that his Iron Cross, which had been given him by the Kaiser, had been 'stolen'. Gilby went to find the matron. She had put the medal, along with watches and other valuables found on patients, for safe-keeping into a safe, where they were all ranged with labels saying which patients they belonged to. He redeemed the Iron Cross and he said he would 'never forget the relief on that poor man's face when he saw me bringing it back to him'.

We walked through the grounds at the back of what had been the royal palace. They were very formally laid out – too formally for my liking, every plant kept neat. Gilby at Versailles was like Colonel Ventris at the Zoo, in his element. The gardeners knew him. He would recall that with some particular plant they had had a problem and asked how they had dealt with it, how it had responded. The gardeners all knew and liked him, and took him into their confidence.

Mother's associations with Versailles were of a different, and less happy, order. To her, it was the home of the doomed French monarchy, and though the day was sunny she felt it full of ghosts.

Back in Paris we went to the Louvre, and my breath was taken by the Winged Victory at the top of the stairs; the air was in those wings, and glory. We found the Venus de Milo a thing of classical beauty, though Mother said that in Gilby's view breasts of that size become pendant. As for the Mona Lisa, if I had been walking along a dark and lonely road and she invited me into her house for a cup of tea, I wouldn't have gone. I mistrusted her looks.

We also found the more modern works in the Musée du Luxembourg and the Musée Rodin.

Back in Brighton, Bonzo continued to call, on his own. Mother said I shouldn't encourage him. He belonged to the Kemps and they might feel we were enticing him. Wouldn't I like a dog of my own, a thoroughbred? I could choose the breed.

I looked through a book on breeds and opted for a Welsh terrier. One with a pedigree was ordered from a breeder. He arrived by train – cowering in his container. Hiding under the furniture, resisting every attempt to tempt him out, he was terrified of me, terrified of Mother. I registered him with the Kennel Club as Taffy o'Cymru, but behaving like that he was never going to be shown. When we took him out, Mother was ashamed of him because whenever he met another dog he lay down and grovelled.

The worst thing was that Bonzo, coming to call as usual, saw Taffy and, feeling himself supplanted, did not come again. I felt, bitterly, that I had exchanged the substance for the shadow. Bonzo, though he did not belong to me, was my dog; Taffy, though he belonged to me, was never my dog.

Taffy was not the only failure in ordering animals from breeders. Seeing in *Fur and Feather* an advertisement for a 'lilac' mouse, I ordered one. The poor thing that dropped through the letter-box, having come in a packet by ordinary post, was a nervous wreck. Terrified of me, terrified – like Taffy – of everybody, it was never able to take its place amongst my other mice.

There was a Drawing Festival held in Brighton annually. Miss Halsey had entered me for it in a previous year without my coming specially high, but now she urged me to try again. The piece set for May that year, 1929, for entrants above fourteen and below sixteen, was 'A Fancy from Fontenelle' by Austin Dobson, beginning

'The rose in the garden slipped her bud'.

When we arrived at the Dome, it was found my name had got left off the printed programme. However, we were assured it would be all right, and the adjudicator – Mr James Agate, dreaded drama critic of *The Sunday Times* – was told there was one more. He did not look pleased, but I mounted the platform and said my piece.

He called a boy back, who had appeared before. Then he called me back. The boy back. Me back. Incredibly, he was choosing between us. How many times he called each of us back I can't remember. Once he turned his back and had both of us repeat our piece while his back was turned. It was difficult to keep up the expression as though it had been for the first time. Or did he want to see if we could vary the expression? There were lines that could be differently expressed. I had decided the rose must not be made unpleasant in her mocking of the gardener or sympathy would be lost for her. She must merely be pathetic.

At last he gave his judgement. I was the winner. The things he said about me were incredibly complimentary. He talked about my feeling for the piece, my 'stage presence' and goodness knows what. I walked on air. My name was in the *Brighton & Hove Herald*. In Miss Halsey's next production I was Mary Queen of Scots.

At school, too, things were becoming more interesting. We were reading Palgrave's *Golden Treasury*. When we came to Vaughan's poem beginning

> I saw Eternity the other night
> Like a great ring of pure and endless light

I felt, instantly, that he had seen what I had seen in Kensington when I was eight. His was perhaps a flat ring whereas mine was an ascending spiral, but there was the same idea of epochs of time being marked on it. I nearly put up my hand and said, 'I saw something like that once', but then an inner voice warned me not to – when I had mentioned coloured sounds it had caused such a lot of fuss. Rather than risk that sort of thing happening again, better to keep quiet and say nothing. Miss Marston said Vaughan was a mystic. Was I a mystic too?

I had by this time found the occult bookshop in the Lanes, that warren of small streets near the Old Steine. Many of the books bore titles that gave me no inkling of what they were about. I was looking for something about Tibet, which would illuminate our prayer-wheel, but did not find anything specifically on Tibet. What I did find were two bottom shelves devoted to books on astrology and palmistry, and I gathered at least some minimum of information squatting on the floor. I bought a crystal, hoping to see visions in it, but never did, which was strange as I saw so many without its aid. I used to call what I saw the 'coloured cinema', because the pictures moved and changed rapidly but were always brilliantly coloured. I remember one of a pediment mounted on two small but substantial pillars. It coincided with the idea I had just formulated for some project but for which I had not really the necessary foundation. It then occurred to me that the pictures were not, as I had always taken it, meaningless, but illustrations in symbol of what I thought, exposing any distortion in my thinking, and that I ought to take note of them, learn from them. Where did they come from? This I asked as I lay in bed in Brunswick Place. Were they impressed on me by somebody else, some other mind? No, I felt they came from me, but from a part of me that knew what I ordinarily didn't. Messages from the me that knew a lot to me that knew very little.

I knew seven was said to be a mystic number, and also its multiples. I was fourteen years old and in another fortnight would cease to be a multiple of seven as I would be then fifteen. I must not let the time pass without making an effort. I opened the cabinet, took the Tibetan prayer-wheel out, and examined it closely. I noticed that the figures carved in the ivory were seated cross-legged. Mother was out and, being unobserved, I seated myself on a floor as nearly as I could in their attitude (I could not copy it exactly). Then I pressed it to my forehead, between the eyes, and said, 'Please Dalai Lama, please holy men in Tibet, hear me and give me teaching. Give me enlightenment.' In case they had difficulty in locating me, I said I was in Brighton, a town on the sea-coast of England. It then occurred to me that the directions should be superfluous – the pull between us should tell them where I was. Nothing happened. Indeed, what had I expected to happen? Some sudden, nirvana-like bliss to descend on me? I was being pretentious.

It was about this time that I became interested in learning languages. French, German and of course Latin I was doing at school, but I bought and did all the exercises in Hugo's *Russian in Three Months Without a Master* and Hugo's *Italian in Three Months Without a Master*. I also bought the Norwegian, Portuguese and Hindustani in the same series, but only to glance through the early chapters. It was not that there was anything I wanted to read in these languages, just a curiosity as to their structure. I did manage the opening lines of Dante's 'Inferno', which I found in an edition that had Italian down one side and English down the other. The Italian was more difficult than in the Hugos.

Renée wrote that she would be in London for a few days and invited us to lunch with her at her club in Dover Street, so we took the train to Victoria. At the club it was as if she had emanated a double of herself, for there were two white-haired, elegant women in black who greeted us in the sitting-room. Mother was in conversation with Renée, I got paired off with the lookalike. I got on well with her and was explaining to her the difference between octopuses and giant squid, when Mother said, 'Evangeline, I am afraid you're getting some information for which you may not wish.'

So *that* was her name. She said, 'It's all right. I'm getting to know Jean.'

Mother said we must decide what I should call Evangeline. 'Aunt Evangeline?'

'Not Aunt,' said Evangeline. 'Just Evangeline.'

'But it sounds insufficiently respectful. She's only a child.'

Evangeline said she did not mind about its being respectful. She did not feel like an aunt, would never submit to being called 'Aunt'. (Renée, on the other hand, insisted on my calling her 'Granny'.)

It was decided we should all go to the cinema, and a newspaper column was searched for what was on. Charles Laughton and Tallulah Bankhead were in something called *The Devil and the Deep* showing at the Carlton in the Haymarket.

Evangeline said, 'Let's go to *The Devil and the Deep*.'

So we set off. Someone wanted to call a taxi, but Evangeline wanted to walk. It was 'no distance at all'.

So we all walked, Mother and Renée ahead, Evangeline and I following.

After the film was over and we had parted from them at Victoria, I asked Mother, 'Who is Evangeline?'

'Lady Northey.' She was Renée's sister and she was married to General Sir Edward Northey, retired now but until recently Governor of Kenya Colony. They lived in a big house called Woodcote, at Epsom. Mother had dined there, sitting next to him, and he had spoken to her of the action in which my father was killed, saying, 'We lost more men that day than in the whole of East Africa in the war.'

She also said that before talking I should think whether what I was talking about could be of any interest to the person I was talking to. In justice to myself, I felt it was Evangeline who, to break the ice, had asked me what I was reading, which was how she came to be subjected to my disquisition on octopuses and giant squid.

The two sisters, Renée and Evangeline, née Cloete, were Boers, but brought up in Paris.

Not long after this, Renée and Evangeline came down to tea with us in Brunswick Place, plus a child who was the daughter of one of Evangeline's daughters. At one moment I left the others in the sitting-room and went into the kitchen to do something. To my surprise, Mother, deserting our guests, followed me into it, appearing upset.

Evangeline apparently wanted, when the time came, to present me and give me a season. She had expressed herself impressed by me, said I was 'unaffected' and very 'douce'. The unusual word was hers. But a season implied a whole string of dances and parties and Mother said I wouldn't like that, would I? I might find myself being expected to marry some young man whom the Northeys thought suitable. Presenting, in itself, was a simple thing; she herself could do it, having herself been presented – in India, in 1911, during the Durbah, in which Gilby and my father were both involved. If I wanted it, she could do it for me. There would be no reason for me to have a season. I didn't want it, did I? She looked so alarmed that I thought she was afraid Evangeline was trying to take me away from her. So I said 'No.' Actually I would not have minded the presentation, by itself, though about the season Mother was very likely right. She said she would tell Evangeline herself that she had told me of the offer and that I had said 'No'.

When, after a few minutes, I returned to the sitting-room, neither Evangeline nor I said anything about it.

But now the question loomed as to what career I was to follow for a living. Miss Proctor had said there were few openings for women at the Zoo, and Mr Pyecroft had not been more hopeful about the Natural History Museum. To obtain a degree in zoology I would have to take 'matric', which meant passing in arithmetic, in which I regularly failed my end of term examinations. The maths mistress wrote on one of my reports, 'Slow and inaccurate but can do sensible work.' Yes, sensible because I could see how the problem had to be tackled, what had to be multiplied or divided by what; slow because my mind then wandered out of the window, and inaccurate because when I came back I forgot where I had got to and misread my figures. My fives looked very like my eights.

I suggested I might become a vet but Mother said people often brought animals to be put down, and I wouldn't like doing that. Farming? If it did not involve putting an animal to death.

Mother had always taken for granted that my career would have to be something to do with animals, but Mr Agate had said I had a 'stage presence'. That suggested an entirely new line of thought. Nevertheless, she wrote to a college that offered a course in agriculture and animal husbandry, and a handsome, glossy brochure arrived. I took it into my bedroom to read quietly, saw that the course included a class in wringing chickens' necks, went into the kitchen to find Mother and told her I would go on the stage. (Margaret Morris, visiting Miss Halsey's class, had told Mother that if I could become part of her own school she would like me to appear in her displays, and perhaps teach; but we had both felt it would interfere too much with my ordinary schooling and that a career in classical Greek dancing would be too limited.)

To enter the Royal Academy of Dramatic Art it was necessary to pass an audition. The date I was given was for some months ahead but I started, at home, rehearsing a passage from Shaw's *Saint Joan*.

In the days between Christmas and New Year I began running a fever of unknown origin which kept me in bed for some six weeks. An appointment was made for me to see Sir Thomas Horder, the country's foremost diagnostician, in London; but whilst I was waiting for it Mother came into my room one night and said she had been thinking about what one would do in India if somebody ran a temperature: give quinine. She gave me a massive dose of quinine, and again, and again, the temperature falling each time. I was nevertheless taken up to Horder.

He said he had never in his life been more tempted to write 'P.U.O.' which sounds like something precise but means precisely 'I don't know'. Ordinarily, he would say a treatment that made the patient better was the right treatment, but Mother must stop giving me the quinine as it would cause me to become deaf, not now but in later years. Mother said, 'Perhaps you wouldn't mind being a little deaf in later years.' I realised she had feared I was dying. But she stopped giving the quinine, and I returned to normal.

We went for a fortnight to Stratford-upon-Avon, for the Shakespeare Festival, arriving with a little time to spare before dinner. I sat on my bed and opened my *Shakespeare*. I had by this time read most of the comedies and tragedies and made essays into the histories. I would try something different, the Sonnets. As I read, I puzzled. There seemed to be more than one person in them. Who were these people? I thought I might understand better if I knew, and turned to the biographical introduction. It said he married Anne Hathaway and had children. That did not help at all. When I rejoined Mother at table, I said it could have been the biography of a different man. She gave me a rather curious look, said, 'Some people think he didn't write them' that they were written by a man called Bacon. 'Was he married?' I asked.

She did not think so, not at the time the Sonnets were written.

I had asked because I had felt in the company of a very lonely man, sitting on his bed, alone, as I was sitting on mine, writing these things to these persons unknown.

I went up to London for the RADA audition, in front of Kenneth Barnes, the Principal, and two other persons. Afterwards I received a letter from Barnes, dated 24 September 1930, saying I had passed the Entrance Test and a vacancy would be kept for me the spring term, 1931.

I had wanted to start at the beginning of the academic year but Mother insisted I must remain at school until after I had passed my sixteenth birthday, as to say I had left school at fifteen would look bad on paper. My sixteenth birthday was a kind of majority for me in another way. My Indian Army Officer's Orphaned Daughter pension was now paid to me direct, into my account at Lloyds Bank, Cox's Branch, 6 Pall Mall, instead of being tacked on to Mother's pension.

Everyone at the school knew where I was going. On the last day there were the usual three cheers for the headmistress and then, unexpectedly, 'Three cheers for Jean Fuller!'

As I walked out along Montpelier Road for the last time, I reflected that the long, initially resented, period of my schooling was done. It had ended better than it had begun.

Three

The furniture I loved, the brass table with the animals, the Japanese Samurai and the Chinese whatnot were packed up and returned to storage, and the viola, on which I had taken introductory lessons, sold, and we moved back to London. It was in a pea-soup fog so thick it hurt one's eyes and throat that we installed ourselves in a small hotel near RADA. RADA was like the Shakespeare theatre in Stratford-upon-Avon in having been burnt down and, pending the reopening of a new home, making do with makeshift accommodation. Mostly it was in and around Malet Street.

The beginners' class was taken by Miss Chester, who always made us do *Much Ado About Nothing*. It had been cast in the autumn term. She could do nothing about a new pupil arrived in the spring term. I would just have to sit and watch. Perhaps someone would fall out. Someone did fall out, and I found myself cast as Don John, the unpleasant man who causes all the trouble.

At RADA the women students greatly outnumbered the men, and as in most plays there were more parts for men than for women, most of the women had to play men – the long parts split between several. I did not fare any better in Ibsen's *The Wild Duck*, where I found myself playing Relling, another unpleasant man. What one needed was to be taught how to move on the stage as a woman, in the sort of parts one might expect to have to play on the professional stage. Norman Page, who took one of the other classes, warned us we were entering the most overcrowded of all professions: 'Only one in ten of you will ever get a job on the professional stage.' Perhaps that was why the atmosphere was competitive rather than cooperative, and very tense.

We also did the *Alcestis* of Euripides. I was in the chorus, but did not enjoy it as I had enjoyed being in Miss Halsey's *Iphigenia*. But now I realised my years at Miss Halsey's were telling against me. Elocution was a dirty word at RADA, and I had become over-elocuted. I realised this for myself, yet in time to get back to my normal speech. Again, that I had just taken the ILAM bronze medal and was entered for the silver would do me no good if known; I took the silver, since I was entered for it, but kept quiet about it, for the ILAM, like elocution, was another dirty word at RADA. I realised for myself that speaking monologues from Shakespeare before judges had got me into the way of looking straight in front of me while speaking, and not, as I must now learn to do, at the other people on stage with whom I must interact.

I had also been rather dried up by my Mother's instruction – after my talking about octopuses and giant squid to Evangeline – to think first whether what I was talking about could be of any interest to the person I was talking to. So instead of saying anything at all I sat wondering what sort of conversation I ought to make, and sounding to myself stilted in my attempts. I had lost a lot of my spontaneity.

I did find interest in the lectures of the history of the theatre.

And to the Bradford Hotel, in Montague Street, near the British Museum, came interesting people. There was a Mr Higgs, who had been in Russia during the Revolution and at a camp where somebody called Krishnamurti had got up in front of thousands of people and said he was not Christ. Apparently he had been brought up by some people who had told the world he was. He had nevertheless given a teaching that was very beautiful. Mr Higgs gave Mother the *Star Bulletin* for March and April 1931. I don't know if Mother read them but I did:

> I know for myself that I have attained, and knowledge of attainment does not depend on the authority of anyone outside myself ...

This sounded like what I was after. But then he wrote:

> You attain liberation when you are no longer under the yoke of experience ...

Was he deriding experience? That was what I thought I needed.

I never had a chance to talk to Mr Higgs, but his son Eddie came home on leave – a junior officer in the Regular Army – and I was at once paired off with him. We were seen off to a cinema together. I could think of nothing about which to talk to Eddie. It was like the Ventrises, saying Michael and me must meet, as though we were the right age for each other which we were not.

Worse was to follow. A Mr Lister, staying in the hotel, asked me to come with him to a dinner and dance at the Hyde Park Hotel. Mother thought I should go, but over the fish he asked me to marry him. Taken aback, I said, 'I'm going on the stage.'

'Not if I have anything to do with it,' he said.

He was trying to take me prisoner. I forcefully rebutted his proposal and we had a miserable evening.

[43]

I told Mother that something dreadful had happened, and was devastated when she said 'Perhaps he was a little precipitate.' I could go a long way and not find a nicer man, he was a rugger player ...

I was shaken and shocked.

For the Easter holiday we went to Stratford again, and for the summer term moved to a hotel in Bayswater to be nearer the Park.

At RADA we had been slowly moving into our new quarters and there was a formal opening by the Duke and Duchess of York (later King George VI and Queen Elizabeth). We, the students, were unable to see this ceremony, if there was one, for we were all herded into a long room at the top of the building, to wait, wondering what was happening, until Kenneth Barnes opened the door to let their Royal Highnesses in and said, 'And these are the students.'

It was during this term Gilby came to see us again. I had been in a class during the morning, but as I emerged from the Praed Street Underground, I was touched to find him standing on the pavement waiting for me. We walked back together to the hotel. He was walking rather slowly, and it struck me, for the first time, that he was now becoming an elderly man. He had been born on 14 February 1858, so he was seventy-three.

Over lunch at the hotel he told us of the provisions he had made in his will, and said he had left it unsigned so that, if any change in our circumstances suggested a possible alteration, he could add that before signing. Then he said he must be off to see his 'son and heir', Hector.

Mother had agreed to our having an adventurous summer holiday. I went to Thomas Cook and bought the tickets we wanted. It was for a round trip, Nice, Rome, Naples, Capri, Perugia, Milan, Lucerne, enabling us to break our journey when and where we wanted. I remember the cheque I wrote was for £31. Mother did not want to be in Rome during the heat of August so we would go in September.

Just as we were leaving something arrived through the post. The letter with it read:

Will you please accept this book of Krishnamurti from me with my best wishes? It is now out of print & I had the good fortune to get the very last copy. You will find in it the whole of his teaching.

[illegible initials] HIGGS

London
29. 8. 31

The book was composed of several titles: *The Pool of Wisdom, Who*

Brings the Truth, By What Authority, Three Poems: J. Krishnamurti (The Star Publishing Trust, Eerde: Ommen, Holland, 1928). The package was of course addressed to Mother, but I read the book, on the eve of our departure and in Nice.

I had to keep going back over it, for I found his train of thought tended to be difficult. Actually, I could have done with some authority. I wanted to be told, with the authority of someone who knew, what happened to us after death and where we went eventually.

Back in the Bradford after our summer holiday I started on a dramatic adaptation of Dostoevsky's *Idiot*; but I was not making any progress at RADA. My report had been unenthusiastic. One was told West End managers sometimes came to the end of the year performance on the lookout for likely talent, but what chance had I of being spotted unless given a part in which I could shine? Two professional actors (unconnected with each other) passed through the Bradford and both said RADA was useless as regards getting a job on the stage. Stage people, apparently, regarded RADA the way RADA regarded schools of elocution and the ILAM examinations. How did one start then, I asked? Mostly through relatives, the stage ran in families. Or through accident. Harry Hanson gave me the name of an agent, Rosa Thornbury. Though the Officers' Family Fund would have paid for me to spend a second year at RADA it seemed more practical to see the agent. She was able, through good fortune, to get me a small part immediately: Barney Lando's company, which toured a play called *Lost Property*, had just lost an actress. I should join the company at Luton, on the Sunday preceding the Monday opening there.

The part proved to be only that of the maid, but it was across the footlights. I was handed it on Sunday, given a rehearsal of it on Monday evening, then walked for the first time onto the professional stage. Jimmy Lannon, the juvenile lead, stood behind me in the wings to push me on at the right moment: 'Now!' And I was on.

Otherwise, of Luton I can remember only one thing: walking, with Jimmy Lannon, under a very dark and grimy railway bridge and being pounced on by him for having named Shakespeare's Scottish tragedy. I said I thought it was only within a theatre that to do so was bad luck. '*Any*where,' he corrected me. Nevertheless he saw me to my hotel and met Mother.

The week in Luton was the last before the Christmas break, and when we reassembled in January 1932, it was in Aldershot. Mother and I took the opportunity to nip over to Farnham and see The Bush

Hotel again – from the outside. Mother said, 'When we were here before, we were important people. Gilby was at the Cambridge. Now we're only theatricals.' I had not realised she regarded the stage as a come-down, and was rather hurt.

Jimmy Lannon came to see us again and gave us some disinterested advice on my career. I must get something better than this. Had I written to the Old Vic? 'Ask Lilian Bayliss for an interview.' And of course write to Stratford. Say I had played Shakespearean roles. And go to a good photographer and have some good photographs taken. Managers liked to have them to put up outside theatres.

Then Rosa Thornbury came up with something better. A new company was being formed. It was a consortium of actors who had taken the Queen's Theatre, Dundee, for a season, and were now auditioning for the juvenile lead. I should go to an address off Piccadilly. There I found a part being put into my hand and was asked to read it, in dialogue, with one of the others, in front of the rest. I was told I had got the part. I was Romo, in A. A. Milne's *Michael and Mary*.

We rehearsed the play for a whole fortnight; then joined the company at St Pancras on a Sunday and all travelled up together, changing trains at Edinburgh and reaching Dundee at breakfast time. We were on the stage that night 25 April 1933.

We were doing one play weekly. Rehearsals for the new play were always started on a Tuesday morning, when the parts would be given out and 'walked through', reading from the scripts. By Thursday we were expected to know them, by Friday to be word-perfect. Monday morning would be dress rehearsal, on Monday night the performance. Then on Tuesday, the first rehearsal for the next week's play and so on, always rehearsing for the following week whilst playing this week's play. Mother and I had taken rooms at the top of Airlie Terrace – she made my dresses for Romo in emerald green. Though it was permissible, after a decent interval, to wear in the town a dress in which one had appeared on the stage, it was not permissible to repeat dresses from one play to another. My salary was £3.10s a week, which in those days was quite good, but would have been eaten into badly had I had to buy dresses. With Mother making them, I actually saved something from my pay each week and put it in Post Office Savings.

I did not have much time to paint – though we made Sunday excursions, to Forfar (where I did manage a sketch), Perth, Inverness and Aberdeen. I was trying my hand at writing a little poetry, and, having read Dostoevsky's *Crime and Punishment* before we came up, was embarking on his *The Brothers Karamazov*.

My name was on the playbills and my photograph too, hung around the town, as well as outside the theatre. James Hayter was our producer, probably the best producer I ever had, with precise ideas of what he wanted, drilling us till he got it. In the weeks that followed *Michael and Mary*, we put on a succession of plays, the titles of which have little resonance with me now – *Honours Easy, The Middle Watch, Murder on the Second Floor*. (I remember *Murder on the Second Floor* because I had to fall backwards out of a cupboard, dead, and the man opening the cupboard failed to catch me as he should have done, so that I fell on the back of my head and hurt myself quite badly. I refused to do another backwards fall in case he failed again; a sideways roll was as far as I'd go.) For Drinkwater's play *Bird in Hand* I had the lead. This was because there was only one female part in the play, the daughter of the inn's landlord, and Mary Wynne, our leading lady, stood down for that week, being a trifle old for the part.

Mary Wynne was back, in a long part, the following week, but in the week after that, half way through the second night of the Aldwych farce *It Pays to Advertise*, it became evident she was ill. What with I do not know but she was sweating and looking as though she was fainting. We were all afraid she would collapse before the play was finished. Then as the last curtain fell she was rushed away in the waiting ambulance and, on the stage, James Hayter, Jack Brown and Gerald Dudleigh (the business manager) were standing talking about what to do. Impossible to get another actress up from London in the time – they would have to close down and telephone the local newspaper to warn people there would be no performance and any who had booked their seats would have their money returned.

I stepped up and said I would play the part.

'You?'

I said I had watched the whole play that night from the wings, as well as during the rehearsals. I might not be able to memorise every word but I knew the plot, the way in which scene followed scene, situation developed out of situation, and in a play like this it did not matter if the words were not exactly as scripted so long as the story proceeded. My own part was so small it could, with a little ingenuity, be cut out altogether, leaving me free to take over the lead.

They jumped at it. Somebody found me the script of the part, and said we would of course rehearse this, not next week's play, tomorrow morning.

Back in our lodgings, Mother thought I would do better to go to sleep rather than make myself look exhausted by staying up all night learning my lines.

I was back at the theatre in the morning, and, while some of them were examining the text to see how the part I was to have played could be cut out, I was given a 'run through' of the lead – down stage left, up stage, down stage, etc.

That evening, Wednesday 8 June 1932, there was a simple announcement made to the audience that there had been a change in the cast and the part of Mary Grayson would be played not by Mary Wynne but by Jean Fuller, and we were away. There wasn't any hitch and I don't think there was anything uncoordinated in the story line.

Thursday morning's rehearsal was of course for the following week's play, *Interference*, in which Mary Wynne was to have been Faith Marlow, the innocent wife of her husband's blackmailer. Obviously, I had to take over as Faith Marlow.

We sent a telegram to Gilby and he arrived, having flown from Le Bourget to Croydon, where he changed to another plane for an airport near Edinburgh, and thence by express. He was not in time for *It Pays to Advertise*, but he was there for the first night of *Interference*, Monday 13 June, and afterwards came behind the scenes to meet the other members of the company, who gave him a wonderfully deferential welcome. Overjoyed to see him, I little knew his own health was about to give way.

Then things took a bad turn. Dudleigh began trying to paw me in the wings. After trying merely to dodge him, I finally asked him to stop it, and the result was a curt note saying I was no longer required as a member of the company. No explanation. Jack Brown spoke to me in the wings, saying, 'It's a dirty trick that's been played on you, after you saved us all from being closed down.' He hoped I knew he had had nothing to do with it.

We were out of Dundee by the Sunday train of 10 July.

At Edinburgh we broke our journey to see our Scottish relatives and were met on the platform by Aunt Grace and Uncle John Laing, sister and brother of my Mother's mother, Jane Violet. They took us by the bus to their home, in Windsor Gardens, Musselburgh. There would not be time for them to take us out to Penicuik, where the family came from, but they took us to North Berwick, to see Auntie Lila. I was never sure where she came into the family tree but I knew she had given my christening mug and, for one of my birthdays as a small child, a pendant heart set with seed pearls and a tiny diamond in the centre.

And so back to London and the Bradford. Harry Hanson now invited me to play Jackie Coryton in Noël Coward's *Hay Fever*, with which his company was opening at Hastings. It was September when the rehearsals started and we found the Ventrises were there. They found us from the playbills.

Colonel Ventris came to join us for morning coffee at our hotel. Michael was now at Stowe. Dora and he had tried separation, but when they were separated they pined for one another, and when they were together they tore each other apart. The solution they had finally arrived at was separate but nearby hotels. They were both in hotels on the front, only a few paces apart, and they would meet on a bench on the front for a few minutes every morning, during which they could take care to be nice to one another. The trouble was, he said, he and Dora were 'both porcupines'. The relations of porcupines had to be conducted with care so that their quills should not stick into each other. (As he was a member of the Zoological Society, he may have witnessed a porcupine coupling.) 'There has never been any third party interference on either side.'

After that he brought Dora to tea with us, and a date was made for a further get-together. Dora said to Mother, 'I'll take Jean out to tea; that will leave you and Vereker free to sit here and talk about India.' At least, as Mother said to me after they had gone, she wasn't jealous.

Dora, good as her word, took me out to a tearoom in the town, and I found her perfectly easy to talk to. In fact I got on with Dora better than Mother did. Dora confided to me that she felt her life somewhat useless and empty; she would like to take up architecture, but at her age hesitated to present herself at the Royal College of Architecture and ask to become a student. They would think she was silly. I said she shouldn't feel silly but should go ahead and do it. But I never heard that she did.

Harry Hanson was delighted at the rehearsals by my performance as Jackie Coryton, who was meant to be a quite brainless ingénue and I played up the empty-headedness of the lines given her. I was therefore doubtfully pleased to hear Hanson say to somebody, 'She doesn't have to act, she *is* Jackie.' The Hastings *Argus* of 11 October 1932 wrote: 'A capital example of a pretty, gushing, brainless debutante came from Jean Fuller. She managed an insane giggle that was amusing and completed the effect.'

I was looking forward to the stronger part in the next week's play when Hanson said he had been persuaded by his leading lady the part should go to a friend of hers, a London actress of more experience. I was out of a job. Though I suspected personal politics, it was possible that by playing Jackie too well I had done myself out of consideration for more serious roles.

We had entered 1933 when I gained an interview with a Mr and Mrs Charles Calvert, who had taken the Empire Theatre, Longton, for a season, and were forming their company. They took me on, and we went up in March.

Emerging from the railway station at Stoke-on-Trent, I had my first view of the Black Country. Soot everywhere, on everything. I realised Longton was one of the five towns in Arnold Bennett's book, *Anna of the Five Towns*. The five towns were Stoke-on-Trent, Longton, Bursley, Hanley and Newcastle-under-Lyme. During my stay there, I had a look at all of them and read the novel. The five towns were 'The Potteries', all pottery kilns. I said I would like to see the inside of a pottery since we were there, and indeed Mother and I were kindly shown pots in their various stages of production, from lumps of wet clay to finished articles. Our hotel looked straight at the side of a metal railway bridge beyond which was the tallest chimney I had ever seen. I got out my paints and painted it. That painting is the only one of mine to have been printed in a newspaper.

On the stage I played the juveniles. The only ones I can recall are Vivian Tompkins in *The Passing of the Third Floor Back*, Betty Farrer in *Hindle Wakes* (quite a strong part, this) and Poppy Dick in the Aldwych farce *Rookery Nook*. While rehearsing this, the last play of the season, one of the small part actresses fell out. No time to get another. Calvert asked me, 'Could your mother do it?' And so Mother, by accident, found herself on the stage. During some time when I was off stage, I nipped round in the dark to the front of the house, and thought she looked distinguished.

Back in London we met Colonel Ventris again, for morning coffee in the Bonnington. He said Dora was tired of a marriage that wasn't a marriage, and if she persisted in this idea, he supposed he would have to play the gentleman and give cause so that she could bring a divorce action against him. He was, however, very ill and might not live long.

I remember that as we walked away, Mother was profoundly sad, for she was very fond of him. When we heard no more from him, we supposed he had in fact died.

The next engagement I got was with Tod Slaughter's company, opening with *Maria Marten or the Murder in the Red Barn*, at Collins, Islington. I played Maria's younger sister, Nan Marten, and Slaughter, abandoning his usual role as the murderer, metamorphosed himself into the comic Tim Bobbin. This was rather too plainly because he fancied playing opposite me as Nan. Consequently the roles of Nan and Bobbin got drawn out with gagging disproportionate to their significance in the play. On the opening night, 9 June 1933, there was some speculation as to whether Sickert would be in the audience. Walter Sickert, the artist, I was told, loved murders and also loved music halls, and Collins was an old music hall to which he used to go. Could he have resisted the *Murder in the Red Barn* at Collins? There was peeping through the little hole from which actors can get a squint at the audience. Some were sure they saw him. I was invited to look. I cannot in any meaningful sense say I saw Sickert, but he certainly saw me.

From Collins we moved up to the Theatre Royal, Norwich. I took the occasion to see the Cotmans and other English watercolourists in the museum. In the theatre, there was a reply with which to shut up anyone who complained of the theatre: 'Have you played Kettering?' Because if not, you had not yet struck rock bottom. I never played Kettering and am ignorant of the special inconvenience which characterised its layout, but the Royal, Norwich, though distinguished, must have run it a close second. The dressing-rooms were all on different storeys, so that one had to keep running up the stairs, and people abandoned their use and changed in the wings.

We went on to do a repertory season of barnstormers at the Lyceum, Ipswich. I took the lead in something called *Moths*. The rest I forget. Mother and I took the occasion to make a trip to the Constable country and see the spot from which *The Hay Wain* was painted.

Then Mother received a telegram from Renée: Gilby was ill and had been brought to a hospital in London. Mother went, at once. I was unable to accompany her as I was on stage. She came back saying he was delirious and had not recognised her. She was glad I had not seen him like that. It had been during a tour of Italy he had been taken by some abdominal trouble. He died on 26 July 1933. Mother had supposed he would be laid at Highgate beside her mother, but Renée said she would not feel happy with that. And so he was buried at Epsom, amongst the Northeys. Hector had whispered to her, 'The Northeys have pinched our father!'

I cannot find that I have an obituary for Gilby, but in the *Who's Who* for 1933 it reads:

Smith, Col. Frederick, C. B. 1918, C.M.G. 1916, D.S.O. 1900, LR.C.P.I., L.R.C.S.I., D.P.H. Durham, R.A.M.C. (retired pay): b. 1858, served Zulu War 1879 (medal with clasp). Boer War 1881, Sierra Leone – Mendi and Protectorate Expeditions 1898–9 (medal with clasp). South Africa, 1900, Secretary to a Principal Medical Officer (despatches, Queen's Medal with four clasps, D.S.O.), Senior Medical Officer, West Africa Command 1901–2, North West Frontier of India, 1908 – Mohmund Expedition (medal and clasp), European War 1914–18, Commandant Trianon Palace Hospital, Versailles, and Senior Medical Officer, Paris Area, 1914, Assistant Director of Medical Services 27th Division, 1915; Deputy Director of Medical Services 16th Corps, Salonica 1917 (despatches four times, C.M.G., C.B.). Address c/o Glyn, Mills & Co, 3 Whitehall Place S.W.

The above makes no mention of his books, of which the most important is *A Short History of the Royal Army Medical Corps* (1929). Earlier no-nonsense titles I can remember are *Modern Bullet Wounds and Their Treatment*, and a paper on *The Sanitation of Forts*. Unpublished was 'The Bloodless Adventures of Colonel Xerxes Wilson at the Back of the Front in the Opening Months of the Great War' (disguised autobiography) and a novel, 'Yemma', considered by publishers unprintable because, set in Sierra Leone in the time of the Hut Tax Rebellion, it featured the rape of a white girl (unfortunately named Pansy) during a sack of the Mission, a lot of 'leopard men' murders and the ultimate marriage of the hero to a black girl, Yemma, who seemed to be the only character any good at anything. One publisher, Geoffrey Bles, expressed the highest admiration for the work but said he dared not. Ultimately, Gilby turned it over to Mother, who bowdlerised it but it still did not get off.

He was the playmate of my childhood, my introducer to caterpillars, chrysalides, moths and butterflies.

Slaughter was making advances to me that I found disgusting; I handed in my notice.

This time I did not have too long to wait for a new job. Rosa Thornbury told me the Bragg-Liddell Shakespearean Company had a vacancy. They were at the moment at the Winter Garden Theatre, New Brighton, playing *Othello*, so I had better be able to take over one of the parts in that. In the train I learned Desdemona and went straight to the theatre. Geoffrey Bragg already had his face blacked for playing in *Othello*. He received me in his dressing-room. No, I wouldn't be playing in *Othello*. 'You're Mistress Quickly in *The Merry Wives of Windsor* tomorrow night.' He had wanted an actress who was older but it was too late to change me for one of the age required for the part. 'You'll just have to paint wrinkles on your face.'

During what remained of the day I learned Quickly. I had one rehearsal, on the morning of 'tomorrow night'. In the last act, Quickly had to metamorphose into the Fairy Queen. 'It's the worst quick change in the whole of Shakespeare,' he told me. The dressing-rooms were too far away. I would do it in the wings. Two people would pull my Quickly dress off over my head and a third would push the Fairy Queen dress down over me (if time, wipe off wrinkles).

On second thoughts, better not draw any in the first place.

'It plays better as a real metamorphosis,' Geoffrey said. More mystical. One of the people waiting in the wings to pull off my Quickly wimple and gown would be his wife, Laura Liddell. Usually she would be Mistress Page in this play but she was pregnant with their first child, had carried on as long as she could but could not go on in her usual parts 'now she's a funny shape'. That was why he had got me in. He would (as Falstaff) be left alone on the stage after exit of Mistresses Page and Ford. He had only three lines to utter after which he could not stand about doing nothing till I was able to enter. If necessary, he would give me the sun, moon and the stars.

As I looked perplexed, he explained.

It was a completely meaningless piece of iambic pentameter which could be used to fill a gap in any part of any play of Shakespeare. It could mean 'I've dried, help me' or 'the dagger I have to pick up is not in the place I should pick it up from' or, as here, 'the person who should enter to me can't be ready quickly enough'. The chance of there being anyone in the audience familiar enough with the play to notice the alien interpolation in Shakespeare's text was remote. It could even be repeated.

I spent most of that night learning the part. I hadn't seen much of New Brighton but was told the mournful sound of a foghorn heard occasionally was emitted from *Bootle's Baby*, somewhere out on the Mersey.

The following morning's rehearsal was more to indicate where I should be on the stage while speaking than to hear me over the line which I was anxiously presumed to know. Entering as the Fairy Queen from right I should proceed to centre up stage but turn right to face the following troop of fairies and elves, to address them the speech beginning:

Fairies, black, grey, green and white,
You moonshine revellers, and shades of night ...

Then fairies and elves should move slightly downstage of me so that I could present the audience with my half-face while delivering the lines beginning:

About, about!
Search Windsor Castle, elves, within and out ...

(twenty lines, I hoped I didn't dry). But then, for my last speech, from up centre, walk straight down to the centre. 'Fie' etc. Got that?

And then it was the evening. His wife did not fail me in the wings. I was suddenly in glistening white, a tiara stuck on my head and a wand into my hand. And then I was on. No, I didn't dry on the long speech. This was nearly the end. At last, the finale: from up centre, straight down centre:

Fie on sinful fantasy!
Fie on lust and luxury!
Lust is but a bloody fire,
Kindled with unchaste desire,
......
Pinch him, and burn him, and turn him about
Till candles and starlight and moonshine be out.

It was over. Nothing more now but to join the others to take the final curtain.

I played the part for the rest of the week. We were not doing a matinée, so Mother and I crossed the Mersey to see a matinée at the Liverpool Repertory Company, and got back in time for the last night at the Winter Garden. It was the last in New Brighton. On Sunday we left for King's Lynn, changing at Manchester and I don't know how many other different places. Mother was not of the party. The Bragg-Liddell Shakespeare Company had its own magnificent wardrobe of period costumes, and she thought I was old enough to take care of myself. I was, indeed, eighteen.

King's Lynn I had visited, in the Kensington years, on a bus trip from Hunstanton. This time I saw little of the town save the street the theatre was in.

Geoffrey Bragg said he felt he had given me in Quickly rather a heavy load to start off with. But this week he would give me lighter loads: the player queen in *Hamlet*, Audrey in *As You Like It* and Hippolyta in *A Midsummer Night's Dream*; the last was for the matinée on Saturday. There was virtually no rehearsing for any of these: just a walk through for me and for anybody else who was in a different part from previously, just to make sure we were on the right part of the stage as we said this or that: up stage, down stage, centre stage etc: no indication of how he wanted the lines spoken. In that, Geoffrey Bragg was the opposite of James Hayter, who would tell one exactly how he wanted everything spoken. In a sense, in the Bragg-Liddell one produced oneself and made of the part what one would.

Just before we broke up for Christmas 1933, Bragg said to me, 'Understudy Gertrude in *Hamlet* and learn Titania.' From this I supposed I was to play it when we reopened with the *Dream* in January.

I learned both Gertrude and Titania.

When the company reassembled in January 1934, in Crumlin, South Wales, it did not, as I had been prepared for, open with *A Midsummer Night's Dream*, but – a change from Shakespeare – Tennyson's blank verse drama, *Becket*. I was Marjorie. I had not brought Tennyson's works with me, and from the typewritten part for Marjorie handed to me could not imagine why this girl kept saying 'Whoops'.

We also did a T. W. Robertson play called *David Garrick*. I wish I knew who the author was, because I was given the lead, the first time I had played the lead in a costume play. We did other things I can't remember. And then we got stuck, because Bragg had not been able to find a theatre for the week intervening between Crumlin and a return visit to the Winter Garden, New Brighton, where apparently we had been a success. In the meantime he was unable to pay us our salaries, as the takings at the box office had been insufficient. A fellow lodger at my lodgings was sure our manager had 'scarpered', but I assured him that was not so: Mr Bragg was respectable and still here, and in touch with us. It was Mother who sent Bragg a cheque that got us out of Crumlin.

Crumlin was a mining village, depressed by the closure of pits, and by the means test. Our landlady told us she had thought to better the family income by taking in her next-door neighbour's washing in addition to her own, but the exact sum she made was deducted from her husband's Unemployment Benefit, so she stopped it as there was no point.

I asked the men at the nearest working mine if I might be taken down it. They would have to ask the management. Permission was given. I was able to induce one other woman from the company to come with me. We went down the shaft, and walked down a long narrow passage to where we could see men hacking at the coal-face.

Then we returned to New Brighton, where a repeat of *The Merry Wives of Windsor* had been specially asked for. I was Quickly as before. The following week we played at the Pier Theatre, Southport, Lancashire. I was Bianca in *Othello*, and wrote to Mother that I had found lodgings at twelve shillings a week and a fishmonger who sold white halibut at fourpence a pound. This alarmed her and she wrote commanding my instant return to London. It was the same mistake I had made long ago, when I had joyfully told her I had ridden Tom into Ashford and received a telegram telling me not to do it again. I was put out as I had been feeling I had found my feet. When I told Geoffrey Bragg, he was sorry too. He talked a bit about himself and said he always felt depressed when he heard anyone had 'settled down', because that meant become dull. No longer adventurous. He would carry on, but thought to change his name from Bragg to Kendal. He was born near Lake Kendal and it was a name associated with the theatre.

When I left, it was in the middle of a scare that Laura was about to give birth to her baby on Southport Pier.

Mother, I found on my return, had made a new friend, Tom, a civil servant staying at the Bradford. I regretted having been recalled there, for here I had nothing to do but sit around with them.

However, my agent Rosa Thornbury said she had another job for me – I was to join Joseph Bloor's company at Macclesfield. Arriving in Macclesfield in the afternoon, I walked endless streets in which I had the greatest difficulty in finding lodgings. I had, for the last week of their season, to take over the lead in I can't remember what, at a moment's notice. Had Rosa Thornbury recommended me as a 'quick study'? The silk town was so near to the potteries that I took a bus in to see old scenes again: black as ever, but looking largely closed. On Sunday we all took the train to Dundee, for me a return visit – though not to the Queen's but to the Victoria. I walked up to look at the Queen's but it was no more. It was a cinema. At the Vic I played Leila, the only female part in *Rope* (a play I disliked), Barbara in *East Lynne* and the lead in a Frederick Lonsdale comedy *Spring Cleaning*. At the stage door, a man accused me of bad behaviour to my parents – 'I seed yer. In there.' It was my first experience of the inability of the simple to distinguish between a part played on stage and the player. We were playing, to my horror, not only twice nightly but two plays and even three plays weekly, which meant no more than two rehearsals as a regular routine. I felt this made it impossible to give of one's best and when I received a telegram from Maurice Hansard inviting me to take the leads in one play weekly repertory at Porthcawl, on the South Wales coast, I accepted it.

I found I would be opening, on 7 June 1934, as Mrs Calthorpe in *The Man from Toronto*. A member of the company warned me the part was notorious for placing an exceptional strain on the actress as she was never for one moment off the stage from first to last. Apart from the fatigue of learning it, I can remember nothing except that I wore for it a primrose and white dress Mother had made me for one of my parts in Dundee.

After the Friday morning's rehearsal of the following week's play Mr Hansard invited me for coffee in the town. It was to tell me that some unfortunate financial hold-up made it impossible for him to pay me my salary that week. At least Mr Bloor's pay packets had been brought round to the dressing-rooms on Friday nights. But I accepted Mr Hansard's assurance my salary would be brought up to date the following week.

Thereafter I played Stasia in *The Passing of the Third Floor Back*, Anne in *Outward Bound*, Joan Danvers in *The Joan Danvers*, Eliza in *Eliza Comes to Stay* ... but waited for pay.

I made trips to Cardiff and Swansea, walked over the sand dunes and looked at what appeared to be the only bathing beach, by the groyne. It was marked DANGER. It did not look dangerous and I stepped in. Never had I swum more easily, made greater speed ... only when I turned and tried to swim back I found it impossible. Now I understood that notice. The current was carrying me straight out to sea. I really feared I was going to drown and yelled. Then I saw my plight had attracted the attention of the coastguard and a rowing-boat was being put out towards me. A lifebelt was thrown to me and I was hauled aboard. That was a five-mile-an-hour current, they told me, and people had drowned there. Never had I felt such a fool. I did not divulge my identity and after drinking the tea they brought me, slipped into the theatre and proceeded to my dressing-room as though nothing had happened.

There was a meeting of the whole company with Mr Hansard and a man from the National Insurance. He said, 'If you prosecute Mr Hansard you kill the goose that lays the golden egg'; but Mr Hansard must at least stamp our cards.

I made friends less in the company than in the fairground I daily traversed between the theatre and my digs. The fortune-telling couple came to tea with me. The woman had been shocked by a man's asking her when his wife would die. She had told him she never predicted death. In fact, to be sure of its never turning up in anybody's fortune, she had removed the ace of spades from the pack. She spoke responsibly, and it was as if some glimmering of an older, sacred mystery transpired through the commercial setting.

I felt it was no good waiting for Hansard to get his money, and returned to London. Almost immediately I was engaged by the Billy Lynne Repertory Company, playing leads for the autumn season at the Westcliffe Theatre, Clacton, for £4 a week. It was, in those days, a very respectable sum. We opened on 24 September 1934 with my teetering on to the stage in high-heeled blue shoes I had bought for the part, as Lady Cattering in *While Parents Sleep*. The following week I was Ming Lee in Edgar Wallace's Chicago thriller *On the Spot* – black wig, Chinese make-up and clothing – and then Crystal in *The Man in Possession*.

At a dinner and dance at the Grand Hotel to which we were all invited, I told a young man that in London I lived in a hotel near the British Museum. He said, 'I don't suppose you spend much time in that!' Actually I did, I knew its every gallery. Useless to say. I was presumed, apparently, to spend my life in an endless round of cocktail parties and dances. My being on the stage was misleading.

Four

I bought myself my first typewriter, from Selfridge's – very smart in its red case. I had not learned to type but the instructions were adequate. I would no longer need to send my manuscripts away, I would type them myself. I was once more embarked upon a novel. This time the title was 'Stage Without Glamour'. All I can remember of it now was that in the first chapter I combined my recollections of two train journeys, with the Bragg-Liddell from Crumlin to New Brighton, the poor wretches trying to sleep being woken at midnight to change trains at Shrewsbury, and with Joseph Bloor's company from Macclesfield to Dundee, two of the members married with children who kept being sick all the way. Through this I wove some kind of a story, with the heroine coming out into the sunshine at the end to declare affectingly, with her face pressed against that of an old donkey, she knew the world was simple. This claimed not the mystical experience I had hoped for when at the age of fourteen I had pressed the Dalai Lama's prayer-wheel to my forehead but an actual experience when, during the time that Mother was away for Gilby's funeral, I wandered into the park at the back of the High Street, Ipswich, and, while I was sitting on a bench, an old donkey came up and pressed his face against mine, as if in sympathy. Waves seemed to flow between us.

An odd note came through the hotel letter-box inviting me to a meeting of The Creative Circle at 64 Springfield Road the following Saturday at 8 pm. There was no signature or explanation, but, hoping it might be something interesting, I went. The front door was opened to me by a man who said, 'I'll show you through', and he took me through the house, out into the overgrown garden at the back and then up some steps into a conservatory. Here were a number of young men seated around a china fountain. This presumably was The Creative Circle. I wondered what it created.

Then it all came out. More than a year ago I had sent one of the poems I had written during my first period in Dundee to 'The Poets' Corner', edited by Victor B. Neuburg; this was a regular feature of the *Sunday Referee*. I can't remember now what it was about; it had not got a prize but had received an 'Honourable Mention' accorded to senders of 'good poems'. A young man seated himself beside me and explained that a number of those who had sent in poems had found their way to 'Vicky's', usually on Saturday evenings, and Geoffrey Lloyd had thought it would be nice to meet everyone who had contributed and said he would send out circulars, inviting people to meet Vicky and each other. 'We're all very fond of Vicky.'

I asked the speaker his name.

William Thomas was what I thought he said but he corrected me. No, it was a special Welsh name, I would never have heard it. He would spell it for me, D-Y-L-A-N. Dylan Thomas. In Wales the y was pronounced more like a 'u', but when he came to London he found people here were pronouncing it as the 'i' in Bill. He'd decided to keep it as the English pronunciation of his name. It sounded more distinguished.

Something began to stir in my recollection of the column. Wasn't Dylan Thomas the prizewinner?

Vicky had got the *Sunday Referee* to arrange with Longman's that the latter should publish a collection of poems by the author selected by Vicky at the end of the year as having sent in what he judged the best poems. The first year's winner was Pamela Hansford Johnson, whose book *Symphony for Full Orchestra* had already appeared. She wasn't here tonight but had been a regular at Vicky's from the beginning. And yes, this year the published author was to be himself and he was very excited about it.

'What is it to be called?' I asked.

'*Eighteen Poems.*'

He asked me what I did.

I said I had acted, in various parts of the country including Wales. I threw in that I had been down a coalmine.

'It's more than I have!' he exclaimed. He did not come from the mining part, but from Swansea, which he thought very nice, except for the railway running along the front.

I have heard tales of the riotous and outrageous behaviour of Dylan Thomas from those who met him in later years; but as I remember him, at Vicky's, he was just a quietly spoken, pleasant young man.

Then the door from the inner rooms of the flat opened and we were in the presence of Victor B. Neuburg. Shorter than the grey-haired lady who accompanied him – Runia Tharpe, alias Sheila Macleod – there was at first sight something disproportionate about him: his head, with its shock of curling hair too big for the rest of him, his hands and ankles, which absence of socks left bare, suggesting a body desperately thin. Features I would say refined Jewish, but the shaded blue eyes carried me to an illusive impression of ancient Egypt, Karnak, the ibis of Thoth. He bowed to us all with graceful, old-fashioned courtesy. How nice of us to have come to see him ...

I knew I had caught Vicky's eye for he came straight over to Dylan and me. Dylan said, 'I've been telling her something of the history of the Poets' Corner.' He told Vicky what he had just gathered from me, that I was an actress; he didn't think we had had an actress amongst us before.

Somebody raised the question, should we give ourselves a name as a group? Vicky said there was a Greek word, 'zoe', meaning life. Zoeists could mean people putting life into things. 'It begins with a z and so few words do.'

It must have been on a subsequent Saturday that someone asked whether we should invite well-known people to speak to us. Idris Davies – a son of a coal-miner, more Welsh than Dylan – said well-known people were not always all that interesting. Hadn't we enough ideas of our own to keep each other interested? Dylan said members must not buttonhole other members and read their own poetry to them, which could force a choice between saying something insincere or hurtful. He didn't think we should become a poetry-reading group. There was The Poetry Society for that. He would not be against an informal discussion group, only he didn't like the name Zoeists, as Zoe could be mistaken for 'Zooey'. Calling us The Creative Circle had been considered too pretentious.

I suggested The Conservatory Club, as we met in a conservatory, but Pamela Hansford Johnson rejected that – people might confuse it with Conservative.

She was in those days very political and very far to the Left. She reported Vicky as complaining, 'You children always bring everything down to politics', and said, 'But everything *does* come down to politics.'

But if she was – as was Geoffrey Lloyd – a Communist, she was not, as the majority of Communists were, atheists. I recall her sitting bolt upright – prim, erect and stalwart – saying, 'I am a Christian.'

Zoeists or Zoists, for want of a better name, we remained (not Zooists, as ridiculously misspelled by Constantine Fitzgibbon).

Most of this was thrashed out at our committee meeting on 29 June 1935, at which we decided those of us present were the committee:

Pamela, Dylan, Geoffrey Lloyd, Geoffrey Pollett, Herbert Corby, Idris Davis, Walter Ford and myself. Members should pay a five shillings a year subscription, to pay for tea, milk and the purchase of a tea-set.

Pamela arrived with Dylan and Geoffrey Lloyd. They had between them five bottles of beer, which they had thought to distribute between those assembled, but the unexpected absence of Vicky and Runia left us without access to glasses. Pollett suggested that as the door between the conservatory and their ground floor flat was probably not locked, we should simply go in and take glasses from the sideboard. Pamela did not think Runia would like our penetrating into their rooms in their absence, and I suggested we had better just drink from the bottles, wipe them and pass them round. So we did.

Then Vicky and Runia came in, and Runia, when she saw us drinking, said our behaviour was 'disgusting'. She stamped. I was dumbfounded. She said the smell of beer was disgusting to Vicky. Vicky said it wasn't and told her to stop making such a fuss. He also agreed to be our Chairman.

A. L. Morton (a neighbour of Vicky's from Steyning days) gave us a talk on 'Poets Town and Country' with extracts from Thomas Hardy, Edward Thomas and – his favourite – A. E. Housman:

> The chestnut casts his flambeaux
> … there's an end of May.

Vicky declared, a little obliquely, that in the stoicism of these lines Housman ranked with Marcus Aurelius, Catullus and Lucretius. His only English peer was Emily Brontë.

Someone gave a talk on woodcraft and 'Men of the Trees'. I talked on something. Then Cyril Moore, advertising manager of the *Sunday Referee*, who had let me in the first evening and had the flat below Vicky's, said that he had met a real yogi in Lyons Corner House.

Mr Rai *was* a real yogi. He explained the laws of Manu. The caste system was originally one of the responsibilities, not privileges, and he classified the yogas as paths to union with the divine through Raja Yoga, exercise of will, Bhakti Yoga, devotion to a teacher (for the Hindus Krishna, for Christians he suggested Christ), Jnana Yoga, study and reasoning, Hatha Yoga, physical exercises (his line), Karma Yoga, action in the world, and something that might interest us as we were poets, Mantra Yoga, the use of sound to create vibrations on higher planes. All were honourable. It was a matter of what one felt came to oneself most naturally.

We wanted to see him perform his exercises. He said he could only do them at dawn. So we went home, to return in the small hours. Normally he did them naked, but somebody lent him bathing trunks. Most of the exercises he performed were simple stretches, but he did one thing I have never seen done by anyone else, not even Iyengar: he sent a kind of wave motion up his spine, apparently moving all the vertebrae to one side then the other, dislocating them, yet bringing them back into order. On this path a vegetarian diet was required, and continence for life. Someone asked if he did not find this difficult; he said no because the energy was not stopped, it was converted into that of a finer level.

Vicky said, 'It's obvious you know something I've wanted to know all my life.' If Mr Rai could spare him time for a private talk, he would like to tell him a long story and ask if he had any advice to give 'for a case like mine'.

Rai said it was strange the way invisible wires pulled. He had arrived from India (on some business for his father), knowing no one, and in this strange city of so many million inhabitants, in the first place where he looked for something to eat, he met Mr Moore, who had brought him to the one house where he could perhaps be of some use.

Something else struck me. During most of the Saturday talks, conscious of knowing less about poetry than most of the others, I said very little; but here now, with Rai, it was I who put the greater number of the questions to him; it was Vicky and I who were talking with him all the time.

The following week Rai was there again and afterwards asked if he could drive any of us home. Two got into the back of his car, and I into the front beside him. When we stopped, outside the Pembridge Hotel, in Pembridge Crescent, where Mother and I were now staying, I asked if I might read his palm. There was insufficient light in the car, so we got out and crouched in front of the headlamps. There were few lines that I could discern, but a plain mystic cross. He told me he felt Mr Neuburg was a very advanced soul, but his body had been wrecked by wrong training in youth. He had felt his own inadequacy to deal with a case so grave and called for help from his teacher; though almost any exercise would be too much for him, he had prescribed something which would benefit him. He gave me his address, in Lahore, and said I should contact him, 'When you come to India.' I had no plans to go to India nor could I afford it. I said, 'I was conceived in India but I do not feel that I am going back there.'

He conceded, perhaps not. My path could lie here.

But did it? It had become evident I was no longer on the stage. I had told Mother I did not want to take any more engagements in the provinces, but I had not succeeded in obtaining an audition for any West End production. I was doing nothing. The Saturday evenings at the Zoeists had become the centre of my life but I had, as it were, forgotten to have a career. My novel, 'Stage Without Glamour', was finished but I had not been able to find a publisher for it. I lent it to Vicky, not without some hesitation as he had all the poems submitted to the Poets' Corner to read. He said, 'It's very sordid', so I supposed he had got stuck in the chapter about the nightmare train journey.

A man who had come in and appeared to be an old acquaintance of his said, 'I'd like to read it.'

He said this with such an air of significant importance that I thought he must or might be a publisher or literary agent, at any rate somebody who would help me get it published. It was handed over to him.

Vicky called him Gussy. His name was Gerard Heym. He drove me back in his car. I told Mother I had been driven back by a man I did not feel altogether comfortable with, who had asked me to tea. Why did I distrust him, she asked.

'He said I had a profound mind.'

'That's not an indecent remark.'

'I hadn't said anything profound.'

Sometimes an impression could be formed on very little. 'Where has he asked you to tea?'

'The Devonshire Club, in St James's Street.'

'It's a very respectable place.'

At the club, he asked me about my background, and when I said my father had been in the Indian Army he asked if he had contact with any Tibetans, had gifts from Tibetans.

I told him about the prayer-wheel and he said that must have been intended for me, so that I should have something in this life to connect me with the land of the Lamas.

I would have liked to think that, but the presentation had been before I was even conceived.

He didn't get down to talking about my novel. He asked me to tea there again next week.

Next week he asked me what I had dreamed.

I told him I had dreamed about the Martello Towers near Clacton, that were built as defences when an invasion by Napoleon was feared.

It was true but it seemed to rattle him. He said this was against him, because he had a foreign name and was seen as an invader.

Perhaps so, but I did not fancy being psychoanalysed and it seemed to be only for some clues as to my psyche he had any interest at all in my novel.

He spoke about some books at his place in Chelsea he would like to show me. I didn't want to go to his place, but agreed to meet him at the Victoria and Albert Museum to look at the Buddhas.

There were a lot of them, and he asked me for my comments on every one in turn. He said the ones I liked were the Khmer, those of the classic period, but I was appearing to warm to the soft smiling ones of the southern Buddhism, whereas it was the stern-faced ones of the north we must follow.

We? I wasn't going anywhere in his company.

He was furious and said I trusted Neuburg but not himself. Neuburg was riddled with sex, though impotent because of his sexual excesses with Aleister Crowley.

I had heard that name; there had surely been a court case reported in the papers. It had to to with magic and the judge had said some very unpleasant things. Was this, I wondered, the 'long, sad story' Vicky had confided to Rai? I did not think Heym should be talking about it in this way. Nevertheless I agreed to meet him at the British Museum where he wanted to show me one more Buddha, a stern one, of the north.

I knew that Vicky regarded me in a special way. He would sit looking at me, and on one occasion when he did so he said, 'I believe that you remember.' I had gathered enough of his vocabulary to realise he meant in Plato's sense.

Then one evening he slipped some handwritten pages into my hand. He had woken up while dreaming the content and written it whilst still half-asleep, in another state altogether. He hadn't had the courage to read it himself, yet. 'Don't let the others see.'

I read it back at the hotel. It was very strange. I felt that he had given me what was really a love-poem to Crowley, but infused with a strain of terrible regret:

> The ways are known
> To one who dreams in autumn and alone ...
> No music and no memory is this,
> Nothing at all; a new begotten kiss.

When I gave it back to him the following week, I knew I had to do it so that no one would see. As he took it from me, he said. 'Don't say anything about it.'

The Saturday after that, as we were breaking up, Runia said a very old friend of Vicky's would be coming the next day, for her seventieth birthday. As some people had taken to dropping in on Sunday afternoons I took this as a warning to keep away as they would not want to be disturbed. Cyril Moore, however, insisted that I come; as his guest if not theirs. If we felt ourselves unwanted we should have tea in his room downstairs.

When I arrived a number of people were already in the conservatory. Runia joined us and said we might find Vicky's guest rather frightening. She was very downright; she was a Buddhist initiate.

A young man I had not seen before, apparently called Donaldson, from the *Sunday Graphic*, asked if she would give him a story about Jack the Ripper. I wondered what a Buddhist initiate might have to do with Jack the Ripper.

Then Vicky came in with Cremers. (She was a Baroness and it would have been correct to call her Lady Cremers, but by her own wish she was always called by simply her surname as though she were a man.)

She was dressed entirely in black, her white hair straight and cut in a short bob. Vicky brought her over to me and said, 'This is a little lady I'd like you to meet.' (He always referred to me in the third person as 'This little lady'.)

Vicky said, 'The last time I saw Crowley, he cursed me with full ritual.'

It was strange he should tell her this in front of me. It was the first time I heard him utter the name of Crowley, so the story of their having been a connection between them was true.

It was just before he – Crowley – left for America. 'In that room, with all those things in it.'

Cremers said, 'You knew a thing or two yourself', meaning he would have taken measures to protect himself.

Vicky said he had been too miserable. When he screwed up his resolve to tell Crowley he was leaving him, he had been prepared for his violent anger, for a stormy scene, but not for a full ritual curse, not for the malice that could have willed upon him death by a whole series of horrible diseases. He had had a nervous breakdown.

Runia joined us and the conversation stopped.

Cyril Moore signalled to me to come down to his sitting room.

[66]

A few minutes afterwards Vicky and Cremers joined us there. Cyril Moore asked helpfully, 'Would you like us to go out? Jean and I can walk in the garden.'

Vicky burst out laughing. 'They think we're a spooning couple, Cremers! They think we want to be alone.'

So we stayed. Vicky drew up a hard chair between us, so that we all faced Cremers. It was her hands that made movements in which there seemed to be so much power that I could imagine sparks coming from them. She said, not unkindly, 'Crowley hadn't the power, Victor.' Her assertion was that Crowley had succeeded in awakening and raising a current but had been unable to raise it above his middle. 'Halfway in everything, Crowley!'

(I didn't, at the time, know what Cremers meant by 'current'. Looking back, I am sure her reference was to the occult force known by Theosophists as 'kundalini', but of that more later.)

Not a black magician, Cremers went on, nor a white magician. A sex maniac. 'It was sex, sex, sex all the way with Crowley.'

Vicky said, 'You're not telling me anything I don't know, Cremers. Why do you find it necessary to say these things to me?'

She said Crowley couldn't curse. Victor hadn't died of any of the diseases wished upon him.

He conceded that. He had 'a bit of trouble here', putting his hand on the lower part of his chest, but none of the things he was cursed to get. But what hurt was that Crowley could have hated him enough to wish such horrible things on him.

She said she set herself to break Crowley. 'I killed Crowley.'

Although I thought she only meant psychologically, it was still quite strong stuff.

Vicky was sitting hunched in his chair. He said, 'You're a beast, Cremers.'

Cyril Moore and I went out into the garden. When we rejoined the others in the conservatory. Vicky said to me, 'This little lady has had a strange afternoon.' He did not know what I had made of what I had heard. It had been the great drama of his life, he said. When he had first met Crowley, 'I thought he was a very fine person, I think you would have thought so, too.' The next moment he was handing a plate around, as though nothing had happened. 'Have a macaroon.'

When I was about to go Cremers took my hand in an iron grasp and held it for some time, looking into my eyes. 'Ha, child, how old are you?'

[67]

'Twenty.'

She continued to look into me for a few more seconds, then said in her bluff, gruff way, 'Goodbye.' It was oddly benign.

On the following afternoon at the Pembridge, Heym called for me. This was quite unexpected. But he drove me off in his car, asking who was at Neuburg's yesterday afternoon.

When I mentioned Cremers, he started. 'She is a black magician. You must not go to her house.'

She hadn't asked me to go to her house, nor did I feel that she was a black magician.

Had I not noticed her hands, he said, they were claws.

She was a bit frightening, I agreed, but I thought she was a protection to Vicky.

I asked, 'Was there some organisation to which you all belonged?'

'You want to know too much.'

And he insisted, again, on my coming to see the old books he wanted to show me. In Chelsea, in Beaufort Street. He said my suspicions of him were 'insulting to a man of my calibre'.

Where he wanted to take me was a library, stacked with shelves running from wall to wall and floor to ceiling, with only narrow alleys between them. The sole piece of furniture was a classroom desk from a children's school. He put my novel on it and said a bit about what he found in it, but then took down from one of the shelves one of his treasures. The writing and deities looked Tibetan. I knew the image of the various entities with their gods were their shakhtis and were not meant to be indecent – there were some in the British Museum – but the red lips given these made them look unpleasant. What was the kind of paint? It was not oil, and yet was so thick it almost stood up, and it had an enamel-like brilliance. And the ground was not paper but something thicker. Heym said it was parchment, and the binding was vellum.

The curtains had been drawn when we entered, 'to keep the sun out' and though he parted them, it was only slightly. I began to feel really uneasy. I looked again in perplexity at the volume.

'It's magic,' he said. 'Everything in this room is magic.'

Suspicious, I asked, 'Where did you get these?'

'They are missing from a Tibetan monastery.'

Did he mean they were stolen? He said their existence was secret.

'Even from Vicky?'

'Most of all from Neuburg.'

I did not like that. Then he said, 'Neuburg and Crowley were very near. Where they failed, we shall succeed.'

That was enough. I said I was going to go. But he placed himself against the door, barring my exit.

He said, 'Are your eyes too sacred to kiss?'

I said, 'Please get away from the door. I want to leave.'

It was a hard staring match. At last he stood aside, and, as I passed him, he shouted curses at me, 'You are blasted! You are barren.'

Outside in the street, I walked, in what I hoped looked a dignified manner, until I had got round the corner, out of sight from his window. Then I ran.

Mother said if I wasn't going back on to the stage, it was not too late for me to train for something else. Art?

I had thought of this when leaving school. I had always enjoyed painting, but the only ways in which one could earn a living as an artist were through commercial art – I did not want to draw advertisements; book illustration – I was a painter rather than a draughtsman; or portraiture – I liked drawing people whose faces interested me, but to succeed at it one would need not only to draw extremely well but have a certain talent for flattery. I feared it would, like the stage, be impractical – more enjoyable as an amateur thing.

Then, said Mother, would I go to a secretarial college and learn shorthand typing? This seemed to me a come-down. However, there was a Major Mackenzie in the hotel who worked at Scotland Yard, and he said if I qualified in this domain he would recommend me for a post at the Yard. This, at least, sounded interesting, and I agreed to go to a college off Victoria Street. Vicky, when I told him, was really sad for me.

One Saturday evening brought a young man called Harold Herzmark. He came only the once, but I met him again at a party given by Walter Ford in Hampstead, and he accompanied me home. He was returning to Oxford now, he said, but would like to meet me again in the Christmas vac. Perhaps we could go to a theatre.

Vicky's was not the only column in the *Sunday Referee* to be concerned with poetry. I saw that in another, a competition was advertised in the column by Templar for a translation from Dante's 'Inferno'. The lines set were from canto v, Francesca to Dante relating how she and Paolo were seduced into an unlawful love by reading a book together. On 13 October the result was announced: three people shared the prize which would be equally divided between them; they would receive 10s 6d each. One of them was Jean Fuller. All I can remember of it now is rhyming 'tender-hearted' with 'He from whom I never shall be parted', and then closing with: 'A pander was that book and he who wrote it.' (The Italian being '*Galeotto fu il libro e chi lo scrisse.*')

Although it was not printed, it was the first time I had won a prize with any kind of literary composition, and Vicky noticed and congratulated me on it.

But then, on 27 October, Mother, who was down before me, greeted me with 'Something dreadful has happened to the *Sunday Referee.*' The whole paper had a different layout. There was no 'Poets' Corner', no Templar.

I went up to Vicky's that afternoon and found almost everybody else there. Vicky told us the first time he and Runia heard of it was that morning. Last night, the type had been set up as usual. They had been to see Hayter Preston, then Mark Goulden. What had happened was this: the proprietors had decided to switch to a policy designed to increase sales; as this must lower its tone, both Goulden and Preston had resigned. The *Sunday Referee* as we had known it was no more.

But in the bus back, Runia and he had been putting on their thinking caps. They hadn't got a lot of money, yet could produce something between them. They wouldn't be able to pay contributors.

By the following week it had all been settled. *Comment* would appear on Saturdays, price 3d. Dylan and Pamela, though now able to sell their work, sent their contributions *gratis*. Reading something Pamela had sent him, 'His clothes were new and nervous', Vicky said that for conciseness this compared with Jane Austen.

The first number of *Comment* appeared on 7 December 1935, carrying stories as well as poems. Herbert Corby and I came on Friday evenings to address the wrappers and stick them round the copies being sent out and put the stamps on. I liked these evenings because of the close contact they allowed us with Vicky and Runia. Vicky would be reading his immense mail, picking out the poems he would print. Dylan was back in Wales by this time, but I remember Vicky opening a bulging envelope from him. 'What's he sent me this time? ... "Grief, thief of time, crawls off ..."'

Vicky kept asking me to submit poems, but I had become very shy of presenting anything in this company. As he was taking stories, I sent him a story instead, 'Many Are Called'; it appeared on 18 January 1936, and stretched over two issues.

Harold took me to see *Lady Precious Stream*, at the Adelphi. Something in the play caused us, as we came out, to be talking of the holy man on his path to attainment. Harold said, 'When he's got there, he ceases to be interesting. He's only interesting on his way there.'

This shocked me. The blessed state must be worth attaining.

Though the difference in our views was apparently dismaying, it did not seem adequate cause for breaking our engagement, for we had become engaged very quickly – though as he was at Oxford on a scholarship, the terms of which precluded his marrying before he had taken his degree, it would have to be a long engagement.

I thought it would somehow shake down ...

He said he would come down again for my birthday.

Mother asked me what I would like to have as a present. I thought that for my twenty-first it should be something lasting – a clock. I walked through Harrods and found one I liked.

Harold didn't like it. A clock seemed to him an unsuitable choice, and he did not like its shape. 'It's got hips.'

I thought it was a nicely balanced shape, and was disappointed that he did not like it. (I still have it, though it has ceased to go.)

On 7 March Mother and her friend Tom joined us for drinks, then went off somewhere on their own. Harold took me to dinner and dance at the Regent Palace Hotel.

It was not really much of a birthday. When next at Vicky's some reference was made to my being twenty. I said, 'Twenty-one.'

Vicky exclaimed, 'She's had a twenty-first!' Something must be done to celebrate it. And he gave me a book of his poems.

> FOR JEAN
> V O Fuller . / .
> From V B N . / .
> For her 21st (7. 3. 36) . / .
> 14. 3. 36 /
> Vicky . / .

I thought the pattern of dots astride slashes must have some mystic meaning.

Vicky had several times asked me to bring Mother, and the evening she chose was 21 March. A. L. Morton was talking about history and whether it was possible to write it objectively. He referred to 'the progress of humanity', which prompted Mother to ask, 'Does humanity progress?'

Vicky chipped in. 'Oh it must, there would otherwise be no point in living, no point in anything.' He conceded we had not seen anyone superior to Plato and Socrates, but suggested that was because as they continued getting wiser and wiser, they transcended the need for a physical body and went on to a non-physical plane. The humanity we saw was composed of those of us who had not made it yet to the Nirvanic state. This was to meet her objection that there appeared no obvious spiritual progress. As they attained, they disappeared.

A *Comment* dinner, to celebrate the third anniversary of The Poets' Corner, was to be held at a restaurant in Dean Street on 9 May. I wore the turquoise blue dress I had worn for Lady Cattering, with the teetery blue shoes that went with it.

I was asked to make one of the after dinner speeches. It was the first I had ever made. As I was not a literary expert, I concentrated on the affection we all felt for Vicky and Runia. I saw I had reduced them to tears – I hope by the sentiment rather than the delivery.

Walter Ford had now taken to inviting people to his place on Saturday evenings. I thought this very tactless, as it was siphoning people away from Vicky's. Indeed, this did herald the break up of the Saturdays in the conservatory.

Herbert Corby and I continued to come on the Friday evenings to address the wrappers and send out *Comment*. But then one evening Runia said there was no need for us to come to do this menial work. The woman who 'did' for them would do it for a few extra pence.

I looked at Vicky, hoping for him to say we must continue to come. He could not have realised this meant we would not see him again. Was she really saving us from unnecessary work or was she getting rid of us because we were a nuisance? I shall never know.

The last *Comment* I received, through the post, was dated 13 June 1936.

It was the end.

In July, Harold and I joined forces with Mother, Tom and his three children for a holiday in Swanage. Then, soon after our return, Mother left London with Tom. He had asked her to marry him and she had at first agreed, but on reflecting that on remarriage she would lose her widow's pension and thereby her independence, and that the upbringing and education of his three children must remain a priority, she decided not to; though when he was moved to a post in another city, she went with him.

I was now alone at the Pembridge. I passed the secretarial examination and got a certificate. Major Mackenzie did recommend me to the Yard, and I was taken on, but solely in the typing pool and I don't think he could have realised how much that was ghettoed. One did not meet people who did interesting things, one just typed what one was given. I remember just one thing, the case of a police officer alleged to have used the word 'f--k'. A subsequent paper on the file provided a 'c': 'f-ck'. I wondered what the obviously missing vowel could be. One letter said he found it impossible to believe a police officer could have used such an obscene word on duty. In a still later paper in the file, the whole word appeared. I still did not know what it meant.

The pay I received was largely consumed by bills at the Pembridge, and while that was for full board I was not even eating the lunches. It was too far from the Yard, and I was having sandwich lunches by the Thames. I must find a less expensive hotel. I found one, the Trebovir, in Earls Court, about a pound a week cheaper.

But now Harold put it to me that living in hotels was an expensive way of living. It was the way I had learned from Mother. But anyway why did I need to *be* in London? With Mother gone and the Zoists no more, what was I in London *for*?

In Oxford, Harold said, I would be amongst people I could make friends with. He had, by the terms of his scholarship, to live in college but would look around and see what he could find in the way of rooms in the town at affordable prices. I could put an advertisement in the local paper and perhaps earn as much as a private typist as I did at the Yard. I might find myself being given somebody's thesis to type. There would be more interesting avenues.

In the New Year 1937 I handed in my notice at the Yard, and, in the spring, moved to Oxford.

I will treat only the peripheral relationships; they were the ones that lasted. Harold's friends in the college were Theo Cadoux and Basil Mitchell. Whereas Harold was reading French and German, they were both reading 'Greats': two years Latin and Greek, switching to philosophy and history thereafter.

When Harold led me into Basil's room, ground floor back, my eye was caught by a row of books in orange cloth ranged along one of his shelves. He said they were by Inayat Khan, a Sufi. Sufism was the mystical tradition within Islam. It had a tendency to eclecticism, which Inayat Khan had developed into his idea of *The Unity of Religious*

Ideals, the title of his major work. He had come to the West preaching this in 1910. Basil's father had been one of his earliest Western converts and Basil had been brought up knowing the Inayat Khan family. They lived in Suresnes, near Paris, and their place of worship was adorned with candles dedicated to all the major religions of the world: the officiating priest would light up each one in turn, saying 'To the glory of the omnipresent God, I light this light to ... the Christian religion ... the Jewish religion... the Zoroastrian religion ... the Buddhist religion ... the Hindu religion ... the religion of Islam (I am not sure if I get them in the right order). Inayat Khan was now dead, but the elder of the two sons, Vilayat, was expected to take it over when deemed old enough (it was being cared for in the meantime by uncles). Basil's favourite in the family was the elder of two girls, Noor-un-Nisa, known within the family as Babali, 'Daddy's daughter'. Something very ethereal about her. Their mother was American.

Theo's father was interesting, too. A Congregationalist minster, he was a tutor in Hebrew in Mansfield College. I feared a Congregationalist minister would be stuffy, but he received Harold and me with ponderous courtesy at his home every Sunday afternoon, and Theo told me that he had upstairs a copy of the four Gospels made in his own hand, using different coloured inks and in different styles of lettering to distinguish what he believed to be the sources of different verses. Sometimes there was a change of ink or style even in the middle of a verse. He was trying to see what, when all the doubtful sources had been pared away and the accumulated myths put on one side, one could reasonably believe to have been the historic life and real teaching of Jesus. This sounded keenly interesting.

I also met Enid Starkie, Harold's 'special subject' tutor.

In the summer of that year I went with Harold to Paris, where I read in the Bibliothèque Sainte-Geneviève, and Basil said he would be talking to the Sufis in Suresnes and asked us to his talk. There was the ritual, as he had described it, and then he had been billed to speak on 'The Virtue of Tolerance' but said he had decided to speak of 'The Virtue of Intolerance' instead. What would have been the use of Elijah if he had been tolerant?

Afterwards, he introduced us to Vilayat and Noor – both very reticent on that day.

A year later, when we went to France for a second summer holiday, we took our gas-masks, which had just been issued to everyone as the shadow of another war was looming, slung over our shoulders. After a while spent in Auvergne – eating deeply into the savings put into my Post Office Savings Account during my first engagement in Dundee with the Shaftesbury Players, which I had earmarked for a time of need. We returned to Paris to find the dustbins stood un-emptied along the pavements. The men had been called up. Hitler had marched into Czechoslovakia. They really did expect a war.

Then Chamberlain came back with the assurance from Hitler that the Germans had no further territorial ambitions. No war. I received a postcard from Mother: 'Thank God. Thank Chamberlain.'

A year later it was obvious I could not remain in a relationship that was utterly destructive to me. The worst of it was that my faith had been so undermined that I could not even say 'put it down to experience' if there was no hereafter in which the experience counted ... nothing at all. I knew only that I had to be on my own again.

I wrote to Mother asking if I could have the use of the furniture that had been in store all these years. It was brought round in a van and decanted in the room I had found in King Henry's Road, London (near Chalk Farm). I felt, at last, a certain relief.

Then there was the Nazi-Soviet pact, 1 August, followed by the invasion by Hitler's troops of Poland, and on 3 September, Mr Chamberlain's voice, tremulous on the radio, telling us we were at war with Germany.

Five

A t first nothing seemed to be happening. It was the period of the
Phoney War. I did what I ought to have done before I left school:
I started to work for 'matric'. I was disadvantaged by not having a
university degree. London took external candidatures, unlike Oxford
or Cambridge, but to be allowed to proceed one needed 'matric'. I
inquired of the university if they had any register of tutors in mathematics. The poor woman who came to me was very patient with a
slow-thinking pupil but I did reach a grasp of some things. I entered
for the exam taking English, French, Latin, History and the compul-
sory Mathematics. I failed on the last, notwithstanding the tuition,
but I felt only by a narrow margin – another effort and I should get
through. I was about to re-enter when somebody drew to my attention that being over twenty-three I could enter for University Entrance
instead, which offered an optional alternative to Mathematics: Logic.
Logic! Basil and Theo had both read Logic as part of their philosophy course. Both had come down from Oxford with a first in Greats.
I had been party to many of their conversations while studying, the
jokes they made about impossible syllogisms and thought I would be
sharp enough to detect an 'undistributed middle'. I asked them what
I should read. Eaton's *General Logic*. I passed, and entered for
London Intermediate, for which the subjects to be taken were reduced
to four. I chose English, History, Logic and Ethics. For the last I read
Plato's *Republic*, Socratic dialogues and, on the recommendation of
Theo and Basil, who had remained friends of mine, Broad's *Five Types
of Ethical Theory*.

In the meantime, the landlord wanted my room in King Henry's
Road, but I was able to find another nearby, at 28 Oppidans Road.
This was even nearer the top of Primrose Hill, though one could no
longer walk on it, as its grassy top had been taken over by the military.
They had guns installed there, in case of an air attack. But on the hori-
zon the barrage balloons looked reassuring. I was of course now not
far from Vicky and Runia's and walked to Springfield Road but found
the whole place had changed.

One evening towards the end of May I had an unaccountable urge to go out and stand there again. This was lunatic; I was making for something no longer there. But I veered off, into Boundary Road, and stood for a long time looking at a building with a porch; then returned. I hadn't the addresses of any of the Zoists, but Dylan now had a publisher: I wrote to him care of his publisher.

I received a reply in his familiar writing:

Laugharne
Carmarthenshire
Wales
20 June 1940

Dear Miss Fuller,

    I haven't heard anything from Vicky and Runia for years until about a fortnight ago when Pamela Johnson wrote to tell me that Vicky had just died. I was very grieved to hear it, he was a sweet, wise man. Runia's address is 84 Boundary Road, NW8. At least, I suppose she is still there. I wrote her a letter, but haven't had a reply yet, probably she is too sad to write.

Yours sincerely,
DYLAN THOMAS

I walked out and checked. 84 was the house with the porch, at which I had stood and looked.

The war had brought Mother back to London, having parted from Tom. She had gone to Ruskin Manor Hotel, Denmark Hill, so that we were now at the opposite ends of the 68 bus route, and on Sundays took it, to lunch alternately at her place and at mine.

France fell. I was cycling down the Chalk Farm Road, when I saw a poster of which only the end letters were visible:

CE

As I drew nearer, I read

NCE
ES

And then I saw:

FRANCE
GIVES
IN

The shock. Was the inconceivable conceivable? Could they get over here? I was never so thankful as to hear Churchill's voice vibrant on the radio, 'We shall fight them on the beaches ...'

On 10 July 1940 Basil told me the whole Inayat Khan family had arrived on the doorstep of his parents in Southampton, had gone on to Oxford now, but Noor and Vilayat were in London for the day. Could I join them at Lyons Corner House? With them were Basil, Theo, Harold and a girl they had met on a boat.

Vilayat and Noor had both had scruples as to whether they should take part in the fighting, but felt they were not neutral in their hearts, so they set out from Paris, finding themselves in a long procession of refugees, whole families, with their old people, their children, their pets, a little dog, a canary in a cage. The German planes came down and strafed them. This seemed so monstrous that Vilayat was conscious of a most non-Buddhistic desire to strafe them back. He was going to get into the RAF. Noor said, her eyes wide with wonderment, 'They came down so low we could see their faces and they must have seen the faces of the people they were killing.' She was hunting down the certificates for a course of nursing which Claire and she had taken with the Red Cross in Paris and which should have got shipped over here. She was also talking about going back and joining 'the maquis'.

Everybody was talking about 'dog-fights' in the sky. The first German aircraft I saw close to was on 18 August, over King Henry's Road, where I was standing: the German and the RAF plane came so low that one could distinguish the black swastika on the one and the blue, red and white concentric circles on ours, and even the faces of the men, and the little jets of flame. I thought they were going to crash into the houses, but they regained height and disappeared in the direction of St John's Wood. Which won? I never heard.

At any rate by August the German planes were coming over nightly, starting just after sundown, continuing till dawn, our guns on Primrose Hill trying all the time to get them. A whole row of houses along one side of Primrose Hill Road was brought down, by a thing said to be a 'land-mine'. A woman who had been in bed on the top floor found herself descended to street level, uninjured. I noticed tied to a railing a hand-written notice saying a rest centre for the bombed-out had been opened up the road. I thought I ought to do something to justify my refusal of some official's well-intentioned offer to evacuate me, so I walked up, looked in at the door, and asked, 'Can I help?'

Yes. People had brought tea in plenty but only a few cups, so they had to be constantly retrieved, washed out and reissued. I stood at the sink, washing cups, until three in the morning, when a Miss Bertha Bowles, of the Church Army, said to me, '*You* lie down.' I lay down on the bare boards of the floor and slept deeply, aroused only by the feet of people stepping over me and the All Clear siren. It was seven in the morning.

After that I worked several nights a week at the rest centre. It was an entirely voluntary gathering together of people without any kind of organisation behind it. Later we got better premises, in the vacated school in Harmood Street, off the Chalk Farm Road. I was given more to do with the homeless. Bertha Bowles said, 'Treat for shock in every case, even if they say they're not suffering from shock.' How did one treat for shock? 'Wrap them in rugs and take them tea.'

The hospitals were filled with the seriously injured and could not take in those whose misfortune was merely that the bombing had rendered them homeless, and, though shocked, had no injury to speak of save for a few cuts and bruises. It was there that we came in. We filled the gap. We were not trained nurses, but some people brought disinfectants and bandages. Some people brought suppers. I brought some of my rations, for instance my sugar which, as I did not take it in my tea, could be given to people who did. An ARP man said that as coming here meant going out in the Blitz, I should have a helmet. He gave me one. I still have it.

One morning a week Phoebe Llewellyn Smith was painting my portrait. She had been brought into our Oxford circle by Basil. Phoebe (Sir Hubert's daughter) had, like Basil and Theo, got a first in Greats, but she wanted – had always wanted – to be an artist and had looked forward to going to the Slade when she came down. Now she felt she ought to be doing war work. She got a job, eventually, as private secretary to Sir Archibald Sinclair, but in this interim had asked me to sit for her – in return for her hearing me over my Latin verbs and declensions.

One morning when there was a string of thuds she started slightly and said, 'What's that?'

'A stick of bombs,' I said, surprised that she asked.

She relaxed. But then said, 'Those bombs may have killed somebody. But one can't do anything about it. I thought somebody had slipped on the stairs.'

Basil called too. He was going into the Navy. Would I like to come with him to see a play. We went out and bought an evening paper and stood trying to read it. Obligingly, a German flare came floating above us, and we read the entertainments guide by its light.

Basil said the flares were sent ahead of the bombers to light up their intended target for them. They must be coming for our guns on Primrose Hill. Sure enough, the sky began to drone and we quickened our steps away.

The play we had chosen was a comedy with Owen Nares. As we came out afterwards and started walking back up Shaftesbury Avenue, a whole house burst into towering flames. 'Oil bomb,' somebody said.

'We can't do anything,' said Basil, and, as the fire engines approached in procession, steered me on.

From Tottenham Court Road we took the Tube, and I saw, for the first time, the people who camped there nightly with their eatables and drinkables and packs of cards. At Chalk Farm Basil was going on, to stay with friends further along the line, but I got out. As I approached Primrose Hill the guns were absolutely blazing, and, stunned by the noise and fearful of being hit by flak, I cowered against the wall, my helmet on my head, then scuttled along till at last I got my key in my door.

Oppidans Road was the nearest road of inhabited houses to the guns. The houses actually facing the hill had all been evacuated by order. But the noise was often deafening.

On 10 September Theo telephoned, very early, said he was in London and might he invite himself for breakfast.

He read aloud a bit of T. S. Eliot, *The Waste Land*, and from Milton's *Paradise Lost* – the fall of Satan, another of his favourite pieces for reading aloud. Then he said he had to call in at the London Hospital; would I care to come with him? (He was, like his father before him, a conscientious objector and serving in the Friends Ambulance Corps.) I had never been to the East End and was a bit hesitant about making my first trip there when it had evidently been pounded the previous night by German bombers. Pain was certain and disorganisation probable.

He persuaded me however. There was not much damage to be seen until after we had crossed Holborn Viaduct. Thereafter it became more apparent. A bomb had plainly fallen in Threadneedle Street. Rubble in the middle and police warning us off.

At Aldgate the police stopped us altogether. No we could not go on, at least not without making a considerable detour. We made it. I was, for the first time, in Whitechapel. The London Hospital looked intact. Theo dumped me in a pub while he went into it. I told the publican I was surprised to see the street so orderly. He said as soon as the All Clear had sounded in the morning, the people had come out of their houses with brooms, and swept up the fallen masonry, pushing it into the piles I could see, to simplify the work of the men who would come with their lorries to collect it.

Theo came out. We were in Jack the Ripper country here, but he thought the sites of the murders were probably now destroyed. We tried to walk towards one of the sites, but the tangle of firemen's hoses and that mixed smell of burning and wet I shall never forget were too much for us. The hospital, said Theo, had been hit in a few places, but only by bits of masonry falling from houses nearby. 'It's a stout building.' Staff were carrying on.

On Sunday 29 December Mother spent the afternoon with me, as usual, in Oppidans Road. Some time after tea she said she would go. 'I'd like to be aboard the bus before the Alert sounds.'

I walked with her to the terminus at Chalk Farm and saw her aboard. The Alert went almost immediately.

I walked back to my flat. From my window I could see that the sky to the east and south was reddening badly. It was going to be another night of heavy bombing. I became anxious as to whether Mother's bus would get through and, after giving it reasonable time, rang the Ruskin Manor. Impossible to get a line. I tried at intervals through the night. Still impossible. Either everyone was telephoning at once or perhaps the exchange had been hit.

Suddenly all the bells of the house were being rung. It was the warden saying we must be prepared to leave if the fire came this way. 'Don't go to bed. Or if you do, sleep dressed.' A lorry would take us.

I asked, 'Where?'

'Away from the fire.'

I looked round the room and chose the treasures I must take: the Tibetan prayer-wheel, my father's medals and sword (I took this down from the wall and practised walking with it) and photographs.

The warden did not come back, so I supposed our firemen were getting the better of the fire.

In the morning I was able to get through to the Ruskin Manor and to Mother. Yes she was all right. The poor 68 bus had broken all speed records as it crossed Waterloo Bridge and the city burned.

She said, 'Let's meet for coffee, at the ABC, half way between us.'

I got on the 68 bus. I had been expecting her to be weary, but she was bright-eyed. 'I can't help it,' she said, 'I feel so well. It's the adrenaline ... Do you realise, dear, we are living through history. HISTORY!'

From the bus, as it crossed Waterloo Bridge, she had seen St Paul's absolutely surrounded by the fire, black against the flames and the flames reflected in the water. 'I felt it dreadful to be an artist. It was so beautiful. Wren's dome never had such a setting!'

On Sunday 5 January 1941 I went to the Ruskin Manor for lunch with Mother. As always by the 68 bus. South of the river the damage was very bad. The Elephant was a festoon of white plaster. All along the Walworth Road houses had lost their fronts, leaving the rooms within all open to view. The lavatory pedestals were hanging, like strange blooms, from the pipes that were their stalks.

At the foot of Denmark Hill was a pub called The Fox under the Hill. Most of its above-ground structure had been destroyed, but from the basement drinks were being served up, and someone had adapted the sign so that it read 'The Fox Very Much Under the Hill'.

Mother said, 'This is a better war than the other. Then it was just the men marching away to be killed. This time we all take our chance together.'

I was during this time still working a few nights in each week at the rest centre, but of course there was no pay. We had no employers, just came and went as we had time. I did not want to be called up for the Army, as it would mean leaving my furniture, so I applied for a job in the Red Cross, and on Monday 17 February 1941 began work at their then HQ in St James's Palace. Then I noticed an advertisement from the Postal Censorship, and wondered if I could fit the bill. It said nothing about having a degree being necessary, only that one should have foreign languages, yet be British born.

I took my birth certificate, which declared me born on 7 March 1915 at Iver Heath, Buckinghamshire, to my interview on 20 May. One could go in at one of two levels: without foreign languages or with a minimum of two foreign languages, and there was a difference in pay.

Hoping to pass in at least two of them, I was offered three – French, Russian and Italian. One just had to translate a handwritten letter. I had expected to pass on the French and the Russian (I had been taking lessons recently on the latter) but not on the Italian, which I had allowed to get rusty. Unexpectedly, it was the other way round. I passed on the French of course but not the Russian. This was because the books in that language I had read (which included the whole of *Anna Karenina*) were printed and I did not recognise the handwritten deformations of the characters. I had, however, passed on the Italian. And so I was in, and summoned to report for duty on Monday, 16 June 1941.

We were given a week of training, which included a security training more rigorous than seems to have been practised in some organisations with more need to be secret. Then we were in King Edward's
Buildings, near St Paul's for three weeks (I ate my lunches on the steps
amongst the pigeons) and then to High Holborn, where there was foreign language stuff to read.

I hesitated before going to see Runia because I had never been sure
whether she liked or disliked me. In the event she received me with
unexpected warmth. What she had to say was exceedingly surprising.
Soon after she and Vicky had decided to live together, she received a
letter, over a woman's signature, saying that as it had come to the
writer's ears she was now the companion of Victor Neuburg, there
were things she ought to know and would be told if she called at a certain address. She was to tell no one. 'I didn't even tell Vicky.'

She said there were the names of three old ladies whom I had to
memorise: Fräulein Sprengel, Florence Farr and Annie Horniman.
When I began to write them down she stopped me. I must write down
nothing. I must commit to memory. She was old enough to die soon
and the story must be passed down to a person able to preserve it –
meaning, apparently, me. She asked me to repeat the names several
times, to be sure I had got them correctly: 'Fräulein Sprengel, Florence
Farr, Annie Horniman.' I took it that she had been talking with
Fräulein Sprengel, but she corrected me. 'No! Fräulein Sprengel never
came from Germany.' (I know today that certain researchers, notably
Ellic Howe and Bob Gilbert, have doubted whether she ever existed,
and Timothy d'Arch Smith has drawn to my attention that Florence
Farr died in 1917. So I have to assume that was Annie Horniman who
wrote to Runia, received her and told her about the other two.) These
ladies, said Runia, had the texts of very ancient rituals used in ancient
Egypt, concealed and preserved – in Germany – throughout the 2,000
years of Christianity. Fräulein Sprengel had passed them on to
England, where they became the basis of a society called The Golden
Dawn. This was the first I had heard of The Golden Dawn, though I
had long supposed that there had been some secret organisation. I
know now that Howe and Gilbert believe the rituals to have been composed not by the ancient Egyptians of the time of the Pharaoh but by
an English Freemason, Wynn Westcott, who gave them this fancy origin to make them more interesting; but my purpose here is to try to
stick to recording, as accurately as I can, what was said to me that

evening by Runia. The head of The Golden Dawn came to be a man called MacGregor Mathers, another new name to me. His, said Runia, 'was a very lonely position'. With so much to keep secret he must have longed for someone to talk to, and he began to talk to a young recruit who was very eager and pressing and whose name was Aleister Crowley. But Crowley was impatient – too impatient to wait to be given the rituals, so he stole them. That, the old lady told Runia, was why everything went wrong for him. Had he waited he would probably have been given them lawfully in due course. As he took them by violence, they went into reverse. Victor, when he was recruited by Crowley, had no idea of this but supposed the succession lawful. 'Vicky was therefore wholly innocent,' Runia was assured. It was just in case anything in Vicky's behaviour struck Runia as strange, the writer thought she ought to know this background.

Although it was summer, it was almost dusk when I rose to go. On the step I said something about its being strange, our having this conversation, and Runia said 'It's karmic.'

It was the first time I had heard that word. I did not know what it meant or how it was written. I thought it must mean something in the sense of fated.

Suddenly she dived back into the house and came out again with a book, with a light blue wrapper. It was a present for me. It was *Winged Pharaoh*, by Joan Grant.

I found the book extraordinary. Narrated in the first person, it apparently told the life of someone who had lived thousands of years ago. Of course, this could be mere novelist's licence, yet the characters in the book believed in reincarnation, and in the possibility of remembering past lives. The teller had been specially trained in this art, hence her ability to practise it now. Was this purest fantasy or could it be true? Vicky had certainly believed in it. If it was so, then every experience, however apparently unrewarding, must in the long run serve for something when brought over into the lives to come.

I went back to Runia's in Boundary Road several times. She said she wished I would help her sort out Vicky's books and papers, arrange them under subject matter so that she could see what she had got, and think what to do with them. There was an empty room at the top of the house. Would I come and live in it?

This I really did not want to do, I was happy in my room at 28 Oppidans Road where I had just had a telephone installed. In this place I would only have the use of the one in the hall downstairs. It would upset my way of life. Yet Runia's insistence made me wonder if it was some kind of a karmic duty or spiritual opportunity she was offering me which I should not refuse. So on 4 November 1941, not really happily, I moved, helped by Mother and by Theo, who happened to be in London that day.

On the top floor there was, as well as my room, a room occupied by a Jewish mother and daughter, refugees from Germany, whom Runia did not seem to like much. She also appeared taken aback by the amount of my furniture being unloaded from the van, and Mother said to me, 'I don't think she was expecting you.'

Then, my father's medals were stolen. I had, with what may have been foolish pride or vanity, displayed them on one of the shelves of the Chinese what-not, which could be seen when the door was open. Runia accused me of leaving the door of my room open and seemed to be trying to put the blame for the theft on to the Jewish mother and daughter. I could not believe that Jewish refugees could have any motive for stealing a British officer's medals. As for leaving the front door open, I thought it would have been very unlike me as I was usually careful to lock up. But even if it had been open I found it difficult to believe anyone from the street would have come in and climbed to the top of the house to take medals. Runia was extraordinarily slow in acceding to my demand she should ring the police, and I believed it was she who had taken them.

So, indeed, did Mother. Only one thing was clear. I must get out of this house. I left it on 14 March 1942, for 1 Taviton Street.

It was Mother who had found me the new flat – for flat it was, a set of rooms, self-contained except for one extra bedroom half a floor below that went with it. The generously-proportioned sitting-room was on the first floor. I bought from Heal's a huge print of Franz Marc's *Red Horses* and hung it over the heavy oak sideboard that had been in our dining-room in Beckenham. And it was of course much nearer to the Censorship, shortening my morning and evening bicycle rides.

It was also much quieter, though strangely I missed the thundering of our guns at Primrose Hill. I could still hear them but only faintly. And the Harmood Street rest centre was now too far away for me to help there after work. However, I learned that there was a group called the St Pancras Fire Fighters. Its headquarters was in an odd little corner called Duke Street, just opposite St Pancras on the south side of Euston Road. I presented myself. Yes of course they were always glad of another volunteer, and I joined a little group being taught by a Mr Murray. The hours at the Censorship were the regular nine to five, Sundays included (we were on a rota for the first choice of which day we should have in the following week for our 'rest day'), so this enabled me to get from Holborn to Duke Street in time to attend Mr Murray's class in fire fighting. I went perhaps a couple of evenings in the week (those I could spare from academic study, for my degree). We were not only taught how to fight fires but given some basic advice on self-preservation – for instance, if a bomb is going to land near you, lay yourself flat in the gutter, face down, with your nose in the angle between the kerb and the road. (Some time later, walking along Guilford Street, I had to put this exercise into practice when I heard a bomb homing in above me. Undignified but salutary.)

Something happened during these first weeks at Taviton Street. I got back my faith. The faith I had had as a child, but which had been undermined and overlaid. I did it this way. I put it to myself that for everything of which one had need there existed that to satisfy it. One needed water; water existed. One needed food; food existed. There was the need to believe; there must be that to believe in. I read the whole of the New Testament.

On 17 April, the doorbell rang. When I heard it I was already on my way downstairs, holding a letter I was taking to the post. The letter was to Harold, to end our relationship completely; for although no longer engaged to him I had received him when he came to London. This had been a mistake. His visits just chewed me up. There must be an end.

I went on down the stairs and opened the front door. It was Vilayat.

Basil had given him my address, he said; as he would be in London for a bit.

I was just going to post a letter, I said.

He would do it for me. He took it from my hand, walked to the pillar-box and dropped it in. That, afterwards, appeared to me symbolic.

He came back, and followed me upstairs.

We talked almost at once of things that were sacred. I said I wanted spiritual teaching. He was the son of a spiritual teacher, a mystic of the Sufi tradition.

He said he was not a guru. He could after the war introduce me to a man he regarded as a guru. This man lived in Paris. In the meantime, he could only suggest to me some things to read, which he would lend me if I cared to call on him for a cup of tea.

He was living in a strange room high in Premier House, on Southampton Row. It had bare floorboards, a large kitchen sink, which occupied most of the space, and one or two hard chairs. He had been in the RAF and had flown and loved flying. But then it had been discovered his eyes were not good enough for night flying, so he could not be a pilot. He could have stayed in that service in a ground job, but to have to watch his pals go up, unable to do so himself, would have been too painful, so he had changed to the Navy. In the Navy he could go in at a higher level if he passed an examination in navigation and some other things, which he could do perfectly well as a civilian. That was why, for the moment, he was back in civilian clothes, studying at Birkbeck.

He could lend me his father's books, of course. He handed me *The Unity of Religious Ideals*, and one or two others. But he did not think Sufism was my way.

'It's too bhakti for you.' He was using the classification of the yogas I had heard from Rai. Sufism was very devotional and emotional. He perceived that I wanted to know the 'hows' and the 'whys' and 'whats' of everything. I asked him questions to which, honestly, he did not know the answers. He thought I would be better satisfied by Theosophy. 'It's more Jnana.' Again, one of the terms Rai had used. 'Raja and Jnana'. That should suit me.

He handed me something else from his shelf, *The Masters and the Path*, by C. W. Leadbeater. It would, he said, be wrong of him to recommend to me this book without telling me the author had been the subject of some scandalous allegations concerning his connection with boys. Whether that meant he could not have had the connection with the Masters he claimed, 'I leave to you.'

I said it seemed to me he had faith in the book or he would not be offering it to me.

He hesitated, then said what he wondered was whether he had permission to publish all this. He suspected probably not, but he was glad he did it. It gave one 'at least an idea'.

If I am honest I have to say that the two books that have meant the most to me are not any of the world's classics but *Winged Pharaoh* and *The Masters and the Path*. I had always thought that to obtain the teaching of the holy ones in Tibet one had to reach them in the physical body, but it seemed that some of them were on the lookout for potential pupils on the path wherever they might be located. A chapter heading was 'No One Is Overlooked'; could my petition to them when I was fourteen years old have been received by them? Could anybody be watching what progress I made?

It was revelation. I gobbled up every page.

I read also what else Vilayat had in that room. Two shorter works by the same author, C. W. Leadbeater's *The Astral Plane* and *The Devachanic Plane*, also *The Etheric Double* by A. E. Powell: 'This man has a synthetic mind' said Vilayat, pointing to the many sources from which it had been culled as he handed it over.

That was all he had with him, but he drew my attention to the existence of the Theosophical Bookshop in Great Russell Street. I might find it interesting to browse there and perhaps attend a lecture or two at the headquarters of the Theosophical Society, at 50 Gloucester Place. 'You might even feel you would like to join it.'

I was soon in both Great Russell Street and 50 Gloucester Place.

I saw a lot of Vilayat and his family that summer; his mother had taken a room at 4 Taviton Street, which made her very nearly my next door neighbour. On 27 May I thought I should call on my new neighbour, and caught Noor, now in the light uniform of the WAAF, just as she was leaving. Her mother told me what a good daughter she was: 'I don't know what I have done to deserve such a daughter.' On another occasion I encountered all four of them, Vilayat, Mrs Inayat, Noor and Claire on the steps of Premier House.

Premier House was on my way back from the Censorship to Taviton Street, so I tended to call on Vilayat between five and half past, which is when I came across another girl there, already taking tea with him. She was slender, with auburn hair, rather pale, and her name was Joan. I will call her Joan Manchester, as she came from that city and and spoke in its accent. She was a teacher, but following evening classes at Birkbeck, where Vilayat had met her. On two dates in August Joan came to tea with me.

Since reading Leadbeater, I had become very conscious of the vibrations of objects, and was surrounding myself with holy things – more than one figure of the Buddha, two Egyptian bronze figurines, and from the same shop, in Cursitor Street, which I visited in the lunch hour on 22 September, some Egyptian figurines in what looked like clay. I brought these to show Vilayat on my way back, as I had brought the others. Joan was there.

Vilayat looked at them, said nothing much. He was sitting by his enormous kitchen sink. Joan began talking about Egypt and particularly about Queen Hatshetsup. She spoke of her doings in such detail that I thought she must have been reading a book about her, perhaps by Arthur Weigall? I had Weigall's book on Cleopatra and had read the one he wrote on Akhenaton, but I could not recall that he had written anything about Hatshetsup or indeed that anybody had. On what source was Joan drawing? She built up the figure in detail: 'She opened up trade with Punt.'

Then something happened. The face that had been Vilayat's began to change into another's. I was more frightened than I had ever been in my life. I was witnessing what was surely impossible, one person turning into another. Was it an ancient Egyptian who had overpowered and taken possession of him? The colour of his skin had changed, from its usual slightly olive brown to something more like parchment, and the eyes had grown so cold.

Suddenly Joan got up from the hard chair she was sitting on and knelt in front of him, saying, 'I'm Mnemis. Please recognise me.'

He looked on her with the same cold look with which he had looked at me.

She got back on to her chair.

Gradually the Egyptian's appearance thinned, and Vilayat began to reappear. He looked now distressed, putting his hands to his eyes, then asking us how we got here. 'Have you been here all the time?' He seemed to resent our presence, and said, 'Please go away. Please leave.'

We got up and went out at the door. On the landing, we looked at each other strangely, and again as we reached the front door.

'Come and see me,' I said.

And she said she would.

When I called on Vilayat again next day, he was a little better, but still not quite his normal self. It was not a possession, he said, it was himself as he had been. The personality that he had been was not very nice and that was why the experience had been disagreeable to him. It was that one he said, touching one of the clay figures distastefully, that 'sent' him. Something that was put in the tomb.

When Joan came to me she was still very shaken. 'Did you see the face?' she asked me.

'Yes, I saw the face.'

But there had been a difference in our way of seeing. For her, the entire room had been blacked out and there was nothing in it except for that face. For me, the room was all the time still there and the whole of Vilayat, including the hands, that changed colour and appearance along with the face. It was the whole body of an Egyptian in Vilayat's clothes.

I referred to her name, 'Mnemis.'

She jumped almost as if in pain. 'My name *was* Mnemis. How did you know?'

'You told us when you knelt ...'

She was dismayed, she knew nothing about this. 'I knelt?'

I assured her she had got up from her chair and knelt down in front of Vilayat.

She knew nothing about this. Only that he was a high priest.

But then she said. 'I know, now, why I always make my eyes up, prolonging them at the sides. We did it then.'

In the days that followed I sought out every book I could find in the public library with pictures of Egypt, and brought them to ask Vilayat if he recognised any of the buildings shown. No. No ... he said, dismissing one after another. The lotus columns of Karnak left him, to my surprise, indifferent. There was only one he recognised. It was in my old *Harmsworth Encyclopaedia* of 1920, under Egypt. 'That's it,' he said at once.

It was a long, low building. I commented how low it was.

'It was higher, then,' he said. 'There was another storey.' He began to read the text below the picture. Yes, it said so. It said there was another storey and an avenue of sphinxes ... yes, that was right ...[1]

He had been high priest, and Joan something in the temple, but who had I been, for I must have had some connection with them?

Joan, with whom I had had, briefly, so vital a rapport, ceased to communicate with me. It was not until long afterwards Vilayat told me what had happened to her. She had been to a dance, got made pregnant by a man she had never met before and whose name she never knew, broken off her course of study at Birkbeck and had a nervous breakdown. Vilayat attributed it to premature exposure to the occult. She had been upset by the vibration from another period and trying to efface it by immersion in the this-worldly.

In the meantime, he had passed his examination in navigation and received his call-up to report to HMS *Collingwood* on 2 September 1942.

I bought myself a huge book, *Egyptian Grammar, An Introduction to the study of Hieroglyphics*, H Gardner (Oxford, Clarendon Press,

1 Deil el Bahri, built by Queen Hatshetsup c. 1500 BC.

1927). It was set out in lessons, each furnished with a vocabulary and a passage from a genuine hieroglyphic text to translate. I did all of them, but had no esoteric revelation. The portals which had opened seemed to have closed again.

Mother said she was going to Scotland to see Aunt Grace and Uncle John, her mother's sister and brother, and when she came back it was with a lot of old family photographs. One she passed me looked like me at seventeen, in the photograph by Navana.

'Who is this?'

Her mother's younger sister, Mother said, 'your Great Aunt Annie. A Theosophist, like you.'

I had always thought I was the only member of the family to have become a Theosophist.

Née Laing, she married a Fred Dick and went with him to Dublin and later to Point Loma, where there was a Theosophical colony.

I had not heard of Point Loma.

But I wanted to know more of Annie ...

Six

I saw less of Vilayat now that he had gone into the Navy, but more of his sister, Noor. On 22 September she rang my bell to ask if I could put her up for the night. Her mother, at 4 Taviton Street, had only the one room, so when she came on leave from her RAF station to visit her, she had always stayed at the YWCA in Great Russell Street; but tonight they were full up. She could not afford a hotel. She still had the key of what had been Vilayat's room in Premier House, where she was clearing up after him, but now that the bed was gone she did not want to sleep on the floor as there was 'a terrible draught under the door'. Then she had remembered that my flat at 1 Taviton Street had an extra bedroom.

Of course she must come in, I said.

After that she always stayed with me after visiting her mother. The conversations we had are recounted in some detail in the book I wrote about her, and I do not want to take space here to repeat what is in the biography. But briefly, she loved all the objects with sacred associations, particularly the Tibetan prayer-wheel, in which she felt peace and blessings. She was fascinated by my facsimile edition of *The Egyptian Book of the Dead*, published by the British Museum. She liked the little Egyptian bronzes, but I did not show her the clay figure which had 'sent' Vilayat or tell her of the occult happening as I did not think he had done. I should also perhaps mention the scarabs. At the same shop, in Cursitor Street, I had brought three scarabs, one bright brown, one grey and one blue. These I offered to Joan (still with us then) and Vilayat, inviting them to choose one each. Joan chose the bright brown, Vilayat the grey, leaving me with the blue, which attracted me the most. But now I found, in a different shop, a fourth scarab, grey like Vilayat's, and I bought it and gave it to Noor. She said she would wear it and it would keep her safe.

My flat, with its curious contents, and our conversations about spiritual things afforded her a refuge from the austerities of regimented life. She said she did not want present exigencies to make her think there was 'nothing in the world but wireless and war'. At the RAF station in Abingdon, she was a wireless telegraphist.

We talked also about what should be the position of Indians in this war (she not differentiating between Hindi and Muslim in this context). According to one view, they ought not to participate. There is a small thing I did not mention in the biography as I did not want trouble with Krishna Menon. He had been furious with Vilayat for enlisting in the British armed forces. Noor trying to understand what he was talking about, went to one of his lectures, and he went on about how wrong it was for Indians to serve in the Army, Navy or Air Force, directing all his sallies at her personally. 'He hadn't got Vilayat to go for, so he went for me. I wasn't in uniform but he recognised me!' He was all the time *'glaring* at me' with his piercing eyes.

Her own view was just the opposite. She felt that if Indians supported Britain, now that she was beset by enemies, in her hour of need, it would make a better atmosphere for talks when the war was over. She wished one or two Indians might do something that was very brave, and would be praised. It might be that because of support now, the long-sought independence might then be given willingly.

The year turned. On one of my rest days from the Censorship I was tempted by the timid March sun to sit outside, in Gordon Square, with a book. Looking up from it, I saw a girl approaching by the central path. It looked like – it was – Noor but she was in khaki, not Air Force blue.

I expressed surprise, and she said she had been transferred to the FANY – First Aid Nursing Yeomanry.

When arrived from the boat, she had talked about Red Cross certificates, first aid and nursing, but since joining the Air Force she had become a wireless telegraphist. It would be odd to sacrifice such a specialist skill and revert. I asked no questions – in the war one had never to ask anybody what they did – but must have looked puzzled.

'That covers many things.'

To a trained censor – trained to recognise words and phrases that though outwardly innocent of any special meaning might have one for a recipient waiting for it – that word 'covers' stood out in what could be its only intended meaning, as 'masks'. She had, with that word, told me something that, strictly by the book, she ought not to have done, though it was safe with me.

To show it was indeed safe with me, I made an instant and total change of subject. Vilayat had told me that when she was a small child she had talked as though she saw fairies, little people within the cups

[93]

of flowers. It put me in mind of Shakespeare's line, 'In a cowslip's bell I lie'.

She saw them, she said, until someone told her they did not exist, except in her imagination. After that, she never saw them again and the garden seemed empty because there were no faces in the flowers.

I walked with her as far as her mother's, where she went in.

She came on 8 May, to ask if I could lend her a dress. She had a few days' leave due to her and wanted to use them to visit a friend she had made in the WAAF, Joan Wynne, who was about to have a baby. But it was in Eire, and it was not permitted to enter Eire in uniform. (Eire was classed by Britain as a foreign country, neutral in the war.) I helped her choose something from my wardrobe and a coat to go over it.

It must have been about ten days later that she rang my bell, said she had just time to return me these things, not to stay, and dashed away.

I assumed she had gone to Eire and come back. She had not. Something very different had happened. It was not until many years later that I learned her leave had been cancelled by an order to stand by for her mission, and that on the night of 21/22 May an attempt had been made to land her in German-occupied France, near Compiègne – abandoned because no landing lights were seen on the field. As these operations were only undertaken when the moon was full, this meant that she would now have to wait about three weeks before it was full again, which it would not be until 18 June.

Some days later the long daylight had already turned into darkness, and I had undressed and was in my nightgown, with one foot in my bed already, when my bell rang. I went down. It was Noor on the step. Could I put her up for the night?

I brought her up the stairs and gave her coffee. She was going 'on foreign service', she said, 'overseas'. Ordinarily, that would have suggested across an ocean, but I feared she meant only across the Channel. She said the worst part of it had been deceiving her mother. She had not actually lied to her, but 'overseas' had conveyed to her mother the idea of a hot country and she had kept giving appropriate advice – 'Avoid going out at midday, respect the custom of the siesta.' Not to disabuse her felt like deceit, and she felt terrible.

Cautiously, I asked, 'Will you have an address where you are going?'

'Yes.' She wrote in my address book, 'c/o The War Office, Whitehall, SW1.'

She did not think she ought to write or receive more letters than necessary as it might put unfair strain on the people who had to carry them, but she would like me to inform her if anything happened involving Vilayat I thought she would wish to know. The waiting had been so long, she said, it seemed as if it would never end. But this time she believed she was really going. 'In three or four days time.'

She wanted what advice I could give her from her palm and horoscope, and after we had shared a midnight supper we went on talking right through the night. She had had difficulty in deciding that it could ever be right to fight in a war, but it was in the *Bhagavad Gita* she found the solution to her problem. Krishna had told Arjuna that as he was a warrior to fight was his duty, only it must be without hate.

She said that as a child she had read the stories of martyrs who went to the stake for their beliefs. She had thought that such tests belonged to the Middle Ages, but now it could really happen to some people that they could be tortured for a secret. She wondered how brave she would be, drew her nails into her fists and said, 'I don't think I would ever speak.'

She wondered how brave she would be in a Nazi concentration camp … It was past the time at which one could think of going to bed. The daylight was creeping in round the edges of the black-out. I drew it back, and made breakfast.

On the doorstep she said she would not be seeing me again for a long time. 'It's the end of a phase,' she said, 'thank you for *everything*.' And she did something she had never done before. She kissed me.

And was gone.

The owner of 1 Taviton Street notified me that she wanted the flat back. This was a bore; moving furniture was costly and I would not have moved in had I known it would be let to me only for so short a time. However, Mother began to look round for somewhere else for me.

Old friends, Theo, Basil, Phoebe, and Vilayat, were dropping in when they could manage it, also one or two new ones made at the Censorship. I see also in huge letters in my diary in 1943:

5 July ENGLISH
6 July LOGIC
8 July LATIN
12 July ETHICS

These were the four papers I had to sit for the London Intermediate examination. It seems a long time after I had began University

Entrance (in 1940) but I had had distractions. I could only study in the evenings after getting back from the Censorship, and one evening a week was claimed by the St Pancras Fire Fighters. Then the time taken for working through Gardiner's *Egyptian Grammar*, which had nothing to do with my studies for university, was taken out of the hours in which I should have been pursuing my scheduled studies. And now, the four days I had to sit the examinations were four days taken out of my annual leave from the Censorship. It was again in the museums in South Kensington the papers were sat, and at the *viva* afterwards I had some contretemps with the examiner for Logic. He said I had not done what was intended in one question; I said I had not understood the way the question was put. It then came out that he was referring to a work on logic by someone called Spedding, whose text it was assumed I had studied. I said it was nowhere stated that that particular book was to be the basis of examination. I had studied from Eaton. He appeared not to have heard of Eaton. How had I come to work from this unexpected book? I had been advised by three friends (Basil, Theo and Phoebe) who had come down from Oxford with Firsts that it was the one they used. It had not occurred to me that Oxford and London might operate on a basis of different books.

Anyhow, I passed, with some relief, in all four subjects, and the way was now clear for me to read for my B.A. Hons. I had first thought to take this in Philosophy. That was why I had chosen Ethics to pair with Logic, reading for it *Five Types of Ethical Theory* by D. Broad (again a recommendation of my Oxford friends), as well as Plato's *Republic* and some of the Socratic dialogues. But I had gathered that the present attitude in academia was very much geared to the atheist logical positivism, and Basil, in particular, having in him something of the mystic though now turning more to orthodox Christianity, had found this irksome and restricting. I therefore decided that the subject in which I would go for Honours would not be Philosophy but English. The downside of this, of course, was that it meant having to do Philology, Anglo-Saxon and even Gothic. I understood the point of learning the classical languages, and even Anglo-Saxon: there was literature in them, but in Gothic there was nothing but the four gospels translated from Greek into Gothic. I took that hard.

It was once again Mother who found me my new flat; or rather, she found me two possibles. We looked at them together, and I preferred the one at 4 Guilford Place, because, although it was on the top floor it was completely self-contained. It was going at a low price because 'bomb-shaken' – though the floorboards seemed perfectly sound – and because it was near to three big railway stations, King's Cross, St Pancras and Euston, which the German planes were trying to get.

'You've got a bargain for after the war,' Knight, Frank and Rutley's man said as he showed us over. People were avoiding this neighbourhood now, but after the war … It was also extremely near the Censorship building. One could see it from the front doorstep and had only to walk straight down Lamb's Conduit Street. And, this time, there was a properly drawn up lease.

I moved in on 2 November 1943.

I had by this time gathered from my Theosophical reading that there was something called 'kundalini'. A force latent at the base of the spine, which was the gateway to the development of all kinds of higher faculties, and which was usually wakened for one by someone in whom it was already functioning. This was obviously the 'current' to which reference had been made by both Vicky and Cremers, and I asked Vilayat if he could do it for me. He said he had not the competence, and rather doubted whether there was anybody in the Theosophical Society in London who had. 'Blavatsky would have done it for you.' There was the man in Paris of whom he had spoken to me on our first evening. There were considerable dangers attached. He had always reserved this man's name.

On 8 January 1944, when he came to see me in Guilford Place, he said spontaneously, 'I'll give you the name and address of this man in Paris – in case I don't come back.' And he wrote a name in my address book, Vivian …

He had been at sea before, but I thought he must be going into some action he considered specially dangerous.

The Blitz proper was over now. Nevertheless, on 18 May 1944, we women of the St Pancras Fire Fighters were summoned by Mr Murray, our mentor. We were to report, not in the evening but in the daytime – so I had to get one of my rest days or days of annual leave from the Censorship – to a bomb site on the south side of the Euston Road. 'Ladies!' he addressed us from a top of a pile of rubble, he wanted volunteers to work in teams of three. Number one to go ahead, carrying a pickaxe with which to remove any obstacles blocking the way; number two to follow carrying a bucket, and number three to follow two, carrying the hose. 'Who will volunteer to be number one?' I put up my hand, was accepted, and two other women fell in behind me.

He then set fire to some of the rubble and clutter in the bomb-site. We went forward, in procession, with the implements provided. Their playing on the flames made such a lot of smoke that it hurt my throat. But anyhow, the fire was extinguished.

When next we met at our usual Duke Street evening rendezvous, Mr Murray told us we had received 'a great compliment'. We might have noticed that round about the edges of the bomb-site were people watching us. What we would not have realised was that some of them were members of the Euston Road Fire Brigade. Having seen how seriously we trained, they asked if we would like to work with them? We were invited to report to them at their fire station. There we were shown the red monsters in their stables, how to get their hose out from its hiding place, uncoil it and fit male pipes into female pipes, then taken on a tour of nearby streets and shown, in every one, one panel in the pavement which we were to recognise covered a hydrant. 'Now, if you could get that up before we came, that would save us time.'

If there was one thing I disliked in the war it was hearing the Alert after I had got into my warm bed. I had to get up again, get dressed and walk to the block of flats in Judd Street it was my responsibility to guard. The other two women, Bucket and Hose, lived in the flats so were always there before me, and handed me my pickaxe, which they garaged for me.

It was some time since I had first written to Joan Grant, but now she invited me home to Trelydan, in Wales, for a long weekend in May.

She opened the door to me, a tall, long-legged, lanky figure, her apparent height increased by the braiding of her hair over the top of her head. Behind her was her husband, Charles Longford Beatty, a big, jovial man. My fellow guests were Ingrid Lind and a Church of England canon who was shortly to be ordained a bishop.

After we had dined, it was the canon who said we should now ask Joan when and how she first became aware of her previous existences.

'At eighteen months,' she said. When her parents moved to Hayling Island, where there was a long, level, sandy beach. Trying to run when she could hardly walk, she had remembered how, as a long-legged young man, she had run and run, practising for an important race. It had infuriated her to find herself in this slow and awkwardly moving body that could hardly hold itself up. From the type of tunic worn, she thought now that that incarnation had probably been in Greece and that it might have been the Olympics she was training for, but she never had any more of that one come back to her. After that there were bits of canoeing, in a red-skinned body – bits of all sorts of things, from a jumble of periods and places. Egypt did not come through early. When she and her first husband, Leslie Grant, returned from a dig in Iraq via Egypt, it occasioned in her only a slight sadness, not untinged with disapproval, that so much had fallen into such neglect that to find it again you had to dig it out of the sand.

It was only back in England, when they were staying with the friend who had been more of a mother than her real mother to her, Daisy Sartorius had handed her a scarab. She had passed straight out, into her re-living the initiation when she was Sekeeta. It was Daisy, then her real mother, who had put it round her neck before the drop-stone closed behind her. When at last she came back it was to hear a man's voice keeping on saying, 'Joan! Joan!' Why did he think her name was Joan? He had been her brother, Neyah, but was now her husband, Leslie Grant. 'Joan! Joan!' He was shaking her. 'Come back!' Daisy's father in that life had been Daisy's brother in this (which was why Daisy never married) – a botanist in both.

Carola had come up by accident. Sir Henry Wood, the conductor, was staying with them and asked if Joan could tell him anything about Egyptian music. Not really musically educated, she confessed herself quite incapable of giving Sir Henry the sort of information he wanted. Yet she agreed to try, and 'changed level' saying to herself, 'Music!' When she came back she asked if she had managed to bring anything about music back from Egypt, and Leslie said, 'You weren't in Egypt, you were in Italy.' And he read her the beginning of what she had dictated, 'I was born early in the morning on the fourth of May in the year of our Lord 1500 ... My name is Carola...' and she was playing a mandolin by the wayside, in company with Petruchio (Charles Beatty) and Luccia ... It was probably the existence in which she had given most attention to music.

She had the material which went into *Life as Carola* before *Winged Pharaoh* was published. The publication cost her her first marriage. Leslie believed absolutely in the authenticity of her recall, but though he shared the secret with Sir Henry Wood, as being a great friend, who also believed in it without question, was horrified at the idea of publication. Other archaeologists would say, 'Poor Leslie Grant, his wife thinks she was Pharaoh!' Even the assurance that the publisher's blurb would leave it open to the reader to assume the text fiction did not reconcile him to it. 'And then *this*', with an affectionate gesture towards Charles, 'turned up.' They 'eloped'.

When he brought her to Trelydan nobody called, as she was not his wife. After her divorce had come through and they married, they began to call, but she and Charles had circulated a note saying Mr and Mrs Charles Beatty would not be at home to neighbours who did not call on them before they were married.

Later in the evening Charles got into some endless and heated argument with the canon, at one moment saying, of bishops, 'If they are what the symbols on their mitres proclaim them to be' – a sarcasm at the expense to the guest about to be ordained – and at another moment rebutting one of his replies with 'That's a damned lie!'

Joan was trying to restrain him, but unsuccessfully.

In the morning, whilst I was still in bed, my breakfast was brought up to me on a tray by Ingrid Lind. She sat down on the bed, and said, 'I was Luccia, the tart.' It was Joan who had suddenly realised it, whilst working on *Life as Carola*, exclaiming unexpectedly, 'My dear, you were Luccia?'

We tended to believe in the authenticity of Joan's recall but not in her opinions upon some disputed points. In particular, in her dismissal of astrology we thought she was much too glib. Ingrid Lind said, 'Astrology had helped me, and I stick up for astrology.

Did she know when Joan was born?

12 April 1907. Moon and Sun both in Aries.

When we went down we found Joan in distress. The canon had gone, without saying goodbye to anyone.

Perhaps he had gone for a walk in the garden?

No. She had looked in the garden. And he was not in his room and the things he had brought with him had gone. He had definitely left. He must have been so upset by that row with Charles.

I had longer conversations with both Joan and Charles over the weekend. She was not able to throw any light on my experience with Vilayat and Joan Manchester. The Egypt of *Winged Pharaoh* was of the first dynasty, that of *Eyes of Horus* a much later one. She had nothing of the period of Hatshetsup. She did not think she had met me before.

What was currently coming through was bit of a life in Greece which would later go into her book *Return to Elysium*. Charles said he had come into that life as a strange shrivelled creature, 'only interested in *things*'.

'I got him out of it,' said Joan.

I left on the Tuesday evening.

I remember my first experience of the V1s, the German flying bombs. I'd heard them in the night, and then halfway through the morning a crackling on the intercom at the Censorship told us our Director was about to address us. It had, he told us, just been announced on the radio that German pilotless aircraft had been active over southern England during the night and were continuing so this morning. As they did not arrive or depart in fleets, and there could therefore be no time at which raids could be said to be beginning or ending, the sirens would no longer sound Alerts and All Clears and we would no longer go down to our shelter as we did usually when there was a raid in daytime. We would just have to carry on as best we could. Ignore the things. 'You can go under the tables if you like.'

I did not see anybody go under the tables. What we were doing was crowding to the windows, telling each other, 'They haven't got men in them' … 'They're bombs with wings.' Our motherly Mrs Marshall, Deputy Assistant Censor of our table, said, 'You know, they're really rather clever.'

A few days later there was a Government announcement that the term 'pilotless aircraft' would be discontinued and replaced by 'flying bombs'. In the meantime, a different name for them had entered the popular speech, 'doodle-bugs'.

From the Censorship we saw one come down so low we thought it should be possible to find the crater, and in the lunch hour four of us set out in search. 'Towards the Viaduct,' Mrs Marshall thought; 'Gray's Inn, among the legal people's offices,' I suggested. We found it, actually, in Greville Street. It was already cordoned off, but we peered in and my table mate said, 'The blast is wide, the penetration shallow in relation to the breadth of the explosion.' I was impressed by her arcane diagnosis.

In a way, the doodlebugs were a relief to me, as the abolition of Alerts meant the end of Judd Street vigils: Pickaxe, Bucket and Hose had no longer to assemble.

On the other hand, our Director, Edwin Herbert, told us on the intercom (I never knew what he looked like, knew him only as the voice coming through that machine) that since we now never went down to the shelters and were consequently in greater danger, he had arranged with the Red Cross for someone to come and give a special course of training in First Aid. It would take place in the building, on the first floor, and the time we spent at it would count as office hours worked. He hoped there would be a volunteer from every table.

I volunteered at once. It was quite an interesting course, included some elementary physiology and, though obviously geared to the emergency treatment of the type of wounds we might have to deal with if a doodle hit, could be of use in later life. At the end of it we took a little exam, and were awarded certificates and armbands – which we always had always to wear so that in an emergency we could be quickly identified.

One day I was rather mysteriously ordered up two floors, from the third to the fifth. A number of other women, who had been similarly extracted from our previous tables, were gathered there, wondering what this was about. Then suddenly it dawned upon us. Every one of us had for one of our foreign languages Italian. That was it. We were the new Italian table. Opposite me I now had Mignon Nevada, an opera singer who had sung, in Italian, at La Scala, Milan, and on my right a Mrs Sabo.

Mother had come to lunch with me at Guilford Place when it was announced on the radio that Paris had been liberated. The Marseillaise was played. We removed our plates from our knees and stood up, to attention. Then we kissed each other, our eyes filled with tears. That was 23 August.

On 8 September I had just got back from the office and was in the kitchen making myself a cup of tea when there was the loudest noise I had ever heard in my life.

I opened the kitchen window and looked out.

In the house opposite, a window opened and a man looked out. He cupped his hands and called to me, 'What was that?'

I cupped mine and called back, 'It must be a V2.'

It was.

In the days following we had a good many of them, but never as loud as that. They came faster than sound, we were told, and that was why we felt the landing before we heard the approach. So they always took one by surprise. The most I counted was eight in a day. I found them a bit unnerving. With the V1s, one heard the approach and could prepare oneself for possible transmission to the next world, but with these things there was nothing before the shock.

Permission was now given to write to liberated France; on postcards only. So, on 11 September I composed a postcard to Vilayat's 'Vivian'.

As it must be read at our tables I said nothing remotely savouring of the occult, but, as if I were someone he already knew, asked if there was anything I could usefully send from England when regulations permitted the posting of parcels. I added (in French of course) 'Vilayat sends his kind regards.' This was to intimate to him how someone he had never heard of had his name and address.

Days passed, and weeks. No answer. Had he moved, or had restrictions not been lifted yet on communications from France to England?

There was a morning when I left the table for a minute and, as I was returning, met Mignon Nevada on the landing. She asked me if I knew a family called Inayat Khan.

Surprised by the question, I said I did.

She had known them in the days when they lived in Gordon Square and the children were just tiny tots. She had found herself thinking about them lately. More precisely, she had been worrying about the two eldest, Noor-un-Nisa and Vilayat, wondering if they were all right. And this morning she had woken with the thought that I could tell her.

'I don't want to know what they are doing,' she said, 'I only want to know if they are all right.'

It was precisely the assurance I could not give her. Vilayat was desperately worried because nothing had been heard from or concerning his sister for a year.

When we returned to the table, Mignon Nevada mentioned what we had been talking about to Mrs Sabo. Mrs Sabo said, 'I have a little niece ...' The little niece had similarly disappeared. She felt sure some people who had lived in France had been secretly sent back there. 'They're probably in the same thing.'

But with France now liberated they ought to reappear – if they were still alive.

They tried to make us work an extra hour that winter, but staying in until six provoked such resentment that the Director told us our work had deteriorated, not only during the extra hour but during the whole of the day. Consequently nine to five was restored. And so we came into 1945 with the war news good and the end in sight.

On 8 May, in the mid afternoon the intercom crackled and the Director said, 'Germany has surrendered. You can all go home.'

As we swarmed out of the building we saw other buildings debouching their human contents. I went home and telephoned Mother, suggesting we should meet to celebrate. 'Tomorrow,' she said. She sounded very faint and far away and I thought she wanted to be alone with memories of my father. I went out again.

From every window, it seemed, shreds of torn paper were floating down. I even saw typewriter ribbons converted into streamers whirled and whirled around and then tossed down too.

And next we were at Downing Street, in front of number 10, calling, 'Churchill! Churchill!'

The curtains on the first floor parted and a man looked out and said, 'Mr Churchill asks you to forgive him. He is very tired and has gone to bed.'

In the morning it was back to the office as usual. The war with Japan was not concluded yet. The Censorship was not disbanded.

Soon after the surrender of Germany it was permitted to send not only postcards but letters to France. Of course, they would still have to be opened by the Censorship, so I avoided reference to Theosophical ideas or abnormal experiences which could trouble my colleagues.

The next thing, for me, was that in a few weeks I would be sitting for my B.A. I had entered for an Honours, not a Pass, degree. As I had had no tutor, I asked for some of the examination papers from years past, to see the type of questions that might be set. I had no expectation of getting a First; my philology was too weak and though I had made efforts with the Anglo-Saxon my Middle English was extremely sparse. I read *Sir Gawain and the Green Knight*, and as there must be a question on Chaucer, I read the *Tales* earlier and chanced to get by without having to give time to reading Langland. I thought I knew too much to fail to get the degree, but hoped at least to avoid a Third.

The B.A. examination occupied four days in June 1945. I had to take them out of my annual leave from the Censorship, and we sat, as usual, in the Museum in South Kensington.

All went fairly well until the paper on English Literature to 1475. The expected question on Chaucer asked for him to be compared with Langland. How could I have been so stupid as to think I could get away with not reading Langland? To scrape a few marks, I wrote an essay on Chaucer.

I agonised over whether my failure to answer on Langland might fail me on the paper? If I failed on the one I would be failed on the whole.

The next morning was the dreaded History of the Language – e.g. Philology. Looking through the past papers I had noticed there was never a question on the Icelandic cognates and decided to devote to more likely questions the time it would have taken me to learn them. But that morning, I woke dreaming there would be a question on Icelandic cognates, and so, over breakfast, instead of revising what learning I had, I opened the *My Grammar of the Gothic Language*, the page on Icelandic cognates, and memorised them over the tea and cereal.

The paper started off with passages for translation from Gothic. 'Jan jainthro i nn gaggands ...' I confess I have no idea what it means now, but I translated it then.

Next, 'Compare the following Gothic verbs with their Old English cognates ...' I did.

Then there came a question of Scandinavian loan-words. This enabled me to give an exhibition, in the most apposite manner, of my breakfast knowledge of Old Icelandic cognates.

I thought that would have got me through that.

In the afternoon: Shakespeare. Well, for me, that was a gift.

On Wednesday afternoon, Middle English: more passages to translate, difficult words and phrases to explain, a question on *Sir Gawain* ... I could do that.

And, on the morning of Thursday 14 June, History of English Literature from 1700 to 1888.

'Support or oppose Pope's claim to be a great poet.' I had read Leavis's *Revaluations* and knew how he had upgraded Pope to the detriment of the Romantics, so I could show some understanding of the issues raised.

Then there were questions on Wordsworth, Shelley, Keats and Coleridge, all manageable enough.

And, in the afternoon, last paper, Special Subject – English and American Literature from 1880 to the Present Day. I answered on Hardy, Yeats, T. S. Eliot and the moderns. Should be all right.

When the paper conveying the results came, in mid-July, I saw that the examiners had awarded no Firsts; but I was among the Seconds. I had my degree. It had been a long haul, since I decided in 1939 that I should do what I should have done at school, work for matric and then for a degree. But I had had distractions.

When the news came through on an August afternoon that an atomic bomb had been dropped on Japan, there was an almost stunned silence. Mignon Nevada said to us, 'We shall live in the shadow of this for the rest of our lives.'

We knew now that the victory over Japan would follow almost at once, but there was none of the jubilation that had marked the conclusion of the war with Germany.

And now the Censorship was really ending, but slowly. Seeing our colleagues moving off, one of our group coined a new collective noun: 'a redundancy of examiners'. Of course, Censorship redundancy did not mean freedom from National Service. We had to find some other Ministry to move to. I had two interviews, at His Majesty's Stationery Office and the Ministry of Food. The former would, as to the subject, have suited me better, but the man at Food was so nice I let myself be persuaded.

I finished at the Censorship on Saturday 23 October with a fortnight to spare before beginning at Food.

A friend Vilayat had made in the Navy called on me, and it emerged from our conversation that his wife had gone down to Cornwall with their children to take refuge from the Blitz. Every hotel and lodging house seemed to be filled with families with the same idea, but she had rung at the door of a private house in Bossiney, near Tintagel, where a Miss Marie Steward took them in – for the rest of the war. She was a really interesting woman, an artist and silversmith, and there were curious Druid spirals hidden by ivy on an outcrop of rock in the valley. The idea grew up that I should stay with Marie Steward for a holiday.

On 20 October I took the train. It was dark when the bus from Camelford set me down at the edge of the Rocky Valley. At first I thought I was alone. Then a shape came out of the shadows holding a torch, and the face was one I had seen in a dream. We climbed her stile and crossed the brook which ran through her ground, to reach her porch, deep in bamboo. The house was built to her design in redwood pine from Oregon. She had small trays bright with amethysts, opals, chunks of amber and cornelians. The coils of silver wire were what she put in the flame of her burner to create the settings for the stones as rings or pendants. She was geologist as much as esoteric.

In the morning I wanted to go down the valley. Impossible, said Marie. The mud was so thick as to make it dangerous. Perhaps if I came again in the spring. But we could walk into Tintagel and see the great headland and Merlin's Cave.

The whole place, she said, lived by and turned upon the legends of King Arthur. Though confessing to a suspicion Arthur was a pre-Christian name for the sun and the knights of the Round Table the signs of the zodiac turning round him (with Guinevere for the moon, I suggested), she was steeped in the Arthurian cycle of Tennyson, and in the evenings read me, by lamplight (for the house was not electric), from *The Coming of Arthur*, *The Passing of Arthur* etc., which she knew far better than I did, though I could still hear some of them in Miss Letheren's tones.

Arthur's table was buried under the hill at the back of the house, which had been cut into it. The table rose and could be seen each Midsummer Eve, she said, straight-faced.

I travelled back to London on Saturday 27 October, and on Monday 29th started at the Ministry of Food. As an Honours graduate I went straight in at the executive level. The nice man who had persuaded me to come to them did not reappear, and his place was taken by a man who seemed to wonder why I was there. I did not see another woman there. At the Censorship I had had for table-mates women of interesting and distinctive personality: Patricia Shelford, the Indian Army colonel's wife, Rita Barton, the Jungian analytical psychiatrist, and Mignon Nevada, a prima donna of grand opera, with their very different backgrounds, were all women of personality; and though we grumbled at times, on the whole we were a jolly lot. Here, the typing pool was presumably composed of women but one never saw them, and my colleagues, the men, appeared not to know what to make of me. The only task brought me was to 'Reduce the Allocation List' of the benefits paid by the Ministry to some group of fishermen; it seemed to me mean-spirited work and consequently I was less than zealous at it. Then I would sit for hours alone in my room with nothing being brought to me to do. Why was the Ministry paying me a salary above the basic rates if it hadn't proper work for me?

The cessation of Censorship had emboldened me to write to Vivian that I gathered from Leadbeater's *Masters and the Path* that progress on it depended on the arousal of a subtle fire within the body known as kundalini, which had to be raised from the root of the spine to vivify higher centres. Would he do this for me?

Vivian replied, 'When you knock on the door of the heavens it is the gates of the hells which first open wide; always, by ineluctable law. If you ask it will be given you', but it meant 'the speeding up of your whole karmic drama'. Karma that might otherwise be eased out over a number of incarnations would all fall on me 'in a lump' as Blavatsky said. 'Do not ask unless you are resolved beyond the point of no return.' If I asked, I must be prepared for troubles of unforeseeable nature and duration. Common amongst candidates were a fall, a motor accident or, the circumstance permitting, a boating accident, an accident with machinery, obscure illness difficult to diagnose, involvement in strange situations. 'Reflect well and wait three days before you answer.'

I had found the letter on the mat just as I was leaving for the office, took it with me and read it in the office and replied at once that I had understood his warning, and asked for the awakening of kundalini. I posted it in the lunch hour.

I hoped he would not be annoyed by my not having waited three days. I was too keyed up. I hoped he would say he would teach me some exercises when I was able to visit Paris. But he wrote no more of kundalini, or anything esoteric. He just asked me to receive the niece of a friend of his who had had a bit of trouble but was now in England. So I asked her to tea and put her in touch with a few other friends.

Then Marie Steward asked me down to Cornwall once again. I had a few days of annual leave due, and on Saturday 23 February 1946 took the train down to Cornwall.

By the light of her oil lamp, she told me she felt an evil had come to possess the valley, the valley which, because she loved it, she had built the house to face. She believed that the slab marked with the Druid spirals hid a sacred temple, but something was spinning evil over the outside ... in an ivy-covered ruin that faced it.

The next morning, while Marie was preparing our hot Sunday lunch (she was vegetarian like me), I went for a walk. I decided to walk down the valley by myself and see whatever it was that was to be seen.

It was as bleak and damp as it had been in October. Through the bottom ran a stream and the flash of yellow crossing it must be a grey wagtail. I was doing not too badly when I came to a place where a trickle of water from above crossed the path and my feet slipped. When I stopped sliding and picked myself up, I found I was facing the outcrop of rock on which were inscribed the mysterious circles, concentric except that there was an apparent path or way in cut from the outer to the near-centre. On the other side of the path was indeed what had perhaps once been a shed and was now covered over with ivy. The ivy from the ruin crossed the path and was reaching the spiral, threatening to obscure it. Ivy was a parasitic plant, and I tore it off, to destroy the foothold of whatever troubled Marie, as I did so bidding it aloud to leave the spiral alone and stop being a nuisance to Marie.

Then, leaving torn tendrils on the path, I went on down the path to the mouth of the valley. There the hillside I was on rose and I climbed it. Beyond, I now had a view of the island crag which Marie (and some other locals) called The Sphinx Rock, from some slight fancied resemblance to the Egyptian sphinx. Marie believed there was a cave where the tide came into the cove. I decided to investigate and lost my footing.

'I'm falling to my death.'

I commended my soul to the care of every holy power and visualised the cross.

I hit the ground with a thud. 'I'm alive,' I told myself. 'But is my back broken?' With a terrific effort I managed to move all four of my limbs. Back not broken. Yes there is a cave. But I have to get back up that cliff. The tide came into this cove. If I failed to get back, Marie would not know where I had gone and nobody would ever know what had happened to me. I searched the cliff-face, found crevices into which I could fit feet and fingers ...

At last I scrambled up to the top and lay flat on the grass for quite a while. I realised there was blood coming from my mouth. My chest felt crushed. Eventually I got up again and staggered back to the house.

Marie was horrified, and while I got into bed called a doctor, who came and examined me. He bound me tight in bandages and said I should later come for an x-ray, to see if any ribs were broken.

I wrote next day to Vivian, and Marie posted the letter. A few days later she brought me to my bedside his reply:

'See, even with a warning so precise and unequivocal as that I gave you, a fall was not avoided. One cannot, even if one would, spare another the pitfalls of the path ... Even now you seem to see no connection between your insouciant rite in the valley ... Do not perform maladroit magics ...' One should never engage a black magician on the astral, an inferior plane; it was his domain par excellence. In such a combat act only from the highest spiritual plane ... There really was a black magician at Tintagel. 'Do not provoke – unless you feel of a stature to remove him; he is vulnerable to the five-pointed star.' The general burden of his letter was that I had been silly; but had he left me, in this last phrase – even if half sarcastic – a thread by which I might redeem myself?

Marie felt sure that a black magician and his circle – 'He must have a circle' – would meet at the midnight of the full moon.

The next full moon fell on 17 March. The doctor's letter had sufficed to convert the days following my annual leave to sick leave.

I lay in bed, watching the spiders come in from the tips of the bamboo which swished my window, and spun their threads between the sash and the dressing-table glass, and wondered what I should do. And when I got well enough to get up again and walk in the valley, in the sunshine, I saw the first primroses were opening. Even against an evil entity, I must do no harm ...

On the 13th I had a frightful dream. I had been dragged (tempted or dragged) beneath the earth by a horned satyr, and above me robed priests were performing the burial service over me. With an effort I freed myself and was back in my body and my bed with a bang. I lit the candle, but it was a long time before I could trust myself to sleep again.

During the night of the 16th, as I lay in bed, a flash of pain tore up my spine from root to nape of neck. It was as if a red-hot poker had stroked me. It must be kundalini. I had read in Leadbeater that a fall could occasion its arousal accidentally, but this was represented as a misfortune, since, to be safe, the process required the supervision of a Master. I had thought that when I went to Paris Vivian would show me some exercises, but now this thing had happened prematurely, when I was alone. I was lying on my back at the time. When I tried to raise my head, it caused the fire to rise into my neck. Each time I tried to raise my head there was this further stabbing. I was afraid it could destroy the tissues of my brain, and visualised the cross, and prayed. My whole back burst into flame. Then I slept.

The next day the friends through whom I had met Marie came to visit and we put them in the picture.

Marie found for me an old copy of *The Herald of the Star*. This was the magazine edited by Krishnamurti before his breach with the Theosophical Society. Vivian had assured me that he was the expected teacher for the new age and pointed out that he had never actually denied it – though the 'devotiose' attitude of so many of those who crowded round him had been something from which he felt he had to extricate himself. He was, Vivian insisted, veritably the Messiah of the age now incoming.

The magazine was bound in pale blue and on its front cover was a silver five-pointed star. I held it on my lap and watched the hands of the clock, my heart thumping. As the hands touched midnight, I said, 'In the name of the Logos, the power of the light, the power of the five-pointed star, I command you, all you who here do serve the darkness, be powerless for evil; be gone.'

The silence lasted a long time. Then Marie said she would make us tea. As she asked me to, I spoke a blessing on the place at noon next day.

I wrote to Vivian. He replied, 'Dear sister and colleague … I think you have changed class as an occultist in these last days. … You asked and it has been given you. … Your precipitate methods have gained you what some students here, not less serious, have not achieved in many years … Your greatest danger now is of inflation, I warn you prematurely rather than tardily … You have still much to learn.'

During the next days the fire seemed to be running down from the top of my head, like golden rain, and the branches of it were coming round the sides of my head on to my forehead, where they were working forwards as though trying to meet in the centre.

Then it started working down my legs and arms. I was alarmed, and wrote to Vivian. He replied saying that I should not attempt to direct or control the course which kundalini took. For no two students was it the same, depending on the individual's ray and karma. To attempt to give advice in detail to a student experiencing the arousal would be folly, but he would give me three precepts which, if I observed them, would keep me safe: '1 Forget everything you have read, 2 Meditate upon the Triple Logos, 3 Be without fear.'

The first I understood. None of the books about the phenomenon were entirely mistake-free and anyway my worries were largely occasioned by the warnings in them. But I had never thought much about the triune nature of the Logos: Father, Son and Holy Ghost – yes, but what were they? Ah, but in the books he forbade me to go on reading, it was said that kundalini was a triune force, so probably its three aspects should develop evenly, not one outstripping or lagging behind the others. But I could not tell which was which. There was just the sensation of fire, which had now reached my feet and hands.

Vivian asked me if I had forgotten the symbol of the five-pointed star I had evoked, and reminded me of Leonardo's design showing a man standing with his legs and arms out so that the feet and hands made the head a five-pointed star.

On Friday 29 March I took the return train to London. As I stood in the corridor, watching the now familiar landscape of Cornwall slip by, the fire clutched at my throat, the chakra that had to do with voice and sound, and on the Sunday morning, in my London flat, suddenly it was my heart that was ablaze.

On Monday I was back at the Ministry of Food, which was to go on for a year.

Marie sent me a five-pointed star she had made for me in silver. She had given me to take with me the copy of *The Herald of the Star* I had used in the rite.

Seven

By combining Good Friday and Easter Monday with some days of annual leave, I was able to go to Paris for a week. I travelled on Thursday 18 April, via Newhaven, Dieppe and the Gare St Lazare, to arrive chez Vivian and his woman colleague in the middle of what was in fact one of their regular Thursday evening meetings. I was motioned to one of the chairs pulled up in a semi-circle for discussion. The next day I saw Vivian alone and we talked at length. It was always so borne in upon us that we should not talk about him, or the group, that even now I feel it would be an invasion of his and other people's privacy to do so. Yet one thing I will mention: though his name was French and his mother was French he was not the child of his mother's husband, whose name he bore: she had, whilst travelling in Spain, been raped by a Spaniard and he was the progeny of the rape. And this I mention because it will serve to distinguish him from another teacher in Paris with whom he might otherwise be confused. Vivian always refused to be considered as a teacher, far less a Master 'even as a polite tribute to my white hairs'.

The younger members of the group took me about with them, on the Saturday to the annual Convention of the Theosophical Society in France, at 4 Square Rappe. 'She belongs in England,' they told a person at the door and swept me in. And on the following evening they took me back there to attend a play.

On my last day, just as I was leaving, one of the younger members, Hélène, put into my hand two photographs. 'They are of the Masters Morya and Koot Hoomi,' she said. To look at when I meditated. Not to show around generally. I have since realised they are (for I have them still) prints of the ones not supposed to go beyond the Theosophical Society's Esoteric School.

Back in London my doorbell rang and it was Vilayat on the step, his eyes nearly bulging out of his head. 'I've found out what happened to my sister. She was burned alive.'

He thrust a newspaper into my hands. I looked at it, tried to make it out … Apparently some members of the staff of a camp called Natzweiler were on trial. They were charged with having put four women to death by lethal injection, and one witness had alleged that one of the women had not completely lost consciousness when thrown into the crematorium. The names of three of the women were given, the other was said to be unidentified.

Noor was not mentioned, I said.

She was the unidentified girl, said Vilayat.

Did he know this?

He had been given reason to believe it.

I did not know what contact Vilayat had with the War Office or whatever department Noor had worked for, or what, precisely, he had been told. It remained in my mind that her end, though perhaps frightful, was uncertain.

I saw during this time a number of Vilayat's friends, both his Sufi people and what one could call non-attached seekers. We would meet for talks or meditation here and there, sometimes in a flat which Vilayat had taken near Victoria Station. One I remember on the grassy side of Primrose Hill, no longer crowned by guns. That was a Sufi group and I had been invited to give the talk and lead the discussion – on a summer evening, on the grass.

One person who had come into this orbit was Oliver Jones. He was the son of Professor Daniel Jones, of University College, London. Oliver told us his father was deeply interested in spiritual questions and talked often of someone he called 'Bill', who seemed at times to be spoken through by beings of greater wisdom. I was a bit sceptical, though not dismissive.

In August I was able to spend another week in Paris.

On 24 October, Oliver brought Bill Pickles to tea with me. He had left for India before the war and this was only a brief return visit, and he was staying at the Joneses, at Gerrards Cross. I would say a yogi, definitely – and a Cockney-speaking one – yet not without his personal problems. He got into violent argument with one of my other guests.

Some time after, Oliver rang again, to say Bill had vanished without leaving word. It seemed so rude … Then he rang again, to say the police had rung and asked to speak to his father. Did he know a man called William Pickles? He did. They had found him flat on his back on the Bow Road. There was no trace of alcohol on his breath and they thought he was simply perished from hunger and cold. All he would say about himself was that he was staying with Professor Jones. Would

Professor Jones have him back? They would bring him over. He had gone straight up to his room without a word. It was so strange, because it was in the Bow Road Maud Macarthy and her husband had first discovered him ... It was as if he wanted to deny his mission and return to his origins. More of Bill later.

I bought myself a Siamese kitten. I had long wanted a cat, and ordered a pedigree Siamese from an advertisement. But when she arrived, I think it must have been in the beginning of 1947, she was a poor scared thing. I called her Bast, after the Egyptian cat-goddess, but though she came with birth certificate and pedigree, she did nothing but suck people's clothing. I have since read that this is characteristic of Siamese that have been taken too soon from their mothers. They never really get over it. I didn't have a good record buying pets through advertisements: first there was Taffy, the pedigree Welsh terrier, then the 'lilac' mouse, and now Bast. Would I never learn?

It was a bitterly cold beginning to the New Year, particularly in my room at the Ministry of Food, in which one of the panes in the window had been broken. Nobody made any effort to repair it, probably because the whole thing was to come to an end so soon. So I had to shiver away the last weeks of my National Service.

Vivian asked me to come for a longer time to Paris. Mother had to leave Ruskin ('Toffs' workhouse' as the bus conductors used to call it) as it was being demolished to make room for council flats, and said she would come and live in my flat whilst I was away and look after 'Bastie'.

On 9 March I took train and boat again for Paris. What can I relate? We met on the Tuesday and Thursday evenings, we talked of Blavatsky, considered the teachings of the Masters ... The attitude was very much that of Krishnamurti. I remember Vivian's saying to one young man, 'When I ask you what you think I don't expect you to answer by telling me what Plato said. Perhaps I know. We are not here to exhibit our academicism.' There was nothing to pay or to subscribe to. At any rate I was never asked for anything. No refreshments were served. If we stayed too long, Vivian would say, 'Terminé! Allez! Ended! Go!'

For those of us free in the middle of the day, there was an hour's meditation, from twelve to one. Those of us who had visions could recount them. Mine were really just what I had called as a child 'the pictures', excepting that, as the days progressed, instead of their just appearing in front of me as on a screen, I seemed to enter and interact with them. When I got back to my lodging, I would write then down while they were fresh in my memory. For what interest it may have, if any, I reproduce one of them here.

A sword. In the blade a new-born child, curled. This became a red lion rampant, then a red candle, alight. Then there was nothing more in the sword, but it was wreathed in flame.

The room in which I wrote these up was bare. Even the floorboards were bare. There was just a bed and a gas-ring, on which I cooked my meals, in which lentils featured constantly because, like the room, they cost little.

A married couple belonging to the group invited me to dine with them at their flat in Montmartre once a week in return for English conversation. Learning that I walked back, all the way to my room on the South Bank, the man was horrified. 'You walked straight through the red light district!' I had not known. No one had approached me. Breathing again, he said, 'At the speed you walk, no one would.'

The woman who had given me the pictures of Morya and Koot Hoomi introduced me to Wanda. Wanda, better known to the public as Marie Olivier, was the leading-lady of the French existentialist writer Jean-Paul Sartre, and was at that time starring in his play *La putain respectueuse* (*The Respectable Whore*). As her social life appeared to begin only after the last curtain came down, and to continue into the dawn, she slept until after midday, waking in just about time to fit in an English lesson before leaving for the theatre. I asked if she had attempted Shakespeare and suggested *Antony and Cleopatra*, and we read it – the scenes with Cleopatra in them, me taking the other parts so that she could be Cleopatra. She paid.

Then there was somebody with a niece who wanted English …

Meanwhile, I had been wondering again if I could take up art. I started with timid pencil drawings in the gardens of the Luxembourg and the Tuileries, and by the banks of the Seine. Then I called at the famous Académie Julien, showed them and asked if I would be accepted as a student. The presentation was less formal than in an English art school. One paid by the day, turned up when one chose, and entered a large room that contained a number of different groups. One was around a still life – an arrangement of flowers, fruits, ceramics, or whatever, changed weekly; others were around a classical Greek statue in reproduction, a live model, naked (and that means really naked without even the loin-cloth of modesty) who might be male or female, and another round a clothed model, usually in the dress of every day. One attached oneself to whichever of the groups took one's fancy, drew or painted, and an instructor came round and made critical comments. I thought I had better limit myself to drawing to begin with, and took charcoal. I joined the group round the nude figure, as that was the only thing that could only be got in an art school. My drawings were not good. The legs, the teacher pointed out, were too small for the torsos. But week by week – the models, like the still lifes, were changed each week – they got less bad.

But I am speaking of the daytime. The exciting hours were those devoted in the evenings to 'croquis', quick sketches. The woman in charge would call out, 'Croquis de dix minutes … croquis de cinq minutes … croquis de deux minutes!' The nude model changed pose every time she clapped her hands, and by the time it came to two minutes we were breathless. It was the two minute sketches that really tested one's ability to see the essential lines of the figure and draw them at once. Invaluable training.

As a student there I was now able to get a student's card, admitting me free of charge to all art galleries and museums in France, and of this I made continual use, in the Louvre, the Luxembourg, the Jeu de Paume – particularly the last as it then held the Impressionists, Monet's *Gare Saint Lazare* and *Nymphes* … I loved their bright, clear colours.

I returned to spend Christmas with Mother. I told her I wanted to try painting in oils. She had oils and we set up a still life with the green Moroccan vase I had bought in Cursitor Street and some oranges and an orange cushion. She did not touch my picture but pointed out that, as well as the lights from the window, and shadows, there were reflections of one object upon another, the orange of the cushion and fruit replicating itself in the green of the vase. It was subtle, but it made all the difference.

But she had something to tell me. At the Chelsea Art she had come to know Florence Humphrey Holland, who had been a friend of Sickert, and had letters from him, and from Conder and George Moore. Mother had suggested they should be published and said she would write a connecting thread between them to make a book, to be called *Letters to Florence* … She had a pile of Sickert's letters on the table beside my typewriter, on which, though not a trained typist, she was labouring to type them out. I held some of them to look at – and never dreamt of the story Florence held in store.

I returned to Paris and the Académie Julien in the New Year 1948. I now set up my easel – a little beauty, bought second-hand at the door – in the group gathered around the still life. I wanted to think not about the difficulties of drawing the figure but the delights of using paint. The oil-paints sold at the Académie Julien were softer than those sold in England and could be used with hardly any medium at all. The 'still' for that week was of a tureen with blue flowers on the white ceramic, with grapefruit and lemons crowded round it, upon a white napkin on a blue cloth – opportunity to use the bright, clear colour that I enjoyed. I noticed the centre of interest had sloped too far away to the left so, to balance it, I entered something that was not in the subject set at all, a tall thin vase on the right. That saved it. The teacher did not stop me.

In the following weeks I did more still lifes, a mandolin propped against music, a cluster of sprouting onions, a bowl full of mixed flowers, a vase with yellow zinnias. Then I became bold enough to attempt nudes in paint, a black woman holding fruit ...

But now I began to wonder why I continued to inhabit a room with bare floorboards and a gas-ring, when I had in London a flat of my own so comfortably furnished. Vivian had for deep reasons discontinued the Tuesday and Thursday evening receptions and also the morning meditations, as not in keeping with the spirit of Krishnamurti's teaching; if the All was in one, as it must be if one was in the All, why did one need to sit at prescribed times with one's eyes closed? So we were all thrown out on our ears, to find our individual ways.

Painting I could continue to learn at one of the art schools in London. So, on 12 April, carrying my suitcase in one hand and my treasured easel in the other, I took the train from the Gare Saint Lazare. As it pulled out of the station I thought how extraordinarily like Monet's painting of the Gare Saint Lazare it looked.

It was perhaps half-past five or six when I arrived back in my flat. Mother had made a special effort for my homecoming. The brass table and the brass animals walking round it had been polished up, the silver shone, wooden things had a soft gleam. She made the supper.

I thought she would want me to tell her more about the Académie Julien, but it was she who was bursting with something to tell me. Something Florence had told her about Sickert. 'She says he knew who Jack the Ripper was.'

'Who?'

He didn't say. Had been afraid to say in plain language.

'How did he know?'

He had seen the bodies. Later he had painted them. The set of pictures called *The Camden Town Murder* series were not of the Camden Town Murder, which merely afforded him a pretext for re-living, in paint, his memories of the murders of 1888, the dreadful bleeding bodies.

How did he come to see the dreadful bleeding bodies?

Florence had not said. In the street, Mother supposed. Perhaps coming home on a dark night …

Why didn't he go to the police?

Perhaps he was afraid to.

I would have gone to the police.

But a man might be afraid he would be suspected.

Did Florence really say 'bodies' in the plural? He might have stumbled over one body by accident, but to have seen all of them … Only one person would have seen all of them. 'That makes him the Ripper!'

'Yes!'

Not so fast … we must not jump to conclusions. Florence said his fondness for Dieppe was not just because he liked it as a place, which he did, but because it distanced him from the scenes in the East End where the murders had been committed. In London, he always had the feeling that a short bus-ride could carry him back into those haunting dark streets.

She said Florence said that never for one day, one hour or one minute of his life did he forget those dark streets and those murders. He had done a series of paintings far worse than any that we knew, which could be of nothing else. Florence could not bear to look at them because she knew what they meant … but he had destroyed them.

But he wanted the truth known after his death and had left clues. In the 1920s Florence had accepted a commission to paint a portrait of Saint-Saëns and afterwards Sickert asked her to come and do one of him. It was just after the death of his second wife, Christine, and he was obviously feeling sad, but while she worked he told her that there was a series of pictures into which he had painted clues as to who the murders were by, and why. No one of them contained the whole explanation, but taken all together they did, and it was for anyone interested to pick out which of his pictures were the ones including the clues and fit them together. It was a riddle.

The supreme clue, he had told her, was a gull that he had put on Queen Victoria's shoulder. It was not in the main picture but in a picture within the picture.

She asked me if I knew of any symbolism attached to a gull? She indicated my shelves of theosophical books. Anything there about a gull as a symbol for something? I shook my head. The only symbolic or mythical birds I could think of were the phoenix, the ibis, the kingfisher. The only literary allusion I could think of was in Chekhov's *The Seagull*, which didn't help. There was the sense of 'to gull' meaning to make a fool of, but if the idea was the Ripper had been gulled that didn't help us.

It was not that same evening but a few days later, Mother having seen Florence again in the interval, that she began to tell me what at first sounded like a different story. When Florence first met Sickert, which was in 1885, he had with him in his studio a girl with a small child. At first glance they might be taken for a conventional family, man with wife and child, only the girl was not his wife and the child was not his child. She was the child of a man who, Florence said, was 'in direct line of succession to the throne'.

What had this to do with the Ripper, I asked.

'She says what she is giving me is the background.' Unless she understood the background, Florence said, she would not understand the murders. She had to be patient.

They knew a girl called Mary Kelly, who worked in a small shop opposite. Although Irish she had come from Wales, where she had been employed in a hospital, scrubbing floors. The child's mother, who was a bit wanting in the head, wandered off, leaving the child on Sickert's hands, so he asked Mary Kelly to come in and act as nanny to the child. Hence Florence came to know her. She thought Mary Kelly was a bit envious of her as she appeared to subsist without a job. 'If she only knew how hard I worked!' Florence exclaimed. But Sickert was failing to pay Mary regularly. 'When I've sold a picture' was no use to a girl who had to pay her rent on Friday nights, and Florence noticed her standing about on street corners, and was horrified to realise she had become a prostitute. Later she disappeared from the district. Florence had never named the street in which Sickert had the studio in which all this happened but it was in walking distance of Warren Street Underground Station, and there was in it a male brothel, a few doors along the road. Sickert told Florence that he was receiving blackmailing letters from Mary, written from some address in the East End. He did a portrait of her, which he called *Blackmail*. He gave the sitter a fictitious name but that picture was of Mary Kelly. He drew her several times. In retrospect, Florence wished she had done more to help Mary Kelly. If she had had the slightest foresight of the ghastly end that awaited her, she would have taken her to the studios of all the artists in London till she found one that would take her on as a model, and pay properly, regularly, not like Sickert. She had a good appearance, 'good hair'. She was in some ways a silly girl yet Florence blamed herself for not having done more for her. She need never have come to that terrible end.

'What end was this?' I asked, still uncomprehending. How did Florence learn of it?

'From the newspapers. It was in every newspaper, the horrible murder, the mutilations.'

'She was one of the Ripper's victims?'

'Yes.'

Then Mother was telling me another story. Florence had thought to take the little girl out to tea at her own flat in the Sloane Square district, but as they were crossing Trafalgar Square in the direction of the Strand Underground, a coach came up on to the pavement. Florence had jumped and tried to pull the child out of the way, but the child was hit by a wheel and slightly injured. When she got back and told Sickert, he told her that was no accident but an attempt at the murder of a child whose father was inconveniently in direct line of succession to the throne. She must never talk about what she knew or she could go the way of Mary Kelly and those other poor women.

She had all her life been frightened by this, and though she had been twice married she had never told either of her husbands. 'I'm telling you things I've never told *anyone*,' she had said to Mother.

The story was made difficult to follow by the failure to give names to any of the characters, save Mary Kelly. At one moment Mother was referring to the illegitimate child as 'he' and I queried this. She said, 'There are *two* illegitimate children in this story.' There was the one by the girl in Sickert's studio and the man in direct line of succession to the throne, that was a girl. There was also one born to the child when she grew up of which Sickert, not her husband, was the father. It was when Florence returned from India after her second widowhood that she had met her again and she had told her the little boy running round her was not her husband's but Sickert's. She had not kept in touch with him but he had adopted his true father's name, and if Mother had any occasion to write to him she should address him as Joseph Sickert. But not tell him anything about this. It was for his sake as much as for personal safety that Mother must never make public what she had told her, as, if he didn't know, it would come as a frightful shock. For me,

[121]

Sickert's innocence or guilt seemed to hang upon one point: whether the bodies of all the murdered women had at any time been upon public display, all together, so that he could innocently have seen them all. I went to Foyle's and asked if they had a book on the crimes of Jack the Ripper. No. I walked the length of Charing Cross Road asking in every bookshop. Everywhere it was 'No'.

I set down all the above to have on record that the story was told to me, in this form, at this date. In 1977 there appeared a book by Stephen Knight, *Jack the Ripper: the Final Solution*, which told the same story, plus certain variations and additions – notably that the murders were carried out by the royal physician, Sir William Gull. Knight's source was Sickert's son Joseph by Alice Gorman, Clarence's purported daughter. The source of both Florence's and Joseph's account can only have been Sickert. He died when Joseph was seventeen and I can understand his feeling it his responsibility to tell him 'Your grandfather was the Duke of Clarence' – if that was the case. A secret marriage may have been invented to pretty the story for innocent young ears but why had the necessity of keeping the matter secret have to be bolstered by the assertion that a string of women in the East End had been murdered by royal servants? The coach in which Gull was alleged to have been driven through the East End to pick up the women had, I thought, evolved out of the one which, according to Florence, mounted the pavement in Trafalgar Square.

I go back to what Florence said that did not come through Sickert. Mary Kelly was angry with Sickert and flounced off. Sickert, in referring to letters he received from her, used the word 'blackmail'. Of whom, concerning what? Was she saying it was ridiculous for Sickert to say he had no money? He should go to the Palace and demand payment of maintenance for that child, and, if necessary, threaten to raise a public stink by telling the world the heir to the throne had fathered a child for whose upkeep he was too mean to pay.

And yet another slant. My mind went back to Cremers. It was Runia who had told me, that day in 1940 at Primrose Hill, that together with her friend Mabel Collins, Cremers and a man (whom she did not name) had formed a business partnership for the marketing of face creams. He claimed to know a lot about magic, talked a lot about the Ripper crimes and professed to know so much about how and why they had been committed as to cause Cremers to think it was he who had committed them. She believed that by representing to him the frightful karma he must be laying up for himself, she talked him out of it, for he assured her, 'There will be no more' – which caused her to think she had been right.

There has been a book about him, *Jack the Ripper, the Bloody Truth* by Melvin Harris (Columbus, 1987). Harris had his information from papers left by the journalist who had cornered Cremers that day at Vicky's and he gave the name of the man, Rosslyn Stephenson, from Yorkshire but believed to have qualified while in France as a doctor. It suddenly struck me as significant that he had expressly excluded Mary Kelly from his list of victims as the mutilations were not as he would have made them. This seemed a highly promising lead but then I found he had been in the London Hospital when the murders were committed. I wrote to the Hospital. Yes, they had had him as a patient, suffering from neurasthenia. He would not have been kept in bed. Yes, in-patients were allowed to go out, but not during the hours of the night at which the murders had been committed.

I must leave the mystery with the reader. The conspiracy theories abound, some of them so wildly far-fetched as to be comic. But Florence's story to Mother is, I admit, still a lingering puzzle.

I made some portraits of Bast, but she worried me. She seemed no happier. I had been away for so long that what connection there might have been had weakened. Mother, now that I was back, would be moving out of my flat into a nearby hotel; she had her eye on the Whitehall in Montague Street. I had Bast mated to a pedigree Siamese and she became pregnant. I watched her give birth, eagerly hopeful, but before I knew what she was doing she had taken every one in her mouth and swallowed it. The whole litter had been eaten.

Oliver Jones had friends in Cornwall who wanted a Siamese cat. And so I gave her to them. But I felt bad about it.

My still life with *Tureen and Yellow Fruits* at least progressed as far as the Hanging Committee when I submitted it to the Royal Academy. As it was only the second oil-painting I had ever done, I was pleased.

I called at the Camberwell School of Art (the one suggested by Mother) and asked if they would take me as a student. It was arranged I should start in the autumn term. And I wrote to the Indian Army Officers' Family Fund asking if they would make me a grant towards the fees from their Post War Re-Education and Training Scheme. They did.

Oliver said his father would like to meet me. If I could fit in with his methods, he could send me pupils for English lessons. Oliver reminded me his father was Principal of the Phonetics Department of University College. An appointment was made for me to call on him there in the afternoon of 11 May.

To know at least something of the subject before I met Professor Jones, I bought a copy of his *Outline of English Phonetics* and spent the intervening days reading and memorising as much of it as I could.

There was almost nothing of him. Small and slight, with a moustache.

We talked about the creative power of sound. I said the ancient Egyptian hieroglyph for Ra was a mouth, which seemed to tie in with the Logos doctrine, and he said, 'In the beginning was the word.' He told me of some experiment in which sound had been made to make ripples, in sand if I remember correctly.

He showed me a chart of the sounds of the Sanskrit alphabet and made me make all of them, particularly those found difficult by English people, the bh and the ao diphthong.

He talked of the difficulties speakers of various languages had in the pronunciation of other languages. Germans found it difficult to pronounce the English 'p', which we make with a little puff of air following the plosion and Germans do not, so that if they said 'pat' it sounded to English ears more like 'bat', with voiceless 'b'. Japanese had particular difficulty in making the distinction between English r and l, because they had neither, but a consonant halfway between them, articulated not by shaping the tongue as for either but by making a flap with it, so that whichever they tried to say when speaking English sound to English ears like the other. He made me make a German 'p' and a Japanese flap.

It had been because of his ability to recognise foreign types of English he had been drawn into the case of Bill. Maud Macarthy had come into the Department about something and had told him of an East End Cockney boy she and her husband had come to know who went into trances in which he spoke with strange foreign accents. Could Professor Jones identify them? Were they Tibetan? He had never heard Tibetan English so could not say, but at least he could distinguish Punjabi English from Gujarati English.

Was it true he was, as Oliver maintained, the original of Professor Higgins in *Pygmalion*?

Shaw's Preface mentioned Sweet, he said.

But Sweet was an Anglo-Saxon man. I had his *Dictionary of Anglo-Saxon* and *Anglo-Saxon Reader*.

He was an Anglo-Saxon man but he had a phonetics side as well. 'Shaw knew him. And he knew me.' They were both members of the Simplified Spelling Society, and Shaw did come into the Department. He didn't show him the play he was writing, 'because he was afraid I'd make a fuss'. He just gave him a ticket for a box on the first night and hoped for the best. Professor Jones confessed to having been somewhat taken aback but said, 'I decided to take it in good part.' He therefore laughed when everyone else did. But Shaw told him afterwards that when he had seen him laughing it was with great relief. He had been half afraid of a writ for libel. In fact, Shaw said, it was after a talk with him in the Department and, as he was travelling back in a bus through South London, that he found he was calling the character Jones in his mind. He pulled himself up – that wouldn't do. Then the bus passed a draper's shop and from the deck he noticed a sign over it, HIGGINS & JONES. 'And he decided to call me Higgins as he couldn't call me Jones.'

He said, 'Don't ever pay to see a play by Shaw.' If there was a play by Shaw on anywhere and I wanted to see it, I should just tell him and he would ring the manager and I would have a box, if there was one, or at any rate a stall. He had a free box or best seat to any play by Bernard Shaw at any theatre, at any time, anywhere in England. He had sent occasional visiting scholars to the play, Americans over for Ph.Ds and the like. He would send them on their own, as he couldn't sit through it again.

'I don't think anybody who knows me could think it was meant to be me,' he said. He had never so badly lost his temper as to throw his shoes at anybody, and 'For the record, I've never had an affair with a student.'

In thinking nobody who knew him could think Professor Higgins was modelled on him, he was mistaken. Just about every one of the students he referred to me believed it, it was the aura that clung around him, and the staff believed it too, even Gimson, his eventual successor in the chair. But he wasn't quick-tempered, I objected to Gimson. 'Ah,' he said, 'we don't know what he was like then.' Gimson's idea was that he had in fact been hot-tempered but that seeing the caricature of himself on the stage he had resolved to make his behaviour as unlike that as possible.

On that afternoon Professor Jones's secretary brought us in tea and cakes. 'Have whichever of those looks to you the least poisonous' (one was a rather arsenical green) 'and come again next week, on Wednesday.' Almost by the way, as I was leaving, he said he would certainly recommend me to foreign students come to take the course who could do with a little general English, grammar and the like, as well. They sometimes asked.

Naturally the students he sent to me all wanted to know who Eliza Doolittle was in real life, and when I told them she was an imaginary character, plainly disbelieved this disclaimer of the great love adventure of Professor Jones's life.

It was, I think, at our second meeting that Professor Jones told me he wanted me to make a career in phonetics. Starting in the autumn term, he would like me to follow the one-year course in phonetics of English for Foreign Students and begin research for my thesis on the Phonetics of Polish, to be submitted in perhaps two years' time for the London Master of Arts.

But I didn't know Polish, I protested.

It didn't matter. There were really only two European languages that hadn't been done, Polish and Dutch, and he preferred Polish for me as there were a lot of Poles in London at the present time so that it should not be difficult to engage an informant, someone who would come and make the sounds of his language for me to describe, and in the autumn we would have in the department a very distinguished Polish phonetician from a university in Poland, a Mr Jassem, who would be of great assistance to me. He worried a good deal about what was going to happen to Phonetics when he was gone. Gimson would succeed him in the chair, obviously, and was friendly, but there were undercurrents he did not like: in the School of Oriental and African Studies there was Professor Firth who was his enemy. I would have to go to SOAS to attend Firth's lectures on Linguistics, but I would realise how hostile to himself he was. He hoped that eventually I might obtain a post in this Department.

I was incredulous. I had looked forward to starting at the Camberwell School of Art, but here was an academic career being offered me, and it seemed sensible to accept. I wrote – not without a pang – to the Officers' Family Fund explaining what had happened and asking if they would transfer the grant from the Camberwell School of Art to the proposed course in Phonetics at University College. They did.

He asked me to come to a session with him one afternoon in every week during the summer vacation, because once term started he would not be able to spare so much time for me. He started every time by making me go over the phonetics of the Sanskrit alphabet, which he considered fundamental, because it was the nearest thing we had to the vanished sacred language. And he was vexed with Annie Besant for getting its imitated pronunciation wrong in her translation of the *Bhagavad Gita*. There were several people at Adyar who could have done it for her correctly. Long and short marks in the wrong place and a fancy spelling as Samskrit, with an 'm' instead of an 'n'. Where on earth did she get that from?* He had been asked to review the book for *The Aryan Path*, and had given it a bad review. In retrospect he had often wondered if he had done unfair disservice to a noble woman, but she had alienated him by her incompetence. He had said to himself, why should he believe what she said about the astral plane, of which he knew nothing, when he found in her treatment of a subject on which he did know something so many mistakes? And he warned me, should I ever write a book, against laying myself similarly open. This may be a suitable occasion to declare that in my book *Blavatsky and Her Teachers* I have said, 'Tibetan is a tone language.' It isn't.

He also talked about Leadbeater. Although unable to see astral bodies he did see small darting points of light which were exactly like those described by Leadbeater, which rather inclined him to think the other things Leadbeater said he saw might also be described. I told him I too saw the tiny points of light that danced everywhere, and had first noticed them on the beach at Brighton in the hot summer of 1930.

Let us see if we could see any now, he said, and we went to the window of his study, which gave on to the courtyard between the parts of the college which overlooked Tavistock Square and Gower Street respectively. Although it was not a specially bright day, when we unfocused our eyes we saw lots of them, darting about everywhere. We saw them in exactly the same way. He said he had always wondered how far or near they were. There seemed no way to tell.

He believed he had been the Korean phonetician Se Jong, who, in 1446, created a phonetic alphabet for the Korean language. It was still

---

* I believe that I have since found the source of Mrs Besant's confusion. It lies in Max Müller's classic work, *A Sanskrit Grammar* (London, Longmans Green, 1886) which she must have consulted. Now it is a fact that in the index, on p. 191 one finds Samskrit written with italicisation. Now that always means something with Müller. To find what it means in this instance, one has to go back to the first chapter 'The Alphabet'. In this, there is, on p. 5, '9(8)'. This is not at first reading easy to understand, but I think what he means is that when 'n' occurs in certain positions it is the custom 'for the sake of more expeditious writing' to draw the character for 'm' instead. The pronunciation remains unaffected by the change. The subject of his reference is surely the shape of the characters, and it is evident from the examples he gives that to form the *n* requires more strokes than the *m*. But when transliterating into the alphabet we use there is no point in maintaining the substitution since, for us, it is not quicker to write *m* than *n*, and to write *m* where *n* is to be pronounced serves no purpose at all, and, unexplained, is misleading.

in use, he said, with just a few modifications. That he could have been Sir William Jones, the eighteenth-century Sanskritist, leapt out as so obvious it seemed to him too glib to believe. The only biography accorded him only virtues and 'I feel that it is in the faults one is more likely to recognise oneself, don't you?'

Returning to Bill ... he had once asked him, 'Is Krishnamurti a Master?' and had got the reply, 'A Master of Masters.' It was always these moments of translucence from other planes that I enjoyed in my conversations with Professor Jones. In comparison, the strictly phonetical work to which I had, beginning with the autumn term, to apply myself under the various teachers was rather foot-slogging.

Eight

It was perhaps about half past five when Omar Ali rang me, and the date was 5 April 1949. Omar Ali was the young Pakistani who shared an office with Vilayat in Pakistan House. I had met him a few times. He said the award of a George Cross to Vilayat's sister was going to be announced tomorrow. It was posthumous. Vilayat had been warned in advance and had left the office early in order to collect his mother and take her away so that the press could not get at her, as she was sobbing and would say her daughter should never have accepted the mission. Vilayat had asked Omar to take any calls that might come for him to Pakistan House, and tell reporters what he could of the family. But, Omar said, he knew very little about the family; could I tell him some things he could tell to reporters? I tried and could feel him trying to get a grasp. Shortly after we had hung up, he rang a second time. Instead of his trying to memorise the things I had said, would it not be better if he put reporters on to me? That was how it came about that my telephone rang for the third time and the representative of the *Daily Telegraph* announced himself.

From the official citation, which I read in the next morning's papers, I learned that she had been set down in enemy-occupied France by Lysander aircraft on 6 June 1943 (that would have been a few days after I had last seen her), that the Gestapo had made mass arrests in the groups to which she had been detailed, that she had been given an opportunity to return to England but preferred not to leave her French colleagues without means of communication, that after three and a half months she had been betrayed, arrested and taken to the HQ of the Gestapo in the Avenue Foch, refused any cooperation, made two attempts to escape from the fifth floor, refused parole and was sent to Germany where, on 12 September 1949, she was shot at Dachau. At any rate that was better than 'burned alive' at Natzweiler as Vilayat had thought he understood.

He rang me that evening. It was of course from the family home, in Suresnes, that he had taken his mother. She did nothing but sob, had sobbed all through the night and had been sobbing all day. A doctor and his wife would look after her. He would have to get back to Pakistan House or his absence would be putting an unfair burden on Omar Ali. In fact he was back the next day.

On the 26th Omar Ali rang to tell me Vilayat had been called back to Paris as a matter of emergency to tend to his mother. Then on 3 May he rang again, to say Vilayat's mother was dead. He asked me to tell Vilayat's Sufi people.

I rang Hayat Bouman. She said she would organise a memorial service for 'the Begum' as she called her. This was held at 5.30 on Sunday 5 June, at their place on Primrose Hill. I attended it and of course Vilayat was there.

The official citation did not name the service in which Noor had served. She was referred to by her Air Force rank, but she had given me her address as c/o The War Office, Whitehall.

In one of the newspapers I saw a reference to Colonel Buckmaster as having been her commanding officer. He was apparently head of the French Section. It did not say of *what*.

On 16 June, I wrote a letter to Colonel Buckmaster, The French Section, The War Office, Whitehall, London SW1, saying I was a friend of the Inayat Khan family and asking if there was anything he could tell me beyond what was in the official citation.

He replied by telephone. There was a person who could tell me much more than he could, a Miss Vera Atkins. He gave me her address in Chelsea.

I wrote to her, and she invited me to come and see her at 6.30 on 19 July.

There was something about both her face and figure that reminded me irresistibly of Marlene Dietrich. She had the huskiest voice I had ever heard, and she chain-smoked, through a long holder.

But the oddest thing was that she had had iron bars set across her window. In case of burglars, she said, catching my glance at them. But she was not on the ground floor. There was nothing in the room of obvious attraction to a burglar so I supposed she held documents that could intrigue some interested parties. I thought she must be the public face of the secret service. She looked at me with appraising suspicion and asked, 'What are you?'

I said, 'I am an Honours graduate of London University, and during the war I was an examiner for the Postal and Telegraph Censorship Department of the Ministry of Information.' I thought that would assure her that I was used to secret work. As something more seemed required, I said I was at present doing a little postgraduate work in phonetics, at University College, London – a thesis on the phonetics of Polish, though it was not a language I knew.

At this she humanised. Her brother did a thesis on the phonetics of Kikuyu, though he did not know Kikuyu. We both laughed.

I said I was thinking of writing something about Noor.

She strongly advised me against trying to discover the detail of Noor's adventures in the field. If I persisted, 'People will find it much the least interesting part of your book.' There was interest in the background of these women, not in the detail of their work. Noor would have gone first to a school for physical training, then on a course of self-defence and finally on a course of security training. She had not been notified that the locations of these training schools had been taken off the Official Secrets list, so would not give them to me.

'It was I who briefed her for her mission,' she told me. And she had ridden with her in the car to the place where she would board the aircraft. It was a beautiful summer's day with all the flowers in the hedges appropriate to June, if I liked to make something of that. I would never learn anything about the people with whom she worked when she landed in France. The group she was sent to join had all been arrested. No, there wasn't anybody who had been in touch with any of them with whom she could put me in touch. She must again advise me not to try to piece together her adventures in the field. She could however give me the name of a woman who had been held prisoner in the same prison as Noor, in a place called Pforzheim, to which she had been sent after her attempt to escape from Avenue Foch. Yolande Lagrave. She would give me her address, in Bordeaux. And she did give me one or two other people, who might or might not have met Noor.

Then she said there was one other person she ought to tell me about, but with reserve – John Starr, who had been a prisoner at the Avenue Foch and her fellow in the attempt to escape from it, but whereas she had afterwards refused the offer of parole he had accepted it. He was not actually a traitor but 'a borderline case'. If I saw him I must make clear it was only 'Madeleine' (Noor's code-name) I was interested in and try not to draw him out on anything else. If he started telling me some fantastic rigmarole in which it appeared everything he did was justified and everything the Section did was wrong, I should know what to think.

The initials SOE were still unknown to me and she was still to me the public face of the secret service. With a curiosity that was not unfriendly, I asked her what she had done before getting into this organisation.

'This and that,' was her reply.

My diary shows me that all through July and August I was having weekly appointments at University College with Mr Jassem and also Professor Jones. He confirmed there had been a student called Atkins. He had gone over to SOAS (School of Oriental and African Studies) for sessions with Jomo Kenyatta, lately known as the suspected mastermind behind the Mau Mau murders of white settlers in East Africa but then just a student following a course of Phonetics of English for Foreign Students, and making a little pocket money briefing Atkins on the sounds of Kikuyu, for he was a Kikuyu speaker.

Apart from these sessions – one of them with Gimson – and giving lessons in English to students recommended to me at the Department who came to my home for them, I was also making a little money taking a class at the West Central Jewish Club, in Gower Street, every Tuesday evening at 7.30.

But I found an afternoon to visit Windsor Castle to see all the relics they had of the Inayat Khans' formidable ancestor, Tippu Sultan. I also wrote to all the addresses I had been given, and received replies to the appeals I had made in *The Times* or *Telegraph*. One was from Fred Archer who had met Noor while they were both in the Air Force, and one was from Noor's friend Joan Wynne who had had the baby in Eire. Both came to see me.

My letters to John Starr and the French patriot I put in the wrong envelopes, but from Starr I had an invitation to come and see him. I decided to go first to Madame Lagrave, Starr afterwards.

I left on 26 August by the 9.35 from Victoria and got into Bordeaux at 7.15 the next morning, booked into a hotel and found my way to Madame Lagrave. She bade me dine with her that evening. Of all the women prisoners in Pforzheim she was the sole survivor; it had been by mistake she had been arrested and this was remembered when the rest were shot. The inmates from Bordeaux became aware that there was a mystery prisoner who was never allowed out for the daily walk around the prison yard accorded to the others. Feeding bowls were circulated from one cell to another and, using knitting needles, they scratched on the bottom of one that in cell no. 12 were three French women. On the bottom of another feeding bowl came back the message: Nora Baker, Radio Office Service RAF, 4 Taviton Street, London.' (Baker was the maiden name of Mrs Inayat, and of course the address was hers.)

In this way, scratching on the bottoms of the food bowls, using the tongue of her handcuffs, 'Nora Baker' was able to say quite a lot: 'Never tell my mother I have been in prison.' The last message they received from her read: 'I am leaving.'

Madame Lagrave had often wondered what had become of her.

I realised Madame Lagrave had given me the material for what might well be the last chapter of my book, and, back in my hotel, wrote it all out while still fresh in my memory.

I thought I should also see a little of Bordeaux, and on Sunday 28th climbed to the top of the Cathedral and from its roof, looked down to see where the river emptied into the Gironde, leading ultimately to the sea – from where the Inayat Khans had left in 1940.

I descended, and walked along the river bank in the direction of the port, for a long way. Then I saw a restaurant and sat down at a table by the waterside. I asked for the *déjeuner à prix fixe*. 'Vous êtes Anglaise?' asked the waitress.

'Oui.'

Whilst I ate she stood by my table and told me she had a friend called William. He was a sailor. He wanted to marry her but she was in doubt. He was a virgin. She was not. It had been her custom on Friday nights when the ships came in to pick up a sailor and take him to the local dance-hall. After they had danced she would take him back to her room. But when William escorted her back he said goodnight at the door. She was very surprised as she had thought he liked her company. But he did this every time; Then he said he would not sleep with her unless she married him. Would she do so? His home was in Cardiff. Would she be happy in Cardiff? she asked me. She wrote down for me the name of a street.

I had to confess that I did not know Cardiff, I couldn't tell her what sort of street it was.

She said she thought it would be respectable because his mother lived in it. She would have to live with his mother. He assured her Cardiff was very like Bordeaux, a big port, with ships coming in and going out. It would be just like living in Bordeaux, waiting for his ship to come in, only it would be in Cardiff, waiting for his ship to return.

'It is a chance to improve my character,' she said. 'If I remain here my morals will deteriorate.' But could she trust herself, during the long days when he would be at sea or in Bordeaux, not to go dancing in Cardiff? William was very passionate and if she slept with another man after being married to him, he might do her some physical harm, even kill her. 'Perhaps fear of being killed will keep me good?'

From the point of religion there was no obstacle. William was Protestant and she was Protestant. Most French people were Catholic but in Bordeaux, for historical reasons, there were a lot of Protestants. So no problem there. I was English. What did I think? It would be a tremendous risk for her to abandon everything she knew, for she had never been out of Bordeaux, yet so tremendous a chance.

Much, I said, depended on the character of the mother, and of the relations between them. If she disliked this French girl, strange to her, whom William had brought home, it would be terrible. On the other hand, if she accepted her, they could be company for each other during the long days when William was away. 'You might then have less temptation to go dancing.'

She wanted me to advise her. Should she go?

I felt it was an occasion when I should feel myself in my pineal gland and integrate myself in the All. I drew myself up and said. 'Go, but take sufficient money with you, if you find you don't like it, to pay your fare back from Cardiff to Bordeaux.'

She said very solemnly. 'Thank you, I will do exactly as you say.'

Strange the responsibility one can incur without expecting it. I have often wondered how it turned out; I never even knew her name.

I cannot now remember how Maria Lloyd came to get in touch with me but she had known Inayat Khan and invited me to spend a fortnight as her guest in her flat in Le Grand Palais, Monte Carlo. So, on 1 September I said goodbye to Madame Lagrave – who was really glad to meet someone who had known her pathetic fellow prisoner at Pforzheim, as nobody either from Noor's family or the War Office had come to see her – and at 8 pm took the train to Carcasonne, where I thought to break the journey. It was a dreadful train, there seemed to be only rattling wooden seats and most of the time I had to stand. However, I left it at a few minutes before midnight to indulge myself in a little tour of the walled city, often mentioned by Vivian, which had played such a part in the history of the Albigenses.

The next fortnight was somewhat idly spent, I sat on the beach and even swam, visited the Jardins Exotiques, Monaco, Nice and Cannes. Beneath the superficial life, there is a deep stillness about that coast. In the evenings we talked about spiritual movements and teachers.

On 13 September I left Monte Carlo, changed trains in Marseilles and travelled through the night – very weary I remember – and arrived in Paris at 8.40 in the morning of the 14th. I booked in at the Hôtel de la Paix and, in the evening, found my way out to Issy-les-Moulineaux, where, at 8.30, I rang the bell of the Starrs' flat.

He was short, blonde, with a rounded face and a moustache. His wife brought us coffee, then moved off to let us talk.

'I'll have to tell you some of my story for you to see where your friend fits in,' he said. Shortly after he was brought to the Avenue Foch as a prisoner, he was shown a map of France on which had been marked off the areas in which the French Section organisers had been arrested; they were numbered 1 to 12 and he was asked to write in his own code-name, 'Bob', and the number 13. This he did. In civil life he was a commercial artist and his lettering caught Kieffer's eye. Kieffer was Sturmbannführer, chief of the Sicherheitsdienst (German Security Service) at Avenue Foch. Kieffer asked Starr if he would copy out the whole map in his artistic hand. This was the perfect opportunity to familiarise himself with the information it gave, which would be important if he could escape with it to London. Whenever the Germans captured a radio operator complete with radio set, they were in the position to work it back to London in the captured operator's name – if they could get the code. Had the codes been explained to me in London?

'No.'

One's messages were inscribed upon the squares of a grid, 'Numbered across and down as in a crossword puzzle.' He drew one. Each operator had not only an individual code but an individual security check and the radios were told before being sent out that if they were captured they might give their codes, so long as they did not give their security checks. The check consisted in a spelling mistake that had to be made in one square of the grid, let us say 8 across and 5 down; if this fell on the middle letter of the word 'man' one had to write not the 'a' but something else, say, 'mtn'. This would assure London one was still a free agent. Now, in the guard-room used to sit a British officer, code-name 'Archambaud' who had a certain amount of liberty and was permitted to choose his own programmes on the radio. 'Archambaud' had told Starr that he had been given not one but two security checks (this because his role was particularly important, as radio to the big chief, 'Prosper'). When he was asked by Dr Goetz (interrogator at Avenue Foch) for his security check, he gave the first one only, trusting to the absence of the second to advise London that he was a prisoner. To his utter dismay, Goetz later showed him the return message which had come from London: YOU FORGOT YOUR DOUBLE SECURITY CHECK BE MORE CAREFUL. After that, he was so shaken that he gave Goetz the second as well. But there was a so-called Canadian circuit up in the extreme north of France which was run by the Germans for a year and drops of arms and munitions and, most unhappily, human beings were being made to it, straight to German reception. It was about this he felt it desperately necessary to tell London if a means could be found.

But how to escape? They were on the fifth floor of 84 Avenue Foch, in what must have been the servants' rooms for it was a commandeered house. There was the room used by Vogt as his office, into which prisoners were shown to be interrogated by him; there was the guard-room, and there were the three cells. 'Madeleine' was in the middle and had on the other side of her a Frenchman, Colonel Faye. The cells had no windows in the walls, but skylights in the ceilings, across which, in each case, three bars had been fitted. How to remove those bars? The three prisoners were able to communicate by means of notes stuffed into a crevice in the lavatory. Then the cleaner's carpet-sweeper going wrong gave Starr the opportunity to help mend it and so steal from her tool-box a screwdriver. This, passed to and fro between the three cells, made it possible to mine around the ends of the bars, but then the damage to the plaster into which they were set began to show. 'Madeleine' asked Vogt for face-powder, and he brought it for her, and she shared it with the other two and they used it to cover over the damage to the plaster. Finally they did get one bar out each – hers stuck and he and Faye had to delay to get it out – and they all three climbed out on to the roof, from where they had to make their way along a very narrow parapet to the place where they could descend on to the flat roof of a building facing the Avenue Foch from the other side of the courtyard. Unhappily, searchlights picked them out and they were recaptured.

He had been given parole but with the thought in mind that he might be able to pass his information about the German control of the radio circuits to some prisoner who was free to attempt escape.

The game ended in the following year, when London, at last perhaps suspicious, had required the operator on the ground to speak to the man in the plane by S-phone. Starr had verbally agreed to do it, but at the last moment, when they were on the field, said, 'No, I can't.' Von Kapri took the S-phone but his English was so grotesque that Morel, who was in the plane, realised it was a German on the ground and told the pilot not to land but return to England. Starr said if he had refused to go out with them they would have had time to whip around and find somebody else. Vogt's English was a good deal better than von Kapri's.

I did not doubt that I had been told a true story, but it was a deeply troubling one. If the fact of the Germans playing our radios back to us had not been made public, it must be a British state secret to which I had become party by accident. I knew now why I had been advised to make clear to Starr that only my friend interested me and not to encourage him to talk about anything else, and if he started to spin a story, to distrust it. I had been given the material for a thrilling chapter about the attempted escape, but would I dare put in anything else about the radio sets?

I began writing the new chapter, in pencil, seated on my suitcase, in the Gare de l'Est, for my next two calls were in The Hague, Holland. Rumbling through the night, my train brought me into The Hague on the morning of 16 September.

My first call was on the brother of Inayat Khan, Vilayat and Noor's uncle, Murshid Musharaff Moulamia Khan. With him was their cousin, Mahmood, Mahaboob Khan. My chief task here was to persuade the uncle to allow me to mention the descent of the family from Tipu Sultan. Vilayat had told me, privately, one evening at Premier House as the sun was going down, but as to making it public, he feared his uncle would object. He felt publication should not be made without the uncle's consent. This was obviously going to be hard to come by. 'I live in a small house,' he said. 'To claim descent from the great Emperor would make me ridiculous.'

But their story of the descent was true, I insisted.

'It is true. By the blood, and through the female line.' Through the daughter of the Sultan, as Vilayat said.

Vilayat had warned me that he did not stand in very good odour with his uncle, but by telling him Vilayat had felt that 'your consent' was needed, I softened him a little.

Mahaboob put in helpfully that descent through the female line was important considering the influence of the mother in the home.

At last, the uncle gave his consent.

After that I went on to see Baroness van Tuyll. It was she who (under her professional name of H. Willebeek le Mair) drew the illustrations to Noor's book *Twenty Jataka Tales*. (Yes, the spelling is correct: *pace* the writers who have reversed the position of the 't' and the 'k', the tales have nothing to do with the capital of Java. Jataka is a word in the Pali language, that of the earliest Buddhist scriptures.) She gave me snapshots of Noor on horseback riding on the beach and of Noor in Indian dress playing the vina. 'I thought her instrument was the harp,' I said. Yes, the harp, seriously. But she did try the vina, because it was the Indian instrument, and put on the Indian dress for the picture. I left The Hague by train at 9.50, sailed from the Hook of Holland an hour later and arrived in Harwich at 7.15 in the morning of the 17th, and so by train to Liverpool Street, and home.

Then it was back to the usual grind, but with a few days in Cornwall to see Marie and back in time to take my class at the West Central Jewish Club on 3 October.

Krishnamurti's name was on the placards. He was talking at Friends House. I attended eight of his talks. I also saw, at last, Colonel Buckmaster. The appointment given me was for 2.30 at the office of the Ford Motor Company in Regent Street. It was on the landing of a staircase, for he had only a few minutes to spare from a committee meeting.

He could not clearly remember Noor as a person; what he remembered was that her radio post, the 'poste Madeleine', went 'on and on and on'.

Was he thinking of counting in the months it had run under German control, I wondered. Had he forgotten or was he still deceived? (His book, *Specially Employed*, published that autumn, said nothing about any radio circuits having come under German control; it was an unblighted success story.)

I asked him, 'What do you think of Starr?'

'Nothing, After he'd been taken by the Gestapo he did everything they asked him for a year.'

He asked me what story Starr told. When I came to his pinching the screwdriver, and sharing it with Madeleine and Faye to enable them to loosen their bars, he said, 'In that case, one wonders why he didn't go with them.'

But he did, I protested.

'You've only got his word for that, and that's worth nothing.'

He warned me that if Starr felt his reputation damaged by anything I wrote about him, he might take legal action.

I remember some of the thoughts that came to me as I walked home. One was of disappointment. My idea of a Colonel was somebody of Gilby's presence. The presence that comes of having taken responsibility. I felt that Buckmaster somehow lacked stature.

I had given up expecting a reply from the 'French patriot' but now one came, offering me an appointment for 6 November.

So I would have to go back. Vilayat suggested a few other people I should see in Paris who had known Noor before the war, the family doctor, Dr Jourdan, and his wife, and a near neighbour, Madame Pinchon, who had housed Noor's harp for her during the war. She would remember Noor's having it carried round to her when they decided to leave for England. There was also Madame Salmon; he didn't have her address but could give me that of her parents, the Grutars family.

So I took the train and boat again on 4 November. On the 5th I went first to the Grutars family in Paris. Yes, their daughter was still in the city and I could call on her at lunchtime. She had caught sight of Noor during the summer of 1943. It was in the Champs Elysées, carrying a heavy suitcase. This, she horrified Madame Salmon by explaining, contained a radio transmitter. She was there on behalf of the British.

At 2 pm I reached Dr and Madame Jourdan's. Madame Jourdan had a lot to tell me. Not only glimpses of Noor before the war, but during. At what must have been a late stage in her mission she had come to beg shelter with them until she was met by the man who would tell her where and when she should go for the aircraft that would come to take her back to England. It was from their place she transmitted what was probably her last message and received the reply, 'May God keep you.' This quite undid her, emotionally – being addressed as a human being.

I then went out to Suresnes and saw Madame Pinchon. She told me she had seen Noor during the German occupation. She had suddenly appeared at her door and asked if she might use her house for radio transmissions to England. Madame Pinchon, terrified, said certainly not. She told her to go away. But Noor wanted to look at what could be seen from her window of the Inayat Khans' house. Madame Pinchon had pulled her away. 'It was the house that drew her,' she said to me. Noor had begged her, should she not survive the war, never to tell her mother that she had come here. It would be too upsetting for her. That was why she had never spoken even to the other members of the family.

But, she told me, Noor had gone on to the home of a Madame Prenat, whose daughter, Madame Lacour, had been at school with her. She gave me Madame Lacour's address, which was only a few streets away.

So I went, and I found Noor's old school friend, who remembered her for the qualities of her character. 'Elle avait eu moralité!' A terrifically high morality. Yes, her mother had allowed Noor to transmit to England from her garden. Noor had set up the aerial as though it were a clothes line – as nimble as a cat; she had a room in the Avenue Richard Wallace at Neuilly, but Madame Lacour could not remember the number. Like Madame Pinchon, she could not tell me the date at which Noor had first come to Suresnes, but obviously it must have been much earlier than the days when she took refuge with the Jourdans.

The next day I had my appointment with the 'French patriot'. His wife insisted on my partaking of an enormous luncheon and more wine was offered me than I thought good to take. Then the atmosphere changed completely as she left me alone with her husband and his lawyer. 'I have made a statement to the police already. Why do you come to question me?'

I knew now why I had been soft-soaped by the wife. A woman, Renée Garry, was in a few days to be tried before the Permanent Courts Martial of Paris, on a charge of intelligence with the enemy; the accusation was that she had sold 'Madeleine' to the Germans. He, the 'French patriot', was giving evidence for the defence. He would say that 'Madeleine' did not need anybody to betray her as she was in contact with two so-called 'Canadians' who were Germans who could have arrested her at any moment they chose. Then he asked, 'Whom did you think I was when you wrote me the first letter?'

'Starr.' I knew immediately that I should not have dropped that name, but it was too late to take it back.

'A short man with a moustache and a face like the moon?'

It was undeniable.

He worked for the Gestapo, the 'patriot' asserted. He had seen him copying things on to a map of France.

I knew he was going to make trouble.

I was staying at the Inayat Khans' house. Vilayat had instructed the doctor and his wife who lived on the top floor to let me in and give me access to the papers on his desk. As I was going through them that evening I came on something unexpected, a letter from a Mr Dennis McFarlin, of Stockport, who had been in Germany with UNRRA just after the war. In Pforzheim he had been approached by a German woman who had told him the prisoner Nora Baker had told her of an escape she had made in company with two male prisoners, over the roofs from the Gestapo HQ in Paris. The testimony of this woman (inmate or cleaner at Pforzheim prison) so closely tallied with that given me by Starr that I thought that, having been the means, probably, of getting him into trouble, I might, with this, be able to get him out of it. So I took it. And travelled back to England the next day.

I saw Vilayat in the morning of the 8th. The date of that woman's trial made it impossible for me to attend. Professor Firth's class at SOAS I could miss, and private pupils I could shelve, but I could not fail to take my class at the West Central Jewish College.

He said he would go. 'Caserne de Reuilly.' I told him.

I called the same afternoon upon Miss Atkins, at her office. This was at 1, Bidborough Street and had to do with arranging holidays for children in foreign countries. When I began to tell her a woman was coming up for trial, she at first began saying she really could not listen to every ... But when I said the woman's name was Garry, she reacted almost as if she had been knocked off keel.

This was important, she said, she would have to tell Colonel Buckmaster at once. No, she could not talk about it with me.

Now I had only to wait to hear of what followed from Vilayat.

Nine

Vilayat telephoned me, I think from the airport, on 17 November, and said, 'She's been acquitted.' Shortly afterwards he was at my place. Before relating what had happened at the trial itself, he must tell me what he had done the day before. First, he had gone to see Starr, whose address I had given him. The chief thing he wanted from Starr was his opinion that Noor had not been tortured. Starr had assured him he never heard screams whilst at Avenue Foch and Vilayat's sister always looking physically intact, quite neat in her little suit, not looking like someone who had been mishandled. This was one very great load off Vilayat's mind. Then he went to see the 'French patriot', with whom he had a most peculiar interview. The man had run his sister down, alleging she had given a friend of his a rendezvous with the Gestapo at Le Pont Levallois. When Vilayat demanded this friend's name the 'French patriot' had hedged and refused. But Vilayat had fairly 'shaken' it out of him. Perhaps he had really thought he was going to get hurt, for he gasped, 'Viennot', and coughed up the address. Vilayat found Viennot, who had told him a story that was totally different; but this I must hear from Viennot himself. He gave me his address.

At the trial, next morning, was Renée Garry, in the dock; she was the sister of Emile Garry, a *Résistant* who was apparently Noor's chief. He had been arrested, as a secondary consequence of the betrayal, and was dead. Madame Margaret Garry, his widow, sister-in-law of the accused, was a witness for the prosecution, as was Madame Aigrain, in whose flat Noor and another had taken refuge after the mass arrests. But the chief witness for the prosecution was a German, Ernst Vogt, who said the accused had given him the address of 'Madeleine' for 100,000 francs. It was his chief, Kieffer, who had told him to go out and meet this woman, who had telephoned his office. Vilayat himself had witnessed for the prosecution. The 'French patriot' appeared for the defence saying 'Madeleine' had been in contact with two supposed Canadians who were in fact Germans, but the trump card held by the defence was a letter to Renée Garry from Buckmaster thanking her for her services to his organisation. Counsel for the defence waved this in the air, asking, 'Which are you going to believe, that German Gestapo man or the English Colonel Buckmaster?' She was acquitted by five votes to four.

During the hearing Starr had come up to Vilayat saying, 'I'm sorry to trouble you in the middle of all this but I've just been charged with intelligence with the enemy.' He was in the custody of the French officer standing behind him, whom he introduced, 'Captain Mercier.' Mercier said he understood Vilayat to have in his possession a paper confirming Starr's evidence. Would he confirm?

'Yes.'

I said, 'As a matter of fact, you haven't. I took it.' I had thought that – rather than trust it to the post – I should carry it to Starr. Perhaps I should hand it to Captain Mercier.

Vilayat wanted to see Miss Atkins and, though it was nine o'clock in the evening, I rang her and asked if we might come and see her. Yes.

She unbuttoned that evening more than she had ever done before.

'What did Renée Garry look like?'

Vilayat said, 'A big woman, with high colour.'

She said, that was exactly what Kieffer had told her. She attached more importance to verbal description than to a photograph.

'Really?' asked Vilayat.

It was through a photograph, she then confided, that she had given him the false information that his sister had been one of the women put to death at Natzweiler. A party of eight girls had been sent by rail from France into Germany, where the group had been divided. She had identified three out of four girls sent to Karlsruhe and subsequently to Natzweiler. She had shown a photograph of Noor to Odette, the only one of eight to have survived, and asked her if this was one of the eight. Odette said it was, and on the strength of this misidentification Miss Atkins had misinformed the family. When she gave evidence at the trial of the Natzweiler camp staff, she had stated that one of the four girls she was still unable to identify. It was only when information came in referring to Noor's having been in Pforzheim it was realised she had not been one of the party of seven, but had been sent separately, earlier.

As for Colonel Buckmaster's letter – he had received after the war lots of letters from people saying what they had done for his organisation and he wrote them polite thank you letters.

Vilayat said Vogt struck him as a more refined man than he would have expected of the Gestapo. He had asked permission to speak with him afterwards but this had been refused; he was, of course, a prisoner of the French.

Miss Atkins said Goetz, whom she had interrogated when he was brought to England as a prisoner, had impressed her as much superior to the ordinary Gestapo type; and she supposed Vogt, whom she had not met, to be the same.

I said I would make a formal application to the French to be allowed to see Vogt.

We talked until midnight. This, she said, was the worst case she knew of save one.

'You know of a worse betrayal?' asked Vilayat.

'Yes.'

She talked about Kieffer. When she had lunch with him he was still a free man. His involvement in the shooting of a party of uniformed paratroopers had not then been brought up. 'If that hadn't come up he would be a free man still today. We had nothing else on him.' (I knew from Starr Kieffer had been hanged; Starr had gone into the box for him to testify that he had been, as a prisoner, well-treated and had not seen anyone at Avenue Foch ill-treated.)

And so, back, for a while, to ordinary life: Professor Jones, Saturdays, Professor Firth, Wednesdays, the WCJC...

On 24 November Lise de Baissac came to see me. She had met my friend only once and only briefly. It was in a café on the Place des Ternes. She – 'Madeleine' – was wearing a light summer dress. 'Antoine' was there also. It was about the arrangements for pick-up by Lysander. 'Madeleine' had stayed only a few minutes. After she had gone, 'Antoine' said all the arrangements for the pick-up by Lysander had been made over her radio. It would have been about the middle of August.

To fit in, then, somewhere between her return to Suresnes and her seeking shelter with the Jourdans. 'Antoine' was a name I had heard in Vilayat's resumé of the trial. He had been someone who, like Noor, stayed at the Garrys'.

Lise de Baissac told me a bit of her own story. The man who had received her when she had been parachuted had after the war been tried on a charge of intelligence with the enemy. Then tried again for the second time, 'not a traitor' according to the more recent verdict.

'One never gets off the mud of having been an agent.' She said this with a movement of revulsion, as though washing herself.

The following day I went to the HQ of the FANY, where a Miss Clarke brought out Noor's file for me and I took notes. Of course her file at the Foreign Office remained closed to me.

I told Vilayat I should see his sister Claire. He was against it as talking of Noor would upset her and she was only just coming out of a nervous breakdown. Eventually he did consent to take me to see her at a flat near Baker Street on 19 December, to talk about their sister, but only very briefly.

On 30 December 1949 I went back to Paris. I had forgotten that its being New Year might make it difficult to get in at a hotel, but telephoned Starr and he found me one, not a tourists' but a commercial travellers' one, the Hôtel de Commerce, at 2 rue de Casablanca in the 15th arrondissement. It had the twin advantages of being inexpensive and near to the Starrs.

There was a brief delay before we could see Mercier, but on 2 January 1950 I saw Viennot. He told me a great deal. Too much to recapitulate here. Yes, he, the 'French patriot' and another man, Vaudevire, none of them of the British French Section but autonomous, had become acquainted with her. As she could not transmit from her lodging with Madame Jourdois at 3 Boulevard Richard Wallace, Vaudevire found her an address chez a Madame Peineau from which she could. Two more addresses for me to visit. About Le Pont Levallois. He had told Noor that if she was arrested and the Gestapo asked her to telephone him as if free and lure him to an appointment, she should indeed say, 'At the Pont de Levallois.' He would then know she was under German control and would come bringing with him a party of toughs sufficient to snatch her from the toughs guarding her. But when he came with his toughs, there was just no one there at all.

It was the 'French patriot' who, after he had been arrested, gave Noor a telephoned appointment at a bench on the Avenue MacMahon. Viennot told her she must not go, but drove her in his car very slowly down the Avenue and up again. The 'French patriot' was there all night, but accompanied by toughs who, when they gave up waiting, closed in on the 'bait' and took him away. Poor Noor was trembling and sobbing: she would not believe he would do it.

In the evening I had my appointment with Madame Garry, the widow of Emile Garry. In broken tones she told me of the unhappy relations with her sister-in-law. She had also some recollections concerning Noor. Theirs must have been about the first address she came to after being landed. She rang at the door but failed to give the opening code-phrase. As her husband's reply was to be in answer to the code-phrase, he didn't know what to do; but eventually he gave the reply without having been asked the question. Noor then explained she had been told her contact would be an elderly lady, and had been put out by being confronted by a young man. She was tired and faint, not having dared buy anything since landing save a bottle of Vichy water which she thought couldn't involve coupons. 'Antoine', who also lodged with them, was a major agent and probably her direct chief after the disaster. Had I met the Balachowskys?

No. Who were they?

It was with them that 'Prosper' stayed when working at Grignon. 'Prosper' was the big chief of the main British network and my friend had certainly been sent out to work under him. 'Prosper' and his helpers had all been arrested and were dead but the Balachowskys could certainly tell me a lot about my friend's early days before the disaster. They lived now at Viroflay, on the Versailles line, last stop before Versailles. She could not remember their address but it should not be too difficult to find them from the description she could give me of the buildings.

After the disaster she and Garry had thought best to leave their flat; they had gone to Le Mans, and their guests, 'Madeleine' and 'Antoine', had been taken in by Madame Aigrain, with whom they must have spent their first days after leaving. Madame Aigrain owned a big woman's shop on the Champs Elysées, the Toile d'Avion, where I could probably find her.

The next morning at nine o'clock Starr called for me with his car to drive me to the Reuilly barracks. On the way he told me that Mercier had told him to tell his story from the beginning, taking his time and including everything. At one point in his narration of the days prior to his arrest, he had mentioned a British officer whose code-name was 'Henri'. Mercier had asked the real name of this officer as there was something he would like to ask him. Starr was not sure whether it was in order to give the real names corresponding to code-names, so went to the British Embassy, explained the position and asked if it would be in order for him to give his *juge d'instruction* the real name of 'Henri'. When he called back for the answer, he was told the one that had come was, 'Leave the country immediately.' Just that and no answer to his question.

This advice particularly shocked me.

We drove in through the portals of the Reuilly Barracks, passed sentries, parked in the courtyard of the Tribunal Militaire Permanent de Paris, and then were in the office of Captain Mercier, tall, blonde, in uniform, very smart. 'You understand what this is all about?' he asked me. 'Captain Starr was held in slightly irregular circumstances, which I hope he will explain to my satisfaction.' He took out a packet of cigarettes and offered one to Starr. 'I wrote to Colonel Buckmaster some time ago, asking whether there was anything he would like to tell me about you. I have not had a reply.'

Starr said, 'I don't think you will.'

There was a moment of intense silence. I felt Mercier had taken in an entire situation. Very quietly, he said, 'It is not indispensable.'

He suggested Starr should have legal representation. 'To protect you against me. I might ask you questions in what your counsel would tell you was an improper way and you had not to answer.'

Starr said he had no fear of the way Mercier would question him.

Mercier said, 'If it is a question of money, you can have one of our people to be your defender. He will charge you no fee.'

Starr still declined.

Mercier looked at me. 'You are my witness. I told him his rights.'

I handed him Dennis McFarlin's letter.

Good. Might he borrow this for his *greffier* to make a copy for his file? He handed it to the *greffier*, seated behind his typewriter.

Mercier said to Starr, 'You are innocent until proved guilty.'

Starr had thought it was the other way about in France. 'Has the law changed then?'

'No, Starr.' It had always been the same. 'Believe me I had to pass an examination in the history of French law as part of my qualification for my job.' It had never been otherwise. 'This is the great Anglo-Saxon myth.' What was different was the role of the *juge d'instruction* – examining magistrate, researching magistrate – which had no counterpart in the English system. He has to instruct himself in the facts of the case, a process usually taking months. At the end, he either signs a *non lieu*, a paper saying he finds no case to send for trial, or he does send it for trial with a précis of what appear to him the salient points requiring to be tried. 'I can be either *juge d'instruction* or president of the court martial, but not both in one case, which would give too much power to one man. The précis may have some effect on the way the president views the case, but even if it is with a hostile eye, you are still innocent, unless and until the panel of judges finds you guilty.'

I said I had heard examining magistrates sometimes went out to view the scenes in which things were said to have happened. Could we go to the Avenue Foch?'

'Certainly! This afternoon, at two o'clock. We can all go together.'

And at two o'clock, in Starr's car, we set off.

As we passed through the Place des Voges he bade Starr stop for a moment and let us get out. He wanted us to appreciate the beauty of the old Paris, the architecture of the houses – so much nicer than what the tourists were always taken to see. He was hardly treating Starr as a prisoner or suspect. And then we were in the Avenue Foch. Mercier declaimed humorously, 'Starr's castle!' And as we walked up the steps of No. 84, imitating the German guards, 'Schnell! Schnell!', it dawned on me that Mercier was treating this as a day out, a fun day.

We mounted the marble stairs to the maisonette comprising the fourth and fifth floors. The place had of course returned to private ownership but Mercier's uniform gave us respectful if startled admittance. On the fourth floor were the rooms in which Kieffer slept and ate. On the fifth, Starr – keen now as a terrier at a rat hole – was identifying the room which had been Vogt's office, in which the prisoners were interrogated, the guardroom, the lavatory with the wash-basin beneath which was the crevice in which he, 'Madeleine' and Faye had placed the notes they exchanged and passed the screwdriver backwards and forwards. He bade us all put our hands into it, Mercier, the *greffier* and me. I put my hand in and imagined Noor's stuffing into it a note or the screwdriver, or fishing it out when left for her. He showed us three cells, his, hers and Faye's. The skylights were still there but to climb out through them we would need a chair, as they had had. He wanted to show us the parapet along which they had walked.

Mercier stopped him. No, Starr was not going to do it again. 'I can see from here that it could be done. But you had the Gestapo behind you. The situation is now not so desperate.'

Instead of risking falling to our deaths we would go round to the house at the back of the courtyard through which they had attempted to descend to the street.

Not to alarm the woman who let us in, Mercier explained that we were just interested in the route taken during the war by some escaped prisoners. The woman looked very closely at Starr, and said, 'You were one of them.' She had thought they were thieves, but then she had seen one of them was a young girl who was crying, and she thought they must be escaped prisoners. It was an unexpected identification, not lost on Mercier.

We went up on to the roof to see the way they had come down, then left the house. Just as we were setting off, Mercier said stop, wait a moment. And he went in through a door on the corner. When he came out he was smiling. 'I've got another identification for you, Starr. The *concierge du Square* also remembers you.' He had been looking from his window on the fateful night and saw the SS drag the three prisoners from the house and take them away. Two identifications. Both unexpected. 'I don't think there is any doubt you were here, Starr.'

The next morning I found the Toile d'Avion on the Champs Elyseés and was able to speak with Madame Aigrain. Yes, the young girl I inquired about had come with 'Antoine' to her flat for shelter. They had laid low there for some days, following the mass arrests. Where they went after they emerged from hiding with her she did not know. But much later, 'Jeanne Marie', as she was calling herself, called in briefly to say goodbye as a plane would be taking her back to England. That was the last she heard of her.

For the next day I had three appointments: Viennot again, Madame Lacour again, Starr again. I always found the repeat interviews valuable, not only for checking over with the interviewees that what I had written correctly represented what they had said, but because very often they came up with additional recollections.

On the next day again, 6 January 1950, I found Professor and Madame Balachowsky at their home in Viroflay. The Professor was a specialist in plant diseases and had been attached to the Agricultural School at Grignand, which was the place from which 'Archambaud' made most of his radio transmissions. 'Archambaud' was the radio operator of 'Prosper' the big chief. He had also with him a girl courier, 'Denise'. Madame Balachowsky told me 'Prosper' had confided to her that his real name was Suttill. She had wondered if this was a pun on Subtle, yet another code-name, but he had said it was his real one: Francis Suttill, real name, 'François Despré' cover name for use with *non-Résistants*, and 'Prosper' to members of the service only. The real name of 'Archambaud' was Gilbert Norman, cover name 'Gilbert Aubin', and the real name of 'Denise' was Andrée Borel, cover name 'Monique' something. It was to this team my friend had been attached, as assistant radio to 'Archambaud', as Archambaud had been complaining to London that he had more work than he could handle without assistance. I had been given what Miss Atkins had told me I would never get, the names, both real and code, of the colleagues Noor had been sent out to join, and I was all ears.

My friend had come out to them only a day or two after her arrival, and, said Madame Balachowsky, she had had to chide her twice on the first day. In the first place, she had left her brief-case in the hall. 'When I picked it up and asked her what it contained, she said, her codes ...' She had no business to leave her codes in the hall. 'Jeanne Marie' – which was the cover-name of 'Madeleine' – said she had supposed that as this had been given to her as the address of a safe house, all the people in it were trustworthy. Madame Balachowsky said she certainly hoped they were, but 'You have no right to assume it. Keep them always close to you.' And then, when offered tea, she poured the milk into her cup first. The French serve it as though it were coffee, tea first, milk into tea after. One could see she had learned to make tea in England.

With her flaming red hair, Madame Balachowsky could look a bit formidable.

It was just before the mass arrests. My friend had told her a British officer called 'Antoine' was coming out to meet them. She said he was a big tall man, and when a big tall man came and asked for her husband, he said 'I've been expecting you' to the Gestapo man who had come to arrest him. He had been sent to Buchenwald, where apparently the Commandant thought him qualified to treat an outbreak of typhus, but he was able to be instrumental in the escape of Yeo-Thomas.

Madame Balachowsky estimated that the arrests following upon that of 'Prosper' and 'Archambaud' ran – taking into account the subsidiary ones – to five hundred. There was talk of a pact. She did not know the truth of it and did not wish to speculate. She had always held 'Prosper' in high regard. An honest, straightforward Englishman. But the last time he had been back to England he had been very unfavourably impressed. He had told her he hardly dared to speak in the corridors. What he really meant, she really did not know; but he came back a changed man. Something had most profoundly upset him.

Her husband, who had let her do most of the talking, concurred. Something was wrong.

The next three days passed in a whirl of appointments, mostly with people I had seen already, to check a point or hear anything fresh they had to say, but there was one new one, with Madame Peineau. Viennot had given me her address after some hesitation as he had not, himself, met her. It was one of his colleagues, Vaudevire, who did so and recommended to him her house – in Bondy, a suburb to the east of Paris

– as a place from which 'Jeanne Marie' (as they called Noor) could transmit with safety.

I found Madame Peineau and she confirmed this was true, showing me with pride the scorch-mark made on her kitchen table. But she said, she had taxed her with insecurity in leaving the transmitter in full view and the book in which she wrote down the message coming through from London, open on that table. 'Jeanne Marie' said she did not think anybody came into that room. Madame Peineau had retorted, '*I come into it. How do you know Monsieur Vaudevire is not mistaken in me?*' Jeanne-Marie must learn not to trust anybody. And, she said, 'Even for myself, I do not like that book to have lain open where I could have read it.'

But 'Jeanne Marie' confided in her, told her about family and showed her, beneath her blouse, what looked like a greyish-white stone, on a string, and explained that it was a talisman. (I thought this must have been the greyish-white scarab I had given her.)

The open notebook had also worried Viennot. He wished she would not keep all the back messages, because, if she was captured, they would be very useful to the Germans, but she said she had been told in England to keep them.

On 8 January I returned to England.

Back to the grindstone: Professor Jones, Professor Firth. I did not actually hear Firth say, as Professor Jones told me it had been reported to him, 'I've killed Daniel Jones.' But he had a way of referring to 'Daniel Jones phonetics,' as though they had measles.

'It makes my blood boil,' said Miss Chapallaz to me as we left his class together. Miss Chapallaz was on the staff of University College, it was she who took the Phonetics of English for English Students I had followed, but was, like me, submitting a thesis for MA: hers on the phonetics of a little known Italian dialect. 'But Firth won't live,' she assured me, 'unless he writes a book. Daniel Jones will live, because of all the books he's written.' We were the two outposts of Daniel Jones phonetics who had to go over to SOAS for the obligatory talks by Firth on Linguistics, and felt ourselves like marked targets.

I had met my Fuller relatives. I had grown up without contact with them, but I knew my father's sister, Dorothy, had married an Italian, and gone to live with him in Italy; and in the family book kept by Mother I had found an address for her and wrote – not really expecting a reply – to La Marchesa Dorothy Brichiere-Colombi at this address in Florence. And a reply came, not from Florence but from London, where she had returned in her widowhood. So I was invited to her flat, in Dulwich, and met her sons, John and Paul. She brought me to my flat some pieces of family jewellery and gave me addresses of further Fuller relatives, with whom the abiding links have proved to be with the ones in America.

Miss Atkins invited me to dinner on 15 February. Over a preliminary cocktail, she asked, 'How's Bob? Starr! Has he been able to get another job yet?'

For a moment I did not understand; he had never been out of one, that I knew of, was a commercial artist, probably self-employed. He had taken a day off to visit the Avenue Foch.

'Oh! He's carrying on then?'

And then I understood. It was she who had sent the message: 'Leave the country immediately.'

As we moved to the dining-table and she sat opposite me it struck me as surprising that she was in full evening dress. And then I thought it isn't really elegant to wear something transparent so that the shoulder-straps of one's slip and vest show through. What she was wearing was a lace dress that went with an underlying sheath sewn to it at the shoulders. I had had one when I was eighteen. But she had lost the sheath that should be beneath the lace. It was not indecent but it was odd.

She asked me, 'Why do you want to see Vogt?' (I had mentioned that I was trying to learn his whereabouts). She thought that even if I did manage to trace him he would have very little to tell me. He was not brain of Avenue Foch. He might come up with a list of prisoner's clothing.

She had spoken very differently of Vogt when I had come with Vilayat. Then he had been a brain. Now she was saying she feared I would have all the expense and fatigue of a trip to Germany for nothing.

I realised she did not want me to meet Vogt, and decided no longer to confide in her.

On 15 April I went back to Paris and on the 16th saw Viennot again, Madame Jourdan again and Madame Lacour again, this time with her mother, Madame Prenat. The mother told me that so seriously had she taken her promise to Noor never to tell her mother she had come to Suresnes that if Mrs Inayat Khan had been still alive, she would have told me, no, she never came here. At six o'clock I saw Madame Jourdois, Noor's landlady at 3 Boulevard Richard Wallace: yes, she had realised that in 'Jeanne Marie' she had an oddly behaving tenant. On the 17th I saw Starr again, he would like me to meet a person from the Sûreté, Mangin (I have this name only by ear) on the 19th, at the Café Weber, at eleven in the morning.

At the Café Weber were two men, Mangin, in civilian clothes, and one in army uniform: 'L'Inspecteur Coupaye'. Army uniform but police rank. They were furious because Buckmaster had not attended the trial of Renée Garry, gone into the box and submitted himself to cross-examination. How well did he know this woman to whom he wrote this letter?

I suggested he had not known in time (though Miss Atkins had told me she was going to tell him at once).

Mangin dismissed the excuse. He said, 'I informed him the moment she was charged.' He always informed Colonel Buckmaster of any impending trial of anybody in any way connected with his Service. There was never any response.

I said he had only given me a single interview, lasting about ten minutes, on a staircase landing.

That's more than we have,' said Coupaye. 'We have never seen him at all.' The people in London had delayed the handing over the German officers of the Avenue Foch staff as long as they possibly could. Goetz and Placke had been held in London and Placke, when he arrived, told them he had been told in London, 'We have to hand you over to the French now but you don't have to tell them very much.' In fact, Placke had talked a lot. And Vogt, who had not been taken to England, was held, in Germany, for an unnecessarily long time. When they wrote to the British to ask them to send them Vogt, they were told they did not know where he was. Yet they afterwards learned he was in British hands at the time. There had been an earlier trial for intelligence with the enemy, more serious than that of Renée Garry, in which the testimony Vogt could have given would have been important and might have made all the difference to the outcome. 'They kept him from us until after it was over and his testimony was of no use.'

I said I wanted to see Vogt. They said they thought all the Germans had by now been released. 'But you are now going to see Captain Mercier. He can get you Vogt's address.'

Before we parted, Coupaye wrote down for me his name, address and telephone number in the Ministère de l'Interieur.

Mangin, Starr told me when they left us, was something quite high up, he believed second to Wybot, the dreaded head of the DST (Département de la Surveillance du Territoire).

I saw Madame Garry again in the evening, and next morning, the 8th, Mercier, at the Tribunal Militaire.

He considered my request. 'Vogt's address cannot be a secret of France.' He told the *greffier* to get him Fresnes prison, then took the line and asked, 'Quelle adresse Vogt a-t-il laissé?'

He wrote it down and handed me the paper. I read an address in Freiburg.

Would I lunch with him? He conducted me into a restaurant by the side of the Tribunal Militaire where he customarily ate – and suddenly he was asking me rapid-fire questions about my whole way of life. Then he relaxed, and said, 'I have questioned you with as much rigour as though I were acting in my function. Now you háve a taste of what it is like to be under the grill.'

As we walked out, he said, 'Miss Atkins knows nothing. Of course not. Colonel Buckmaster knows nothing. Naturally not. And me? Naturally I know less than nothing about anything at all. It is the first qualification for my job. But YOU, you go round talking to first one person then another, hearing different things and already you know a lot. Already you can be dangerous, and you don't know for whom.' He pulled my arm and said, 'Don't walk on the outside of the pavement. A car could come up and knock you down. Remember that when you go to Germany – and everywhere you go.'

He said this jocularly; yet not entirely so.

Ten

On 24 April I travelled back to London and, on 26 April 1950, composed a letter to Vogt. I explained that I had been a personal friend of the young girl he would have known under the name of 'Madeleine' and would be very grateful if he would let me come and see him, to talk about her. I mentioned I was writing a book and emphasised that I was not official.

On Monday 8 May there was a letter from Germany. It was from Vogt. It was in German, but I made it out. During the five weeks she had been held at Avenue Foch, he had questioned her daily but she had conducted herself as 'a good brave Englishwoman'; he had great admiration for her and would like to meet someone who had been her friend.

In the meantime, I had sat the exam, tidied up and handed in that wretched thesis on the phonetics of Polish and on 15 June had to present myself for the *viva*, the oral examination. There were three persons questioning me: Professor Jones, Professor Firth and one from a university somewhere in the Midlands, who would obviously have the casting vote.

The next day, 15 June, I set out from Victoria Station. In Paris I took a taxi from the Gare du Nord to the Gare de l'Est, from which the train drew out as the shadows were descending. I thought with what heavily laden feelings Noor must have set out from this station, a prisoner, leaving France for Germany.

At 8.30 in the morning of Saturday 17 June 1950, my train drew into Freiburg. A white-haired lady came towards me. 'Are you Miss Fuller?' She was Vogt's aunt. Gestapo men and aunts somehow don't go together. She engaged a cab, saw me into my hotel and asked what time I would like her nephew to call on me. He would not be free until midday and it was agreed he should come at three.

He came. Tall, very thin, with spectacles. He had flat brown hair. He said he thought I might like to hold our conversations in the English Institute. I had never heard of it but we walked there. We entered a large sitting-room and I sat in a chair.

Not so near to the wall, he demurred. In a wall, a microphone could be hidden. There was absolutely nothing he had to tell me that was secret but still one did not like to be recorded.

I moved to a chair right in the centre of the room and sat in it.

'Not just under the light.' There was one just over our heads. Ah, of course a microphone could be hidden in an electric light.

I looked around for a chair away from both walls and lights, and sat down for the third time.

He sat for a moment, but then said, 'On the underneath of a chair a microphone can be hidden.' Would it attract too much attention if he knelt in front of the chair and felt with his hands underneath it? Or just simply turn the chair upside down, to look?

I said, 'I think you would feel more at your ease if we left this place and walked in the open air.'

We walked up a leafy lane to a bench overlooking the roofs. This seemed to be risk-free.

He asked me. 'Do you believe that "Madeleine" is dead?'

'Oh yes, the telegram was received at Karlsruhe from Dachau.'

He stopped me. 'It was not my meaning. My meaning was, do you believe in the immortality of the soul?'

'Yes.'

He had been born Catholic, but when he was a child a priest had told him animals had no souls. That put him off religion. It seemed so unfair we should survive, they not.

'Perhaps they too survive,' I said.

'That's it. It's all of us or none of us.'

Why did she throw her beautiful life away, he asked? Her sacrifice made no difference to the outcome of the war. They used her radio set to lure further men and women to their deaths.

Did she know?

He thought not. 'I did not tell her. It was not in the interest of our service she should know.' When he told her she had forfeited her life for nothing, she said, 'I have served my country. That is my recompense.'

'My admiration for her was of such a kind that, if I had not been a married man and if she had not been my prisoner, I could have fallen in love with her.' He permitted himself a moment's fantasy. 'If I could equate myself as being as much use to Kieffer as she to Buckmaster, it would be taking one from each side and so doing harm to neither if we went away together to a neutral country. Why do I talk like this? She would not have done it. I would not have done it. The proof is, we didn't.'

If 'Madeleine' were alive she would be sitting here with us on this bench now. Perhaps indeed she was? 'I cannot imagine anything nicer than to be haunted by "Madeleine".' She would not reproach him for her death.

But there were some people before whom he would be ashamed if he had to meet them again in the next life. People to whom it was promised their lives would be spared. Kieffer and he (as the translating intermediary) had been questioning 'Prosper' for forty-eight hours when Kieffer made him a proposition. If he would hand over the addresses at which had been stored all the arms and munitions the British had been parachuting for months, neither he nor any of those whose addresses would have necessarily to be disclosed as guardians of the dumps would be killed. All would be kept in prisons until the end of the war. '"Prosper" turned to me, and asked, "Can I trust your chief?" You can say it was a silly question. I could hardly say no, with my chief standing by, but if I had not said yes with so much conviction, adding bits of my own, "I know Mr Kieffer. He means it. It is a good offer he is making you", he might have refused the bargain.' That made Vogt feel a moral responsibility. It really had seemed to him a good offer. To collect and bring in all the arms that were hidden before they could be used to kill German soldiers seemed to him good. 'That gave me energy in explaining it.' Kieffer said he would contact the Reichssicherheitshauptamt in Berlin. The proposition was ratified by telephone. '"Archambaud", the radio operator of "Prosper" was brought in and the deal explained to him. Kieffer signed his name beneath the paper, and I' – he could not find the English word for witness – 'wrote my name beneath his.' Then 'Prosper' wrote his name and 'Archambaud' did the same for him. 'This thing was stamped with the seal of the Reichssicherheitshauptamt. Where is it now? They were all killed. In Germany, at the end of the war when they were no longer in Kieffer's hands. If I meet "Prosper" again, when I too am dead, I shall be ashamed. If when he knew he was going to be killed he thought of Kieffer and me, he must have thought we tricked him. We did not mean to trick him. I know I didn't. If I have to meet "Prosper" again, will he believe I did not mean to trick him?'

'Perhaps in the next world one will no longer think about Avenue Foch.'

He permitted himself his first glint of humour. 'Ah no, that would mean we were in Hell.'

I asked him how he had got into that service and he told me the story of his life. He was on his mother's side, Swiss born on 28 June 1904, in Laufenberg, a small town on the Rhine. 'It is very narrow where it runs between Germany and Switzerland. You can shout across it.' Once, when a boy, he had swum to Switzerland. The Swiss guards had told him he could not stay there; he was a German child. He had not the strength to swim back, so they rowed him back to Germany. In his teens he had worked on his father's farm, milked the cows. But then he had gone to Paris, where he had worked, for the first few years, in a patent attorney's, then in a bank; married a French woman and applied for French naturalisation. It would have come through in a few days, then war was declared and all naturalisations suspended. He volunteered for the French Foreign Legion, but was turned down at the medical, short-sighted and colour-blind. Then some people who had a flat in the same building as his wife and himself reported him as being a German at large and he was arrested and interned at Pau. When the Germans entered France in 1940 he was liberated and told to report to a military recruiting office set up for Germans found in France. Again he was – this time to his relief – turned down at the medical: short-sighted and colour-blind. He was then directed to report to the office of Kieffer. There were no prisoners to question at that early date. He had simply to go with Kieffer everywhere and interpret between him and the French people he had to meet, as he spoke only German.

After he had been with him for a little time, Mr Kieffer, face like thunder, said, 'Come into my office. I have received a letter about you.'

It was from those same people who had denounced him to the French as being a German still at liberty who now denounced him as having applied for French nationality and to join the Foreign Legion. They finished up by saying he was a British agent.

He had assured Kieffer he was not and never had been a British agent, but said it was true he had applied for French nationality and to join the French Foreign Legion.

'Mr Kieffer was very angry with me, but after the manner of a father to a son.' He told him he was born German, remained German and had no moral title to judge the morality of the government of his country. If he had been accepted by the French Foreign Legion he could have found himself in a position where, in the fighting, he might shoot Germans, and that Kieffer found shocking.

In the end, Kieffer returned the letter to its envelope, put it in a drawer of his desk, and said, 'Be loyal from now on.'

'So I was always in the hand of Kieffer.' He could have brought that paper out at any time, yet did not lean upon his advantage. He always treated him nicely, and he felt that he came to trust him.

'How did you become an interrogator?'

He had been interpreting between Kieffer and 'Archambaud'. As they broke off for lunch, Kieffer said, 'Why do we learn so little?' It was rhetorical. 'He did not expect an answer, but I gave him one. "Because it is impossible to do an interrogation through an intermediary. I can sense sometimes that you put the questions obliquely, at an angle to what you want to know but I cannot know what is in your mind and so I repeat as the curé repeats the mass!" He asked me then if I thought I could do an in interrogation on my own. There was a training for our interrogators, yet 'There is nothing we can lose but our time and that we lose anyway.' He asked me what I needed. I said, tea. To offer whisky or wine would be worse than useless. From captor to prisoner alcohol is given only to make someone talk. The prisoner would refuse it. 'But tea is innocent. And *yet* it is relaxing.' He had before the war spent a fortnight with an English family in a suburb south of London. He had seen tea being made and believed he could make tea.

How tea, which the French do not drink, was found in wartime Paris he would never know but a team was sent out to scour likely places and about three in the afternoon the SS brought up a packet of tea, and milk and a tea-set. He unlocked the door of 'Archambaud's' cell and said, 'Will you take tea with me?' He had on his desk no paper or anything to write with, and yet when later in the afternoon he went to show Kieffer the few things he had afterwards jotted down from memory, Kieffer was pleased and said he could take over the interrogation of all the major agents of the French Section. And so he did. The agents operated normally in teams of three, organiser, radio operator and courier. He interrogated all the organisers and the radios on the non-technical side of their work, for it was Dr Goetz who conducted the radio game. The couriers were questioned by August Scherer, who had taught German at a school in France. Goetz was like himself a civil auxiliary. Kieffer used his civil auxiliaries to do the interrogation of prisoners instead of the SS, and when the time came for the German retreat from France, the prisoners were sent ahead to concentration camps in Germany; the auxiliaries spent some days dividing their papers into those to take with them, those to destroy or those to leave. Kieffer asked him if he thought it wise to leave his wife in France. His answer had been that as she was French she would be better there than dragged into Germany. Kieffer asked if he had enemies in France. No

– well except for those two people who had twice denounced him. In retrospect, he was sure that was what had caused Kieffer to have them arrested. It was ironic that his action, intended to protect her, should have been the cause of the French charging her after the war with intelligence with the enemy, accused of betraying those two people. She was still in a French prison and he was trying to get her out.

He himself had been in the south of Germany when the war ended. First he got himself a job on a farm, milking cows. 'I did not know if they would give me their milk.' But they did, and the life he had lived at Avenue Foch began to seem like the life of another man. Then the Americans identified and arrested him. They questioned him at length, then gave him a paper certifying that having examined him they did not want him for war crimes, and released him to the British. The British held him in their camp at Staumüller for three months, then issued him with a similar certificate, but sent him back to the Americans, who asked him why he had been returned to them. 'I felt like a postal package being sent back and forth.' They returned him to the British, who wanted him gone. He asked if he might return to his home. Where was his home? In what was now the French zone. Then, no. He asked then for an allowance to live on and was told he could live in his cell, only with the door open, so that he would walk around the town and come back for meals, free. Finally, they said, 'Get out. We want to close the camp.'

The French were asking for him so he decided to go to France, as a 'voluntary prisoner', hoping to help his wife. He was greeted by a French officer with the words, 'So, you are a British agent!'

'No!'

'We have proof.' The 'proof' shown him was a copy of a letter they had sent the British asking for him, and a reply from the British saying they did not know where he was. That was sent at the date of their returning him to the Americans.

He insisted that he was not a British agent. Then he was asked if he would care to work for French Intelligence. He said, not for that, either. Not for any intelligence service, of any country.

They kept him in solitary confinement in the prison on the rue du Cherche Midi. Between interrogations, he had nothing to do but to sit and stare at the wall, hour after hour, day after day, week after week … for how long? The food was ample and his treatment correct, but he had nothing to do but think long thoughts.

In the last week before their release he and others from the Avenue

Foch had all been put into one large cell together. They felt sure this was to overhear what they were saying amongst themselves, so they all herded into the middle of the room and put their heads very close together when they wanted to talk. 'You would have laughed at us if you could have seen us.' Yet it seemed to them sensible. When the French officers finally escorted him to his train, a train that would not stop until it reached Germany, they suddenly relaxed their formality and waved him off, crying, 'Bon voyage! Ne revenez jamais! – Have a good journey. Don't ever come back!'

But he was summoned to come back, just once, to Strasbourg, to collect his clearance. He nearly refused. But there was no trap. He was handed his certificate that he had been examined and was not wanted for war crimes. He had also to collect his de-Nazification certificate testifying that search had shown him never to have been a member of the Nazi party.

He showed me the four certificates, which he was carrying in a wallet in his pocket.

'And these are now your most valuable possession,' I said to him.

With a ruefully comic expression, he agreed, 'They are, really.'

When he was put off the train in Germany, it was without a coin in his pocket. His parents were dead so he had told the French his father's brother was his next of kin, and the uncle was there to take him to Freiburg. The uncle had been a schoolteacher and had been demoted for refusal to join the Nazi party, so was not very pleased with him for having got himself into 'a crevice like that'. And he had to live on his uncle's charity till he found a job. But, walking down a street in Freiburg, he had noticed on the other side a bank. 'Why, in a bank, should they not need a man speaking French and English?'

So he crossed the road and went in and asked to see the manager and asked if he needed a man speaking French and English.

'Yes!' Their man who handled the correspondence with banks in England and France had left them suddenly and there was a great pile of letters waiting to be answered. 'Can you start at once?'

So he started at once, first of all writing brief notes to each saying a fuller reply would follow in days, thus giving himself the time to understand the business. The manager had asked him for his *curriculum vitae*, and he had made this out honestly. If the manager had been surprised by the reference to Kieffer's service, he did not show it. 'Some days have passed, and still he had said nothing. He is not going to dismiss me.'

He had received his first pay packet and when he found a room would move out from his uncle's. But his aunt and uncle invited me to take coffee with them one evening. 'I told my aunt you were probably a Foreign Office agent. When she came back, she told me she did not know what a Foreign Office agent would look like but she thought not like you. You looked a nice girl.'

We walked to my hotel and he joined me for dinner.

He had, he said, seen an article in a Swiss magazine about one of the French Section women, Odette Churchill. Could I tell him something? Were she and Peter Churchill really related, as they claimed to be, to Winston Churchill. Kieffer and he looked in reference books and could not find that Winston had a brother who had a son called Peter, but still Kieffer advised him to feign belief, treat with appropriate courtesy – just in case. 'And he told me always to keep arm's length between myself and Peter, so that by no accident could I touch him and give him a claim to have been ill-used.' First of all Kieffer and he questioned the two of them together – it was mainly about their identities as they claimed them – then they were separated. 'I took Peter Churchill' and Odette, as she was his courier, was taken by Scherer. But now, seeing that article, he wondered if there was not really some connection with Winston Churchill – to explain why she had been picked out.

'You know what happened to her?'

'No. Did she have some special adventure?'

'She had all her toenails pulled out.'

'What? Where does she allege that this happened?'

'Eighty-four Avenue Foch.'

If ever I have seen a man jump, almost literally, it was then. He almost upset his soup. 'That was *our* house! Why have I never been told of this allegation officially? Why do I hear it first from you?'

I did not know and was indeed puzzled.

'Who does she say did it?' he asked.

She said it was actually done by a young Frenchman, but under the supervision of a German. She did not know his name.

'Then we would all have been questioned,' he said. The young Frenchman sounded like Pierre Cartaud, whom they called 'Peter', whom she might have seen about the place. 'About him I would feel less sure. But Scherer – I put my hand in the fire if Scherer did a thing like that.'

Scherer was dead. He and Scherer had gone together to arrest an operator named 'Hercule'. He was actually transmitting to England when they burst in on him. He drew his pistol and killed Scherer with the first bullet. Vogt said 'I then drew mine and shot.' He had always been told he must always carry a pistol but had never been shown how to use one and in any case he was short-sighted. Facing each other across only a narrow table he and 'Hercule' emptied the entire contents of their revolvers into each other's bodies and neither of them was killed. When he recovered consciousness they were both in beds, side by side, in the Hôpital de la Pitié.

He did not believe this thing about Scherer. He didn't believe this story at all.

It was in the official citation, I said. And our King and Queen attended the premiere of the film.

And Winston Churchill, he asked?

No. He had a prior engagement. That was, indeed, odd.

I said a point was made in Gerard Tickell's book on Odette that she was the only one of the agents to be given a trial. At 84 Avenue Foch.

He did not believe that either. 'We were not a juridical body.'

The floors of the Avenue Foch underneath Kieffer's apartment were, so far as he could remember, occupied mainly by secretarial staff, typists and filing clerks. Also, down below, some SS, such as Otto. Never could a court martial have sat there. None of the prisoners were sent to face a trial.

That made their execution illegal, I pointed out.

'Why we should have done illegally what we could have done legally I don't know.' But – he made a sudden point – if they had sent them before a court, it would have meant that all of them would have been shot, since, working in plain clothes, they fulfilled the definition of spies. Whereas 'We sent them to concentration camps.' The conditions in the camps might have been deplorable, but at least they had the chance to survive and some did.

About the conditions in the camps. Without appearing to be trying to defend the indefensible, might he say a word? 'You saw our camps at their worst.' The Allied bombing had destroyed communications. Food was not arriving. Of what arrived, priority went to the Wehrmacht. 'Our soldiers must have the best.' Then came ordinary German people. Last, very last, came the prisoners in the camps. Bad food, inappropriate food and food no longer fit for consumption caused the inmates intestinal illness. The bunks and the persons were covered with vomit and excrement, the baths and the lavatories totally insufficient for the numbers and their condition, and although it was not their fault that they were in this condition, they looked degraded and that caused staff to treat them as though they were degraded. He believed that was at the root of the apparently sadistic brutality of the guards in Belsen and some other places. 'There should be training for staff ... precautions should start with care to keep everything very clean.'

We parted, agreeing we should start seriously to work in the morning.

I waited for him the next morning with paper and pen.

'What do you want to call me in your book?' was the question with which he arrived. He was averse to having his family name published. It was not fair on his uncle, who thoroughly disapproved of his wartime role, and he himself felt soiled by the negotiation with 'that woman' for the sale of 'Madeleine'. Would I just call him Ernest? 'It is my real name, the one I was given at the font.' And it was the name by which his prisoners knew him. He refused them his real name and they would say, 'But I must have something to call you.' And he would reply, 'Call me Ernest.' Pronounced in the English or French way, not as in German.

I agreed, and he started with Kieffer's having told him he had a phone call from a woman who said she would sell them 'Madeleine'. She had said she would be standing behind the Trocadero and would say 'Renée'. He had told her the man who would go up to her would identify himself by saying 'André'. Vogt was to be 'André'. Otto would follow him with a revolver, in case it was a trap.

He met the woman, who said 'Renée'. She needed money and would give him an address at which he could arrest 'Madeleine', for a price. He knew that to be the code-name of a major agent of the French Section, but to be sure, asked, 'Who is "Madeleine"?' She said, 'Phono's radio operator.' He knew that 'Phono' was the new code-name being used by Garry, so it was the right 'Madeleine', and said his service would pay between 50,000 and 100,000 francs. She told him 'Madeleine' was living under the cover-name of Jeanne-Marie Regnier (which he knew already) and that she worked sometimes from a flat in the rue de la Faisanderie belonging to a certain Solange. She did not want him to arrest Solange. He promised not to do so, and she said she would telephone on a day when either they were both out or 'Madeleine' was there alone.

The next day she telephoned to say they were both out and she would show him the flat, if he would meet her in a café. When they reached the flat she showed him where the key was hidden under the mat. Then she took him in and showed him 'Madeleine's' radio transmitter in the kitchen.

A few days later she telephoned early in the morning saying they had both gone out, Solange for the day, but 'Madeleine' returning. He thought this was a Wednesday, 13 October, at any rate one of the middle days in the week in the middle of the month. He referred to Kieffer, who said he should call Pierre ('Peter') Cartaud. He took Cartaud to the flat and, using the key left where he had been shown, let him in, locked him in and replaced the key under the carpet. Then Kieffer came into Vogt's office to say there had come a phone call from Peter who was apparently having difficulties. When he got back, covered by Otto from the SS, Peter was standing covering 'Madeleine' with his revolver from the furthest part of the room, his wrist bleeding, and 'Madeleine' was sitting bolt upright on the divan, her fingers arched like the claws of a tiger. He was sure Peter was afraid for his eyes. Seeing Vogt enter, she said, 'This would happen at the last moment. Another few days and I would have been in England!'

He begged her to come quietly as otherwise if she created a scene people in the other flats would see she was being arrested and would warn Solange, so they would have to arrest Solange to prevent her from alerting Garry.

She understood that and, though trembling, placed her hand on his arm, as he told her. So they all four walked out, taking with them the notebook and papers found in a drawer of the table, and her radio transmitter. They got into a waiting car and drove to Avenue Foch, where they walked her up to the fifth floor. She was saying, 'Have me shot as soon as possible!' But then, 'Can I have a bath?'

This seemed a strange request but he let her into the bathroom. She demanded removal of a brick that kept the door ajar. He told the guard to remove it. 'On your responsibility, then?' the guard asked, as it was against his orders, which were, when a prisoner bathed, always to keep the door ajar with a brick.

'Yes,' he said, but then felt he had been unwise. He went into the lavatory and saw from its window that she had already climbed out of the bathroom window on to a narrow parapet, risking a fall of five storeys. But, making for the roof, she was coming towards him, 'Think of your mother – Pense à ta mère. Give me your hand.' She took it, and he dragged her head foremost in through the lavatory window, now sobbing and lashing herself with reproaches for being a coward. She should have let herself fall. 'I don't know why I took your hand. It was just because you held it out.'

Renée now telephoned again, to ask for her payment. He went to meet her but said they did not pay in the street. She would have to come to Avenue Foch to collect – with identity card. She hesitated but came. When he saw the name on her identity card, the name in which she signed the receipt, he felt sick.

Back with 'Madeleine', he was making no progress. She was just saying 'I will tell you nothing.' As she would not talk, he talked, 'I was making a monologue.' About things unconnected with the war, to loosen her up. Then he asked, 'When you are not working, when you have an evening at leisure, do you like to go to see a play? Or a film?'

'A concert,' she said.

'Oh, so you like music.' What sort of music? Classical?' Who were her favourite composers?

'Beethoven and Bach.'

It came over to him that she had had musical education. 'If someone gave me a ticket for a concert of classical music I would go, and enjoy it, but I could not afterwards talk knowledgeably about what had been played. She could. I thought she might have been at the Ecole Normale de Musique.'

In this he was right. But if he had followed it up, he would not have found Nora Baker amongst the students.

Why had she given him this as being her real name, he asked me?

I thought because she had a younger brother, who had not come to England with the rest of the family in 1940. If he was living obscurely somewhere in France, the coincidence of the unusual name Inayat Khan might cause him to be investigated, even arrested and used as a hostage against her.

He told her the names of the training schools through which she had passed in England. Wanborough for physical training, then Arisaig, a small place in Scotland, for how to fight with the bare hands and with the feet, then Beaulieu for security training.

Miss Atkins had told me only Wanborough, saying the others were, she believed, still on the secret list.

'You can take it from me,' he said. 'Arisaig, then Beaulieu.'

How did he know?

'Kieffer told me.' He had been surprised by the Beaulieu, as it looked to him French, but Kieffer told him he should pronounce it not as in French, but 'Byooly' and see the effect it had on English prisoners. He did. 'Madeleine' was appalled and said, 'But you know everything! Have you an agent in London?'

He had answered, 'Perhaps.' In fact, he did not know.

He referred to her having been to Ringway, near Manchester, for her parachute training.

I said she did not go to Ringway and did not parachute. She was landed from Lysander aircraft according to the official citation.

That puzzled him for a moment. He had assumed she parachuted and she had left him in his error. 'She must have thought she had to keep from me the secret of the Lysanders.' He knew they came but had not realised she came by one.

She was most upset when he showed her a photocopy of a letter she had sent home to her mother. 'She loved her mother very much.'

How did he come to have a photocopy of a letter she had sent from France to England?

'It was routed through our office.'

He asked me to lunch with him at a restaurant in the town.

It had come to him, lying awake during the night, that he could have let 'Madeleine' go. He could have invented some pretext to take her out, then just said 'Run.' He had been asking himself what Kieffer would have done if he had come back and said, 'Madeleine ran away from me.'

'He would have been very, very angry. But he would not have had me shot. He would not have thought I had done it on purpose.'

But it would have been a terrible treachery against Kieffer. 'The difficulty lay in "Madeleine's" being a major agent of the French Section.' If she had been a sub-agent recruited locally to perform minor service for the agents of the French Section, Kieffer would not have said too much, even if he had suspected. He was not inhuman. But 'Madeleine', free, would have alerted London that the 'Madeleine' radio was being worked by the Germans. The whole of Kieffer's game depended on keeping 'Madeleine' close.

He was between Kieffer and 'Madeleine', and it had begun to worry him, even at the time. There had been an evening when he had unlocked her cell and said, 'Will you have supper with me?'

She had sat down to table with him in his office, eaten with him. He had not talked about the war during that time, only about things unconnected with it. Suddenly he noticed she was crying.

He asked, 'What is it? What have I said?' For he had not been saying anything to distress her.

She replied, 'It's not you. It's just everything. I was thinking of my mother.'

He had taken her back to her cell, and at the door had placed just one kiss on her forehead. Then suddenly he was afraid. He said, 'Never forget I am your enemy, Madeleine.'

She said, 'Thank you.' Meaning for reminding her. She had not drawn away from that one kiss.

He locked her into her cell hastily for he had become afraid of the situation that could develop.

'And that was against Kieffer. My warning her was against Kieffer. Kieffer wanted me to get on well with her.'

He was off the case for some while following the pistol duel with 'Hercule' when he was kept in bed at the Hôpital de la Pitié. When he returned to Avenue Foch he heard all about the attempted escape of 'Madeleine' with Starr and Faye, and only Starr was still there – who assured him that the idea of escaping over the roofs was hers. This he had no difficulty in believing, having seen her climb out of the bathroom window five floors up on the first day.

I was able to tell him something he did not know. It was she who thought of using face-powder to mask the damage to the walls, caused by their mining around the sockets into which the bars to their skylights were fixed.

It was, exclaimed Vogt, he whom she had asked to get her face-powder. 'She told me the shade – Rachell. Simple as I am, I thought it was to put on her face!'

He had said that to avoid his having to go into a woman's shop to ask for face-powder, it would be better for her to write a note to Solange, saying she was away for a few days, and asking her to give her face-powder and other toiletries from the dressing-table to bearer. And he gave the note to 'Peter' Cartaud to take round. Peter came back in a great state of excitement, saying, 'Phono is there, with his wife.' So Kieffer told him to go back with Peter, taking three other men, to arrest them. This was on Monday 18 October, and the Garrys were still breakfasting leisurely when he arrived with his party. He put handcuffs on Garry, something he did not do with every prisoner. Garry had derailed a train and a lot of people had been killed. Madame Garry was such a gentle person, he had often wondered if she knew, and, if she knew, whether she approved. Did I know what had happened to Garry?

He had been hanged in Buchenwald.

Even if he had a trial, said Vogt, he must have been condemned.

He told me a bit about Cartaud. He had started in the Resistance but after his arrest had gone over to the Germans completely, wanted to be called not Pierre but Peter, filed an application for German nationality and asked for his years in Kieffer's service to be counted towards the years that had normally to be spent in Germany in order to qualify. He was killed accidentally when he came running out of a house they were besieging. One of Kieffer's men, not knowing Peter had gone in, thought it was one of the usual occupants coming out, and shot him. He was in very bad odour with Kieffer for a long time after, having killed one of his best agents.

We came to be talking again about 'Madeleine'. He said, 'I suppose she was the best human being I have known in my life.'

We had still some minutes before he had to go to his bank. Would I like to see inside the cathedral?

We entered, looked at the windows, a painting, and stood for some moments in the religious gloom. As we came out, he said it was strange that though the houses all around had been destroyed by the RAF bombing, the cathedral had not been hit. The same had happened in other towns.

And in London, I told him. The houses all round St Paul's were set ablaze and yet St Paul's scarcely damaged. And the same in other cities.

He asked, 'Can prayers going up turn aside bombs coming down? It could almost make one a believer.'

We walked again for a bit after he got out at five, and then, on the following day, lunched again at the same place.

'There is a question I would like to ask you,' he said. 'That comes badly from me, but you are not my prisoner. You don't have to answer.'

'What is your question?'

'We were told that our people had invented a bomb that flew by itself, directed itself and dropped itself down on London. We were told that the reason why we never saw any of these passing overhead, in Paris, was because the launching pads were nearer the coast. It could have been true. But under Dr Goebbels we had a very developed propaganda. I did not want to be taken in by our own propaganda, that would have been too silly. But I would like to ask you, as you were in London, did any of these things fall on London?'

'Yes.'

'Have you seen them yourself?'

'Yes.'

'How did you know they were bombs, not aeroplanes?'

'They looked different. Sounded different.'

'You saw one come down? Saw damage?'

'Yes.'

He thanked me. He thought, 'It could have suited your propaganda to sustain our propaganda.' To say what damage they had done and claim compensation for it. 'We would have been ill-placed to say we never made any, having said so much about them.' He said this was the first time in many years that he had believed something because he had been told about it. He would believe his uncle or his aunt if they said they had seen something but nobody else. 'But I believe you. It is established.'

I was going on to Pforzheim, I told him. How did I say in German, 'Where is the prison?'

'*Wo ist das Gefängnis?*'

And how did I ask to see the cell in which she was kept?

'I will write it for you,' he said; and did so. He would have liked to come with me and ask some questions of his own, but could hardly ask at the bank for a two-day holiday so soon after starting. His aunt would see me on to the train. But I would come back to Freiburg, wouldn't I, and tell him what I had learned. 'If Madeleine has been ill-treated I want to know about it.'

I broke the journey at Heidelberg, to see the castle, and figured in a photograph taken of a party of tourists; spent the night in a hotel in Heidelberg and was in Pforzheim on the morning of 22 June. '*Wo ist das Gefängnis?*'

I found I had to see some civic authority first, but the civic authority telephoned to the prison and freed the staff to answer my questions.

I found my way to it. But this was the first time I had had to deal with persons who spoke only German. One of the present guards came forward. He had been on the staff when the prisoner Nora Baker was here. Was the only one still on the staff. I pronounced the sentence Vogt had written out for me and was conducted to a cell. Clean, with white-washed walls but window set so high that nothing could be seen from it. He was telling me something and making explanatory gestures. What was he saying? I caught the words, 'Ketten' and 'Fesseln'. Those words meant 'chains' and 'fetters'. He was making movements to show me her wrists were fastened to her ankles, handcuffs to fetters. I could hardly believe what I was being told. He gave me his name, Friedrich Fässer and promised to send me his information in writing.

After that, I went on to see the ex-Governor, Krauss, in his home. He was very old and his palm was wet. She had come, he said, from Karlsruhe, her hands in handcuffs, her ankles in fetters and a chain from the handcuffs to the fetters. In all his years in the prison service, he had never known another prisoner kept like that or heard of one so kept elsewhere.

He had instructions from Karlsruhe that she was to be kept isolated from possibility of contact with other prisoners, the cells on either side of hers empty and those above and below hers empty. This meant that she was in effect occupying five cells, and in a prison built to take only so many, it was leaving him short of space for others. He complained about this. He had been told she was a spy but nevertheless could not think why she should be considered so very dangerous. He sat down beside her sometimes and she talked with him a little. She said her father was a teacher of some kind of Indian mystical philosophy or religion. To him, she seemed a nice girl and he risked taking the chains off while she was having her meals, and sometimes to let her have a little walk around the yard. Then the man came from Karlsruhe who took her away.

When I got back to Freiburg and told Vogt about the chains the expression on his face was indescribable. When at last he found his voice, he said, 'It was too strong. Too severe.' He did not believe Kieffer had ordered chains. What he thought was, Kieffer had said she had to be kept under strictest security – he used a German phrase for that – and that was how the requirement was interpreted at Karlsruhe.

But something was puzzling him. How did she scratch those messages on the bases of the food bowls that were received by that woman now in Bordeaux? Suddenly, he was sure he knew. The handcuffs had a kind of tongue which fitted into a slot and she turned her wrists so that the tongue of the handcuffs became a writing instrument. 'Can you see now into the mind of Kieffer? Everything, everything she would subvert. I say you could sooner keep a cat so she does not have kittens than Madeleine so she did not communicate with the War Office. She was kept suspended in a spacious honeycomb, chained hands to feet, so she turned her handcuffs to write a message which reached the War Office!'

As I had just one day more he suggested we make an excursion. And he took me by cable-car to a height from which we walked over a hilltop. 'Do you feel we are alone?' he asked me. 'I feel that "Madeleine" is walking with us.' She was not a reproachful ghost but warm and friendly. He would have liked to show her this country. See the little cows. 'Did you ever see cows like these? They are so delicate they are almost like deer. She would have liked them.' Had he really some telepathic touch with her? She *would* have liked the little cows like deer.

We lunched at an inn near the top, then descended to the lake, Titisee. Would I like to go on the lake? He hired a rowing-boat. As we put out an enormous black and yellow striped insect landed on my knee and stayed there. He thought it was a queen wasp, I thought it was a hornet, and we discussed this all the time that we were on the water. As we returned to the shore it deserted its post as mysteriously as it had come.

Would I be leaving from Basel? Laufenburg, where he was born, was very close to Basel. Would I not like to see Laufenburg and call on his brother and his family? He would ring them to expect me.

Would I be seeing Madame Garry on my way back through Paris?

'If she would receive it from me, if she would not take it as mockery, if you feel you could say it, will you tell her I am sorry her husband was hanged?'

Eleven

I had made the detour through Laufenberg and Vogt's young niece had shown me the Rhine and the point from which he had as a boy swum to Switzerland.

And now as I sat in the train pulling out of Basel in the fading light, I asked myself how much of what I had learned I could put in my book about Noor. Nothing about Odette. Nothing about the radio game, which was probably still an official secret. Names of the training schools Arisaig and Beaulieu?

Though Vogt had first said I could take the information from him, on further thought he had said that if they were still British official secrets it would be better not. 'Put only what Miss Atkins told you.' The root shock had been to me that I had been discussing with Vogt how much of our conversations I should disclose to our people. By 'our people' I understood Miss Atkins and Buckmaster. The trouble was, I was believing him, not them. Buckmaster had appeared in the film *Odette*, getting out of a hammock and saying the story we were about to see was true. The King and Queen and whole royal family had attended the premiere. It kept me awake throughout the journey.

In Paris, I deposited my case in the Hôtel Confort, then went straight to the Tribunal Militaire, but found Mercier was not in his office. His *greffier* telephoned him and gave me an appointment with him for 4.30 that afternoon.

I telephoned Starr and he came in his car, picked me up from outside the Tribunal and drove me to a café.

I told him Vogt had told me that whilst he was in Staumüller he was visited by a British NCO who questioned him about Starr, in a way that sought for answers detrimental to him. 'He told you things, didn't he?' to which Vogt had said, 'No'. And, 'He enjoyed a great deal of personal liberty, didn't he?' to which Vogt had replied that he never saw Starr leave the fifth floor except under guard. In the end, he wrote out a statement that was for Starr. 'And he asked me to give you his kind regards and say he is glad to learn you are still alive.'

Then I said Vogt didn't believe Odette's toenails were torn out.

'Neither do I,' he said.

He had glimpsed her when first brought to the Avenue Foch, remembered Peter Churchill standing talking with Kieffer and Vogt, trying to persuade them he was related to Winston Churchill. Much later, he had seen Odette again when she was one of a party of girls brought up from Fresnes, and they were all given a cup of tea – made and handed round by Vogt – before starting on their journey to Germany. That was of course about a year after the alleged torture so the nails could have grown again but wouldn't she still show some discomfort in the feet?

And whatever would they have tortured her *for*? The alleged incident was dated in Tickell's book six weeks after her capture. She was said to have been asked 'Where is Arnaud?' meaning Rabinovich. But he would not have sat glued to one spot. He had seen her and Peter Churchill captured and made off, back to London. Starr had spoken with him when, much later, he was captured on a second mission as a victim of the radio game. Agents were all told before setting out that if captured they should try to avoid giving any addresses for forty-eight hours, and colleagues of any agent captured had to make good their departure from any address known to that colleague within that period of time. In fact, 'Arnaud' had seen the couple arrested, immediately decamped and made his way through the Pyrenees and back to London.

In Dijon, where first questioned, Starr had been roughed up, and in Mauthausen, a death camp, where he spent the last months of the war, he had heard the guards discussing how many of the intake of prisoners they had food to feed, and decided half. To reduce the number, they had driven them, naked, through hot and cold showers alternately until the weaker began to drop from exhaustion. As soon as a man dropped, his head was broken by a pickaxe, until the number had been reduced to half. But Kieffer's prisoners were not ill-treated. 'John' – Starr's radio operator – refused to tell them where he had stowed his radio, something they really wanted, but they did not torture him.

I said I was seeing Mercier at 4.30.

'By the way, I had a piece of paper from him this morning,' he said. It was his Non Lieu.

At 2.30 I saw Madame Garry, and, with difficulty, gave her Vogt's message.

She shrank a bit but, the voice coming from very deep within her said, 'I believe he is sincere.'

The worst moment of her life had been when she saw the handcuffs fastened round her husband's wrists. But Vogt told him the number of notches needed to secure him and said if anyone tried to make them tighter he should say Ernest had said that was the number and direct him to ring Avenue Foch and ask for Ernest.

'He treated us as the enemies of his country. Which we were. But without brutality.'

After a moment she added, 'The shoe is now on the other foot. Would he like me to visit his wife?'

I was back at the Tribunal Militaire at 4.30. Mercier was late coming in and the *greffier* served me a cup of coffee. Then Mercier came in, with apologies. He had had to take some prisoners to Fresnes.

When I told him I had seen Starr, he asked, 'Has he received something from here yet?'

'Yes.' It had reached him by the morning's post.

'That was quick. I only put it in my out-tray yesterday evening.'

He added, 'I do believe Starr is a loyal Englishman. And he loves France, too.'

I asked him if he believed Odette's toenails had been pulled out.

This was something of which he had no knowledge, he said. He believed a film was shown in a cinema in Paris in which something of the sort was depicted on the screen. 'But we have no official knowledge of it. It is not something we have been asked to investigate.' Neither she personally nor the British government had asked them to ask any of the Germans they held prisoner if they knew anything about this. 'It does not exist, for us.'

I returned the next day, 28 June, to London.

I had asked Mignon Nevada for her address before the Censorship broke up, and now saw her again and obtained her recollections of Noor as a tiny tot and of the Inayat Khan family at that time. I also saw another of Vilayat's Sufi people, Edith Clarke; Fred Archer, who had been with Noor at the RAF station at Abingdon; and her friend Joan Wynne, who had the baby in Eire.

And about this time, late 1950 or early 1951, I met Selwyn Jepson. It was he who, recruiting agents for SOE, had written to the WAAF and obtained from them details of a girl called Inayat Khan who had been brought up in France, and asked her to come for an interview. This he detailed to me, as appears in my book. Later, he wrote the Foreword.

And now I heard from University College. I was not really surprised that my 'Phonetics of Polish' had not been accepted. Nor had it been failed. It had been 'Referred'. The same thing had happened to Miss

Chapallaz, with hers on the phonetics of the rare Italian dialect. She came to tea with me to talk about it. She was going to re-submit it next year. I was not. I had not been giving it priority attention and would not in the coming year either, which I would be spending in writing *Madeleine*.

It helped that Gimson had told Professor Jones he believed I was slightly deaf. Professor Jones held his watch at varying distances from my head, asking if I could still hear its ticking, and decided Gimson was right. He decided this was a sign phonetics were not my true path and that the other work upon which I was embarked was of greater importance. He was very sweet about it.

I did however – much to my surprise – receive a letter from Gimson (Professor Gimson I should rather call him as he had now succeeded Professor Jones in the professorial chair and was head of the Department) inviting me to be one of the teachers engaged by the College for the three weeks' summer school crash course in English for foreign students. He must have thought that having been for so long specially tutored by Professor Jones I must have learned at least something.

It was throughout most of July, all day and every day, tiring. The pupils were mainly undergraduates – and graduates – from Continental universities. At the end we issued them all with a diploma – not to be confused with a degree – as something they could exhibit as proof they had not idled during the summer vacation. And a group photograph was taken, which I still preserve.

I was painting again, inspired by memories of the dark conifers and very blue lakes of the Black Forest, and produced a set of seven: one of the cable-car, one of the hilltop near the inn at which I had lunched with Vogt, two of the Titisee, one of the Feldsee, one of a glade and one of Freiburg itself. I used postcards to assist my memory, but did them in a kind of *faux naif* style, exaggerating the blue of the lakes and the sky they reflected. I submitted (probably three) to the Women's International Art Club, and one of them, the Feldsee, was accepted and hung.

Starting on 24 April (1951) I was now also lecturing once a week, on Thursday, on the phonetics of English to the Speech Fellowship in Portland Place – I think in the old premises of the Poetry Society wherein I heard Dylan Thomas lecture to it. This was the reason why, when thinking of joining a Theosophical Lodge, I could not join Blavatsky. Its meetings were on Thursday evenings. So I joined, instead, Astrological, which met on Mondays, and very near to my flat. In the years to come I would become a committee member, secretary and vice-president and give it generally two talks in every session.

My book was finished, but I had difficulty in finding a publisher for it. Six turned it down. Reasons given were that it fell into two parts: the Sufi background would be tedious to readers who wanted a war story, and readers interested in the Sufi background would not want a war story; it was too soon after the story of Odette – another of the same type – and the apparent softness of the Germans towards her at Avenue Foch was a travesty: 'We know what happened to Odette.'

I wrote a desperate letter to Victor Gollancz telling him of the reasons given elsewhere for its rejection. I got back a letter saying there was no book it would give him greater pleasure to publish. Would I send it?

I packed it up and sent it to him on 23 July; on 3 September I was received for the first time by Sheila Hodges, who would be the copy editor, and a contract followed.

One of my diversions during the months during which *Madeleine* was going through the press was reading *The Secret Doctrine* of H. P. Blavatsky. To be sure, Vivian had given me at our first meeting his own copy of *Anthropogenèse* (in his French edition, the second volume), enriched by his marginal notes in red ink, but in French translation.

We had studied it a good deal in Paris, but I had never systematically read it, beginning at the first page of volume one, and this I now set myself to do.

I also wondered if I could write a life of Gilby, and appealed for anyone who could remember him. I had nice letters from two colonels, Northey and Foster, but there was not enough to make a book.

Madeleine was published on Monday 29 September 1952, and got off to the best possible start with an excellent review in the *Observer* of the Sunday before. It was the sort of review one dreams of, headed by her photograph.

Others followed thick and fast, provincial as well as national and foreign ones too. This must have contributed to the book's going into six impressions in four months.

But when I saw that the nearly full page review in *Time and Tide* was by Odette's biographer, Gerard Tickell, I thought here was where trouble might begin. Indeed it came, towards the end:

In writing of that grisly building, 84 Avenue Foch, Miss Fuller seems to have accepted the reminiscence of some of its late occupants with a naiveté that is astonishing. Of one tormentor and sadist she says tolerantly: 'he would become excited and slap prisoners' faces, minor brutalities ...' The War Office have greater knowledge of this person's activities. War Office officials ... brought her tormentors to answer for some of their crimes.

My question had been from Vogt's letter to me mentioning Cartaud as having been put onto interrogations during the time that he (Vogt) was in hospital. He had proved unsuccessful in this job as his behaviour to the prisoners only put their backs up. It was, however, important to me that Tickell obviously equated the man I had named as Cartaud with the one alleged to have pulled out Odette's toenails. I replied in a letter published on 25 October 1952:

> In fact there has come not even a suggestion from any official source that she [Noor] was tortured ... no persons have been charged with ill-treating her. Ernest and Goetz, her two interrogators, were both examined by both the British and the French military authorities and their statements were found satisfactory. They were discharged with a clean sheet. One is employed in a bank and the other is teaching in a school in the British Zone of Germany.

There was no reply from Tickell.

The November issue of *The National and English Review* carried a review by Odette herself:

> I think Miss Fuller has written of Madeleine with affection, simplicity and honesty. I can only regret that her knowledge of the temperament and behaviour of some of the Germans one encountered at 84 Avenue Foch is seen through their eyes rather than those of their victims. I knew them all and my experience is not of such gentlemanliness as Miss Fuller would have us believe. I do not think that one can, in fairness, build up their character from their appreciation of Madeleine given five years after the end of the war. It is true that she was not tortured and it is quite possible that in her case they were what they claimed to have been. But this did not typify the general attitude and behaviour of the Gestapo.

This was a cleverer piece of work than the other. I suspected Miss Atkins had something to do with it. Odette had no authority to say 'It is true ...' She had no knowledge whatsoever of Noor Inayat Khan and could have affirmed nothing as true or untrue concerning her.

I had sent Miss Atkins a complimentary copy of the book a fortnight before publication and she wrote me what, considering I had not been near her for two and a half years, was a nice letter – though the end was mildly reproachful:

> I wonder why I was not given the opportunity so freely extended to other informants of seeing the text before it was published.

I had shown the full text to no one, but to certain people, the Balachowskys, Madame Garry, Starr and Vogt, I had shown the parts that incorporated what they had told me, so as to be sure I had not made mistakes in reporting them.

Miss Atkins continued:

> I also wonder you say that the War Office – and for this purpose I should be identified with the WO – made available very little information, did not trouble to find out the facts about the fate of its agents. The very opposite is true.

My feelings had not been that she had not troubled to learn, but of what she must know she had made a minimum available to me, dosed with discouragement of any attempt by me to learn more.

She hoped I would make an occasion for us to meet.

I owed her a dinner from two and a half years ago, so I invited her to dinner. She came on 10 November. It was one of the stranger encounters of my life.

I was braced for her being critical of my book, but it seemed as though she was not going to bring the subject up, letting the conversation, as we sat down to dinner, range over general topics. Klaus Fuchs came into it. 'I don't think of him as a traitor,' she said. We were facing each other across the narrow table from which I had moved my typewriter in order to lay it for the meal. I was so surprised that I said nothing at all. She gave an explanation. 'During the war we shared all our secrets with the Russians and after it he just went on. I don't call that being a traitor.'

I was looking at her very narrowly now. Whilst Britain and the Soviet Union had been allies in the war against Nazi Germany, I did not suppose that our respective intelligence services had shared all their secrets with one another, and it could not be for a private individual to take on himself disclosure of knowledge he had obtained through his work for the Government. To have passed over particulars of our research into atomic secrets seemed to me an enormous treason. Even if he was an ideologist, not a mercenary. This was at the height of the Cold War.

We finished eating and moved into armchairs.

She had at one of our earliest meetings dropped a remark that she did not like Marshall Aid as it would make America too dominant on the Continent. This mild expression of anti-Americanism I had not, at the time, sensed as important. But she was saying something now that was very much more serious. She had never been to America. Probably never would be let in to America. To get into America one had to answer questions such as, had you ever been a Communist, had you ever known a Communist. 'You just have to decide whether you want to get in to America and if so tell the necessary lies. I don't think it worth it.'

Why was she, who never uttered a word without prior reflection, committing the extraordinary indiscretion of disclosing to me that, if the truth were known about her, she would not be allowed into America?

She went on. 'I do believe in democracy. With perhaps a little more freedom for the individual than is in the Soviet Union today. And', leaning forward in an eager way towards me, 'I don't see why that should be impossible to achieve.'

It was that word 'achieve' that hit me. Most English people, talking of democracy, would have said 'preserved'. 'Achieve' implied something needing to be worked for.

I went very quiet. Hardly answering a word to anything. Just waiting for her to go.

At last she stood up. Said there was a minor matter of which she must speak. She opened my book and said, she was sorry I had said nobody was tortured at 84 Avenue Foch.

Guardedly, I said that I had not said that.

'You have given that impression,' she said. She accepted that I had given Vogt's statement as being his own and would not therefore comment, but where Cartaud was mentioned she would like, in any future edition, to see a footnote saying he had after the war been tried by French court martial and shot by firing-squad, after having been found guilty not only of treason in itself but of the most hideous and atrocious crimes.

It was a very odd experience. I knew she was lying, and that she wanted me to print this misinformation in my book as a cover for Odette's story about her toenails having been pulled out. She did not know that I had already been to the Tribunal Militaire and raised the matter of Odette's toenails and been told they had no official knowledge of this story.

As I remained silent, she embroidered. It had been in the late autumn or winter of 1944. Another man was tried alongside of him but all attention was riveted upon Cartaud and the court listened in horror to the recitation of the terrible cruelties of which he was guilty …

It was extremely unsettling listening to a normally intelligent woman making this up as she went along.

I asked her, very deliberately, 'Are you sure?'

Looking me straight in the eyes, she said, 'Quite sure.'

I wondered if she knew I knew she was lying.

At last she went. As she turned to go down the stairs, she said, 'I'll be keeping my eye on you.'

As soon as she had gone I wrote to both Vogt and Starr about Cartaud. Starr wrote: 'He was not only dead but buried before D-Day in a cemetery near Paris, with German military honours.' He had heard of the incident in which he was killed when it happened, and been shown a photograph of the funeral.

Vogt wrote giving me further details of the incident. It had taken place outside a hairdresser's shop in the rue Royale, in which Kieffer's people were interested. A party of their men had been raiding their premises, which was being used as a Resistance letter-box. There was some trouble, and one of their men, not realising Cartaud had already gone in, shot at someone he saw coming out. Too late, he realised that he had shot Cartaud. He gave me the name of a Frenchwoman still living who was eye-witness to the incident in which Cartaud was mortally wounded. He died later in the Hôpital de la Pitié.

I would take this to show Mercier – now promoted to Commandant (Major) – when in Paris.

French translation rights had been sold to Corrêa, Paris, I had been invited to speak on *Madeleine* in the BBC's afternoon programme 'Woman's Hour' (and later in one of their evening programmes) and the rights had been bought from Gollancz to make a television play from my book. It was to be produced by Duncan Ross and he introduced himself to me in a letter I received on 22 November. He would like me to show him some of the places in Paris mentioned in the book, particularly the Avenue Foch.

I flew to Paris a couple of days ahead of him, on 11 December, Mercier had invited me to lunch, in a restaurant at some distance from the Tribunal, at 12.30.

He was glum, silent and bad-tempered. He sent away the soup. Savaged his chop. If he had not wanted to see me why had he invited me?

Unexpectedly he broke his silence with the words, 'I saw three of my countrymen shot this morning.' There was a rule of his service that if, as president of the court martial, one pronounced the death sentence, one had to see it carried out. To make one realise what it means. Not do it lightly. As if one could. 'In this case, there was no redeeming circumstance. At least none perceived by me.' He could not know if that applied to the eyes of God. 'It is very miserable. You have to get up before it is daylight. Drink a cup of black coffee. Impossible to eat breakfast before an execution. You take cigarettes. It would be unforgivable to go to an execution without cigarettes. You say "Good morning" and it sounds ironical, because for them it is the worst morning. At the end, there is almost a collaboration. You both want the same thing – that they will walk to the wall against which they must stand to be shot without making a too awful scene. They want to cut a last figure as a man. Afterwards you have to go to them and shoot each one in the head to make sure he is dead. I thought I would, by this time, be able to eat lunch ...'

He said, he had never pronounced the death sentence without feeling his identity with the man he sentenced. The springs of treason were so common in human nature. In the cases he had to hear usually either fear or cupidity. 'Have I never feared, both morally and physically? I have. Have I never coveted luxury and ostentation I could not afford? I have.'

'But you have not done things that have brought you to stand where these have stood.'

'Thank God, who has not tempted me too far.'

He added, 'I get very Jansenist as I get older. I think we are all born with an innate tendency to do wrong, simply because we are men and descend from Adam.'

I asked him about Cartaud. They knew about him of course, but had not tried him for the good reason he was dead before the Germans left France. A traitor, but not known to have been employed as a torturer.

He read Vogt's letter carefully and said, 'I think he tells you truly?'

Might he borrow this for a couple of days, to show to some of his colleagues?

When I saw him again two days later, he said his colleagues believed as he did that the details given by Vogt were exact.

Duncan Ross was in Paris by the 13th (December 1952) and we went, with Starr, to the Avenue Foch. The owner, Mr Chaix, led us up to the fifth floor. He had been all through this before, he said, when the film *Odette* was being made. She took them into the room in which she had been tortured. Which one was it? The one he indicated was that which had been Vogt's office.

Ross could not get over Kieffer's choosing for his living quarters a set of rooms on the fourth floor of a building without a lift. 'Must have had good wind.'

Starr said we would go somewhere nice for tea; and the place he drove us to was the Grand Trianon Hotel, Versailles. I meant to use the occasion to persuade Starr to let me write his story. Ross said, 'Write a brave book, Starr, and it'll go round the world.'

Ross was saying he believed he had discovered the name of the man in charge of SOE – which was what he believed the organisation that sent the agents was called. Gubbins. Both were new to Starr. They were told, when recruited, that the head of it was Winston Churchill, but who might be in charge, between Churchill and Buckmaster, he had no idea. And he had never heard the organisation given a name.

What did everybody call it, then?

'The thing, the organisation ...' Nobody knew if it had a name.

Special Operations Executive was what Ross had gleaned the initials stood for.

Starr agreed to the book's being written. I flew back to England but returned on 9 February 1953 and lunched with Mercier, not now at the Tribunal Militaire but at the Palais de Chaillot, where he was helping to see in what ways French and German military law could be brought into line within the new Europe in formation. I told him of the project.

I went to the Starrs each evening at eight. Madame Starr made us coffee and then he dictated his story and I scribbled it down. The next morning and afternoon I would produce a text from these scribbles on my typewriter (I had brought my portable) in the hotel bedroom. The hotel served no meals other than breakfast but I found a Russian restaurant nearby in which I could eat. There was one road nearby which I found impossible to walk up; it was as though some inner sense said that way murder lies. I was puzzled, as it, the rue Vaugirard, was neither the place where the aristocrats had been guillotined during the Revolution nor the hostages shot in the recent war. Then I discovered what it led to, the place where poor horses who had finished their working days were led for slaughter, as meat. It was the horses' terror I had been picking up.

The book was finished by 9 March, when we took it to the Palais de Chaillot to show Mercier. He said, 'I don't think I ought to be reading this', but read some parts and was plainly tickled pink.

I flew back to England on the 11th and handed it in to Gollancz, where Sheila Hodges sent it straight to their legal adviser, Hilary Rubinstein of Rubinstein Nash.

When he invited me to come to his office he opened by saying the note from Victor Gollancz that had come with it said he was not afraid of action for libel in the ordinary sense but didn't fancy ending up in the Tower.

I therefore went down to H. M. Stationery Office on Kingsway, applied for the Official Secrets Act, read it and wrote to Rubinstein. I gathered from it that one would be liable for prosecution if, having signed the Official Secrets Act one divulged the secrets of the work on which one was then employed, or learned from a person who had done this. We had not. The playback of the radios was not an official secret confided to Starr by the British. It was from the enemy he had learned it. And I had learned it firstly through him and then from Vogt, who, being a German, was obviously not a signatory to the British Official Secrets Act.

Rubinstein congratulated me on my 'masterly analysis of the Official Secrets Act' and Victor Gollancz became more sanguine about our chances of escaping prosecution if the book went into print.

It helped us that there now appeared *London Calling North Pole* by H. J. Giskes, former chief of German Military Counter Espionage (Abwehr) in Holland, Belgium and Northern France, in which it was claimed that the whole of the SOE network in Holland had been in German hands, all its radios were operated by the Germans, further agents arriving having been met on the field by Germans and escorted straight to prison. This, of course, was what Starr said had been happening in France. This book by Giskes assured Victor Gollancz that the playback told of by Starr was a possible thing, which had happened elsewhere. Asked in the House of Commons whether the claim made by Giskes was true, Eden had stood up and said yes, and this lessened the extent to which the disclosure in our book was of an official secret. Nevertheless Sheila Hodges implored me to submit the typescript to Selwyn Jepson.

When he handed it back to me it was obvious he had shown it to Miss Atkins. Starr, he said, was a continual source of information to the Germans. Other prisoners, left alone with him, would let their hair down and drop the bits of information that were picked up by microphones. 'There were four in the guardroom.' It was the bits captured on the microphones that kept the radio-game going. 'I don't see what's left of your book. You could call it "The Unconscious Traitor".'

I wrote to Starr. He replied by telegram, HAVE IT SENT FOR PUBLICATION IMMEDIATELY. And by letter he assured me it was not normal custom to leave other prisoners alone with him. They would be under escort of Vogt or Goetz, and hadn't it struck anybody the guardroom was full of guards? On the one occasion when his radio, John, had been put in a cell with him they had been so very conscious of possible microphones they were extremely careful not to drop any information, and in fact John's was one of the few radio circuits never played back by the Germans.

After many months of hesitation, *The Starr Affair* was sent to the printers.

Twelve

On 10 September 1953 the newspapers reported that Phoebe Llewellyn Smith's body had been washed up, together with that of a male companion, both apparently from the wreck of the *Ennis*, stuck in the Buxy Sands. The body of another man believed to have been aboard had not then been found, though it subsequently was.

I knew about Arthur, the male companion. Phoebe had told me that an earlier admirer had told her, in a moment of annoyance, that what she wanted was 'not a husband but a male mistress'. It wasn't meant to be nice, but it struck her as being true. What she wanted was a man who would let her paint all day but yet be there for companionship in the evenings. In Arthur she seemed to have found it, because he was somewhat the same. It was a relaxed relationship. She had made her psychiatrist laugh by saying, 'If Arthur had money he wouldn't buy me, he would buy a boat.' Indeed he had, for months, been working on an old boat to make it seaworthy; he was going to take her out in it.

It was the first funeral I had attended: the service in the church, the burial, the flowers thrown on the grave. I said my own prayer for her.

Lady Llewellyn Smith had wanted each of Phoebe's friends to take something in memory of her, and Rosemary Tubbs, Phoebe's flatmate, said that of course what I should have was her painting of me. It had been done with great care yet I did not think was as like me as the earlier one she had destroyed. But yes, it was the obvious thing.

I read in the papers that there had been an inquest, and wrote to the man from Trinity House. He came to see me, and explained lots of things. He had been aboard the wreck and also on the sandbank in which it was stuck. If they had stayed on it, people would have seen them in the morning and come and rescued them. But plainly they had thought it was going down and that they had to abandon it. As to how the 'unsinkable dinghy' had sunk, which had occupied the newspapers, with three people in it, it would have been low in the water. The edges of the sandbank were not firm but very loose and there was a lot of loose sand swirling about in the water. The little waves were quite choppy and would have been coming in over the sides, filled with the sand that was in them. It would have been sunk by the sand.

On 4 February 1954 I received a telegram from a firm of solicitors in Launceston, Cornwall, saying MARIE STEWARD DEAD. My presence was requested, at their office and at the funeral. I travelled on Sunday 7th to Launceston, and put up at a hotel there. She had left me her house absolutely; her stocks and shares she had left in the trust of her solicitors, to be administered by them: the income from the investments to be equally divided between her sister, 'Lulu' Peters, and myself, and on the death of either, to the survivor absolutely.

I was taken by surprise. She had said something about a trust but I did not know what was involved and had not thought of anything coming to me. Earlier she had said she had considered leaving everything to the RSPCA, but then on consideration preferred somewhere where it would 'make a difference'. It never entered my head she would have selected me.

After the cremation one of the partners in the solicitors' firm handed me the keys and said, 'It's all yours now.' It felt strange to be using her key to turn her lock … 'I threw a dead bird out,' he said. I looked at the Mongolian goddess on the mantelpiece. That too, was mine now. All the contents, the furniture …

There remained the scattering of the ashes. She had stipulated she wanted them scattered in the Rocky Valley. This rather worried the solicitor, as the way was wet and slippery and he did not know how far down we had to go. I knew she wanted it done by me, so I told him not to worry. I knew the exact spot she wanted and he did not need to come.

The way was a bit slippery. But I was careful at the place where the trickle of water from above ran across the path, and did not slide. When I reached the strange spiral I opened the urn and scattered the ashes, and uttered words on the wind I hoped she would be glad to hear.

I really did not know what I could do with Marie's house, Ferny Park. If it had been in the Home Counties I might have lived in it, but the six-hour journey made it too far from London, where I really needed to be. And the Celtic environment – despite my rite – was just too pixilated for me to feel at home in it. I decided – hoping Marie would forgive me – to put the house on the market.

The American rights in *The Starr Affair* were bought by Little, Brown, who changed the title to *No. 13*. British serialisation rights had been sold to the *Empire News*, which began its serialisation, under the title, *If I'm a Traitor Try me*, on 18 July. From Miss Atkins I had a letter threatening legal action if she found her reputation damaged, and Buckmaster wrote a letter to the *Empire News*, saying: 'To say that the French Section deliberately sent men into the hands of the German security police is of course monstrously and libellously untrue.' But we had not said it was true, Starr had said to me he 'sometimes wondered if they were doing it on purpose', but that was not a remark included by me in the book.

From Guernsey I received a surprise invitation from Colonel Spooner, to spend a few days with him and his wife. I knew that Spooner had been head of the Security School at Beaulieu, so supposed I was going to be ticked off for having breached the Official Secrets Act.

Nevertheless I took the plane, on 25 August, to Guernsey. He was there to meet me, and from the moment we drove off in his little car bumping over the dusty road, I knew it was going to be all right. 'If I had had my way, your little friend would be alive today,' he said. He had made his report on her adverse. He did not want me to take that wrongly. 'To be an agent is not humanity's finest flower.' To play the harp might, in the eyes of the Almighty, find far more favour. But as an agent she was too emotionally vulnerable, too little conscious of security, too nervous. He had come up behind her on one occasion and she had made a nervous start; if that happened with a German it could give him the idea she was up to something. 'I am old-fashioned enough to feel women should be kept out of danger, not sent into it'; but given the premise that his trainees had to include women, he would have preferred one that was 'harder'. Miss Atkins, however, had insisted on her suitability and it was her judgement which Buckmaster had preferred to his.

We had hardly reached his house, I had hardly been introduced to his wife, Marjorie, when the telephone rang. It was the *Empire News* – for I had given them Spooner's number in case of emergency – reading me the text of a letter just received from Buckmaster, which would be printed in their next issue:

She states that the French Resistance was not under the command of Colonel Buckmaster ... Miss Fuller has no knowledge whatever of the chain of command ...

She says that not one but a number of our networks became German controlled. I know it was only one and consider I am in a better position to know the facts than she is.

Telling Spooner, I gasped, 'There were at least three whose radio circuits were German controlled, 'Archambaud', 'Valentin', 'Madeleine' and I believed 'Leopold'.

He said, 'I did not know there was *even one* that became German-controlled. You can chalk that up as a point to yourself.' The chain of command he would give me after we had had lunch.

Marjorie, discreetly, left us to work.

At the bottom were the agents in the field. Above them were the heads for different countries, France, Belgium, Holland, Norway. For France there were two: F for French Section, controlled by Buckmaster, and RF (République Française) controlled by J. R. H. Hutchinson of Jardine Matheson. Whereas F had mainly English agents, though a few French, RF had mainly French, though a few English. Those in RF thought of de Gaulle as their chief, and of course they were not under Buckmaster. Above all the Heads of Country was Nathan Sporborg, a lawyer, and above Sporborg was Major-General Sir Colin Gubbins. Ultimately it went up to the Ministry of Economic Warfare, a temporary organisation headed by Lord Selborne, and, so, of course, to the War Cabinet and Churchill.

Coming down again to Miss Atkins, he told me her real name had been Rosenberg, until at the end of the war she changed it by deed poll. I had assumed her English. Romanian, he said. Jewish. She was 'the only brain in SOE,' he said. '*She*'s your enemy.' Meaning Buckmaster might make more public bluster but she would be more adroit.

She had been his own adversary. The difficulty lay in her not belonging to an armed service and having a rank. 'If she had been Major Atkins, I would have outranked her. Nobody can outrank a Miss.'

As I looked puzzled, he explained. 'You don't know why she's there or who she's been put in by.' It might be some tremendously powerful person who had put her in and whom you would be angering if you put her down. He had no idea by whom she had been put in.

He gave me his own CV. Born 10 July 1893, Sandhurst. Indian Army: 30th Lancers. After leaving the Army, training horses, then for a while managing a branch of T. B. Ford, manufacturers of blotting paper. Back to horses: stud manager. When war had been declared, he offered his services to the War Office and found himself posted to

Beaulieu. By the time he knew my 'little friend' he was commanding officer of all 'Group C' training schools. He left SOE in 1945 and was now growing daffodils for export to the mainland. From his Army days he kept up acquaintance with Field Marshal Sir Claude Auchinleck.

Had Vogt told me how he came to know the names of Arisaig and Beaulieu?

I said I thought he was simply told them by Kieffer, but I would ask him to confirm.

'You can tell him it's not to take any action on. Just for my own satisfaction, if I can call it that.'

Could I give those two names, Arisaig and Beaulieu, in anything else I wrote? Or were they still British Official Secret?

'Could be,' he said with a wry smile. 'Put it on to me. Vogt told you, but of course you didn't believe Vogt until I confirmed. They won't do anything against me, I'm too senior.'

The question of how the Germans came to know the training schools was galling him. He had a suspect. André Simon, a conducting officer. He had to escort the trainees from one school to another, so knew all of them. He was given to careless talk. 'I cautioned him more than once, and finally reported him. It's no pleasure to me to report a man.'

I let slip my doubts about Buckmaster. Spooner burst out laughing and called in his wife. Marjorie had been in SOE earlier than Frank and knew Buckmaster before Frank did. She told me that Frank had to meet Buckmaster on a railway platform and asked her how he should recognise him. She had said, 'Look for a man who looks as if he'd lost his knitting.' And afterwards Frank had telephoned her saying, 'Splendid! I picked him out at once.'

Buckmaster, declared Frank, was 'an overgrown boy-scout'. He was industrious. 'I will say that for Buckmaster, he was industrious.' But not realistic. Thought in clichés. Used phrases from gangster films, such as, 'I think we must "rub him out".' In fact, too ready with the cyanide pill ...'

Desmond Young, author of *Rommel*, had invited me to stay for a couple of days with himself and wife on the neighbouring island of Sark. Like Spooner, he knew Auchinleck and said he had just had a telephone call from Spooner suggesting we take the Field Marshal into our confidence and he might be some protection to me. (It was

Desmond who took me to tea with Auchinleck, at the Field Marshal's flat off Piccadilly. Strangely, all I can remember of the conversation was Auchinleck confiding he was teaching himself to paint in oils and asking how I cleaned the brushes. I told him I used washing-up liquid.)

As we approached, it reminded me of Capri, rising steeply from the sea, though actually when one had climbed from the beach to the plateau it was flat and almost featureless.

Desmond was interested in a character called 'Gilbert' mentioned in *Colonel Henri's Story*, Ian Colvin's translation of Bleicher's memoirs. I had earlier read this in the German original from which it was translated, *Monsieur Jean*. Monsieur Jean and Colonel Henri were both aliases used by Sergeant Hugo Bleicher of the Abwehr. It was he who had arrested Peter Churchill and Odette. He had referred to a double agent in the service of Sturmbannführer Kieffer, whom he called simply 'Gilbert'. Apparently this was a man working also for London. Colvin's translation was supplemented by a note:

> Colonel Buckmaster has identified Gilbert to the Editor as the
> code-name for his air movements officer … Gilbert, a Frenchman
> is today at liberty despite the suspicions that Bleicher tried to cast
> upon him.

Air Movements Officer! An irritant in the back of my mind had been that photocopied letter written by 'Madeleine' to her mother which, when Vogt showed it to her, so greatly distressed her. I tried to remember exactly what it was Noor had told me on that last evening about mail. She had given me her address, c/o The War Office, but asked me not to use it unless the matter were important as it might not be fair to over-burden the person responsible for delivering and collecting the mail. Letters to her would go in a bag that would be delivered once a month. This once-monthly service was probably both ways. The same person perhaps picked up and delivered. Was that person the pilot of the aircraft, or a person intermediary between the pilot and herself and others with whom she worked? Vogt had said 'Prosper' and 'Archambaud' had been shown copies of mail they had sent to London. Yes, the Air Movements Officer intrigued me. Who was 'Gilbert'?

Desmond Young suggested I call to see Louis Burdet, the manager of the Stafford Hotel in London, who had been involved in these operations. He would write him a line.

On Friday 3 September I had lunch with Louis Burdet in the

Stafford Hotel in St James's Place. He had belonged to RF Section, which was differently organised from F. Whole areas were under a DMR (Député Militaire Régionale), and the DMRs always had for code-names terms used in geometry. Burdet had been DMR for the whole of the region from Marseilles to the Italian frontier and his code was 'Circumference'. He knew nothing whatever about any of the Buckmaster people I had worked on, yet he had a story to tell me.

In 1944, during the run up to D-Day, he was given a series of programmes of action to which were allocated colours – green, red, blue and so on. But on receiving through his radio operator Plan Yellow or whatever, he would order particular action like blow up bridges, blow up railway lines. When Plan Black was announced, he had to call all his men into open insurgence against the Germans, so as to distract their attention from the disembarkation of our troops on the Channel coast – for this would be D-Day. He received Plan Black and sent all his men into action. They were cut down by the German panzers, for no troops were landing on the Channel coast; this was not D-Day. The Communist networks had not risen up. If Plan Black was transmitted in error, how did they know it was to be disregarded? When eventually D-Day came, they were able to rise up in full strength, appearing as the ones who had acted correctly, whereas his people had been so debilitated as to be unable to do much again, and though it was they who had acted correctly, appeared as having risen prematurely.

What did he make of it, I asked?

To this day, he did not know. If the Communists had better intelligence, a private tip off that Plan Black was to be disregarded, he did not grudge it to them; he would just have appreciated if they would have shared it with him.

On 8 September Colonel George Starr, elder brother of the one I knew, telephoned and came to tea. He had been 'Hilaire', organiser of a big network that operated south of Bordeaux, which was one of the few to survive and rise in support of the eventual D-Day invasion. He told me he had at one moment warned London that an adjoining network was, through the radio, German controlled, and got the reply, 'Mind your own business. We know what we are doing.'

But he told me another story. Shortly after the war ended he received an appeal for help from three French members of his former network who found themselves locked up charged with murder. He hastened to contact Buckmaster and ask him to confirm it was he who had given the order for the killing of a man, believed to be betraying them.

Buckmaster was unable to remember anything about it. The authority had come by radio so there was no proof from whom it came. So George Starr had gone to Bordeaux and told the police there it was he who had given the order for the killing, – 'a Resistance killing' – on his own responsibility. They did not look pleased, but motioned him to a table, put paper and pen in front of him and told him to write that out. The three men were then released.

Squadron Leader F. F. E. Yeo-Thomas, they told me, was now in England for an operation for a stone in the kidney. He had been given *The Starr Affair*, which he had been reading in bed. He was a figure of immense prestige in the Free French world and he would like to see me.

On 16 September I rang the number they gave me. It was Barbara Yeo-Thomas who answered the phone. 'I'll get Tommy,' she said, and his first words were 'I can't see anything wrong with what Starr did.' He gave me an appointment for 12.15 on the 18th at his favourite pub, The Friend at Hand.

I arrived too early and had to wait. Then they came in: she fragile, fair, elegant in black, with dark glasses; he short, tough. If there was an inquiry he would give evidence for Starr. But he said, 'By the way, people *were* beaten up at Avenue Foch, because I was.'

I told him I had sent a copy of his book to Vogt, and Vogt believed this had happened to him not in 84 Avenue Foch, to which only F Section prisoners were brought, but in 86, to which all the RF prisoners were taken.

Yeo-Thomas thought this might be right. When he travelled by rail from Paris to Buchenwald it was in a carriage with twenty-eight other prisoners. They compared experiences and it surprised him very much to learn that none of the others had been beaten up, though all had been at Avenue Foch. Then it dawned upon him that the twenty-eight others were all F Section men; he was the only one from RF. He had been taken in and out of Avenue Foch a number of times, and thought he had certainly been at one moment in 84, where he had seen Starr. He could easily have failed to notice if sometimes he had been taken in through a different entrance; and for that matter there was a corridor between the two houses so that he could have passed from one into the other without noticing. It was one room down from the top, therefore the fourth floor, on which he was beaten up; but that, in 84, was Kieffer's private suite; and the bathroom in which he had been ducked in the bath between beatings was differently situated from the bathroom on the fifth floor of 84. He had glimpsed Goetz, who was correct in his behaviour, possibly glimpsed Vogt, but not to speak to; the bullies who beat him up were a different crowd.

Afterwards I wrote up a résumé of our conversation as I would include it in what might become my next book, just to be sure I had not got anything wrong.

His only objection was one that took me by surprise: I had referred to Barbara as his 'wife', which unfortunately she was not. His legal wife, who had threatened to denounce him to the Gestapo when he called, refused to divorce him, and could sue Barbara for impersonation and, possibly libel, as if she pretended to be his wife it would imply that she, the legal one, was not. Barbara Yeo-Thomas would be all right, as she had taken his name by deed-poll..

He suggested there was a matter I might be able to take over from him. Through his job at the Federation of British Industries, in Paris, he had come to know Mr Maurice Norman, of a firm of solicitors, who was desperately upset by allegations his son, Gilbert, was a traitor. That was 'Archambaud' of the Buckmaster Section. Yeo-Thomas had met 'Archambaud' in the prison van which conveyed him and the others from Fresnes to the railway station from which they would leave for Buchenwald. They had sat next to each other in the van and 'Archambaud' told him he had given Germans the first, only, of his two security checks and was devastated when shown the reply which had come from London: YOU FORGOT YOUR DOUBLE SECURITY CHECK BE MORE CAREFUL. (For me, this was the third time of hearing this story, once from Starr, then from Vogt, now from Yeo-Thomas.) But, said Yeo-Thomas, he knew absolutely nothing of the network to which Gilbert Norman had belonged. As I had been studying it, I might be better placed to make out what was the trouble. Norman was in London now, if I could contact him.

He also suggested I see André Simon, conducting officer, who must have known a good many of the agents.

It was Simon I saw first, on 18 September in a pub. He was a wine merchant and plied me with champagne. Had I heard of Déricourt? The name was new to me. Miss Atkins had assured Simon Déricourt was a traitor, said she had proof, but Simon was not convinced. He would drink a glass of champagne with him any day. 'I've been tight as a tick in his company more times than I can remember.' Miss Atkins had maintained that though the agents were not arrested on landing they were trailed; Simon maintained it was impossible to trail a man for weeks and months without being noticed.

Trailed from the fields ... It did not immediately click, but Simon had given me the real name of 'Gilbert' accused by Bleicher but asserted by Buckmaster to have been his Air Movements Officer ...

Burdet thought I should meet an RF man, Jacques Robert, and on 14 October 1954 I dined with them at the Stafford. Robert deplored the antagonism which had persisted between F and RF Sections and thought any investigation into happenings within F should be approached with and through Buckmaster. But in the taxi as he was seeing me home he said what he did find troubling was the extent to which Buckmaster was arming the Communists. 'When we asked for deliveries of arms or munitions there always seemed to be some reason for delay; when the Communists asked, they got it right away. Why were they favoured?'

On 21 October 1954, I met Mr Maurice Norman in the Stafford Hotel, in its lounge and afterwards for lunch. Very old and tremulous, he had brought with him five bulging files of papers concerning his son. It was particularly the Abbé Guillaume who had branded Gilbert Norman as a traitor. Jointly with the brother of Francis Suttill ('Prosper'), Norman had considered whether legal action could be taken in respect of the defamation of their respective relatives, but had been unable to get help from official quarters.

The files he left with me centered very much upon a quarrel between two members of the 'Prosper' network, Maurice Lequeux and Pierre Culioli, each accusing the other of having betrayed arms dumps in the Touraine. Apparently someone called Flower had asked London for a means of being rid of Culioli and a lethal pill had arrived, carried by 'Archambaud', who was, however, horrified when he discovered that what he had been carrying was a pill intended to poison the man who had helped him out of his parachute. He had persuaded the others in the group he was sent to join that they should not administer it. Mr Norman expressed a wish his son *had* administered the lethal pill to the man who later defamed him. Culioli had apparently been put on trial but acquitted.

I told Norman that if he liked to write a letter to Vogt and give it to me, I would send it on to him. He did this, and I sent it. Vogt sent me a carbon copy of the reply he had sent to Mr Norman. It was a nice letter, but the phrase, 'I have never considered Prosper, Archambaud or any of their colleagues as traitors' contained, I thought, the latent warning some people might consider them so – it was a matter of opinion; and the pleasing characteristics in Norman's son that he recalled included 'gentleness', not, in the circumstances the one the father would most wish to read. It would be unlike Vogt to be unaware he had missed out what the father most wanted to hear, that his son had betrayed no one. Something lurked behind this. In his covering letter to me, however, Vogt said that Mr Norman's son's christian name, Gilbert, had been much confused with that of another Gilbert, much to Gilbert Norman's disadvantage. I asked him about this other Gilbert. He said the case was far graver than that of Renée Garry. He did not want to put anything on paper about this but would tell me about it if I came again to Germany.

On 12 November I arrived by train in Freiburg. Vogt and his wife, Lily, now released by the French, were on the platform waiting for me, and, talking nineteen to the dozen, escorted me to the hotel where they had booked a room for me. I dumped my things there and we went on to their place. On the corner was a Christian Science bookshop. Vogt asked me, 'What is it? Christian Science? Do you know?'

I told him it was a movement founded by an American woman, Mary Baker Eddy, who reasoned everything came from God, God was good, so everything that came from Him must be good; if one thought one saw evil one must be mistaken since evil could have no existence.

Vogt said, with a rueful smile, 'If everybody thought like that, it would save all of us a lot of trouble.'

Incidentally, Noor was distantly related on her mother's side to Mary Baker Eddy. It was her mother's maiden name, Baker, she had given Vogt as her own. Vilayat believed it though he had not the family tree of either family. They both thought of themselves as having in their background not only Sufism but Christian Science. And incidentally again, there was a certain consonance between Noor and Baker Eddy in their make-up. I remembered an evening, on Vilayat's balcony in 1942, when he had said, 'Noor-un-Nisa is a saint, but she is still a negative saint. She does not *see* evil.' In order to pass from that blindness she would have to encounter the worst evil the world had to offer. He knew it to be necessary to her evolution, 'but as her brother I shudder.'

Vogt now plunged straight into the subject of Déricourt. When 'Prosper' and 'Archambaud' were arrested, Kieffer gave him photocopies of letters and reports in their hands which they had sent to London. These bore on the backs the reference BOE 48, which meant forty-eighth agent of Boemelburg. He was also given aerial photographs of country premises which meant nothing to him but which

Kieffer said the prisoners would recognise: these bore no reference on the back. Later 'Gilbert', who he was told was BOE 48, became Kieffer's agent directly. He was the man responsible for receiving the British aircraft which landed, boarding on them British agents returning home, together with the mail, and receiving the incoming agents who were then trailed from the field, though usually not arrested. Vogt met 'Gilbert' only once, when Kieffer told him to accompany Goetz in case 'Gilbert' who was about to return to England intended any mischief towards Goetz, his usual contact. They met 'Gilbert' in an empty flat, and he gave them the expected time of arrival of the next aircraft which would be landing, and the place of the landing. Following this landing, three arrests were made.

He urged me to be very careful of anything I wrote about 'Gilbert'. His real name, he had learned whilst in Paris after the war, was Déricourt. He had been tried and acquitted, and could sue me for libel. In Vogt's opinion it must have been because of the mail that 'Prosper' and his colleagues were arrested.

We talked until late, and on the following morning he wrote a statement out for me.

Back in Paris, I met Mercier, and showed him Vogt's statement. He read it with interest but had reservations about it. Coupaye, whom Starr had introduced to me in the Café Weber so close to the beginning of my researches, had said that had the English let them have Vogt in useful time, his evidence would have made a difference to the outcome of a certain trial, which now I realised must have been the trial of Déricourt. Mercier disagreed. 'I don't think it would have made a difference.' There was too much 'reported speech'. In France 'reported speech' was inadmissible from the witness box. I assured him that applied in English law too; we had a name for it: 'hearsay'.

He looked at Vogt's statement again and said, 'It breaks into two parts. Vogt saw a lot of handwritten papers in photocopy with BOE 48 written on the back of each. That is evidence.' Then, 'Vogt went with Goetz to an empty flat in which they met a man who told them a British aircraft would at such and such a date and time land on such and such a field and men would land from it, etc. There is evidence.' In between, there was a gap. That this man and BOE 48 were one and the same man whose code name with London was 'Gilbert' was surmise. Forget about the three men who were arrested. Vogt did not see them arrested. 'If it was before me that this case had been heard and Vogt had gone into the box to say what he says here, these are points at which I would have stopped him; utterances which I should have had to tell my colleagues to disregard. One cannot kill a man on a "Kieffer told me".' He thought, as did his colleagues, that Vogt gave his evidence honestly. But, 'Vogt has not the capability to say what Kieffer told him was true. Or that it was the whole truth. Kieffer could have had another agent, of whom Vogt never knew. It could have been this agent unknown who gave the address of "Prosper".' Before one led a man out to stand against a wall to be riddled by bullets, one had to be so terribly, terribly sure.

It was true that Vogt had told me, at our very first meeting, 'Kieffer told me only what I needed to know, in order to do what he wanted of me.' It was Kieffer, Mercier said, they needed to have had in the box, alive and able to answer questions. But the British had hanged Kieffer without giving them the opportunity to question him.

Slightly to change the subject, he did not believe Kieffer wanted to arrest 'Madeleine' as early as he did. He had known about her for some while and was waiting for the apposite moment. 'When Renée telephoned she put him in a spot.' He could not say he did not want to arrest 'Madeleine'. That would have given his game away to someone who could have spilled it elsewhere. So he had to go through the farce of instructing Vogt to meet the woman and negotiate a price for the information he did not need. I then returned to London.

I flew back to Paris on 6 January 1955, chiefly with the intention of giving myself some days to spend in the office of *France-Soir* looking through its back numbers until I came to the coverage of Déricourt's trial. I also saw a good deal of Barbara and Yeo-Thomas. He drove me out to Puteaux to see Roger Hérissé who had received and despatched aircraft for RF. On the way to Puteaux Yeo-Thomas remarked that it was the Communist networks that seemed to be favoured in speed of delivery of arms. That was what Jacques Robert had said.

I found Déricourt's trial in *France Soir*. It had been on 8 May 1948. I bought the back number and, armed with this date, went round to all the other newspaper offices, obtaining the relevant issues of *Parisien Libéré*, *Paris-Presse*, *Le Monde Libération*, *Figaro*, *Franc-Tireur*, *Combat*, *Humanité*. The prosecution had relied mainly upon Goetz, but he said the accused had interested his service in so much as it was hoped he would one day be able to tell them the date and place of the Invasion. But then the English Major Nicholas Bodington had gone into the box and said that Déricourt had told him of his contacts with the Germans and he had authorised him to maintain them. 'If I had to start all over again I would start with Déricourt.' After this there was only one possible verdict, and the panel of nine military judges gave him a unanimous verdict of 'not guilty'. Laden with all these, I was home on 25 January.

Gleaning from the French papers that there had been an earlier trial, in England, for attempted smuggling, I went down to Croydon, looked through the files at the offices of the *Croydon Times* and *Croydon Advertiser*, where I thought it might have headlines, and having found the date, went up to the newspaper library of the British Museum, at Colindale, to look through the national papers of the same date. What emerged was that on 10 April 1946 Déricourt had been caught attempting to smuggle a considerable quantity of gold and platinum nuggets and bullion. He was defended by Derek Curtis Bennett. It was appreciated by the magistrates that, having been allowed to fly his passengers to France, he had returned in order to face the charges, and he was let off with a relatively light fine.

On 16 February 1955 that I opened a House of Commons envelope to find within it a letter signed 'Irene Ward'. She was, she said, writing a history of the FANY corps. Might she quote in it a passage from my book, *Madeleine*, and would I come and have dinner with her at the House of Commons? The answer to both questions was naturally yes.

I looked her up in *Who's Who*. She was a Conservative, the Member for Tynemouth. This was just before she was made a Dame of the British Empire (DBE).

Little did I guess how important she was to be to me.

It was on 21 February that I went to dine with her for the first time at the House of Commons. Blue eyes, radiant smile and forthright manner. She was, of course, including in her book a chapter on the girls who trained for SOE under the cover of the FANY uniform. She herself had had a curious accidental contact with SOE, back in 1941. Jacques de Guélis, whom she had known earlier, came up to her and asked her if she knew Eden well enough to put a letter into his hand. 'Yes,' she had said. 'Not into the hands of a secretary or any intermediate person, into his *own* hand?' de Guélis insisted. 'Yes.'

'I never saw that letter,' she said to me. He had given it to her in a sealed envelope, and she had no idea what she was transmitting. 'I put it into Anthony's hand.' A few days afterwards, he had told her she could tell her friend that he had read his letter but would not be replying in writing. De Guélis should go straight to Lord Strang, who would be his regular contact. Lord Strang was the head of the Foreign Office Secret Intelligence Service. So Anthony came to have a man in SOE. De Guélis.

The name was familiar. I had met in Paris a man called Gilbert Turck. He had not served in SOE but in MI9, Escapes Section, and he had been parachuted into France in August 1941 with Jacques de Guélis. Turck's mission was to organise an escape route for shot-down airmen and the like, and to this end he rented a house, the Villa des Bois, in Marseilles.

Though he did not say what he had written in that letter, de Guélis did tell her of a matter of his concern: a house in which a lot of people, men of the Buckmaster Section, had been arrested. It seemed to me that this house in which these people had been arrested must have been the Villa des Bois. But what was so secret about it, that Buckmaster had to be bypassed and a secret link with Eden established?

I happened to mention *The Starr Affair* and her eyes opened very wide. In connection with her book she had asked in the Foreign Office if she could see some file and had been told that all files had been closed since publication of *The Starr Affair*. She had not realised the book was by me. It was obvious we had a lot more to say to each other. She hoped I would come back to dine with her again very soon.

She did not think it would have been Anthony who ordered the closing of the files. In fact, she favoured taking him into our confidence. 'Not now, but when he has taken over from Churchill as Prime Minister.'

That would make things easier. She felt Anthony had never been happy about the creation of SOE. 'I think he felt it would impinge too much ...'

My next dinner with Irene was on 8 March. She had now read *The Starr Affair* and thought better of her first idea of taking Eden into our confidence. Obviously he could help if he would, but this thing could be awkward for him and she would not take the risk of his trying to suppress us.

De Guélis had been sent some time in 1942 to Morocco, which would have left Eden without a man in SOE. She felt sure he would have wanted to find another to let him know what was going on, but who would the successor have been?

On 16 March I left from Waterloo to arrive at 6.30 the next day in Guernsey, where Frank and Marjorie were waiting for me. Spooner was absolutely fascinated by the French newspaper reports and suspicious of the role played by Bodington. He could not possibly have authorised

Déricourt's maintenance of relations with the Germans. As an emergency thing, if he had just been arrested, yes, till it was possible to get him to England, but not as a long-standing arrangement. Bodington ought not to have been in the field, anyway. Senior officers should not place themselves in jeopardy.

I said it was noticeable Déricourt had not been charged with the betrayal of the 'Prosper' network – it was Culioli who had been charged with that – but with the betrayal of Agazarian. Now Vogt had talked to me about that. Through their control of the radio 'Archambaud' they knew that Bodington intended visiting France by the July moon, and offered him a rendezvous – supposedly with 'Archambaud' – in the flat of a Madame Ferdi-Filipowsky in the rue de Rome. They were all excited by the prospect of this important capture, and were very disappointed when they discovered the man who had walked into the trap was not the important Major Bodington but the unimportant Lieutenant Agazarian. Agazarian had told Vogt Bodington had been afraid to keep the appointment in case it was a trap and so had sent him instead. 'He was not pleased with Bodington.'

Spooner said, 'Militarily, if someone had to be caught it was better it should be Agazarian than Bodington. Bodington was the second in command in F Section and knew the composition of every network in the field. If he had broken under interrogation it would have been the end of F Section. Agazarian knew about nothing except just what he had to do.'

I could not think why, if there was doubt whether 'Archambaud' was free or sitting as bait in a trap, consent had been given to the rendezvous being in a house. It seemed so silly. 'I'd have insisted on its being in the middle of a large field with no bushes people could be hiding behind.'

'Of course,' said Spooner, 'that would have been sensible if it were possible.' But supposing there was some reason unknown to us why someone had to enter that flat, it was better a less important man should be caught. But Bodington should not have been in the field *at all*. Why did he go? Did he have some reason to want to go? Was there perhaps some link between him and Déricourt? A link from before the war? A common interest? Something at which Reuter's man in Paris could have met the airman? Bodington had a great enthusiasm for dirt-track racing. A thing at which one could have picked up an anomalous acquaintance. I can see him now, pacing his sitting-room and then stopping still as he said, 'I'll bet it all goes back to dirt-track racing!'

I flew back on 28 March and on 20 April dined again with Irene at the House of Commons. She had been irked in her researches by constant reference to Miss Atkins. Who was this Miss Atkins?

I told her Spooner told me she came here as Rosenberg, a Romanian citizen, only naturalised towards the end of the war.

'He must be mistaken. That would make her an enemy alien.' was her response. (Romania was an ally of Germany in the war.) But she would ask the Home Office.

She sent me their reply, which confirmed Spooner. Vera Rosenberg first came to this country in 1938 and was naturalised on 27 March 1944. The name of the sponsor was withheld. This surprised Irene very much. She would have thought the responsibility of sponsorship should be public.

I recalled that to get into the Postal Censorship one had to have been born British.

On 16 May I received a letter from the Abbé Paul Guillaume. This was a name familiar to me from Mr Norman's files. He had apparently written of Norman's son as though he was a traitor and Norman had sought legal advice as to whether he had grounds to bring an action for libel on his son's behalf. But the Abbé's letter to me was perfectly friendly. He had read *Madeleine* (in the French translation for he knew no English) and sent me copies of the deposition to the DST of Josef Placke, saying that he and Karl Holdorf (another of Kieffer's men) had impersonated two captured Canadians of the French Section, 'Bertrand' and 'Valentin' (Pickersgill and Macalister) and in their names built up in the northernmost part of France a network apparently British but actually German. Amongst the genuine British agents whom they met in this way was 'Madeleine', who had been instructed through the radio from London to meet them at the Café Colisé. She talked with them without suspicion.

The Abbé said he had further documents he would show me. Also I had a letter from a Madame Fourcade. On 16 May I flew back to Paris. First the Tourets, proprietors of Chez Tutulle. Mme Touret said that Colonel Buckmaster had called and assured them they could not have known the man who came to their restaurant asking for 'Gilbert' was a German. Indeed he had recommended her husband for a medal and they understood he preferred they keep some things to themselves. 'I never dreamed of a German speaking French like that!' She had told him that at this hour 'Gilbert' would be playing cards at the Square Clignancourt. 'Tout au nord.' On the northern boundary of Paris.

I found the house in the Square Clignancourt, but nobody in it who knew anything about this matter.

On the 16th I took the train to Orleans, and from there by a very long taxi ride through the district known as the Sologne, very flat, with silver birch trees, ponds and marshes, to Ardon and the house of its Abbé.

The Abbé was slight of figure but burned with an inward fire. His resources were limited by his inability to speak or read English, but he spoke with the authority of pinpoint knowledge. His housekeeper picked some asparagus from his garden to form a first course to our meal. Across the table he said, 'I suppose Mr Norman says very bad things of me?'

'Yes.'

He understood that a father did not like to read bad things of his son but some of the things done by his son were inexcusable. As to the pact, he thought 'Prosper' would have had the strength to keep to its terms, strictly, but scrupulously, Norman's son had surely gone beyond the terms that must have been agreed by 'Prosper'.

This was really what Vogt said.

The Abbé was very pro-Culioli. He had been arrested after the war by the DST (one of the officers of it who came to arrest him and took part in the initial interrogations was L'Inspecteur Coupaye, whom I had met) and they referred him to the Tribunal Militaire, where the court martial had found him not guilty of treason yet guilty of acts prejudicial to the Resistance. He walked out but demanded a retrial and obtained, at Metz, by five votes to four, a simple verdict of 'not guilty'. The chief witness for the prosecution had been Mona Reimeringer, a French-woman, mistress of the chief of the local Gestapo at Blois, who said she had been present at his interrogations and that he had led a party to the Hôtel Mazagran where they arrested 'Prosper'. The Abbé said Culioli, suffering from a bullet wound in his leg, could hardly have led anyone anywhere; when this point was made by the defence she had said, 'from a stretcher'. The Abbé did not believe her at all. He thought a lot of the faults alleged as Culioli's were those of Norman's son. I said I thought the reputation of Norman's son could have suffered from confusion with the other 'Gilbert' – Déricourt. The Abbé put me up for the night and I returned to Paris the next morning.

On 19 May I saw Madame Aigrain again. What was it she had said at the trial of Déricourt? That she had been handed, by a colleague of hers, Monsieur Andrès, a report on the effect of the Allied bombing of

Courbevois for transmission to England. She had passed this to 'Jeanne Marie', who later told her she had handed it to the man who handled the departures of aircraft for England, to put aboard. After her arrest, Madame Aigrain was shown a photocopy of it by the German who interrogated her.

'Vogt,' I said.

She had not known his name and was surprised he remembered her.

He remembered her, I said, as a totally uncooperative and irritating prisoner. He had noticed she was wearing rings set with small stones that looked to him real and, thinking they might get stolen in prison or concentration camp, had suggested to her that if she handed them to him he would put them in safe custody in her bank for her, if she would tell him where she banked, so that she could reclaim them after the war. She had recoiled, plainly thinking he meant to steal them and he gave up trying to persuade her, thinking to himself, 'She can wear her rings to concentration camp!'

She recalled the incident and said, yes she did think he was trying to steal them.

On 4 June I called on Madame Fourcade; her flat was very elegant, the furniture upholstered in pale blue silk. She showed me the papers Faye had stowed behind the radiator of his cell in Germany. They confirmed the triple attempt at escape. Faye put the blame on 'Madeleine's' failure completely to remove her bar, and Starr's insistence that 'We can't abandon the girl', which delayed them. Madame Fourcade said that, after a period of depression, knowing him caught, she had experienced on that night the surge of immense exhilaration, the conviction that 'He's free' followed suddenly by the clamp down, the immense depression: caught again.

This dream or psychic experience interested me because it paralleled one Vilayat had told me: that he had seen Noor walking along a very narrow strip of roof and knew she was escaping from Gestapo head-quarters, having escaped from the top, over the roofs, only he said pursued by two men trying to catch her. I now knew the two men were her companions. It was, to me, an example of the way in which clair-voyants can see something that is real, yet misinterpret it as they bring it back. I think it happens often because there is a translation in terms of preconception.

She said that whereas the 'Buckmasters' were concerned with action, piling up deposits of arms and munitions parachuted and storing them for usage on D-Day, together with a little immediate sabotage,

L'Alliance, of which she was head, was concerned solely with intelligence, which it gathered and transmitted to London, where her chief was Dansey. Had I met Dansey?

'No.' Indeed I had not heard the name before and did not realise what a figure he was in our Secret Service.

Some people, she said, did not like him but she had always found him easy to get on with. He always gave his attention to anything she said.

She thought the weakness of the Buckmasters lay in their belief that numbers corresponded to strength, as it did in the Army. In intelligence it was the reverse. The ideal number, for any task, was one. Perhaps a helper was needed, but then two were weaker than one, three were weaker than two. The more there were, the more the danger of getting a double among them.

Had she ever heard of a man called Déricourt, code name 'Gilbert', I asked.

'No.' Not until after the war when reports of his trial were in the papers.

The only double agent she had had to deal with was a man called Blah, from Staffordshire. She had a cyanide pill to administer to him, which she did, in his coffee. It must have been too dilute, because instead of instantly dying he rolled about on the floor, moaning, and she had to ring for two men assistants to come and take him away. They later told her they had dropped him from a boat into the Mediterranean.

She was pouring me tea, into a delicate porcelain cup as she delivered this robust account.

It was while I was still in France that I received, sent on from Cornwall, a letter from the lawyer's saying Marie Steward's sister had died and the whole estate was come to me. I had to go back to England anyway, as the play by Duncan Ross was at last to be shown on BBC television and there were things I had to talk to him about.

On 9 June I collected a written statement from Madame Aigrain and later in the day flew home.

With Marie's legacy I could give up teaching. Yet some of my pupils had been interesting people. I recall with sympathy Babu Kapadia, a young Parsee law student who told me so much of the Parsee religion and asked my advice on so many problems, Dr Sousa, a Brazilian Freudian psychoanalyst with whom I argued so many matters, and Jaime Alba, of the Spanish Embassy in London. It was always to his place, in Knightsbridge, I went to give him his lessons. He asked me once to compose something for him. The matter concerned some scheme to which a lot of countries were invited to contribute money. He saw nothing in it for Spain and did not think Spain should contribute money unless she received some advantage. How could he say that? He had just said it, I said. But it needed to be put in polite language so as to sound diplomatic and courteous. Would I express it for him in suitable language for the conference table.

I said: 'I have read this and do not see in it anything for Spain. Spain will not contribute money unless she receives from it some advantage.'

But he couldn't say that, he protested. It would be too blunt, too rude ...

But the next time I saw him, he had, and it had gone down very well. The delegate seated next to him had said afterwards that if everyone expressed themselves so succinctly these conferences would take up less time.

Where are they now, my pupils?

Thirteen

Amongst the communications that reached me following the transmission of the play Duncan Ross made of my book, two gave me especial pleasure. One began, 'Are you *my* Jean Fuller? Overton was a family name.' Could I remember putting a toad on a table laid for luncheon? Yes, it was from Miss Letheren; from her beloved Devonshire. The other was a telephone call from Joan Manchester. She had known Noor only as the sister of Vilayat, it had felt strange to have been so near yet not near ... yes she was all right ... married ... She rang off. But at least she had rung.

My diary shows dinner-time dates with Irene on 20 June, 8 July and 28 July. Not all of these need have been in the House of Commons, for sometimes she would now come to me, but it was in the House that I told her what had happened to 'Antoine'. He – Major Antelme – had been loved by a lady in SOE with whom Irene had put me in contact, and this lady told me he had confided to her his unease concerning his last mission. Though Buckmaster was confident the 'Madeleine' circuit was safe, she said Morel – *de facto* second in command since Bodington had been taken out of SOE to lecture on French politics – shared 'Antoine's' doubts. 'Antoine' had arranged with Morel a phrase which, if he landed to a safe reception, he would have his radio operator include in his first message from the field. If that phrase was not included in the message, Morel was to know he was in German hands. Morel had never found that phrase in any message sent over the circuit of 'Antoine's' radio operator. Now Vogt had told me, during our first series of conversations, that 'Antoine' had, of course, been parachuted to a reception committee composed of Germans, who brought him straight to Avenue Foch. He had, Vogt told me, been in a towering rage, saying he knew he ought not to have jumped and seeming to imply that he had been sent into German hands deliberately. Vogt could have got this wrong, but was firm on the point that 'Antoine' was very angry with those who had sent him.

As I was talking to Irene about this in the House, she gave me a violent kick under the table. Following the direction of her glance, I saw

Eden sitting alone at the table behind and a little to one side of me. He was now Prime Minister, and had just returned from a trip to some part of Africa. He must have heard everything I said. Irene had at first thought of taking him into our confidence, but was then somewhat against the idea, at any rate till we were more sure how the land lay. It would have eased the atmosphere if he had just come over to our table and said, 'I couldn't help overhearing ...' But he had heard the gist of it anyway; and it must have been more meaningful for him than either of us knew until much later.

Now there was a new mystery. Amongst the Abbé's papers was a copy of a deposition by Richard Christmann of the Abwehr in Holland. According to this, the head of the Dutch Section in London had asked for one of its agents,'Anton', to come back from Holland. It was agreed that the French Section should help him on his journey. Christmann himself was to be 'Ainaud' and escort 'Anton'. Everything went according to plan except that at the Square Clignancourt they met Gilbert 'Archambaud' instead of 'Gilbert' the Air Movements Officer. Several meetings were necessary to clear up the misunderstanding. I read this against what I found in Giskes's book, pp. 111 ff. London's demand for the return of one of its agents put him in a fix because the agent was a prisoner; so he replied that the agent would leave for London via Spain, but his plan was for a 'misfortune' to befall the agent in Paris, where he was to be seemingly arrested, in full view of genuine *Résistants*, who would report the sad event to London.

Why, if he was supposed to be heading for Spain, did he have to make contact with 'Gilbert', who arranged the repatriations by air across the Channel?

I wrote to Colonel Giskes, care of his publishers, and asked if I might see him, and if he could put me in touch with Christmann.

He wrote back that he would, and on 21 August I flew to Hamburg.

Colonel Giskes was at the airport to meet me, very chagrined that a German airline had brought me in three hours late. I explained to him the departure from London had been three hours late because, it was explained on the loudspeaker, an essential part had been found to require replacement and to fetch it required three hours. He was even more chagrined. With him was his sister, Frau Eghart, who would see me to my hotel and look after me generally during the times that he was busy, which included tomorrow; for the day after tomorrow I was invited to lunch by his literary agent, Frau Liepmann.

The morrow I spent entirely with his sister. She took me all over Hamburg, showed me the old town, took me to a restaurant on the bridge between the two stretches of water, then out upon the *aussern* Alster in a rowing boat.

The luncheon with Frau Liepmann proved unexpectedly interesting. She was Jewish. She had left during the persecution but had now come back to what she still felt as her home. She had no compunction about handling the rights in Giskes's book. 'Herr Giskes is a gentleman,' she said, 'in so far as it is possible for a spy to be a gentleman. If he had the choice between doing something in a more disgusting way or in a less disgusting, he would choose the less disgusting.' He now worked, she told me, for the Gehlenpolitzei. What was that I asked. 'American Intelligence.' They were all in it, the important Abwehr men. All excited and eager. It was the new thing.

It was at five that afternoon that Giskes saw me, in his place. With him he had Herr Huntermann, who had been in charge of the radio game, and would act as interpreter between us – Giskes's English being of the same order as my German: we could each read the other's language printed, but were without experience in trying to converse in it. After a little time, however, Giskes began to understand my English, and we progressed to the point where we did not mind making ourselves ridiculous by the mistakes we made in forming sentences in each other's language.

We talked a little about Nordpol. He said he had feared that because the messages from the captured agents were all composed by himself, the similarity of style would become suspicious to the people in London; so to make them individual he had created personalities for them. One he made timid, fearful of carrying out instructions that seemed to him dangerous; one he made fearless to the point of recklessness, eager to do impossibly dangerous things; and one he endowed with moral scruples concerning every task assigned to him. He hoped their handler in London would get to recognise the tone and say, 'Yes, this is our man.' He had observed them in captivity, of course, and tried in conversation to form some impression of their real personalities and then exaggerated them. 'I tried to imagine them at liberty.' He was deeply distressed and ashamed to learn that after they had been taken out of his hands in the last stage of the war they had all been murdered. (It sounded like what had happened to the Prosper group after they were taken out of the hands of Kieffer.)

I said that what amazed us in England was that in a country so highly civilised as Germany there could have occurred the mass murder of the Jews without the ordinary people apparently objecting.

Giskes' sister cut in. They did not know, she said. They heard rumours but did not believe them. *She* heard rumours but did not believe them. On the corner of the street in which she lived was a Jewish family. They were all taken away. Was it possible they had done something against the law despite seeming so respectable? It must be some mistake. 'They will be back,' she had assured other people in the street who were disturbed by their disappearance. 'They'll be back. You'll see.' But they did not come back. Ever.

Giskes referred to the concentration camps established by the British in South Africa during the Boer War. Probably they were not as bad.

That seemed to me a double-edged remark. I had not heard that we had established concentration camps in South Africa during the Boer War, so I did not reply, but made a mental note to check on this when I got home. (Yes, we did, and they were the object of criticism.) But it was hardly like putting people in gas-chambers that must have been purpose built.

Coming back to Nordpol, Giskes said it still amazed him that the British had been deceived. Now that we were both on the same side, he would be more comfortable supposing the British were cleverer than that. Because, in the next war, we were allies. I felt he was geared to playing a role in it. He did not mention America and I did not give Frau Liepmann away.

I had told him in my letter that mine was a purely private inquiry and that I did not belong to the Intelligence Service, but I could tell he was uneasy. 'How many people know that you are here?' he asked, '*Which* people?'

'My mother, Field Marshal Sir Claude Auchinleck, Colonel Frank Spooner – head of the training school at Beaulieu, and before that Indian Army – Brigadier Desmond Young, Dame Irene Ward – a Conservative MP – Le Commandant Mercier of Le Tribunal Militaire Permanent de Paris, and Vogt.'

I thought this might sound a rather odd bunch of confidants, but at any rate not like Communists, which would be what, as an American agent now, he would be on the look out for. Indeed, it seemed to reassure him.

I was, I said, autonomous. I did not represent anyone or anything. I had no one above me. I was just *me*.

He decided to trust me.

His instructions to his two men Bodens and Christmann were to go to Paris and make contact with the Resistance group there as instructed by London, and pretend to them to be wanting to leave France for England through Spain; but they were first to have arranged with the Abwehr in Paris to come and 'arrest' Bodens before the eyes of these *Résistants*, who would then radio the news to London.

Coming to 'Gilbert', he asked if he was paid by the Germans?

I had never thought about it and did not know. 'Is it important?'

'Yes. It is important.'

He would not wish to give away anybody who had acted from disinterested love for Germany. If I could show a receipt for money …

I thought it unlikely such services were signed for.

Could Vogt remember any words spoken by Kieffer showing the regard in which he held 'Gilbert'?

Kieffer had warned, 'He betrays the English and his own compatriots to us; he would betray us to them the day it suited him better.'

Giskes looked interrogatively to Huntermann, who nodded. 'It's enough,' Giskes said to me, 'I will give you the means to contact Christmann.'

He would give me Bodens's address – he did not have Christmann's – but Bodens was in touch with Christmann. Bodens might tell me little, but what he said could be trusted. Christmann, he should warn me, he had found, as an agent, marvellous at missions involving impersonations, but not reliable in his reports. It got to the point that if Christmann said that when something happened he was in such and such a street, you would feel sure of only one thing – that he wasn't.

'He is our enemy,' Huntermann said unexpectedly. Giskes's silence suggested he agreed with that.

As we were finishing, Huntermann said it came back to him that the message from London said 'Anton' was to contact 'Marcel'. After a considerable silence, he added, 'and "Gilbert".'

Giskes asked, 'Has Herr Huntermann told you anything?'

'Yes.'

'Have I told you anything?'

I gave him the answer he so transparently wanted, 'No.'

It would be better, he said, if I did not mention to Christmann that I had seen him.

This made me uneasy. I did not know what I was getting into. I took a train early next morning to Bonn, and posted cards to my Mother and a number of people, including Mercier, saying where I was. I had the feeling that in case I disappeared they should know from what point to follow my track. Then I found Bodens's house. He and his wife greeted me. He was fair, with rather high colour, rosy cheeks. I asked if Giskes had explained the matter to him.

No; he waited to hear how he could help me. As I told the story of the mix-up between the two 'Gilberts' at the Square Clignancourt, as I had gathered it from Christmann's deposition to the French, I saw his face cloud. Though he was very polite and his wife asked me to stay to dinner, he did not like this at all. It was Christmann, not he, who had entered the flat at the Square Clignancourt. Christmann, not he, could tell me what had happened there. He had waited at the foot of the stairs. I said I had understood from Colonel Giskes that his mission was apparently to be arrested in front of *Résistants*; the arrest had to be visible.

'Es war sichtbar,' he said, in a very peculiar tone.

He asked, 'Will you tell Christmann you come from Giskes?'

Colonel Giskes had thought it would be better I should not. That made it difficult.

Yes, it was difficult, he said. Then, as though he had thought of the solution, he wrote a letter, put it in an envelope addressed to Christmann, and handed it to me. The address he had written on the envelope was in Frankfurt, and the next morning I took an early train there. On arrival I again sent postcards to everybody including Mercier saying I was in Frankfurt.

I bought a map and found the address, but the name Christmann was not against any of the doorbells. When some people came out, I asked them in my halting German if Christmann lived there. They said all the numbers in the street had been changed and that I should try twelve houses along – and that was the beginning of a search that occupied me the whole day as I was constantly set on a new trail. I did find a violinist by the name of Christmann, but he was obviously not the right one. In the end I sent a telegram to Vogt saying I would be arriving ahead of schedule.

He was not on the platform to meet me, and there was no light in the window of his flat. I took a room in a hotel opposite. In the morning the mystery was resolved. He was on annual leave from his bank and he and Lily had been on all-day excursion. They had called at the hotel guessing I might be there, but being told I had gone to bed decided not to disturb me before the morning.

But he did not at all like the story I had told him. What was written within that sealed letter? Would I let him steam it open? 'I could do it the way we did it at Avenue Foch. It was never noticed.'

I said I would feel uncomfortable presenting a letter that had been steamed open. 'I don't suppose it says "KILL BEARER".'

He smiled faintly, but still was worried for me. He did not like the printed address of the sender. 'Gesammelt Deutsch.' It did not, he said, mean anything.

'They are both German words,' I said.

'But put together like that they do not mean anything. This is not something real.'

Then suddenly, as he paced the floor, he stopped. 'Yes, it does. Espionage headquarters. That is what it means.' Germany was divided into two halves, dominated respectively by the Western Allies in the west and the Soviet Union in the east. Anything that talked about gathering Germans together meant liaison between the two halves, espionage from the one half into the other ... He had known there must be something like that, but not what it was called or where it was headquartered. What had I fallen into? He did not like it at all.

I asked him to ring Bodens and say I had been unable to find Christmann and ask again for the correct address.

He was reluctant to make contact with anybody in an organisation he did not want to be in contact with. He told me – as he had indeed at our first meeting – that the French had solicited him and he had turned them down. Turning to his wife, he said, 'I could have got you out of prison a year earlier.' He had said to the officer who tried to recruit him, 'You dare ask me to work for the French while you are holding my wife in prison!' and was answered 'That could be adjusted', meaning she would be let out if he agreed. But he had thought she would not want to be rescued at the price of his working for the French. (Lily, hearing this, nodded.) 'And if the British came and asked me, I would give them the same answer. No.' (This also he had said at our first meeting.) The Americans or any others. Actually they had not solicited him but he would, if they did, still say no. He had worked for Kieffer. Full stop. He was not going to be reimmersed in secret intelligence, not for any money, not for anything.

But he did in the end take the telephone and ask for further directions for me. He was not on the line for more than a couple of minutes, then he hung up and said to me, 'He says you should have asked for Fräulein Rother.'

Indeed I remembered that he had said Christmann was living with a Fräulein Rother, but he had not put her name on the envelope and I had not thought to look for it amongst those by the doorbells. I handed Vogt a draft of my book as it had progressed so far, then took the 1.41 from Freiburg to Frankfurt, and shortly after 3.00 found myself back at that door where my searches of the day before had started. Indeed I did find one of the bells marked 'ROTHER', rang it and a young girl appeared. Yes, Herr Christmann was with her. She took me into her flat and indicated a man who lay in the bed. 'Herr Christmann.'

As he leaned out to offer his hand, I felt as if I had met him before, as one of a group of theatricals on a station platform on a Sunday morning waiting for the train to take them to the town where they would play next week. This was impossible, yet there was in his manner something of the theatrical.

He had, he explained, been knocked down by a car whilst crossing the street and was confined to bed by his injuries. Eva, his fiancée, was looking after him.

After some initial skirmishing, I referred to the deposition he had made to the French concerning his meeting with the *Résistants* at the Square Clignancourt.

He had not actually gone in, he surprised me by saying. It was Bodens who went in. He waited outside. This wasn't what Bodens had told me.

When I said 'Gilbert', whom did I mean, he asked.

Taking the bull by the horns, I said 'Both of them.'

He looked at me very narrowly.

There was a very complicated background to this incident, he said. He would have to give himself a little time to consider. Then after a silence, he exclaimed, 'I can do it. It is detachable.'

The instructions from London were for him to meet 'Gilbert' who arranged the air passages to England; instead he had been put in touch with Gilbert 'Archambaud' by mistake. The latter had said he would get in touch with the other one and it was agreed they should all meet, about a fortnight later, at the Café Capucines. There, 'Anton' (Bodens) had been arrested, by the Sicherheitsdienst. He, Christmann, had had to go to the Avenue Foch to try to get him out of his predicament and had a very nasty job in trying to explain.

This was obviously not at all what Giskes had talked to me about, not a prearranged mock-arrest by their colleagues in the Abwehr, but a real one, by the SD, which had taken them both by surprise. Now I understood the peculiar tone in which Bodens had said, 'Es war sicht-bar.'

But if the confusion to some extent tallied with Huntermann's words, it did not at all with anything Colonel Giskes had said. They should have been pretending to be making for Spain. Why meet the man who arranged cross-Channel flights?

He needed to visit London, Christmann said. Just to talk with his opposite number there about some gemstones. He had in these days been smuggling and there had arisen some point of dispute, which could be settled if he went over and spoke with this man face to face. It would not have taken long ...

So that was it. They had been pursuing some personal activity unknown to Giskes.

'But you have a letter for me,' he said.

Reluctantly, I handed over the letter from Bodens.

He opened it. 'He has a nice way of showing his sympathy. He says it will teach me not to cross the road without looking where I am going. Ah! You have seen Giskes!'

So that was what Bodens had done. He had put in a warning. I have dealt with Christmann's statement in my books *Double Webs* and *Déricourt: The Chequered Spy* in greater detail than I need here. The essential was that one of the party whom he and Bodens surprised at the Square Clignancourt, 'Marcel' (code-name of Jack Agazarian), undertook to see 'Gilbert' the Air Movements Officer and tell him these two *Résistants* from Holland (as the *Résistants* of the 'Prosper' group playing cards at the Square Clignancourt supposed them to be) were all going to meet again in a fortnight's time at the Café Capucines and begged him to be there; and that he did not come. It suddenly occurred to Christmann, so he said, that this 'Gilbert' the Air Movements Officer might be a German agent.

How he passed from this to the Battle of Arnhem I cannot remember, but next he was telling me how he had accidentally come to learn that there was to be a big landing at Arnhem of British airborne troops, and he had driven all through the night, pressing his foot down on the accelerator of his little car to do all it could, till at last he reached the head-quarters of the German military and gave them the information usefully in advance. And now he felt the responsibility for all the deaths in that action lying heavily on his conscience. He stretched out his arm as though asking for forgiveness.

I took a train which pulled out of Frankfurt just before midnight, and had a sleeper, but did not sleep. If true, this about Arnhem was a very big story; but was it true?

I arrived back in Hamburg at 8.37 a.m. and after breakfast at my hotel slept at last. It was for luncheon on the following day, Wednesday 31 August, that Colonel Giskes came to collect me in his car and take me to a restaurant where we lunched at one of the tables on the lawn running down to the shining water of the Alster. When I told him what Christmann had told me about the arrest of Bodens by the SD he kept thinking I was making a mistake. He tried to correct me, 'By the Abwehr, by our colleagues at the Hotel Lutecia, as arranged.' No it wasn't, I had to tell him. It was by the SD from the Avenue Foch. It was not arranged. Bodens was taken to the Avenue Foch and Christmann had to follow to the Avenue Foch to talk and get him out of it. Giskes was very much disturbed by this revelation, and more so when I told him it was the man who arranged the Lysander passages across the Channel whom Christmann wanted to meet, because he wanted to go to London. To reassure him it was not to give away Nordpol, I hastened to add he had said he would have come back. It was only to talk about some matter connected with gem smuggling that he wanted to go to London.

Giskes was tight-lipped. 'And I learn this from an Englishwoman!' It was true he had never told them to make out reports. He just assumed, when they returned, that they had done what he told them. 'If he had been to England, and he came back, and I found out, I would have sent him for trial before court martial.'

When I told him of Christmann's claim to have given the Germans the information concerning the landings at Arnhem, he said, 'I can neither confirm nor refute it.' Something had slipped through his fingers those last days. If it was not by the purest of bad luck for the English that they chose to land just where the German military force was massed, the information should have passed through him. But his *Vertrauensmann* (trusty) Lindemans, known as King Kong, had ceased to communicate and was probably trying to reingratiate himself with the Dutch *Résistants*, hiding from them his long relations with the Germans; he could have bypassed him and given the information to the military direct. The same with Christmann. 'He could have bypassed me.'

He drove me to the airport. There I caught a plane for Amsterdam, changed there for London and was home by midnight.

From Christmann I received a typescript in German with a request to translate it into English and find a publisher for it. Starting with the unconditional surrender of Germany, it was the story of the year during which he eluded capture. As capital to fall back on, he bought a large sapphire from a Jew in Amsterdam, and decided to hide not in Germany, where he would be looked for, but in France. He reached the Mediterranean coast, and took the sapphire into a jeweller's in Nice to ask how much it was worth. 'Nothing,' said the jeweller. 'It's a fake.' As he was leaving, two toughs assailed him, saying they knew who he was and would denounce him unless he paid for their silence. He replied, 'I haven't much money on me. But I have something else.' He gave them the sapphire, and they made off with it.

Although it contained a few good stories, I returned it to him saying it was an awkward length, too long to go into a magazine but too short to be produced as a book. There might be a book in his whole life story but it would have to be true. To this there came no reply.

The party at Auchinleck's on 27 October was Desmond Young's idea: Spooner, Irene, me, himself and the Field Marshal, to assemble in the Field Marshal's flat at 5.30. Desmond Young arrived with the news that Spooner had rung to say he was fog-bound in Guernsey, no aircraft or ship leaving, but he would telephone his contribution to us later in the evening. After preliminary drinks we all crossed the road to a small restaurant where we dined. I noticed Desmond Young picked up the bill. Then we all trooped back into Auchinleck's flat for coffee and serious conversation. Spooner rang. As Auchinleck was rather deaf, Irene took the instrument and repeated what Spooner said, one sentence at a time, in her clear voice which Auchinleck could understand. Spooner's contribution concerned SOE's finance and method of making payments. 'I never saw a cheque or a banker's order during the whole of the time I served in it.' Having been accustomed, in the Army, to see his pay appear as credits in his monthly bank statements, he found it surprising to receive it in banknotes. Some people brought suitcases in which to take theirs away.

I picked out, from all that had been said to me by diverse people, instances of what seemed to me peculiar behaviour.

Auchinleck said to me, 'The evidence pulls both ways. To Germany and to Russia. Which is it?'

I said to him, 'There were two wars going on. The open one, in which *you* played a part, and underneath that a hidden, non-military one, a struggle between the Western powers and Soviet Union for the domination of Europe after the war ended.'

Irene said, 'It's like a jellyfish. Amorphous.' She had earlier said the same at my flat.

Our watches told us it was two o'clock. We had talked for nearly eight hours.

Fourteen

On the files lent me by Mr Norman I found letters from Madame Guépin, *liquidatrice* of the 'Prosper' network, and I wrote to him asking if he could introduce me to her. He agreed and I flew to Paris on 19 November 1955. At my hotel I found welcoming messages from Starr and Mercier.

The next morning I called at the Tribunal Militaire and asked for Le Commandant Mercier. We arranged to meet the following morning.

At our meeting I showed him the statement Christmann had made for me. I hoped he would not make trouble for Christmann now Christmann had admitted the one he made for the French was partly false. No, he said, but what made me think the one he had made for me was true? All I could say was that it was different.

We talked about Giskes. He said that after the war there had been keen competition among the Allies to sign up those members of the Abwehr and Sicherdeitsdienst whom they had not hanged. Vogt, for instance, he would have supposed to have been solicited by the British. 'If we think a man is working for the English – the English are our friends and we do not trouble him.'

I said that Vogt told me he was solicited only by the French, and refused them. The British never solicited him and if they did he would refuse them too, or any other country's intelligence service.

Mercier gave a rueful smile. 'Marianne and John the Bull! It would be very funny if, because each suspects the other, Vogt were to be left in peace.'

The next day, 24 November, I saw Madame Aigrain again to show her the English text I had made from her statement.

Then I met Mr Norman. From the Gare St Lazare we took a train packed solid with home-bound commuters, for Gisors and Madame Guépin. She had not only been the *compagnon* of George Darling but, on a number of occasions, hostess to 'Prosper'. He had come there with 'Denise', just before his last trip to England, and had warned that 'Gilbert' was not to be trusted. At which 'Denise' exclaimed, 'That's what I have been telling you for months.'

Which 'Gilbert' did he mean? Madame Guépin had always supposed 'Archambaud' – Gilbert Norman, hence her intense embarrassment at having to tell Mr Norman. Or did he mean Déricourt? The difficulty about its being Déricourt is that Madame Guépin had never heard of Déricourt. The difficulty about its being 'Archambaud' is that a number of people express themselves certain he and 'Denise' were lovers. To complicate matters still further, Elizabeth Nicholas, who was writing on SOE girls, had told me she understood from 'Denise''s sister, Madame Arend, whom she had visited, that 'Denise' was lesbian. I give up trying to understand ... After her arrest, 'Denise' had managed to speak a few words to her as they passed in a passage in Fresnes, 'C'est Gilbert qui nous a tous vendu.' ('It is Gilbert who sold us all',) which she took to refer to the only Gilbert she knew, though in a note she had managed to get smuggled from the prison to her sister, she had said, 'Gilbert me protège' ('Gilbert is protecting me'). This could only have referred to 'Archambaud' – as giving his evidence to the Germans in such a way as to minimise her responsibility.

Madame Guépin suggested I should see a Madame Lebras who had been a prisoner in Fresnes and had shared a cell with Odette Churchill.

'Were her toenails pulled out?' I asked.

'No.' She remembered Odette being fetched from the cell and returning to it saying she had been at the Avenue Foch for interrogation. She was walking as usual, and when she took off her shoes and stockings to go to bed, Madame Lebras detected no sign of injury. 'She did say "qu'on lui avait tappé sur les pieds" or "contre les pieds", whatever that meant, but she reported it more in a tone of slight irritation than after the manner of one who had suffered appalling agonies. After having seen the film *Odette*, Madame Lebras said accusingly to Odette as they were coming out of the cinema 'Whatever made you say your toenails were pulled out?' and Odette replied, 'They were. You didn't know.' (What particularly annoyed Madame Lebras, incidentally, about Tickell's book *Odette* was the misrepresentation of Rosie Scherer, the wardress at Fresnes, as a horror. It was Rosie who had made life in the prison bearable. For instance, learning that Madame Lebras had pet dogs and cats whom her arrest left abandoned Rosie made it her responsibility to arrange for them to be looked after.)

Madame Lebras made the point that she and Madame Astier, the other cell-mate, benefited from sharing the cell with Odette, it meant sharing her privileges. One of them was that after the general 'Lights out' the light in their cell was not extinguished, so all three could continue to read.

Madame Astier now worked in the police station at Versailles, if I liked to see her.

Before doing so I saw Yeo-Thomas again, Madame Aigrain and the Tourets; and on 26 November I went to the Hotel Mazagran, where 'Prosper' had been arrested. The proprietress, Madame Fèvre, took me up to room 15. 'The Germans went up past me and waited for him here, and seized him when he re-entered.'

I also received a letter from Marjorie Spooner saying I might find it interesting to talk to the Baron de Malval, with whom she had exchanged some words some years ago. She did not make plain what she expected him to talk to me about, and this must have made me, when I called at the address she gave me, sound a bit mysterious. Then suddenly something seemed to click and he said with tremendous excitement, 'If it is to DESTROY THOSE TWO I will do anything.' By 'those two' he meant Peter and Odette Churchill. It was because of the way they had hogged all the publicity, with their books and that film, making people think they were the big stars of the Resistance! Why was it always those two whom the public heard about and never about the many who had done as much or more, at enormous risk to themselves, without asking anything for it? They were passed over, forgotten. Besides, he added with particular feeling, it was Peter Churchill he had to thank for the loss of his eye.

He was the owner of the Villa Isabelle in Cannes, and had played host to a number of British agents. When he was eventually arrested he was shown a message which had been found in one of the pockets of Peter Churchill, who had been arrested earlier. It read: 'The seven felucca passengers to proceed directly to the Villa Isabelle.' That must have been the transcript of a message radioed to him right back at the time when a party of French Section agents, which included Odette, arrived by felucca. Churchill should have destroyed it immediately. De Malval had had Odette taken in by his friend Suzanne. Later they had both moved on elsewhere. Peter Churchill had returned to England and parachuted back again still with that message in his pocket. It was the fault not only of Churchill for retaining it, oblivious he was doing so, but of the people in London for not going through his pockets to make sure he was not carrying anything incriminating before re-parachuting. From the beginning of November, when those felucca passengers landed, until mid-April when he was arrested – 2 November until 5

April – he had carried that paper in his pocket and it was the Germans who found it. They came straight to the Villa Isabelle and arrested de Malval on a charge of having received seven British agents arriving by felucca. And he came out of it alive but less one eye.

Was it at the Avenue Foch he lost it?

No. He never reached Avenue Foch. It was at a place on the way. He tried to escape, there was a scuffle and something came up and hit him in the eye. It was an accident, but still the eye was gone.

Had he been in a concentration camp? How had he come out of it with his life?

'I bought myself out,' he said with admirable frankness. He offered the German who seemed to be in charge some shares in a coalmine; whereupon the German decided his arrest had been a mistake and he was allowed just to walk out and return to the Villa Isabelle. 'Being a Baron helped, too ...'

But if ever he met Peter Churchill he would tell him it was his fault he had lost one of his eyes.

I had to confess that my purpose in calling had not been to 'destroy those two'; the most I could do to help his cause was to tell him that Odette's toenails had not been pulled out. But could he explain to me what it would mean if somebody's name was spelt usually Déricourt but sometimes d'Héricourt?

He said d'Héricourt was the name of one of 'les deux cents familles', the true aristocracy of France. Déricourt did not exist.

I felt sure Déricourt was the right spelling, though I had seen d'Héricourt in some papers.

'A bastard!' de Malval exclaimed. 'Somebody who knows he has the right by the blood though not through wedlock.' He suggested I see a Madame Odette Fabius, a friend of his friend Suzanne. Also Francis Basin, alias 'Olive'.

I found Madame Fabius in her office, very chic. She had been not in the French Section but in L'Alliance, therefore working, under Madame Fourcade, for the Intelligence Service. Her cover name had been 'Biche' (meaning nanny-goat) and she had been awarded a Croix de Guerre. After capture she had been sent to Ravensbruck. No, she had not seen Odette there, or heard anything about her. She was the only woman to have escaped from Ravensbruck, though she was recaptured, and on recapture flogged with a leather whip, 'I'll strip off for anybody who wants to see *my* scars,' she said.

She looked so dainty, with a faint whiff of eau de Cologne, I found it difficult to associate her with the punishment meted out to sailors tied to the mainmast in the bad old days of Captain Bligh and the Mutiny on the *Bounty*.

'I don't complain,' she said. 'As I am Jewish, and as I worked for the Intelligence Service, I am lucky to be alive.'

But, passingly, she had referred to 'Carte'; that was the code-name of André Girard, chief of an important independent French network with which French Section agents had to do, not always amicably. Since the publication of *The Starr Affair* I had received a number of letters from him, from New York. He remembered Starr well from the days of Starr's first mission. He sent him his regards and said the pains he took to alert London that certain radio circuits were German-controlled were fruitless because it was already known in London. He added cryptically that from high up it was not welcomed that the Resistance would 'not be too strong at the end' and so the game was kept up 'even at the cost of many lives'. He could not be more explicit on paper. I mentioned this to Madame Fabius. She knew him. What did he mean?

'Communism,' she said. He feared the Communists would take over Europe after the war, feared their presence in all the existing Resistance organisations and was trying to build up something of his own, together with officers of the regular French Army who would certainly not be Communists.

On the following day I saw Francis Basin, now in a wheelchair. He assured me he was wholly French though baptised with the English spelling of his name. He had been 'Olive', the organiser of 'Urchin', one of the earliest of the SOE networks, and of course had had some relations with 'Carte' though they were not always in agreement. About 'Gilbert' Déricourt: 'My position is very delicate. I owe my life to him.' He had been on the run from the Gestapo, together with Claudette Menessier, who had made possible his escape from prison. They had heard that there was this man who arranged air passages to England and they managed to meet him and threw themselves on his mercy. He had no instructions from London to take them. They could not give him the required passwords; only plead. The Gestapo were on their heels. They would be seized unless he took them. He had to make a decision on his own. He made it in their favour. OK, he would board them. He told the others to move up to make room for two more. Now Basin realised it was probably through some arrangement with the Germans he was able to arrange these flights so regularly, but he had taken on his own responsibility to save their lives.

In the afternoon of the same day I took the train out to Versailles and found my way to the Préfecture de Police. Madame Astier received me in her office there. Yes, she had shared a cell in Fresnes with Laure Lebras and Odette Churchill. The latter was very much the pampered pet of their gaolers because of her supposed relationship to Winston Churchill. It was unthinkable that she would have been submitted to any physical violence. The privileges allowed to her were to some extent shared by her two cell-mates.

The next day, 3 December, I flew back to London.

After Christmas, something odd. Madame Guépin gave me the address of Jacques Weil. I had first heard of Jacques Weil from Vogt. After his arrest, he had asked to be allowed to speak with 'Archambaud'. Now 'Archambaud' had made an attempt to escape. Taken down the stairs to the van that was to take him to Fresnes, he had run. He was followed by shots and brought down, and so was now not in Fresnes but in the Hôpital de la Pitié. Vogt conducted Weil to the Hôpital de la Pitié, where they saw 'Archambaud' in bed, and Weil told him that he had, prior to his arrest, denounced him to London as a traitor. Now that he, too, was a prisoner, he realised he had been mistaken and asked his forgiveness.

I thought it would be nice to have a statement about this in Weil's own words, so I wrote to him, telling him what Vogt had told me and asking him to confirm.

His response was to arrive at my flat in London, plus the unexplained presence of a friend (always a bad sign, Elizabeth Nicholas agreed with me). I greeted Weil with 'Vogt writes to me that he is very pleased to learn you are alive, and asks me to give you his best regards.'

He said, a bit grumpily, he was lucky to be alive. We talked in a general sense about I cannot remember what and I was handing them their second cups of coffee when he said, 'I was never arrested.'

I could hardly believe my ears. 'Then you never knew Vogt?'

No answer.

If he was not the man of whom Vogt had talked to me, why had he not said so when answering my letter, or when he came in and I gave him Vogt's regards.

It was the following April that somebody told me that Déricourt's radio operator, Arthur Watt, was still alive and gave me his address. This was important, and on 22 April I flew back to Paris.

The next day I saw Watt, in his office. He was of below average height, straightforward but reserved.

Déricourt was a controversial figure,' he said. Some people were for him, others against.

'Did you *like* him?' I asked.

For the first time, he was direct: 'Yes. I liked him.'

And he gave me some superficial information. It was on the night of 16/17 October 1943 he had been parachuted to reception by Déricourt, to work as his radio operator. With them worked also 'Marc' – Rémy Clément – Déricourt's assistant. His own code-name was 'Geoffroi'.

I flew home the next day.

And the rest of the year I spent mainly at my typewriter. Regular dinners with Irene. Increased contact with Elizabeth Nicholas. I formed part of Dr Corona Trew's Secret Doctrine Study Group. Then, at the beginning of December, my great-uncle John died. Mother, Hector and I took the night train from St Pancras, arriving at Edinburgh at 6.40. My Great-Aunt Grace was not at the cremation. We went afterwards to a place where she had been taken to be looked after. Indeed, she was in bed. As we were all three taking our leave, she signalled to me to come back, by myself. 'I want to be christened,' she said.

I was surprised and puzzled.

She insisted. She wanted to be taken into the Church.

I thought she had always been in it.

'Only kirk,' she said. Plainly she thought of this as inferior.

'You want to be baptised into the Church of England?' I asked, to be sure.

'Yes.'

I was sure the Church of England would be very happy to receive a convert. I would write to the Church and ask for her to be visited and baptised.

'I want to be with John on Christmas Day,' she said.

So it was not exactly a surprise when I received a letter from a lawyer saying my great-aunt Grace Laing had passed away. What was a surprise was that, apart from a particular legacy to a woman neighbour who had become something of a home help, she had left everything to me.

It was not a great deal, just some War Loan, but on top of the legacy from Marie, I had never expected to receive more from anywhere. My lawyer, Mr Franklin, said War Loan was miserable stuff, I should sell it and put it into something with a better yield. I had been reading a book on diamond smuggling and it came to me that if illegal diamonds were worth so very much, perhaps even legal ones were worth something. So I said, 'Put it into De Beers Consolidated Diamond Mines.'

That was a bit more adventurous than Mr Franklin had had in mind. But he gave me an introduction to his stockbroker, who bought them for me. And they went up ...

I returned from Edinburgh on 9 December 1956 and on the 11th received a letter from de Malval saying he was coming over. On the 15th he was having tea with me. He wanted to see Irene to talk about Odette. 'Does Dame Irene realise what sort of woman she is?' When I told Irene she said he had better come to dinner with her at the House of Commons. She told me afterwards she had found him sweet but he had tried to pay the bill for the dinner which just went on her account. 'He's not used to being entertained by women.'

Déricourt had all this time been supposed to be in Indo-China (though his address remained constantly in the Paris telephone directory, the flat was thought to be occupied only by his wife); but suddenly the French newspapers reported that 'un gros Armagniac' aircraft had crash-landed at Orly. The casualties were only two, thanks to the skill of the pilot, Henri Déricourt. So he was back and I ought to give him the chance to comment on the accusations against him featuring in my book. He had apparently been taken to hospital for treatment of his injuries, so decency required the interval of a few weeks.

In the meantime George Adam of the *Figaro Littéraire* offered to contact Bodington for me. He told him he was expecting to translate a book dealing with the downfall of the 'Prosper' network. Bodington said, 'Oh I don't like that at all', but agreed to come to see Adam at six o'clock the next day. However, though Adam waited in for him the whole evening, he did not come or ring or write to excuse himself.

Adam then rang Déricourt's number and found he had Déricourt on the line. He had read my *Madeleine* and, yes, he would come to meet me, at Adam's house, at two o'clock on 7 May 1957.

I flew over on the day before. Adam met me at the airport and drove me to the Terrace Hotel, on the Buttes de Montmartre, to be conveniently near his house in the rue Villa Léandre.

Déricourt was punctual, a shortish stocky figure, with blue eyes and fair hair that curled upwards. I focused on the point that whereas he had stated at his court martial that it was in June he had been arrested and obliged to feign to work for the Germans, I had a statement, from Christmann, from which it was obvious he had been in contact with the Germans in mid-May, a month earlier than he had told the court.

His reply was unexpected and disarming: since the arrest was fictitious it could only have a fictitious date.

But he was admitting to perjury, I pointed out.

'Perjury means lying to God. That is impossible. God knows all.' He did not feel embarrassed at making up a bit of a story for the panel of judges. He invited me to consider the historical plays of Shakespeare. They were not true in all the details. A scene would be put in here or there to make a better play, though without the general picture being falsified. 'To make better theatre! The courtroom was my theatre.' He had provided a simplified version of what had happened, one with simplified scenes, easier to follow than would have been an attempt to render everything exactly. 'The important thing was to be acquitted.' He had provided a basis on which it would be easy for them to acquit.

He said he had been, in a sense, a prisoner of a situation. He had known Boemelburg before the war. Karl Boemelburg of the Gestapo, was Kieffer's direct chief at 82 Avenue Foch.

At dirt-track racing. Bodington also watched dirt-track racing, and sometimes afterwards they would go to a café near the stadium.

I remembered Spooner saying, 'I'll bet it all goes back to dirt-track racing.'

And sometimes he got invited to the Boemelburgs' house, in Neuilly.

I told him the substance of Vogt's statement: that he was BOE 48, later just 'Gilbert', who handed over the mail.

He denied all of it.

I said, 'I know it is true.'

He said, giving me a very deep look, 'It is true for *you*.' Though this could be understood in different senses, just for an instant it was as though it was in the shadows of the pillars of Karnak I had had conversation with him before; then the impression was gone, but our argument had changed level.

I said what was important to me in the story was why Bodington protected him. 'That is the nub of the question.'

'Yes,' he said simply. 'That is the nub of the question.'

I said the question for me was whether it came from higher up; because I felt that, wherever it came from, it was to prevent his disclosing things in court that the protector did not want known. How high up did it go?

I could not draw him on this. He was protecting Bodington.

Finally he presented a solution, 'Call me Gilbert and say all the bad things you like.' He just didn't want his real name in the book. That people who had been agents would know who was meant did not matter to him; it was just his colleagues on the airline or the baker from whom he bought his bread to whom he did not want to have to explain.

We had talked for almost six hours and were exhausted. I said I would type out a summary of our conversations and show it to him.

He said he would be free at 10 a.m. on the next morning but one.

'I won't,' said Adam, 'but you are grown up enough to talk without me.'

That night and the following day I typed out what we had said to each other. I also wrote to Mercier, who was now in Algeria for some time.

On 9 May Déricourt was at my hotel punctually at ten. I had found us a secluded table in the lounge but he said, 'We have nothing secret to talk about,' and took one in the window, from which he watched the people coming in and out.

He said that when Adam had first rung him, talking about a book, he had thought it was blackmail. He expected to be asked to pay compensation for the book's being put aside. He had had a lot of intending blackmailers, but had his way of getting rid of them. He simply told them he would kill them, and they did not risk pressing further.

He had been acquitted, I said, and could not be re-arrested.

'That's true,' he said, 'but I can be assassinated.'

I thought he meant by the Foreign Office, if he talked too much, but he laughed. Not by them no, but there were two people with whom he had 'a balance of silences'. He explained what he meant. 'They know some bad things about me, and I know some bad things about them. The bad things we know about each other are of equal weight. Therefore there is balance of silences.' It all went back to 1941, in Marseilles. Later he named these two persons, the brothers de Vomécourt, Philippe and Pierre. If they thought he was talking to me, the balance was broken and they might take measures to stop him.

Did he really mean murder him?

He made a face. They were not bold types. No, he did not think they would have the daring. 'But, if your book comes out, they will do something, something unpleasing to me and perhaps to you. You do not know what you are putting your finger into.'

That was true enough.

Yes, it was to keep an eye on the door in case those two people should enter that he wanted to sit near the window.

We talked a little about 'Madeleine' and I mentioned that her father had been a Sufi teacher.

'I have ideas about religion,' he said.

'You have a religion?'

'Yes.'

'May I ask what it is?'

'Christian Science.'

This was unexpected but provided a basis from which we could talk at a different level. Somehow we came to be talking of *The Papyrus of Ani*, with special reference to the tableau depicting the weighing of the heart by Anubis against the feather of truth, Thoth standing by, recording. He knew who Anubis and Thoth were, the dog and the ibis. Yes, it was a picture of the Last Judgement. The Last Judgement was something he had thought a lot about. He did not fear it because although he had done bad things he had done enough good ones to tip the scale in the right direction. 'St Peter, when he sees me coming, will let me creep in and find myself the very lowest corner, but of the right place. Perhaps, listening to the converse of the good – if we are allowed a continuing evolution – I shall become good.'

He had mentioned his birth date, 2 September 1909, and I asked him the place, as I would like to do a horoscope for him.

'Can you give me spiritual counsel on the basis of that?' he asked. The place was Château Thierry. 'You won't find it in the register so it is useless to write, but I assure you it was there.'

Had there to be a mystery concerning everything about Déricourt?

He would not admit to being the lowest of the low. 'The curé de Saint Maur confessed the Résistants and gave the confessions to the Gestapo. That's lower than me.'

I had made two copies of my *compte rendu* of our previous conversation, one for him to keep and consider at his leisure, and so we parted, agreeing to meet the next day at Adam's at six.

He came, bringing with him not only my text, covered with remarks and suggested emendations of his own, but a complete text of his own in red ink. Adam took this amiss. Déricourt said he had not proposed it as a substitute but to provide a talking point.

It became evident that Adam's wife was wanting to lay the table for their dinner, so Déricourt and I left them and walked together to my hotel, where we went, not into its restaurant, which would be expensive, but into its café. There we had a light supper, continuing a conversation we had started while descending the steps on T. E. Lawrence, whose *Seven Pillars of Wisdom* he had been reading. He had now to fly again to North Africa, but if I could stay we could meet again in four days' time. As we walked to his car, I happened to mention having seen Watt. For a moment there was fear in his eyes. What, I wondered, had Watt seen that could be awkward? Though it was a May evening, the light was already going. Without a further word, he got into his car and I wondered if I would see him again.

I had four days to fill in. On the 11th I called on the Yeo-Thomases and told them what had happened. 'I can't get over his being so nice about it.'

What Yeo-Thomas could not get over was Déricourt's own handwritten script, on the headed paper of his airline, Sagetta.

If this appeared, the French could charge him with perjury. He was thinking particularly of Wybot, who had interrogated Déricourt for the DST before he was transferred to the TMP. He could be nasty about this.

Barbara suggested they 'confide it to him, rather than have him come on it'. Wybot had, she told me, 'come to dinner here' and they could ask him again – tell him they had a story to tell him and suggest the way in which he should take it.

Yeo-Thomas said only if Déricourt asked him to. But he had to be careful. It was his doing that Déricourt had been suspected by the British. One of his colleagues in RFF had happened to see three of the Buckmaster men arrested as they got off the train that brought them into Paris. How could it be known they were arriving? Yeo-Thomas had asked his own people in London to tell Colonel Buckmaster and suggest to him the loyalty of his Air Movements Officer be investigated. Déricourt had been recalled from the field. Later he had been arrested and tried by the French, and acquitted. That should be the end of it. 'If I meddle in his affairs now, I am hounding him.'

On the next day I had dinner with Adam and his wife. On the next, with Starr.

And then, on the 14th, Déricourt was back, very punctually as always. The appointment was chez Adam but, as before, we left him to his dinner and went down to the café of the Terrasse Hotel for a snack supper. We were seated side by side eating our omelettes when he pointed to his lapel. I had not noticed that the thin red ribbon was no longer in it. 'I removed it', he said, 'to make a better atmosphere between us.' He would have to wear it in public or other people would notice. Whilst the de Vomécourts wore theirs, he would never give them the satisfaction of seeing him without his. He would have to carry a pair of scissors to unpick it just before his meetings with me, then sew it on again. He was smiling as he made rueful jokes about this.

As we went through the text – which was changing from a memorandum into the text for publication – he expressed concern that it showed three meetings between us prior to the present: 'One can give one interview without saying much, but if one gives three, one must have been talking about something. It's almost a collaboration! Could I not put it as though everything that had been said between us had been on a single day?' He was worrying lest those two – by which he meant the de Vomécourt brothers – imagine he had been telling me about *them*. He really had these two persons on the brain.

His main defence was he had got out of France people who had no other way of getting back to England. He had saved more than had been arrested through his activities – without admitting his responsibility for them.

I begged him to think of the three men who, according to both Vogt and Yeo-Thomas, had been arrested as they descended in Paris from the train that had brought them from Angers or whatever the nearest station to the field on which he received them. 'Don't you *feel* anything about them?'

He said anybody who volunteered for work like that knew the dangers of being plunged into that morass of turpitude and did so with his eyes open.

I said they did not expect the man who handed them down from the plane would have told the Gestapo when and where to expect their arrival in Paris. That really was treachery. And I repeated. 'Don't you *feel* anything for them?'

'I am sorry for them. What else can I say?' It was not meant to happen. He was given a promise there would be no arrests of agents incoming. Something must have gone wrong. 'Peut-être qu'on m'a roulé' ('Perhaps they took me in'). It was, in a back-handed kind of way, the first clear admission that he had in fact done a deal with the Germans.

After a pause, he asked, 'What do you think of Haig?'

For a moment I thought he meant whisky. 'Haig?'

'Field Marshal Haig. In the First World War. Passchendaele. He killed 240,00 of his own men and 240,000 of the German. And all to gain a ridge. Lost again in a short time. 480,000 he killed, and for nothing. How many is it you charge me with having killed?'

Vogt only mentioned three.

'Three! Let's make it four, or a round half-dozen, in case there are any you haven't found out yet or I don't know myself.' He said, 'I want to put something to you in a way that may seem childish but is the way in which I have often put it to myself. Suppose that all the people who have ever lived are, on the Day of Judgement, arranged on a giant staircase leading from lowest Hell to highest Heaven, in order of their real wickedness or goodness in the eyes of God. Which of us stands above the other, me or Haig?'

'I don't know.'

'I don't either. But I am not eager to change places with him.'

'Je ne vendais pas des têtes,' he protested. 'I did not sell heads, that would make me vile! You must think I am a monster. I am not a monster.' He did make some money out of the Germans but only by helping some of them in some illicit business. He would give me a clue, a key to the mystery. The name of the key was diamonds. They could be sold in France for ten times what they cost to buy in England.

Had he been diamond smuggling in association with Christmann?

Not in association with Christmann. But he had been diamond smuggling before the war, and during the war it was more profitable. Not for putting in my book.

We worked again the following morning from nine to twelve, finalising the text for publication, and he told me I could write to him care of his airline, Sagetta.

I lunched with the Yeo-Thomases, then had, at five o'clock, one more appointment, with Armel Guerne, in the Quartier Latin. The Abbé had told me he had given evidence for Culioli *in camera*. He told me 'Prosper' had come to see him after the two Canadians hd failed to turn up, very distressed because he had been told or had gathered in London that the invasion was not to be this summer. He had threatened to bring the whole of the French Resistance out into open conflict with the Germans. It was, in Guerne's submission, to prevent his doing this that 'Prosper' had been betrayed to the Germans from London, from 'the top office', and it was before saying this he had asked for the court to be closed. This left me a little shaky and I talked about it with Irene, who was concerned too; but then I thought of writing to

Madame Balachowsky – she referred to Guerne as a 'half made person'. She was sure the story came from his imagination. 'Prosper' was upset because he did not think he could hold his network together for another year and feared we should all be arrested, but he would never have contemplated such a folly.

I thought that in his angry frustration 'Prosper' might have uttered some wild words which Guerne had made the mistake of taking literally.

I had one or two meetings with George Whitehead. He told me on 15 June the Queen Mother would be unveiling a plaque to the members of RF on the house in Dorset Square and had allowed them the use of part of Clarence House for a party afterwards. He suggested I come.

But I was not a member of RF. What did I say if asked why I was there?

'Say you were invited. I invite you.' It was, in fact, he who was sending out the invitations.

At the party I noticed a man wearing the star of some order and realised this must be Major-General Sir Colin Gubbins. Indeed it was, and he came over to me and said he wished people would not congregate just inside the door, making it difficult for further arrivals to get in. Couldn't I make them go out into the garden at the back? He couldn't have known who I was; but I cupped my hands and said in a strong voice, 'General Gubbins would like you all to go out into the garden.' They went.

I wrote to Déricourt asking him if he would like to write a paragraph to go at the end of my book, and he sent me one, written in English, beginning:

I read the whole script of Miss J. O. F. and for the part of the events I have been mixed up I put my signature on ...

But he had read only the last chapter, not the whole book, which might contain matter more injurious to himself than he knew. That a man who had lived his life in a world of duplicity should display such trust amazed me. I wrote back saying he must read the whole of what he was signing for.

He wrote back that he would call me and on 24 August I received a call: 'C'est Déricourt.' Could I get up early enough tomorrow morning to take a plane that would get me into Orly at eleven?

He was there to greet me and see me through the customs. He had with him a young woman, rather tired-looking, without make-up. 'My secretary. I am writing a book in rivalry with yours. A novel. She will type it and then send it to you.' He hoped I could translate it and find a publisher for it in England.

As we got into his car, I asked him if he would like a percentage of the royalties on my book?

'No.' It would mean nothing to him. He might be broke now, but he had had big money.

At the Terrasse Hotel the secretary stayed with us for a time, then withdrew. He read the typescript on the table before us from the beginning, and actually found in it some things he quite liked.

He thought a basic mistake in SOE was to give military ranks. Because these increased with the number of men commanded. This gave to those in London a terrible motive to keep on sending more people into the field, regardless of security. 'Seniority should have been marked and rewarded in some other way.' (This tied in with the observations Madame Fourcade had made.)

When we came to Vogt's statement, I had brought it to show him. It was in French and he ought to see the original to be sure I had not translated it tendentiously.

'No,' he said, gently putting aside Vogt's pencilled sheets. 'I know you will have done it honestly.'

Had he any comment to make? 'There is nothing to say about a statement like this.'

He would, however, say the submission of the mail could not have brought about the arrest of 'Prosper', 'Archambaud' and the rest. That network was German penetrated from every side anyway. 'I will not be made responsible for that carnage.'

I granted that the mail probably did not explain how 'Prosper' and his colleagues could be arrested, but the effect on them of being shown photocopies of the reports they had sent to London was devastating. Demoralising.

'The man who betrayed the mail wasn't thinking about the psychological effect on prisoners.' It was his first really overt admission. But then, he said that did not excuse the pact. 'I put myself in "Prosper's" shoes. It's the first time I've done this. I have been arrested, perhaps roughed up. I am in a state of shock. I am shown photocopies of reports I sent to London. I see the mail has been betrayed. Does that mean I have to betray everything else? Everything he betrayed. The arrests run into hundreds. I will not be made responsible for that carnage!' And he scorned the notion of a pact.

But, I said, he himself had made a pact with the Germans.

'I played a game. But I was *free*.' Anything in the nature of a deal or contract needed both parties to be free. Between prisoner and captors, impossible. Was he given his half of the contract? Did he keep it in his cell, where anyone could take it away from him?

'When did you decide to contact the Germans?'

Before his second mission. When he was recalled by Verity to discuss the accident with the tree, he managed to get an interview with somebody higher than Buckmaster, 'the one between Buckmaster and Gubbins'. He tried to tell him he had been in contact with German Intelligence and could resume it to British advantage. He did not of course say this in so many words but phrased it in a way which, if thought about, could only mean that, and ought to have elicited a sharp questioning as to what he meant. He could only assume that meant hidden links with the Germans were known and not objected to – which must mean the British were playing their own double game in a sense that was not fair to the agents.

I said, 'Perhaps he just didn't understand you. Your hints can be too subtle for most people to grasp.'

He choked. If it was that, it was hardly reassuring. He decided to take his own measures. He was still in England when he knew what he would do on his return.

Meaning, I prompted him, that he telephoned Boemelburg, said he had got himself mixed up with this ghastly British organisation and asking what he could do to put this right.

The silence seemed to last a long time. Then he said with conscious artistry, 'You have given to my words an interpretation on which I don't have to comment.'

About the intervention of Christmann and 'Anton'. Had I not wondered how the Gestapo came to know they would be with the others at the Restaurant des Capucines? Only one of those at the Square Clignancourt that night knew of the rendezvous fixed. 'Denise' – it would be unlike her to give anything away. 'Archambaud'? Nothing known against him prior to his arrest. Agazarian? Very simple and honest. 'That leaves only me. Only I had the capability and the motive to do it. Agazarian had come to tell him about how these two had arrived, wanting to make contact with "Gilbert" – meaning the Air Movements Officer. London would not have confused the two "Gilberts", so the two strangers were obviously telling a fishy story, and their entry upon the scene was over-complicating a situation complicated enough already. The arrest of "Anton" was just to give them both a fright and make them go away.' To have got Germans to arrest Germans seemed to him funny.

Coming to Bodington: had he told Bodington he was in touch with the Germans? I asked.

He had told him in such a way he would know it for himself yet be able to say he had been told or not been told as suited him best. He had said, 'I've been meeting old friends again.'

He said, 'I saved his life. By testifying to it he saved mine ... Well he had to so *something*, but he might have done something a great deal less agreeable to me. I shall always be grateful to him.'

Finally, he wanted me to understand that what happened in the Loire Valley in 1943 had its roots in what happened in Marseilles in 1941. Did I know what was meant by a *souricière*?'

'A mousetrap.'

There was in Marseilles a house used as a mousetrap. A lot of people walked into it and were arrested ...'

I had begun to jot 'Marseilles' on a loose sheet of paper, but he stopped me. 'In case when we leave this table that piece of paper should get left behind, and the de Vomécourts, if they chould come into this place, should find it.' If they knew he had talked about them that would put us both in danger. He warned me to be very careful not to let the name de Vomécourt come into my book. They would suppose anything I said was against them.

We had talked for fourteen hours and we were both tired. It had gone past midnight, the time at which he had said he must leave in order to fly an aircraft to Jeddah. I said, 'Don't have a motor accident through the rushing to get to Orly on time.'

Collecting himself, he said with calm assurance, 'Take-off will be a few minutes late.'

I said, 'I don't think of you as the worst kind of traitor.'

He blushed, very deeply, and said simply, 'Thank you.'

And was gone.

Fifteen

Gollancz had decided they did not want another war-book, but Yeo-Thomas, to whom I had lent a copy of the typescript, wrote a letter to John Pudney of Putnam's, introducing it with the words, 'It is a masterpiece.' I took it to him on 18 September 1957, at midday; he was just going off for his lunch and invited me to join him at a pub in Museum Street. He had some slight connection, he said, not with SOE, but with a film being made about one of its heroines, Violet Szabo; he had been commissioned to write a poem for use in it.

He rang on the 25th to tell me the book was accepted. But then there followed a long period of consultations on legal matters. On 7 November 1957 I was called to read a report from their legal adviser and had to consent to the exclusion of a lot that I put in. The result was to narrow the case to Déricourt, excluding issues touching persons higher up and likely to sue. I wrote to Déricourt about this. He had gone back to the Far East but had given me the address of his airman's club in Paris, the QBG, care of which letters would always find him, wherever he was, as well as that of his airline, Air Laos. Correspondence between us became regular. Meanwhile Irene and I met constantly.

On 13 January 1958 I received a telephone call from Colonel Oreste Pinto. He came to tea with me on the 16th. He had during the war scrutinised refugees arriving in this country to be sure we were not admitting spies in disguise, and was the author of two books, *Spycatcher* and *Friend or Foe*. He was concerned to prove it was 'King Kong' – Lindemans – who betrayed the landings at Arnhem. I told him Giskes just didn't know. If it was Lindemans, it should have gone through him, but did not. Lindemans could have cut him out, but he rather thought the reason Lindemans failed to report to him in the last days was that it was obvious Germany was going to lose the war and he had rejoined his Resistance group, hoping to hide that he had worked for the Germans.

On 30 June there was some kind of function at the Special Forces Club. Madame Guépin wrote that she was coming over specially for it, and hoped to see me there. I told her I was not a member. She said she was, and invited me to be her guest.

When I arrived, she was not alone, and introduced her companion as Baron de Vomécourt.

Philippe de Vomécourt! Déricourt's enemy. We had to engage in social conversation but I endeavoured to say nothing of consequence. He struck me as officious and fussy. He spoke disapprovingly of Elizabeth Nicholas, who had come to interview him in connection with her book. When I got home, I telephoned her to warn her. And then I wrote to Déricourt to tell him what had happened.

I had asked Déricourt if he could send me some kind of a plant from Laos that I could grow in a pot on my window-sill. On 5 September I received a letter from him saying Laos plants grew only in wet heat; he enclosed something else. It was a bracelet, in soft Laos silver and white enamel. It was not a valuable thing or I could not have kept it, but it was pretty.

And then *Double Webs* was out. I spent 30 September packing up copies to send to all my friends – Déricourt, Yeo-Thomas, Vogt, Giskes, Irene, Elizabeth, George Whitehead, Adam, Mercier, Christmann and everyone else who would be interested. A Mr Richard Findlater from the *Sunday Dispatch* telephoned, and on the following day arrived at 4.30 and stayed until 6, followed by their photographer.

The picture was on the front page of the issue for 5 October, against the headline MISS FULLER RAISES CLOAK AND DAGGER STORM.

My party that evening was a small one: Mother, Irene, Elizabeth, George Whitehead and a friend unconnected with these operation, Dr Patricia Thompson, the Wyatt scholar. I remember her saying what puzzled her was why, if so much had gone amiss, Colonel Buckmaster wrote books. 'If I had done something and felt I had not done it very well, I would just keep quiet and hope that if it came to be discussed nobody would think of me in connection with it.'

To which Elizabeth replied, 'But you have a brain, ducky!'

Irene proposed to table a motion in the House of Commons to establish whether the Air Movements Officer had been a German agent or a Foreign Office one planted in SOE. She gave me the text so that I could send it to Déricourt. who might be seriously thrown by her inquiry.

Selwyn Lloyd asked her to delay until 12 November in order to give him time to read *Double Webs*, and it was on the morning of the 12th that I received a frantic letter from Déricourt:

Dear Jean

I ask you, I pray you, I supplicate you, if you wish me any good, not to bring the Foreign Office into it ...

I took a taxi to the House of Commons and was in time to prevent the motion going on the table in its originally proposed form. Irene amended it to propose, simply, that the question of whether the Air Movements Officer was a German agent should be cleared up.

From the moment it became public, telephone calls were ceaseless. Failing to get from Irene or me the name of the Air Movements Officer, the newspapermen had rung Elizabeth Nicholas, Yeo-Thomas and Mr Norman. Thank God nobody broke ranks.

Vogt now wrote to me that, having read my book, he was 'no longer so sure of the guilt of Gilbert ... I have now to suppose that the arrest of Prosper, Archambaud and their colleagues was above all things the consequence of the intervention of Christmann, Anton etc of the Abwehr ...'

Some practically parallel reflections reached me in a letter from Thackthwaite, who suggested that, provided Déricourt was able to make a judicious selection of the mail to be handed over to the Germans, not much harm might be done thereby, and he was getting major agents out of France.

Irene gave a party in Room C at the House of Commons on 19 November, to mark my book and Elizabeth's *Death Be Not Proud*, identifying the long-unidentified fourth girl executed at Natzweiler – Sonia Olschanesky. Just as I was leaving for it, Elizabeth rang me and said, 'To Waterloo!'

I took with me Vogt's letter and read it to the assembled representatives of the press – only to realise afterwards they hadn't a clue what I was talking about. I had assumed that they would have read the books of the two authors they had been invited to meet and would therefore be able to appreciate subtle points. But no, they had come not having read the books and hoping to pick up as the evening went along some idea of what the books were about. Their absence of grasp was evident in the resultant publicity; nevertheless there were intelligent reviews of *Double Webs* in *The Daily Telegraph*, *Tribune* and *The Cape Argus* (South Africa) and I was later able to reproduce the whole of Vogt's long letter in a new last chapter appended to the paperback edition *Double Agent?*

On the 10th I had been woken by an early morning telephone call from de Malval, saying he had made a statement to the *Sunday Dispatch* attacking Odette and Peter Churchill, but if it interfered with my book he could retrieve it. I thought it probably would interfere, but a deplorable impression would be created if he now tried to withdraw it, and on the 23rd Elizabeth woke me again from my sleep – to tell me it was all over the front page of the *Sunday Dispatch*: FRENCH RESIS-TANCE MEN CHALLENGE EXPLOITS OF ODETTE. She and Peter Churchill were challenged to 'name one single act of effective sabotage' carried out by Peter Churchill or herself. There were said to be six signatories to the document but the only ones named were Captain F. Basin, MBE and Baron Henri de Malval. In the following week's issue they had Odette's reply, headed on the front page: NOW THEY WANT ME TO PROVE THAT I WAS TORTURED. But they hadn't – yet – brought this question up.

De Malval sent me cuttings from *Paris-Presse l'Intransigeant*, in which she claimed to know the identity of the man named in Dame Irene's motion. She was suggesting he was one of the unnamed signa-tories to the attack and that it had been launched by him as a 'smokescreen'. I could not think why she should claim to know Déricourt, with whom she could not have had contact; but Elizabeth rang suggesting, 'She thinks Irene was talking about Roger Bardet.' Bardet was a Frenchman who, after being arrested, worked for Hugo Bleicher of the Abwehr and was responsible for the arrest of Peter Churchill and Odette. He was not the Air Movements Officer but had, Elizabeth seemed to remember, at one time been an airman. I told de Malval he must, absolutely, divulge the names of his co-signatories, so that it could be seen Déricourt was not one of them – or for that mat-ter Bardet either.

Ironically, Déricourt, though relieved the pressure had been taken off him in this unexpected way, began to feel a bit sorry for Odette now that the gunfire had switched to her: at least she went to France to work with the Resistance, which was more than most girls did.

Meanwhile, Buckmaster had not been silent. I missed the interview with him on 'Panorama' as I was out at the Lodge – but my Mother saw it, told me what she could remember and I got a tran-script from the BBC. The curious thing was that when the inverviewer asked him whether he had authorised his Air Movements Officer's contact with the Germans, he said he had – it was thought it could be useful. I sent this to Déricourt, who was fairly whooping with delight, exclaiming that the best, the funniest part of it was what 'I can't tell you'. In a separate letter he wrote of an officer's saying he had authorised a subordinate's contact with the enemy, although he had not, 'in order not to look a fool'. I knew I was meant to apply that to Buckmaster.

Then I got a very distressed letter from de Malval saying the people from Libre Résistance, of which Philippe de Vomécourt was President, had visited him, trying to obtain his signature, below that of others, to a document attacking not only me but Dame Irene Ward, which they were going to hand in at the British Embassy.

And from the Abbé Guillaume I received a letter saying he had been under pressure from Philippe de Vomécourt to write a complaint against the use of his name in my book. As he could not read one word of English, it was no use his looking at it, but he was told his name was on every page. Was this so? I was able to assure him it was not. There was only a short chapter on the Abbé of Ardon, and he was not quoted for anything compromising. They had also reproached him for having lent me the typed memoirs of Mathilde Carré, 'La Chatte'; and I was able to tell him I had learned the story before I met him from the book by Erich Borchers (Bleicher's chief) *Monsieur Jean*, which despite its French-sounding title, was written in German. The typescript I had found interesting only from a psychological point of view.

Shortly afterwards John Profumo came up to Irene in the Commons and handed her an envelope marked 'FOREIGN OFFICE SECRET'. He broke the seal himself and handed her the contents. It was a petition handed in at the British Embassy in Paris, that the British Government should suppress the books *Double Webs* by Jean Overton Fuller and *Death Be Not Proud* by Elizabeth Nicholas and take punitive action against Irene Ward for having advertised in the Commons a book for which she had written a foreword (mine). The list of signatories was headed by Baron Philippe de Vomécourt.

Profumo said she could have the letter.

'Can I show it to my friends?' she had said.

'You can do what you like with it,' was his answer, smiling.

She brought it to show me. 'I'll show it to Elizabeth, too, and then destroy it, don't you think?'

Déricourt, when I told him, was immensely relieved. He had felt sure the de Vomécourts would take some hostile action, but what? Now they had shot their bolt and it had failed. In France Philippe de Vomécourt was an important person. In England, it was now evident, nothing.

Irene had posted a copy of *Double Webs* to Harold Macmillan, and gave me, to keep, his reply saying he would read it, followed by a second, saying he had read it, and 'I share your concern'.

He made an appointment for her to be received at the Foreign Office by Lord Lansdowne, the Permanent Under-Secretary (generally believed to be the head of the Secret Intelligence Service). With him he had Robin Hooper, of the permanent Foreign Office staff.

Irene had some questions for them. First, did the Foreign Office send Bodington to give evidence at Déricourt's trial? To this the answer was no. Moreover, Bodington neither asked their permission nor informed them of his intention to go.

Second: was Déricourt employed by the Foreign Office? Again, no. Hooper had served in the same squadron as Déricourt, but had never suggested to him he work for the Foreign Office, and he had at no time been on the Foreign Office payroll.

Then: had Déricourt told anybody in England that he was in Intelligence with the Germans? To this the answer was 'Yes'. Lord Lansdowne had spoken with one or two people, one of whom said Déricourt had told him he had contacts with German Intelligence, which he could resume in the British interest. Rather surprisingly, this offer had not been taken up. If Déricourt had thereafter made or re-made contact with German Intelligence, it must have been on his own responsibility. They bore him no malice, intended him no harm but wished he would stop pretending to have been one of theirs. She could tell me and I could tell him. (They had my book on the desk, various passages flagged and marked.)

Irene had an idea, which she first put to me at my place, that an official history of SOE in France should be commissioned, because for this Foreign Office files would have to be opened to the historian. She had terminated her motion with the suggestion and put it also in letters to the Prime Minister. Lansdowne now gave her his consent, in principle, and she picked up her motion from the Order Table.

On 2 February de Malval phoned to say 'Carte' had joined them – from New York – all old quarrels forgotten and he had got an article, 'L'Affaire Odette' into the paper *L'Express*, a copy of which he was sending me. It was a two-page spread and carried, at last, a full list of the signatories, which had grown from the original six:

André Girard, 'Carte'
M. Henri de Malval
Capitaine Francis Basin, 'Olive'
Docteur Piccard Fils
Docteur Fourrest
René Casal
Henri Goudron
Mme. Expection
Mlle. Odette des Garrets
M. Chef de Gare de la Bocca [Stationmaster of de la Bocca]

From the brief descriptions of their functions beneath their names they had all belonged to the Cannes Resistance. A second group, comprised of persons who had known Odette not in Cannes or its neighbourhood, but in prison. Of these the most important was Mme Laure Lebras who said, 'Odette n'a jamais été torturée' (Odette was never tortured). A Mme. Maryse P said, 'Odette ment. Elle n'a jamais été torturée ni brutalisée' ('Odette lies. She was never tortured or brutalised'), and Mme Fabius said Odette could not have been ill-treated in Ravensbruck.

This was followed on 13 March by another double-page spread, in *Noir et Blanc*, under the title 'Odette est-elle une fausse héroine?' (Odette, is she a false heroine?') This was illustrated by a centre-page photograph of Laure Lebras over the citation from her statement: 'Odette n'a pas été torturée.' ('Odette was not tortured'.)

The feelings of the signatories were summed up in the words:

Odette symbolise aujourd'hui pour tous les Francais qui l'ont connue 1942/43 l'exploitation dans un but publicitaire et lucratif du travail fait en commun dans l'ombre avec les Résistants français qui considerent n'avoir fait remplir un devoir.

I translate:

Odette symbolises today, for all the French people who knew her in 1942/43, the exploitation, for publicity and money, of work done in common with French Résistants in the shadow who thought only to have done their duty.

I should add, if our people really believed Odette's toenails to have been pulled out at 84 Avenue Foch, of which Kieffer was Commandant, why was it not so much as mentioned by the prosecution at

Kieffer's trial? He was charged only with having relayed an instruction to have six uniformed parachutists shot, but one would have thought the prosecuting counsel, seeking to worsen his character, would have brought up the matter of Odette's torture. I have a transcript of the whole trial, in German and in English (from H.M. Stationery Office), and there is no mention of Odette in it. M. Chaix, the owner of 84 Avenue Foch, when I went for the second time, mentioned that when Odette came with the company making the film *Odette* the little room on the fifth floor, which Starr identified as the one in which Vogt had his office, she said that was where her toenails had been pulled out. I saw the film again to make sure and it was indeed that room shown on the screen. It was right above Kieffer's head and he could not possibly have been ignorant of such a thing being done in it. For that matter, why did our people not charge Vogt? Why had he to learn of the story she had told from me?

In the late summer of 1959 Elizabeth's old illness had come on her. She had been in hospital but on 7 September telephoned me to say she was out, still in bed at home but had been asked to review Buckmaster's new book, *They Fought Alone* (Odhams, 1959), for the *Sunday Pictorial*, and wondered if I would care to come that afternoon to look at her advance copy and add my thoughts to hers.

When I arrived, she was sitting up in bed, very excited, but about something quite different. Irene had just been in, and had something to tell her. She had been to the Ministry of Defence and had found herself in conversation with Denis Healey. Somehow they had come to be talking about Odette, and he had told her something of major importance.

Soon after the end of the war she had written to Winston Churchill, apologising to him for having made use of his name by pretending to the Germans that she was married to Peter Churchill and that Peter was his (Winston's) nephew. Somehow she got an invitation to see him. It was to him she said her toenails had been pulled out, and he took her straight to the King and said this woman must receive the highest decoration there is; and that was how her George Cross escaped going through the normal channels and vetting.

This seemed to me so enormously important that while I was writing this book I wrote to Lord Healey saying I did not like to cite him through third party transmission in case I got some story wrong or introduced into it some inaccuracies, and asked him for his comments on the above paragraph.

His handwritten reply came by return of post. It is dated 22 March 2004.

Dear Jean Overton Fuller,
　　Thank you for your letter.
　　I think the quotation you send me is OK – so use it if it is useful.
　　Best wishes,

yours sincerely
DENIS HEALEY

I wondered if it had weighed on Churchill that the whole Royal Family had attended the premiere of that film. That he did not had occasioned some mild surprise. Vogt had suggested to me that it was because he suspected something unsound, Elizabeth's suggestion to me was that it was when he made that pious pilgrimage to the hotel at Saint Jorioz where she and Peter Churchill were arrested that he heard from the people there something he did not like. Indeed, Peter Churchill, in his memoirs, makes it ungallantly plain that by meeting him on his re-descent from the skies and going back with him to the hotel where they had stayed but where, too, she had had conversations with Hugo Bleicher during his absence, she was responsible for his arrest.

From the solicitors of the de Vomécourt brothers I received a letter requiring me to remove from future editions of my book a phrase used by Déricourt to refer to an early network as 'Noble One where "La Chatte" was', as it could be used against Pierre de Vomécourt in a libel action he was bringing against Hugo Bleicher. I had seen in the *News Chronicle* that Pierre de Vomécourt was suing Bleicher who had said somewhere that Pierre de Vomécourt, after he had arrested him, had betrayed to him eight of his comrades. I took this in to Mr Franklin, who replied to the French lawyer, on my instructions, saying the phrase in my book was in no way derogatory to his client and Miss Fuller would not remove it in order to oblige one of the parties to a lawsuit with which she had nothing to do.

　　Déricourt, when I told him Pierre de Vomécourt was suing Bleicher, replied, 'What a fool that de Vomécourt is.'

　　Elizabeth, similarly apprised, said to me on the telephone, 'They're both so repulsive, if only there could be some result by which they could both lose!'

In a way, there was. Pierre de Vomécourt's defence was that the persons had been betrayed by 'La Chatte' (Mathilde Carré). She had just been released from prison, after a death sentence had been commuted to imprisonment for life and finally to twelve years, now served, and de Vomécourt tried to induce her to come to this court in Germany and say it was she who betrayed them. This she declined to do, and de Vomécourt did not carry on with the case.

Both Elizabeth and I had a sneaking sympathy for 'La Chatte'; because once she confessed, everyone else taxed with a fault put it on to her, 'It was "La Chatte" did it.' Pierre de Vomécourt was one of them.

But now I received from Paris a letter signed 'Robert Lyon', saying he had information of importance to give me. A curious thing about this letter was that it contained a question about what was meant by the phrase 'Noble One where "La Chatte" was'. So I took it that Lyon was in consulation with the de Vomécourts and their solicitor.

He arrived on 27 March 1959. As to the phrase that worried him, I said that whereas the Interalliée, in which 'La Chatte' was, was in truth not an SOE but an independent Polish network, it was Déricourt's opinion that SOE wanted to take it over, through its own agent Georges Begué, code-name 'Noble'. It was just Déricourt's shorthand for what he thought of as Begué's first network. This seemed to relieve Lyon.

Then he said he could give me material for a new book. He opened a briefcase full of papers, the purpose of all of them being to indict Gilbert Turck as the man who had betrayed all the SOE agents arrested in 1941 in the Villa des Bois, Marseilles. He had even photographs of Turck and his wife, and copies of their passports.

I said I was not thinking of writing a further book on SOE.

Then he referred to a statement made by Déricourt to the DST that at 9 a.m. on 24 June 1943 he had met 'Antoine' at the Gare St Lazare, who told him he had just seen 'Prosper' arrested there. This, he pointed out, was incompatible with his having received a Lysander and its two passengers, a Colonel Bonoteaux and himself, at about 2.30 on that morning at Amboise. There was no train from Amboise to Paris that could have enabled Déricourt to be in the Gare St Lazare at 9 a.m.

As soon as he had taken his leave, I wrote to Déricourt about this. If the St Lazare story was just one he had made up, should I simply omit it from the paperback edition?

He said he would prefer me just to say that there was conflict of testimony. He made the statement just to help Culioli. Then I understood.

Once in Paris he had said plaintively that people gave one bad marks for the bad things one had done; should they not give good ones for the bad things one had not done? Culioli was coming up for trial at the same time as himself. In the various ambiguities in his evidence he had not tried to shift blame on to Culioli. I understood this better when the Abbé sent me copies of the statements made by Bony and Laffont to the DST before they were executed, concerning occasions on which they followed agents from the country stations near the field up to Paris. The statements did not say whether these agents were parachutists or had been landed by aircraft. It was Culioli who received the parachutists, Déricourt who met the aircraft. Over this issue, I saw now, Déricourt had made it up to Culioli with a statement that would help him defend himself against a statement made by Mona Reimeringer that she had seen Culioli lead the Germans to arrest 'Prosper' at the Hotel Mazagram. A typical Déricourt way of adjusting the scales.

Both Lyon and Bonoteaux had reached Paris and passed out through the barrier in safety, but Bonoteaux had later been arrested. This was presumably the fourth I did not know about when I told Déricourt there were, according to Vogt's statement, three arrested because of him.

With apparent reference to the allegation against Turck, he warned me to be careful, as he felt an attempt was being made to draw me into an area where I would be vulnerable to an action for libel. I did not need that warning. I had told him what Turck had told me and asked him if the 'mousetrap house' in Marseilles of which he had told me was the Villa des Bois. He replied, on 5 April, in English: 'I don't know anything about that story – even if it look like mine.'

Those words 'even if it look like mine' were by far the most revealing Déricourt ever dared to pen, yet, though they puzzled me at the time, it would be years before the penny dropped.

Meanwhile Irene was keeping up the pressure for a history of SOE. John Profumo disappeared from the Foreign Office in the Christine Keeler/Stephen Ward scandal, which, she said, 'was a pity' because he was favourable to us. And very shortly afterwards another member of the Foreign Office staff disappeared in a scandal concerning his relations with a guardsman in St James's Park – only minutes, she told me, after he had given her his personal assurance he would push the project through. And he went out, through the Park, and this happened! She received from him the most abject, contrite and altogether pathetic letter.

Despite these setbacks, Edward Heath was now put in charge of the project, which, for the time being, was not publicly announced. But as time passed and nothing seemed to be happening, he told Irene that he had not been idle: he had been to several universities, including naturally Oxford and Cambridge, seeking advice on the choice of a historian. What was rather holding him up was that he did not want to choose a Conservative, or people would criticise him for having chosen a member of his own party; but neither did he want to choose one flaming red. What he was looking for was one with appropriate credentials as a historian and no obvious political colour, or towards the middle of the party spectrum.

And I? I did not really want to write more books on SOE. Though I kept all the contacts I had made – and new ones formed because people brought me information – I felt that as the war receded public interest in the subject must wane. I should find something else to do.

In the summer Mother went to see some people in Lincolnshire and suggested I come too. I did not go, but just afterwards it occurred to me that if there was a place in Lincolnshire I ought to see, it was Horncastle, where Gilby came from. And so, on 2 June, I took the train to Boston: thence to Horncastle by bus. I remembered Gilby had said the reigning powers in Horncastle had refused to let the railway be built through their town lest it take trade from the canal, and in consequence it became a backwater. Indeed, it seemed a bit void of interest, though in addition to letting Mother know I was here, I sent picture postcards of the streets to Irene, Elizabeth, Mercier, and Déricourt. I asked around, whether anyone remembered the Smiths and the Overtons, and was directed to 'Overtons' Corner', a large white house with black beams, on the market square, today a fish and chip shop, by odd chance the one in which on the evening of my arrival I had supped in what had been my great-grandmother's home. An old man told me John Overton gave him a toffee-apple when he brought the papers.

Mother joined me and we spent some time in the churchyard looking for graves with familiar names, and she said she felt we were like two characters out of fiction, two women looking for their ancestors.

On 4 September I received a letter from Daniel Antelme, nephew of 'Antoine', come from Mauritius hoping to learn something of his uncle. He came to tea on the 14th. I undertook to write both to Vogt and to Déricourt to ask them what they could tell him. From Déricourt

I received a nice letter I could give him and Vogt offered to see him if he came to Germany.

He then went on to see Miss Atkins, and when he came again to me he said she had told him Vogt would be able to tell him nothing worth the pains and expense of going to Germany. That was what she had said to me so many years ago, but I had gone, notwithstanding; Daniel accepted her advice and did not go. I thought it was a pity because Vogt had interrogated his uncle and could certainly have brought the scene alive for him.

It was a long time since I had painted, but in October I began again with a few small pictures of the fuchsia I had grown. Also I became a member of the British Astronomical Association.

Early in 1960 I was correcting the proofs of the French translation of *Double Webs*, rights of which had been sold to Fayard. There were obvious mistakes: 'airfields' being everywhere mistranslated 'aéro-dromes', which was absurd; 'terrains' or 'terrains d'atterrisage' was what Déricourt called them when writing or speaking in French; even 'champs' would have been preferable for that was what they were, just fields. But there were subtler points meriting discussion and I sent the whole lot out to Laos for Déricourt's comments. These were not all self-regarding. I don't know if their number – they covered six pages – discouraged the translator (who was not George Afam), but after all the pains we had taken over it, the book never appeared.

In *The People* on 21 February 1960, appeared an article 'Dead or Alive' by Nicholas Bodington, in which he wrote of his visit to the field in July/August 1943. It referred to the arrest of Agazarian, when he went to keep a dangerous rendezvous with a person who might or might not be a free man. Bodington wrote that he and Agazarian spun a coin to determine which would go, and the coin made it Agazarian. Déricourt wrote in the margin, 'No coin – I was there.' He asked me not to spread this around as he wished no harm to Bodington; but now that Bodington has passed away it seems to me important to make this known since it explains what has puzzled so many – why Bodington went to witness Déricourt's trail. The prosecution was trying to pin the arrest of Agazarian on Déricourt, who would have to say, 'Not me, Bodington,' had not Bodington come forward with a story that got them both off the hook.

On 8 April, when Irene came to dinner with me, she told me she had seen that 'Antoine', when he went on what was to prove his fatal mission, was on his return to report to Anthony Eden. (I think this may have been in a secret history of SOE by someone called Mackenzie, that had achieved an under-cover circulation.) She had, she said, always thought that after the departure of de Guélis for North Africa, Eden would have looked for a replacement. 'I didn't know who it was.' It could have been 'Antoine' – Antelme. In that case what Eden overheard me telling Irene in the dining-room of the House of Commons that summer evening in 1955 must have had more significance than I had realised. If he had not known before, he had learned from me what had happened to his man: he had been one of those parachuted to German reception.

From Bangkok, Déricourt wrote to me on 24 August that his novel, now finished, was being typed; and on the following day he wrote again to say his secretary would send it to me. He added, 'I hope you make a good job of the translation [of *Double Webs*].' He would then have one last look at it before sending it to Fayard.

From Christmann I received a letter, not from Germany but Tunisia, saying he could offer me a Tunisian subject for a book which he would tell me about if I could pay a visit. I had never been to any part of Africa and the night skies would be less polluted than in London enabling me to see more stars. So I packed my telescope when I flew to Tunisia on 11 October. This was a new enthusiasm. I had written to the British Astronomical Association the previous year and was set – their usual task for new members – to monitor the fluctuations of a small variable star which, through the telescope I had bought myself, I could only just perceive. As I stepped from the aircraft I saw indeed, in the unpolluted night sky, a greater spread of stars than I had ever seen.

Christmann met me at the barrier and drove me off into the night, delivering me to the Byrsa Hotel, Carthage. It was all in darkness, but given the key I groped my way to my room. In the morning I was to join him and Eva at their villa, nearby.

I found it impossible to sleep that night; I kept getting up to see if I could yet discern the scenery of Africa. Gradually the silhouettes of palms emerged, and then the bright smack of the light disclosed a crescent-shaped water, moat or harbour, by which a boat was moored. On the white verandah climbed a scarlet poinsettia and purple bougainvillaea, while bunches of bananas hung from the palms.

I found the Christmanns. Richard and Eva were married now and had with them a small daughter. Their house was piled up with boxes of Complan and he showed me a paper appointing him Glaxo's representative in Tunisia. He drove us round Carthage and we went into

Tunis. He was a bit slow in coming out with the story he had for me but I began to fear it was to do with the political situation in North Africa, which I did not want to be concerned with.

On the second morning I climbed the Bursa, the hill on which stood the remains of Dido's citadel. *Carthago delenda est*? There was quite a lot of it, though crumbling. In the afternoon I walked the other way and came to a garden, as I thought. The gardener, as I took him to be, invited me to come in, and began showing me urns; they contained, he said, the ashes of the children sacrificed. I realised with horror I was standing in the Tophet. He was showing me the place where the children's throats were cut. An ideogram of Tanit, she to whom the sacrifices were made. He had a disturbingly proprietorial air.

I was sick day after day in Carthage. The Christmanns assured me this was usual with new arrivals. It was of long standing, had affected the Roman legions when they came to attack. The residents were inured to it; it wore off after a few months. The only thing to stop it was Vichy water. 'Drink the whole bottle,' said Christmann. It did stop it, but the proprietor of the hotel confided to me he did not understand why foreigners were always sick when they arrived.

Eva now suggested I should write her husband's life. He had been born in the disputed territory of Alsace-Lorraine; a miserable, wretched baby. His father had said, 'It's dead.' The doctor said, 'It's dead.' They were about to throw him away with the rubbish when some movement was discerned in him, I think he said by the midwife. But his father always regarded him as rubbish.

The biography went no further, perhaps because he as well as I had doubts as to the advisability of writing it; but what had been said in these opening lines could have explained a lot.

On the 16th he drove us, including the little girl, on an all-day excursion to Zagrouan and then to Khairouan, the second holiest place in Islam. He was a rather frightening driver as he could not endure any other vehicle to be in front of him on the road and had always to overtake. Eva begged him to desist, but in vain. He drove us one evening to a café in a neighbouring village on a hill. I did not notice his having an exceptional amount to drink but as we came back he was driving the car diagonally from side to side of the road and as there were ditches on both sides I was afraid we were going to crash into one or other of them. It was the worst driving I have ever seen.

He offered me an FLN badge, to take home as a souvenir, but I wouldn't take it. I wasn't sure exactly what FLN was, but I thought it was probably an illegal organisation, at any rate an organisation dedicated to expelling the French from North Africa. If the badge were found on me at the customs, it might create a misleading impression.

When my return aircraft brought me into London airport, I was never so glad to set foot again on English soil. And as I walked across the tarmac it was suddenly clear to me that the new explanation of the Square Clignancourt affair was incompatible not only with the new statement he had made to the French but the one he had made me in Frankfurt.

At home I found a slip from the post office saying three attempts had been made to deliver a registered parcel to me. I called the next day at the post office but they had returned it to sender. This worried me. I had told Déricourt I was going to be in Tunisia and surely he would have warned his secretary.

Using his horoscope as a basis, I had been trying out astrological measurements to various dates in his life, by different systems. To obtain the time of his birth, given on French certificates to the nearest half hour, I had written to Château Thierry for a copy, which I obtained without difficulty. His father's name was given as Alfred Déricourt – so if de Malval was right about the name's masking a noble bastardy it must have been farther back – occupation, postman. The calculations had involved me in masses of arithmetic, but it was done, the book was out, under the title *Horoscope for a Double Agent* (Fowler, 1961), and I sent him a copy.

On 10 March I received a letter from him sounding perfectly normal; he enclosed letters for Putnam and Pan saying he had no objection to the publication of the paperback edition of *Double Webs*. Then another letter arrived to say Air Laos had closed down. I had always addressed my letters to him there but I was now to write to him at the Hotel Constellation, Vientiane. Then I received one dated 8.3.61:

Dear Jean
 I am very sorry – really sorry – but it happens I have to ask you not to write to me for some time. I can't tell you why and ask you not to try to find out ...
Your good friend,
HENRY

This did not altogether take me by surprise, as a few mornings before I had woken with a dream of an aeroplane losing height and descending into the sea to the words, 'The poor flying-fish is going down.' The aircraft must, I felt, be a symbol for Déricourt, but in what sense was he going down? Was his aircraft to be lost? The descent was too gradual for a crash. Was he dying? The letter seemed to explain – only hiding. From what? I was not to try to find out. Enclosed was:

I give by this present instrument power to Miss Jean Overton Fuller of 4 Guilford Place, London, WC1 to act in my stead and sign in my stead and place in what concerns

1 All facts concerning me, their relation and interpretation from 15 August 1941 to 9 June 1948.

2 All modifications, corrections, alterations which she wishes to make to the original edition approved by me of her book *Double Webs*.

3 *id* for *Horoscope for a Double Agent*.

4 The use of 2 and 3 in other domains, such as cinema, radio, television, etc.

On the other hand I formally forbid that my real family name be written or pronounced in any circumstances whatsoever. 2 that the name 'Gilbert' appear in the title or in display, the name 'Gilbert' being authorised in the text.

Signed in Vientiane, of the effect to whom it may concern,

H. DÉRICOURT

It sounded like a farewell.

Sixteen

Irene had been quiet for some time, then had Elizabeth and me to dinner with her at the House of Commons on 14 March 1961. It was to assure us she had kept up the pressure and had now been told a historian had been chosen. She had not been told his name. (It was M. R. D. Foot.)

On the morning of 31 July she rang to say she had just come out of the Foreign Office, where 'the historian' had been presented to her. She thought she shouldn't speak his name over the telephone but she had invited him to lunch at the House of Commons on Thursday next, 3 August, at 1 p.m. and hoped I would join them.

She introduced him to me simply as 'the historian', but as we stood waiting for a table to be free I asked him, 'What is your name?'

He made downward jabbing motions with one hand.

'Shoe? Foot?'

He made a shushing noise. 'My very existence is an official secret.'

We were careful of our talk at table. Yet merry.

After we had lunched we walked out on to the veranda that overlooks the Thames, and pulled up chairs. I cannot even remember what we talked about. He had not yet permission to tell Buckmaster or even Gubbins, though he supposed that would be given later. At about four o'clock Irene ordered tea, then said that she must leave us as her Parliamentary duties required her presence in the Chamber.

Foot suggested he and I go for a second tea into a teashop nearby. He told me a bit about himself. He came from Manchester University, and was a member of the Liberal Party.

He gave me a date at his Liberal club and also came to see me at my flat a couple of times. I gave him what help I could in a sense, though reserving things said to me in the confidence I was not passing them to some official body. I lent him a table of dates I had made for my own use, but before doing so removed from it the card relating to Bonoteau's arrest. No need to expose Déricourt's faults unnecessarily.

Meanwhile, I had decided to change subject completely and write a biography of Victor Neuburg. Fr. Brocard Sewell, editor of a periodical called *The Aylesford Review*, had evinced heretical interest in the Golden Dawn and so was one of the first persons whom I told of this. (We had been in touch the previous year, and he had invited me to a Conversazione in Westminster which was memorable for giving me my first sighting of Tim d'Arch Smith.) On 8 August I received a letter from Sewell saying if I wrote a biography of Neuburg he could offer me contacts. And he did. The first addresses that he gave me were of my namesake General J. F. C. Fuller, Mrs Wieland, née Ethel Archer, Vicky's son, and Anthony d'Offay. I wrote to each of them and from all four I had replies.

In the midst of this new activity, George Starr, John's elder brother, came to see me and told me of the trouble he was having with de Gaulle and the Pan paperback *Double Agent?* There had been a last sally over this from the de Vomécourts. Philippe de Vomécourt had written demanding advance submission of the whole text, declaring that, as President of Libre Résistance, he had the right to vet every book on SOE before it came out. I assured the publisher of Pan Books that he had not, and without his interference it was in my hands on 8 September. I risked posting a copy to Déricourt at the last address I had for him, the Hotel in Vientiane, though without much hope he would receive it.

Victor E. Neuburg, Vicky's son, came to see me on the 19th. On the 22nd I saw Runia, but she would only have cooperated if she had control and this would have meant excluding the homosexual element in Vicky's relationship with Crowley. I wrote to Hayter Preston and to Pamela, no longer Hansford Johnson but, since her marriage to the Labour peer (as he had recently become), Lady Snow. Both Pamela and Preston replied. I also wrote to *The Times Literary Supplement* and *Daily Telegraph* asking people who had known Victor Neuburg to contact me which brought further response.

Brocard Sewell now asked me down to Aylesford Priory. I went on 19 September, not knowing what to expect. When I was shown into his room I was certainly surprised to see propped up prominently Baphomet, the goat-headed symbol the Knights Templar were accused of worshipping, which looked as if blown up from the reproduction in Eliphas Lévi's *Transcendental Magic*. I supposed he was not worshipping it and a Catholic monk could have what he liked in his room, but I found its presence oddly disturbing. The accused Knights Templar had ended burned. What had I got into? Yet his conversation was perfectly sensible.

I might have a rival, he told me. Anthony d'Offay had had the idea of writing a life of Neuburg. He did not know how he had got on with it. Actually he thought him rather young to be handling such peculiar material and he thought it would be better if I did it.

D'Offay wrote to me that he had collected some material with the thought of writing a life of Neuburg but had not made the progress he hoped, and would be willing to sell out to me: the collection consisted of some of the books by Neuburg, a book that had formed part of Neuburg's library and bore marginal notes in his hand; and letters from Neuburg to sundry. £100 the lot. I sent him a cheque.

On 2 October I received from General Fuller an unexpected treasure. It was a manuscript diary that Neuburg kept at one time of his visions, under the title *The Magical Retirement of Omnia Vincam*.

I had more than once been asked – first by Vicky – if I was a relative of Major General John Charles Frederick Fuller. I thought the confusion (not by Vicky but by some people) rose from my father's father being John Charles Fuller, army surgeon, who after retirement re-offered his services for the Crimean War and was accorded the local rank for its duration of Inspector General of Hospitals. Note the similarity of Christian names: both John Charles but my grandfather not Frederick. Being now in correspondence with General J. F. C., I thought to mention this and sent a copy of the Fuller family tree going back from John Charles to Francis Fuller, born 1715, freeholder in Washington, Sussex, and invited him to look and see if there was any point at which his tree joined to it. He wrote back saying he had not his handy for consultation but as his, too, was a Sussex family – he was born in Chichester – it looked as though we might be distantly related. He invited me down to Crowborough, in Sussex, for lunch. I took the train on 24 October.

He was a small man, slight of build, with white hair, accompanied by his wife, Sonia. I had been warned he was – or had been – a Fascist, so I was on my guard. They drove me to a hotel. Mrs Fuller apologised for the lunch being in a hotel and not in their home, to which they would take me afterwards. It was because they now had no servants. I said neither had I and neither had any of my friends; I thought they rather belonged to an age that was gone. This seemed to reassure her.

The General had obvious embarrassment in any talk about Crowley and was at pains to distance himself from the esoteric. He said he had at one time practised yoga, adding 'for health', as if excusing it. But then he burst out that the evil in the world was so much greater than the good that, if he believed in anything beyond the physical, he would ally himself with evil, because it was so obviously going to win.

I was shocked. One should never concede defeat to evil. Evil was temporary, good eternal.

When we repaired to their home, he returned to the theme: 'Every animal dies of starvation.'

Drawing on my recollections of the book I had loved in childhood, *The Adventures of a Lion Family*, I said the younger lions permitted the elder to come up and feed though they had taken no part in bringing down the kill.

They did not take the meat back to them when they became too weak to leave the lair, he retorted. So they died of starvation.

I said humans took food to their elders when bedridden.

He said that was 'artificial'. Founded on an idea of kindness that was artificial.

Why think of it as artificial? 'It's human behaviour, which is different from lion behaviour.' It was the behaviour of the more evolved.

I could not lift him from his gloomy, bleak viewpoint but further points I might have made: the domestic cat dies not from inability to eat food but refusing to take it from the plate its owner sets before it – and I should have instanced the herbivore horse dies not from inability to reach grass but cessation of will to eat grass beneath its feet. I think the animal dies because it knows its time is come, and therefore has no will to eat. It wants peace in which to pass.

He had not a lot to say about Neuburg: he had known him in 1906, a Cambridge undergraduate; later at the shows given by Crowley in his flat in Victoria Street – 'which were so respectable I took my mother to them.'

He apologised for having referred to Neuburg in one of his letters to me as a 'colourless personality', saying, 'If one says someone is a colourful personality, that is not altogether a compliment. Crowley was a colourful personality.' Wore showy clothes, dominated the room, whereas Neuburg would sit quietly unless one spoke directly to him, probably didn't say anything. Crowley loved to be thought wicked and thoroughly disconcerted an unfortunate member of the circle called Jones who was bringing a libel action against *The Looking Glass*, which represented the general entourage as immoral. Crowley opted not to go to the witness box to give evidence for Jones but turned up to sit in the court with folded arms, beaming all over his face as though the evil things being said of him were so many compliments. The hapless Jones had to drop the action, choosing to be 'non satisfied' at some cost to his finances as well as his reputation.

But they were certainly an odd lot, he said. Some of them would hoard little bits of paper, compromising letters or memos, which they could use against each other. 'They seemed to think blackmail a normal form of social intercourse.'

He had been going through papers in a box, passing to me any on which he recognised the handwriting, and with sudden alarm asked, 'What's that I've given you?' Somebody had been very cross with him for passing over an obscene paper unwarned.

It was the obscenity that had been the cause of his giving up the aquaintance. Crowley wrote him a letter from Egypt. 'It may, late at night when one is drunk, seem funny to send someone a packet of obscene postcards; but in the morning when you're having breakfast with your wife you open an envelope, to have a lot of obscene post-cards fall out is merely disgusting.' The package might have been opened by the customs and it might have been wondered why he should be the recipient of such stuff. 'I decided to drop him.'

He wished me luck with my biography of Neuburg, and said 'I am writing one of a very different man, Julius Caesar.'

We talked about Caesar. He seemed to be classing him with modern dictators. I said, 'There is one big difference. Caesar showed his ruthlessness when on his way to power, and afterwards surprised everyone by his clemency to those who had opposed him. With tyrants like Hitler it is the other way round; they promise everything that's wonderful whilst canvassing for votes and only after they get into power do they show their ruthlessness.' It was the nearest we got to a possibly dangerous topic. I left feeling he was a man disappointed in his spiritual quest.

On 14 November I had dinner with Vicky's son, generally called Toby, and his wife, Anne. Toby was pretty fed up with having had to be brought up by Colin Evans, for whom his mother had left his father.

On the 15th Gerald Yorke arrived, bringing me on long loan an immense mass of Crowley manuscripts; he had, he explained, parted company with Crowley yet had made him a promise he would not let his papers perish, to which he remained faithful.

On 11 December I saw Mark Goulden in his office at the publishers W. H. Allen. In Vicky's time he had been editor of the *Sunday Referee*. He remembered Hayter Preston, his literary editor, bringing him Victor

Neuburg and so inaugurating 'The Poets' Corner'; and he remembered the latter bringing him Dylan Thomas. I told him it was the Art reviews that had first attracted my mother to the paper. That pleased him and he said it had an important magazine section.

The following evening I was invited by Pamela to her home. She talked a good deal of Dylan, and of that weekend that she and her mother had spent with him and his parents. 'His father was senior English master at Swansea Grammar School'. She felt Dylan attached an importance to this which made her feel inferior.

Then she asked, 'What had Vicky done that people thought he ought not to have done?'

'Had homosexual intercourse with Aleister Crowley.'

She was obviously quite stunned, and for a long moment silent.

'You didn't know?' I asked.

She shook her head.

'Didn't you have any idea?'

She shook her head.

At last she found her voice, '*I* wasn't in any danger, then!'

'No.'

Someone had told her mother there was something in Vicky's past. She had been afraid he might make an attempt to seduce Pamela. 'Right to give a warning, though. Something very peculiar.'

Yes, peculiar. One could grant that. As a matter of fact, I could have done with a warning myself. Though Vicky himself was harmless and, as Pamela said, 'good and wise', he was a magnet attracting people I had found rather frightening.

Pamela said she was still a Christian. She went to church and felt the services had value. She could cope with people who just didn't believe in all that, the atheists and agnostics, better than with the adherents of occult religions.

Remembering that she used to be a Communist, I asked her how she felt about becoming her ladyship.

Impishly, she said, 'It helps one to jump the queue at the hairdresser's.'

Snow came in, and remained with us. He said Pamela had talked to him so much about Vicky he almost felt he had been at the Zoists.

The following March the Snows came to my place. It was just after F. R. Leavis had made his historic attack on Snow. Should I pretend not to have seen it? That would be hurtful tact. I left it conspicuously open on a table and when I went down to let them in greeted with him, 'You're still alive after Leavis!'

He fell on my neck and kissed me.

Had there been a long-standing quarrel between them, in which this was the latest sally?

'No, it came out of the blue.'

'Have you attacked the English School?'

'No.' Leavis did take against some people in an extraordinary way. He always went for Shelley.

'Shelley's dead,' Snow said, 'I'm alive.'

'It's so unfair,' Pamela put in. 'Leavis says he can't think. Charles can't reply, "I can think." It would sound so silly.'

I remarked that it was notoriously impossible to reply to vulgar abuse. That was what made me think it wasn't worth bringing an action for libel.

I happened to have read Snow's *The Two Cultures* which seemed to be what had infuriated Leavis. All I could see it was the observation that the literary people and the scientists were so ignorant of each other's worlds they didn't know how to talk to one another. 'With perhaps a suggestion they ought to get closer together. Isn't that it?'

'Yes.'

Perhaps specialisation was encouraged too early. But even within the two big groups there was almost as great division. Those who had taken 'Greats' at Oxford didn't tend to know much about modern history and astronomers and botanists had not much to say to each other.

I had been told about the Institute for the Study and Treatment of Delinquency, of which Vicky had been a founding member: the Society for the Prevention of Cruelty to Criminals he called it. On 19 March I called to study its archives.

On 27 March A. L. Morton called. The only visitor to the Zoists group who had known Vicky back in the years he lived in Steyning. He spoke of Kathleen's infidelities. I reported that Toby's wife, Anne, had told me she felt Kathleen 'really thought he wouldn't mind', based on the way he talked.

Morton said, 'There are times when a woman is wiser not to take a man at his word.'

D'Offay's collection of Vicky's books lacked the earliest one, *The Green Garland*.

Walking homewards along Wigmore Street one day in mid-April

1962, and passing The Times Bookshop, I remembered it had a rare books department and, though I really did not expect to find the missing volume, decided to look in.

I was turning over one or two of the books on display when a very educated voice asked, 'Can I help you?'

It was Tim d'Arch Smith, the delightful young man I had glimpsed at Brocard Sewell's Conversazione.

I said, 'I'm looking for a book called *The Green Garland* by Victor Neuburg.'

He said, 'So am I.'

The Green Garland was, he believed, a very rare book. Perhaps only very few copies had been printed.

I didn't really need to have it, I said, it was just that it was the only one of Victor Neuburg's books not included in the collection I had bought from Anthony d'Offay.

He knew Anthony d'Offay. A very keen collector.

I could perfectly well just read it at the British Museum, I said. All I needed was to have read it and be able to say something about it. I was writing a biography of Victor Neuburg.

This aroused his interest. He found the whole background to Neuburg fascinating.

Yes, he remembered the Conversazione. No he was not an intimate of Brocard Sewell's circle. The friend who had taken him along that evening was Leslie Staples, a very keen Dickens collector with some valuable Dickensiana.

He would certainly look out for any Neuburgiana and let me know of it.

'What's your name?'

It sounded like Dark Smith, but could not be. I went on thinking about it after I had got home. There was nothing foreign about him. He spoke the good class English known as Public School.

When next I visited the shop I asked him how it was spelled.

'Small d, apostrophe, capital A.' It was his grandfather who had assumed it after some fancied French connection. Before that it had been plain Smith, which was really better. But it was his grandfather who became Colonel d'Arch Smith.

Well, Smith really did need something to go before it. My grandfather thought his parents might have had the imagination to call him Valentine as he was born on St Valentine's Day. Actually, he could have taken on the name Overton, which was his mother's before she became

Mrs Smith. He had my Mother baptised with it, so she was Violet Overton Smith till she married Captain Fuller and that was how the Overton descended to me: Jean Violet Overton Fuller. Tim's father had been a Major d'Arch Smith, rather a missing quantity. Not killed in action, like mine, but gone off with another woman. So we were both brought up by our mothers, both with some influence of grandfathers, who were colonels, though his on his father's, mine on my mother's side. Both only children.

More important was that we both had a feeling for the spiritual mysteries.

October brought renewed contact with Hayter Preston. It was he who suggested that instead of starting my book with Victor Neuburg's birth in 1883, which sounded so long ago, I should use a flashback technique, start with something more exciting. His Crowley contact. I thought about it, rang him and said I was going to start with my own meeting with Neuburg, and the Zoists.

He said, 'Excellent!'

I had always been fascinated by the stars, and finding that Goldsmiths' College of the University of London ran courses for beginners I signed on for classes on Stellar Evolution, starting on 27 January 1963. It was interesting in itself and there was the added perk of being able to go up on to the roof to look through their huge telescope which enabled one to see the stars in the belt of Orion. On 9 March we made an expedition to Mill Hill Observatory to look through its greater giant. Unfortunately the sky clouded over.

Otherwise 1963 seemed to go in the writing of the book about Vicky, while still seeing more people connected with him. It was, I am sure, 'Teddy' Preston who persuaded Goulden that W. H. Allen should publish it.

I joined the Poetry Society, and then the Dulwich Group of poets. It was a long dark trek from the bus stop down to the pub in Dulwich, but the atmosphere, under the presidency of Howard Sergeant, was welcoming; I started writing poetry again and sent him a collection which later in the year he published, under the title *Venus Protected*. A good deal of my newly acquired astronomical knowledge is in it, as well as reminiscences of the hatching of the magpie moth from the caterpillars Gilby taught me to rear, and other creatures. Imagery from the natural world.

From Herbert Corby I heard at last. Amongst the Zoists he had been the one I knew best. He wrote from the Far East, I think Singapore or somewhere like that, but would get in touch as soon as he was back in England.

On 13 May Irene rang me from the House of Commons in great excitement. Could I come there right away? She would like me to be there at two o'clock, when Question Time began. She was going to ask a question of the Foreign Secretary to which there would be a favourable answer and she would like me to be there to hear it. No, not in the Public gallery; in the Serjeant at Arms' Private Box. She had the invitation ready to hand me.

I read:

HOUSE OF COMMONS
Admit
Miss Overton Fuller
    to the Serjeant at Arms' Private Box
    On Monday, 13 April 64

The words were framed within gold borders.

I looked down upon the scene within the Chamber from a box of lonely splendour. I saw her rise and ask

the Secretary of State for Foreign Affairs whether he will now supplement the existing official histories of the late war with an official account of the United Kingdom's contribution to the resistance movements on the continent?

The Secretary of State rose and said:

Her Majesty's Government have given a great deal of thought to this question. Some three years ago they commissioned a professional historian to write an account of the achievements of the Special Operations Executive in France. The draft has now been completed and Her Majesty's Government have decided in principle that it is suitable, subject to further detailed scrutiny for publication by Her Majesty's Stationery Office.

Irene then said:

Will my honourable Friend convey to my right Honourable Friend the Member for Bromley (Mr Harold Macmillan) the appreciation of, I am sure, those connected with the Special Operations Executive and the resistance people whom they helped in Europe of the fact that this decision has been taken. Would he also convey my thanks and those of my two friends who were associated with me in this, Elizabeth Nicholas and Jean Overton Fuller, and pressed the former Prime Minister to take this action? Would he convey how grateful we all are that at last the Government have decided to let the world know something of the work done by the British in conjunction with our European friends?

To which the Minister replied: 'Yes.' (I think she had taken the precaution of asking me on the telephone if she might join to hers my thanks to Harold Macmillan.)

And so the public knew on 15 April 1964 what we had known since 3 August 1961. It was all over the papers the next day, *The Daily Telegraph* having for its prominent sub-heading: NAME OF AUTHOR SECRET.

Both *The Telegraph* and *The Times* mentioned Elizabeth and me. *The Daily Telegraph* reported Irene as saying Mr Macmillan had been a big help and listened to representations from Elizabeth and me. 'He extracted from the Treasury the money required for the History to be compiled. Even then, it took a bit of pressure to get the project past the Foreign Office and the Cabinet Office. Secret files had to be opened up.'

After Irene fetched me back down from the Serjeant at Arms' Private Box, she took me into the tea-room and it was there I screwed myself up to tell her what I knew I must, that in the coming General Election I was going to vote Labour. It was a shock to her, but she was very understanding, said, 'I quite sympathise,' and, when we parted, put her arms round me and kissed me with more than her usual warmth.

On 2 March 1965 I received a letter from Irene:

Dear Jean,

I have a very sad piece of news to tell you, which came my way only last Thursday. 'Gilbert' is dead. Apparently it happened in South Eastern Asia two or three years ago, and was reported in *Figaro*.

I have no other information, but this accounts for the fact that you have had no news … I am so sorry to send you this news but wonder if you had in any way anticipated it.

Love,
affectionately,
IRENE

It was the death of a friend, and I said a prayer for him. I inquired of *Figaro*'s offices in London and Paris. The obituary had appeared in their issue of 18 February 1963; he had been killed in an air accident in Laos on 20 November 1962. I told Irene when on 10 March she took me with her to the Covent Garden Opera House to see Margot Fonteyn and Nureyev dance.

Tim told me over the dinner table at my place he had been introduced to a group of people interested in the Golden Dawn. 'The leader is Golden Dawn through and through.' She was Russian, had something of the same heavy build as Madame Blavatsky. Could she have occult powers? Even the way in which he had come to meet her was mysterious.

It was, he thought, probably through the agency of Gerard Heym he owed his introduction to her circle. This was not, in my eyes, a recommendation. Nor was it altogether in Tim's. Heym was not regarded by the Antiquarian Booksellers Association as a speedy payer. However, he had brought to The Times an antiquarian book to sell, and they had bought it from him and he had invited Tim to tea at the Devonshire Club, where he talked mysteriously of the Golden Dawn (Heym, Tim assured me, was mysterious about absolutely everything). Tim then found himself the recipient of an invitation to an address in Hampstead, where indeed he found a circle, presided over by Tamara Bourkoun.

It was she who telephoned me, and I invited her to tea with me on 16 March. She was rather heavy in build, not at all sophisticated. She told me, encapsulated, her life-story. Born of Russian parents in Manchuria, then brought up in Shanghai, she had sought wisdom of the Theosophical Society but became impatient because its members only talked about ideas, never practised magic (wisely, in my view). In New York had made contact with Israel Regardie, who told her all about the Golden Dawn. But she had become impatient with him too, because he was making no practical contact with the unseen powers. She felt a new order had to be founded, and her problem was there was no one living with the authority to do it, for, as in the Catholic Church, priests have to be created by a practical contact with those that have gone before. As she was pondering this problem she saw a stirring in the atmosphere and there materialised a piece of vellum, inscribed with words appointing her as the founder and head of this new order.

Up till now she had been talking simply and perfectly sensibly, and indeed this was said in the same simple manner. I do not automatically discount all stories about miracles, but this sounded to me unlikely. I said little and just let her run on.

Her manner was not boastful and indeed at one moment she actually sought my opinion on something. In Mozart's opera *The Magic Flute*, why did the hero have to have constantly with him, while on his great spiritual adventure, that dreadfully inferior clown?

I offered a guess: 'Perhaps for the same reason that Don Quixote had to have with him Sancho Panza.'

Did I mean the lower part of himself, that had to be sublimated?

With perhaps, also, some common sense. Quixote was prey to illusions all the time. And illusions could lead one off the path one sought.

As she was putting on her coat to go, she said, 'I have never had a husband – or anything like that.'

I took her to mean she was a virgin. But though she had a good deal of authority in her manner, I thought perhaps she felt her inexperience.

W. H. Allen had begun sending me manuscripts they had received from other authors, to give my opinion, for a small fee, whether they were suitable for publication. This gave me rather the same feeling as when, before I got started on my SOE books, I was for one year one of the examiners in English for the Cambridge Higher Certificate. I had so often sat for examination that this reversal of roles mde me feel with the poor wretches striving to produce what was required. As publisher's reader I could, at least, be a little bit helpful by tacking on to a criticism a suggestion for possible improvement. On 21 April I went into Allen's office to return a manuscript by hand with my report on it, and as I handed the package to the publisher's literary editor, she took the opportunity to tell me she had now read my *Shelley* and found it 'very good indeed'. It was puzzling therefore when on 29 April I received a letter from W. H. Allen saying my biography of Shelley had received an adverse report and they were consequently not publishing it. Then something occurred to me. The literary editor had told me she was setting up as a literary agent. I told Mother I suspected her of having given it a bad official report in order to get it away from Allen's and handle it herself, for profit.

Mother said, 'I don't like that.'

'Neither do I,' I said.

But now there was the launching of *The Magical Dilemma of Victor Neuburg* to think about. In the weeks running up to publication day,

Tim had been pushing it in every way he could think of. He had obtained from The Times Bookshop, conditional on the bookshop being mentioned, permission to circularise its customers with 1,500 leaflets advertising the book, and he found me the printers, Jonathan Vickers, who printed the leaflet.

The launch was to be on Monday 10 May and I was sending out invitations to the party Mother was giving for it at my place at 8.30 that evening. Pamela wrote that she and Charles would come 'if humanly possible'. General Fuller wrote that he and his wife would be 'delighted' to come (but at the last minute cancelled because of some emergency). Irene rang to ask if it was required to be in evening or cocktail style dress, 'because I will be coming straight from the House of Commons'.

I said, 'That's all right. Snow is probably coming straight from the House of Lords. Have you met him?'

'No, but I've met his wife.' Pamela and she had been momentarily on some committee for something.

The Snows were the first to arrive. I said to Charles, 'It's good of you to have come.'

'My wife would never have forgiven me if I hadn't,' was his reply.

Irene came in an elegant hat and a bit of emerald lace in the neck of her blouse. (When she was young people used to tell her that, as she had fair hair and blue eyes, she must always wear blue but she had got so bored with it that she thought she'd try out emerald.) I had on the evening dress made for me by Mother to wear for the author's photograph that appeared in the book.

Tim helped Mother uncork the champagne. I said, 'To Victor Neuburg' raising my glass to his photograph, and Pamela promptly proposed the return toast, 'To Jean'. I then read aloud Vicky's poem, 'Druids'.

The Snows, who had arrived half an hour early to help with the preparations, the first to arrive, were the last to leave. Happening to stand by the window, I saw them on the pavement below as they walked away. When they thought they were out of sight, they suddenly linked hands, like children, and skipped along.

On the following day the BBC collected and drove me down to Steyning. The last part of the climb thence to Chanctonbury Ring we had to do on foot. I had not been up there since I was a child, with Cousin Arthur. But that, I felt sure, was the place of Vicky's inspiration, and so, with my back to the strange grove atop the hill and my face to the television camera, I read, again, the whole of Vicky's poem, 'Druids' from *Songs of the Groves*, sandwiched between the answering of questions that formed the main part of the interview.

The programme was transmitted, on Southern Television. The subject-matter of the book was obviously controversial, but there were prominent sympathetic reviews.

On 25 May Tamara telephoned to ask if I was coming 'tomorrow'. I think this must have been to one of her evenings for those she was gathering around her, which she was trying to make a regular thing. But no, I couldn't. It was a Dulwich Group night and Sergeant had put me down to share the platform with Leo Abse (the Labour MP), to read from *Venus Protected* and other poems, he from his latest book of poetry.

On 28 May I was invited together with Mother to spend the day with the literary editor turned agent at her home in the country. As I expected, she was very keen to be the agent for the *Shelley*. We thought it best to accept but we both felt the atmosphere was fishy. Only one thing was interesting about that day; the agent's son was a pianist and every time he sat down to the piano, provided he avoided a syncopated rhythm, the cows from a neighbouring field came up to listen. If he played anything with a syncopated rhythm they apparently retreated to the far side.

Tamara had made the acquaintance of an expert on Mithraism, and was giving a course of lectures on it at the Ivanhoe Hotel, Bloomsbury. She hoped her friends would attend. She had asked Tim to take the chair; so on 2 June I went.

On 9 June Tim rang to ask me if I could take the chair in his stead that evening; so I did. The lecturer said something that disturbed me: he was, he said, giving these talks for nothing. This was an odd point to make and there was a touch of resentment in his voice. He must be giving these talks on someone else's initiative. Tamara's? The hire of the room must cost something; who if not he paid it? And something was being charged to people to attend; who received the money, Tamara? Was this a commercial enterprise? Suddenly the whole enterprise seemed somehow tainted.

On 11 June I left for Iceland. When as a child I had studied maps in the atlas I had been fascinated by this island which looked like a pendant from the Arctic Circle. I wanted to find what it was like, and perhaps to be alone for a bit.

Leaving London Airport at five in the afternoon and passing over Scotland and the islands beyond it was a five-hour flight to Reykjavik. The landing field was all buttercups, the temperature cool but not freezing. I walked over the buttercups to the customs where the man asked, 'What have you come to Iceland for?' I said, 'Adventure.'

I booked in at the University Hotel, went out and walked around for an hour. The air was so pure that distances looked less than they were, things a long way away appearing near. I went to bed with the sky still light. People said 'Good night' to one though it was daylight. In the morning I tried the beach; it was possible to paddle – but dangerous because all the world's unwanted corrugated iron and tin cans seemed to have been thrown into the water.

On the 15th I made an excursion to Gullfoss, where the waterfall spray rose so high there was a rainbow in it, then to Geysir, the hot-spring whence the steam came bubbling out through the boiling bog. The spring supplied the hot water which issued from my hotel bath-room taps.

On the 17th I made an all-day trip from Reykjavik by air to Akureyri, the town furthest north. Reykjavik was lapped by the Gulf Stream, Akureyri not, and the drop in temperature was sharp. We went on by bus, stopped at Lake Myvatn, were invited to get out but the mosquitoes were too much of a problem. The country was black lava desert, and in a natural hoop of the lava I saw a ram, with magnificent curled horns, standing as if it had framed itself. Then the black turned to yellow as we reached the sulphur springs of Namaskard, all bubbling up through the lava, while beyond rose a most magnificent flat-topped mountain, a black hulk with pendant diamond of snow. I asked the driver to write its name. He wrote 'BURFELL' and said it was almost on the Arctic Circle. We saw also the largest waterfall in Europe, Gotafoss; and then the bus hurtled back; it had come through on the radio a blizzard was expected straight from the Pole. We reached Akureyri before the blizzard, hastily took off, and I saw passing below me the largest of Iceland's glaciers before we landed back in Reykjavik.

I had purposely brought no reading matter so as to give a rested mind some idea about what I should do next. In order to keep company with Tim, should I go further with this Golden Dawn thing? I saw a small white skull, bleached by the elements, roll down the shingle beach of Reykjavik and into the sea; that seemed to indicate something not beginning but ending. The Golden Dawn was very nineteenth century. Perhaps like Masonry, Martinism and many suchlike things, it was not needed in the age of Krishnamurti.

I had come to Iceland partly with the thought that I might use the time alone and, with no commitments, do a bit of meditation. In Paris, in 1947, I had particularly long runs of visions. Doubtless that was because sitting with Vivian, his great woman colleague and their best clairvoyant, the atmosphere had been conducive. Yet the source must always be possible to tap. At midday – it was at midday we always sat – I thought of them and of the Masters of wisdom, and sitting on the side of my bed closed my eyes. From behind my right shoulder passing in front of me was a girl, descending to the white bridge across the fjord. Although her back was to me, I saw that over her white dress was the black and green box-jacket that was mine. She was me. Her white plimsolls were very down at heel, as she had walked so many hundreds of miles through the millennia, through so many lands. In her left hand she held by their strings a bunch of balloons, pale blue, pale pink, green, yellow and violet, rising up on their strings. She had kept them aloft through the millennia. It had seemed to her the one thing she had at all costs to do. As she crossed the white bridge on to the other shore I knew what those balloons were. They were ideals, concepts, concepts of ideals, that waved above her head. Why had she thought she could not walk without them? As I asked this question they vanished. When reading Krishnamurti I had wondered why he used the terms 'ideals' and 'concepts' and 'conceptual thinking' in a pejorative sense. I understood now, and as I did so a rowing-boat, without an oarsman, came in from the right and she stepped into it.

I had had what I wanted of Iceland and returned by the next plane, on 20 June. On the plane I sat next to a woman who had wintered there; she said what was terrible was not so much the cold as the absence of daylight. It made everybody edgy. I felt a bit the same about the absence of darkness.

Tim cannot put an exact date to his breaking with Tamara, but it was between my return from Iceland and the ending of the cricket season that it was wearing thin. Cricket was Tim's favourite sport, he was enormously knowledgeable about it. He was a member of the MCC and during the season spent every Saturday afternoons at Lord's whenever there was a match.

On 23 June there was a last talk on Mithraism, in Tamara's flat, because they had been unable to cover their expenses at the hotel. (So they had hoped to bring in the public.)

On 19 July she came to see me, telling me that her charter derived in some way that I did not understand from one of the less orthodox sects within the Islamic mysticism. That was the last time I saw her.

But in the meantime, Tim had told me she had taken over a co-Masonic lodge, so as to have its charter. But why did she need to dissipate her energies in these sideshows instead of leading her pupils into the mysteries of the Golden Dawn? I thought because she herself was frightened. And why did she need to get herself another charter if she had had one miraculously delivered, on vellum? She wanted Tim to join the co-Masonic lodge and help her oust the existing members: 'Housewives, Timothy!'

Tim was not attracted by the plan to take over the existing members or the ritual itself. To me, he burst out: 'And it's on Saturday afternoons. Shan't go.'

Cricket to the rescue! I was grateful to the game.

Seventeen

I made paintings of my recollections of Iceland, though the landscape did not easily lend itself. The one that meant most to me was Mount Burfel, but Mother observed dampingly, 'It's a quite singularly bad composition.' Well yes, I knew it was just that hunk on the sky line with no foreground, the patterns made by the black lava desert and yellow sulphur not serving to give an idea of distance. But Rita Barton, colleague from Censorship days, said, 'It's got trolls in it.' Thank you Rita. I hadn't thought of it, but perhaps there could be.

I also went back to the Shelley landscape, and started one of a pool I thought I remembered in the Shelleys' grounds. But why was I mixing the alizerine crimson with white to produce a range of pinks, in different shades of which I was creating the pool itself, the vegetation round it and the sky? I was creating a rose dawn – and it was not of Shelley I was thinking.

With my typescript *Shelley* all was not going well. The newly established agents, having manoeuvred to get it, seemed to be having no success. I asked for it back. It came back – with a note saying if I thought to send it to any of those firms just as from myself, the response might be different. So they had not sent it. So what had been the object of the manoeuvre?

I sent it to Oxford University Press, and received a very nice letter from Jon Stallworthy saying it was too much of a research work for the general reader and he had sent it to their academic house, the Clarendon Press. This was flattering, but then Clarendon returned it with a letter saying that for their narrow academic lists there were too many excursions from Eng. Lit.

Well ... in reading Shelley's fragment *The Assassins* I recognised its source in a little known anonymous French work, *Le Vieux de la Montagne*, which I had read in the British Museum in quite another connection. This title appeared moreover in Mary Shelley's reading list for 1816 but no previous Shelley scholar had thought to look at it: it was revealing because it gave a picture of this Islamic sect quite different from the usual, and so explained why Shelley had done this. It was the French work he was following. Moreover, it made suddenly plain that the Ariel of whom Shelley wrote was not the sprite in *The Tempest*, though he knew his Shakespeare, but the Ariel in *Le Vieux de la Montagne*, a sort of angel in Islamic mythology. To explain this involved me in a few pages that had nothing to do with Eng. Lit., yet were needed if the reader was to understand what Ariel meant here: from works I consulted, it appeared Ariel was the Islamic equivalent of Greek Cupid, but raised to a spiritual level. Platonic Love might one say?

The other excursus concerned the Nairs. Shelley had read a book about this Indian people amongst whom there is no marriage. But the author of the book had never been to India or met any Nairs. Mother had, on the Malabar coast where my father was stationed in 1914. She understood that there was no marriage amongst them, the women chose their own lovers and a Nair man visiting a woman left his sword outside so that no other would enter. The children belonged solely to their mothers. Yet the Nairs were very modest, they would not allow my father to photograph them but signified by signs that it would be all right if the camera were passed to Mother. I agree this was nothing to do with Shelley since he did not know it, so – unwilling to drop it altogether – I banished it to a footnote. But looking at that photograph Mother took there is a thing that haunts me. Each of the two women stands with one breast bare. Am I looking at the originals of the Amazons? From Malabar to Greece is a long way, and the Amazons had one breast not just bare but sliced off, but the look is the same as in the famous marbles. It is a very long shot but is it possible the very ancient Greeks had contact with a tribe of women who had some of the ideas of the Nairs? Beneath the photograph Mother has written that all young 'Naya' (as she spells them) women wear one breast bare, elder women being bare to the waist. (So unlike all other Indian women, Hindu or Muslim, so much wrapped up and property of their husbands.)

On 6 April 1966, after a long silence, Foot telephoned. He asked me to lunch with him at a restaurant in Soho. He said his book would appear later in the month and he was taking this occasion to express his respect and admiration for the work I had done, the research that had gone into my books.

I was therefore unsuspecting of what was to come. On the morning of 28 April, publication day, I walked down to Her Majesty's

Stationery Office to buy my copy of *S.O.E. in France*, by M. R. D. Foot. I brought it home and began reading the preface. It started off by saying, in the first paragraph, that the reason for the Government's departure from its usual policy of keeping such archives secret was that there was not 'a whole discreditable history to be hushed up'. Certainly mistakes were made, but a number of writers had fastened upon one or two of these mistakes, that bore on less than five per cent of the SOE's effort in France, and inflated them – for lack of balancing evidence – into phantasmagorical sketches of SOE as a kind of Moloch that devoured innocent children for evil motives.

Whilst I was wondering if I was included here, Elizabeth rang, furious: 'That's meant for you and me.' Yes. I knew it was.

More surprising was that Irene's name nowhere appeared. She was the mother of the whole project. If she had not conceived the idea, put it to Macmillan, who put it to the Foreign Office, there would not have been a history. Her name should have appeared first amongst the credits. There were only two: to Major-General Sir Colin Gubbins and Lieutenant Colonel E. G. Boxshall (Foreign Office). I felt the omission of her name an insult to Irene.

For myself, what vexed me most was that in his Bibliography he said *Double Webs* 'investigates Déricourt mainly through the evidence of Bleicher and Christmann'. I never met Bleicher, never had any correspondence with Bleicher and used none of Bleicher's statements. Foot meant, of course, Vogt. Vogt I regarded as much the more honourable character. I telephoned Irene at the House of Commons and she asked me to come right away.

As she met me down below, she said, 'I worked so hard to get it. Is it worth having got?'

'Yes,' I said, it contained dates of people's passages to and from France that could only have been got from the files. I had written solely from my conversations with people involved in the operations and my dates were only as accurate as their memories. Foot had written entirely from files, without meeting any of the people – except, apparently, Gubbins.

We went into the tea-room.

Irene's diagnosis of what had happened, as she put it to me over our tea, was that the influence of Gubbins had made itself felt. On that morning of 3 August 1961 Foot was told his appointment was still an official secret and that he had leave to talk about it only with her, me and Elizabeth. We were the privileged three. He had not, at that date, permission to talk to anybody in SOE about it. I would remember from that lunch how excited he was about it all, the sense of a privileged get-together. But obviously the matter could not long be kept from Gubbins, nor should it have been. Irene thought Foot must have been very favourably impressed by Gubbins; and been assured by him there was nothing seriously wrong. And that it was the Gubbins view that affected his presentation of Elizabeth and myself in the *History*. Plus the attitude of some of the elements in the Foreign Office. Though in no way responsible for SOE, and its mistakes, once the SOE files had been, on its dissolution, transferred to the Foreign Office, the Foreign Office took responsibility for them – poor Mr Eden had had to get up and answer questions about the German control of the Dutch Section. Among the stuffier elements in the permanent staff, too, there was a tendency to resist Harold Macmillan's urging to open them to a historian. It was not only Irene's name that was absent from Foot's book; so was Harold Macmillan's, and he really should have been given a credit. She was glad that she had expressed our thanks in the House to 'the member for Bromley'. (It was not permitted within the Chamber to mention any member by his or her name.)

I did find in the book the things I most wanted to see. The radio-game was admitted. It was admitted the radio-sets of 'Archambaud' (Norman), 'Valentine' (Macalister), 'Madeleine' (Noor) and 'Leopold' (Marcel Rousset) – the ones I had learned of from Starr and from Vogt – had in fact become German controlled; plus one more, found by Elizabeth, 'Arthur' (Steel).

It was twelve years since, after the publication of *The Starr Affair*, Buckmaster had told the *Empire News*: 'She states that not one but a number of our networks became German controlled. I know it was only one and consider I am in a better position to know the facts than she is.'

The official history had admitted to five.

I just wished Foot had given names of all the men and women dropped straight into enemy hands.

Having left the envelopes open, I showed Irene the letters I intended delivering to *The Times* and *The Daily Telegraph*, if she did not see anything wrong with the wording:

Sir,
    I am puzzled by Mr Foot's statement to the press that he had only two years in which to complete his history, *S.O.E. in France*.

On August 3 1961, that is nearly five years ago, Mr Foot was introduced to me at the House of Commons by Dame Irene Ward as the historian officially appointed by the Foreign Office. Dame Irene had previously shown me the correspondence between herself and Mr Harold Macmillan who was then Prime Minister, in which my book *Double Webs* was mentioned also her suggestion that there should be a historian appointed to undertake an official history.

We talked through a whole afternoon, having both lunch and tea as Dame Irene's guests and, after her Parliamentary duties required her to leave us, he and I continued our conversations over dinner in a restaurant nearby. I understood both from Mr Foot and from Dame Irene that disclosure had been authorised by the Foreign Office to practically nobody but ourselves and Elizabeth Nicholas, author of *Death Be Not Proud*, who would have been of the party that day had she been available.

On August 22nd 1961, Mr Foot came to tea with me to consult with me further. At his request I showed him the original of a statement written out for me by hand by a former official of a German service, and he appreciated the accuracy of the transcription of it printed in my book *Double Webs*. I also lent him my own card index of dates in SOE history, which I had built up for my own use; later he returned it with expressions of gratitude, saying he had copied it out.

After I received practically no spontaneous communications from Mr Foot until the beginning of this month when he rang and asked me to lunch with him on April 6. When I arrived he said at once that he had asked me because of his admiration for the integrity of my researches, which transpired through my books. I would have been better pleased had he said this within the covers of his own book, which I have seen for the first time today, wherein such comments as he has made on mine are without exception belittling and no hint whatever of his admiration appears.

She saw in the text nothing that needed changing, so I sealed both envelopes up and delivered them by hand to the offices of *The Times* and *The Daily Telegraph*. It was printed in *The Times* of 30 April, and I think it appeared in the *Telegraph* also, though it is the cutting from *The Times* which is pasted in my album.

Foot wrote apologising for having in his Bibliography given Bleicher as my source where he should have said Vogt, and undertook to change Bleicher to Vogt in any future edition; but he said it was not dinner but a second tea we had on leaving Irene on 3 August 1961. He was perhaps right, though I remember being handed the menu and hesitating as to whether to choose an omelette or a welsh rarebit – perhaps what country people call high tea.

A new printing of his book was required earlier than expected, but from an unwelcomed cause. On p. 431 he had written:

... stories of torture come from the prurient imaginations of authors anxious to make their books sell; apparently with one exception, the story that Mrs Sanson had all her toenails pulled out at the Avenue Foch. She did return from Germany with some of her toenails missing; unfortunately her experiences in Ravensbruck had induced in her a state of nervous tension so severe that she had considerable trouble for many months in distinguishing fantasy and reality, and it is likely enough that she got the two confused in trying to give an honest account of what she had been through. In her formal interrogation on her return she made no reference to this incident at all. The story has now become a well established part of the folklore of the war; the principal villain of it, a young French double agent, was undoubtedly killed in a gunfight with the resisters in the rue de Rivoli, and it is neither charitable nor magnanimous to complain as some brave men and some vindictive gossips do that her GC should never have been given her.

What was Foot trying to say? That she did lose some toenails, not through having them pulled out during her interrogation at Avenue Foch, as an inducement to talk, but later, in some other way? Elizabeth had always expressed to me her belief that Odette's story of having had her spine burned with a red-hot poker at Avenue Foch had been designed to tally with some scar she had got in some other way. Could the same be true of the toenails, that she really had lost some though in some other way? Anyway, Foot confirmed that the alleged torturer, Pierre Cartaud, had been shot, as Vogt told me and Mercier confirmed, in a shooting incident in the street whilst the Germans were still in Paris, and had not been after the war charged by the French with torturing prisoners. Why had Miss Atkins felt it incumbent upon her to cover up Odette's lie? That to me was the biggest mystery. It was presumably not she who had told Odette to make this story up, so why should she cover for her – and try to make me ruin my reputation by printing, as being true, the false story she told me? There was also something unpleasing in the choice of Cartaud to put the blame on: a traitor to France, he would have fewer than most people rushing to his defence.

Anna Neagle, who had played the part of Odette in the film called the passage in Foot's book 'character assassination', and Odette demanded an apology, retraction and damages.

Elizabeth and I discussed on the telephone what line we should take. Although he had been nasty to us, if he pleaded justification and the case came to court we would go into the box for him.

But he retracted and apologised, the whole edition was called in and the Foreign Office paid Odette £12,000 in damages. 'And that means the taxpayers, you and me,' said Elizabeth, disgusted.

Tim, on 22 May, over dinner at a Chinese restaurant in Soho, told me he had finally broken with Tamara. Some time after that he told me he had heard she had had a stroke: sunk into a coma, unable to recognise anybody or anything. Later again, he heard she had died.

Truly, I was sorry to hear it; yet all the more thankful Tim had got out when he did.

In the meantime I had become a member of Writers' Workshop. This was not part of the Poetry Society though it held its meetings in a room on the premises, on Friday evenings at eight, so that if one had attended the Poetry Society's meeting at seven one could easily go on to it. The atmosphere was at once more cosy and more professional. No applause. We all knew each other and would discuss the poem just read; had it come off well? If not, what was wrong with it? Was it too much rhyme-led or were too many of the lines end-stopped? Members included George MacBeth, Alan Brownjohn, Shirley Toulson, Hannah Hobsbaum (secretary), George Wightman (in the chair), Fleur Adcock, Donald Ward, and, later, Martin Booth. MacBeth was the presenter of the programme 'Poetry Now', broadcast regularly on the Third Programme, and it was because he liked the poems I offered that I more than once appeared in this. (These attendances at Broadcasting House were actually paid, at so much a minute.)

I wrote to Chatto and Windus saying I noticed they had published Swinburne: would they be interested in a biography of him by me? I was invited to an interview with Edmund Grey on 14 June. We talked for perhaps half an hour and then he said, 'I suppose you'd like us to make you an offer?'

I said, 'Yes.'

That was the simplest placing of a book – not a line yet written – that had come my way. And the strange thing was, that just after that my *Shelley*, having been turned down by twenty-one publishers, was accepted by Jonathan Cape, whose Graham Greene (not the novelist but related) liked it very much.

But now Chatto asked to see my *Shelley*. By my contract with them I had to give them first refusal of my next book, but I had offered *Shelley* to Cape before I approached Chatto about *Swinburne*. In the end it was sorted out amicably in correspondence between the two publishers: Cape were to do *Shelley*, as a one off, the first refusal on my next to remain with Chatto.

One of Tim's customers at The Times was a Mr Mayfield, a big Swinburne collector, and we all had dinner together in a hotel on 19 June. Mayfield tipped me to have a look at the letters written to Swinburne by his cousin, Mary. I would, in any case, have looked at letters from all his relatives but something in Mayfield's tone alerted me to take special note.

Tim saw me home afterwards and handed me a present. It was a first edition of Swinburne's *Love's Cross Currents*.

It must have been soon after that, in the Students' Room of the British Museum, in the queue before the issues desk, that I happened to see Foot. I didn't think he had seen me, so I took no notice. Later Elizabeth rang me and told me he had told her on the telephone that I had 'cut' him. No, it was not meant to be a cut. It was only that I had put in for a Swinburne manuscript, was eager to hold it in my hands and did not want to be delayed by conversation.

As I began reading the letters from Mary Leith to Swinburne in the British Museum I was at first puzzled because they all began, 'Cy merest dozen'. Then I realised it was not merely in the salutation but in the text that initial letters of words had been transposed. The salutations should be read, 'My dearest cousin', and in the text below it took one only a moment to see which letters needed to be put in their proper places to make a comprehensible text. It was a cipher, but so simple, so childish that they had perhaps invented it when they were children, and kept it up. In the first she thanked him for sending his 'Eton book', and from what followed it was obvious this was all about flogging and that this delighted her.

Tim, meanwhile, had been becoming concerned over the future of The Times Bookshop. There were rumours it was being sold to Truslove and Hanson, a subsidiary of W. H. Smith. It was doubtful whether they would want to keep on the antiquarian department, and even if they did he did not really see himself working for that firm. There was a difference of attitude. If only he had the capital to set up on his own ... 'If only I could get together £1,000.' I said, 'Couldn't I let you have that? We could go into partnership.' This was over tea at the Wimpole Buttery on 16 November 1966.

When he came to dinner with me on 24 November, I told him I could put in £4,000.

It was our rose dawn.

Mother and I took it in turn to have each other to lunch on Sundays. It was at her place, on the first Sunday in September 1967, that she mentioned that, as she had been walking along the road, she had had a moment of feeling rather faint and had turned into a chemist's, just to ask for a chair on which to sit down. The assistant, who was an Indian, thought she was suffering from the heat and stood before her chair fanning her with a paper. This charmed her – it was like being back in India again, where if anybody seemed about to faint it was always assumed they were suffering from the heat.

I suggested she might see her doctor, and she said she would but could not have thought the matter urgent since, in the ensuing days, she did not do so.

On Sunday the 10th, as Tim was coming to dinner with me in the evening, she said she would come for our lunch on the Saturday instead. She asked what I was giving Tim to eat. When by myself I was vegetarian, but I wanted Tim to have something he would like and so had bought a couple of grouse. She took an interest: what was I going to give him to drink with it? Would I serve it with red currant jelly? A bit of watercress might be nice. ... And so on.

Afterwards I walked with her to the Russell Square underground station. I saw her buy her ticket and watched her step into the lift, and slowly go down in it.

On the Monday Mother rang about midday, just to ask how the dinner went. It was a lovely day she said and she had taken a chair down to sit in the sunshine on the doorstep.

On Wednesday, midday, there was a phone call from a hospital. 'Are you Miss Fuller? Your mother died at 11.40 in the morning, yesterday.'

The author's father with his men of the 88th Carnatics, Indian Army

LEFT The author's mother: photo by the author's father RIGHT The author aged six

'Gilby': the author's grandfather, Colonel Frederick Smith, 1918

QUEEN'S
THEATRE
Week Com. MONDAY, JULY 4

THE
SHAFTESBURY
PLAYERS *Present*

JEAN FULLER

JAMES HAYTER

=THE=

CHEERFUL KNAVE

A COMEDY IN THREE ACTS

By KEBLE HOWARD

NEXT WEEK MISS DOROTHY MATHER, A BRILLIANT LONDON ACTRESS, WILL JOIN THE COMPANY
TELEPHONE 4985   ENTRANCE—HERMONHILL AND HAWKHILL

WILLIAM H. COX, PRINTER, 21 NORTH TAY STREET, DUNDEE.

Playbill for the Queen's Theatre, Dundee, 1933

The author, Paris 1947

Phoebe Llewellyn Smith

The author, 1954

March 1957: Waterloo Station promotion

Tim d'Arch Smith, Paris, 1967

The author, same occasion

The author and her mother, December 1963

Tim d'Arch Smith, 1992

LEFT Irene Ward   RIGHT The author at presentation for wartime graduates (see p.354)

The author, having played Cyril Scott's 'Lotus Land'
at a Theosophical Society meeting, May 1999

The author at home March 2001 – with some of her paintings on view

The author with Barry Humphries and Tim d'Arch Smith, 2006

I was quite unprepared for it. I dashed there in a taxi. I do not know what I had expected but I had not expected her cheek to be cold, her body stiff, a strange almost ochre colour. Hoping she was still near enough to it to hear, I said all the things I wanted her to hear.

Then I was beset with paperwork. My signature was required on an authorisation for a post-mortem. It seemed she was dead when she arrived from her doctor's in the ambulance. Then I had to walk to the Town Hall and register her death, and then to an undertakers. 'She wants to be cremated,' I said.

Then I went to her flat, used my key and let myself in.

On her big easel, the easel that had been Sickert's, which he had left to Florence and she had left to Mother, was a painting of some fruits, dark plums and lemons, obviously unfinished, the paint still wet, the tubes of oil-paint she had been using still without their caps and the brushes still unwashed. She had been working up to the last. Pinned to the easel with a drawing-pin was a note saying that in the case of her death I was the person to be informed, with my address and phone number. That had been there for a long time.

All around photographs of myself at every age stared at me bleakly: as a child, in my stage days, with Tim side by side during our weekend in Paris last spring. What to do in this empty room? There was the little oak-tree she had grown from the acorn she had picked up in Kew and planted. She had tried, by trimming its roots, to keep it as a bonsai in the Japanese manner but its will to grow defeated her and she had transplanted it from its first tiny pot into a hyacinth bowl. It was her child. I picked it up and took it back to my flat in a taxi.

It was violets I would have liked for her coffin, for Violet was the name given her at her birth. But in September there were no violets. African violets, then. They are not a kind of violet that grows in Africa but a different botanical species, saintpauliers, yet they look very like violets and she was born (because of Gilby's being in the RAMC, in Africa) in Cape Town. They flower in the autumn. I could not get a bunch anywhere, but I did find a small plant in a pot and picked the flowers off it. As the coffin was going through the hatch into the furnace I walked up and laid them on it.

One bud on the plant that I had missed opened, its centre like a yellow star. It seemed symbolic of resurrection.

I remembered a dream she had told me, perhaps a few weeks ago. She had seen my father again. It was so many years since she had seen him, but there he was, in his scarlet uniform, small, in the distance.

Much of their courtship had taken place during the Durbar; they had met on a tennis court in late 1910 but were engaged within three weeks, during the Durbar. He was in his scarlet uniform riding his horse in the parade, in the procession accorded the King and Queen of England when they came out to be crowned Emperor and Empress of India; and after she had made her curtsy to the King Emperor and Queen Empress, he was in the pool of officers in their scarlet uniforms waiting for their partners, and took her arm and led her into the Court Ball. He was in scarlet when – two years later because first the death of her sister and then one thing after another had caused the swift courtship to be followed by a long engagement – at last they were married in 1912, in St Peter's Church inside Fort William. They left under an arch of his men's raised swords – during a crashing thunderstorm. Their marriage was brief because he was killed in 1914. She said to me once, 'A world came to an end in 1914.' Indeed, though it must always be strange to be a posthumous child, in my case it is stranger than most, for my father belonged to a world I have never seen; a world that had vanished before I was born. He was in the distance, in the dream because of all the things that had happened and all the people she had known in between; but it did not make any differences. He saw her, and came up and took her arm. A few days after, she saw a bandsman pass, in a scarlet uniform. It seemed to her an earnest that her dream was true. Because, for her, scarlet was Jack.

Her birthday was 13 October. I always tried to give her something nice. A necklace with some artistic touch to it. Extraordinary that 13 October was the date I was given to come and choose a memorial stone for her. I had not thought that this year it would be a stone. She would have been eighty-two. She had lived through five reigns. She had seen Queen Victoria and she had seen the Beatles. She had wanted to live to see men land on the moon, but that was still in the future.

I brought all her things to my flat, to sort out. I hung my father's sword on one of my walls, found a place for the silver cups that were trophies he had won at this and that. The silver spirit kettle I placed on the brass table which she had let me have already; it was the piece of furniture I loved most.

But the easel that had been Sickert's was uneasy in my home. Far too big for my sitting-room and unneeded by me as the pictures I painted were never more than 18 x 14 inches. Mother had tried to get me to paint larger, as she herself did, saying that in galleries only larger ones were noticed. But I did not paint my pictures for them to be hung in galleries. I painted them to hang on my own walls and did not want them to occupy too much space. The small easel I had bought in Paris at the Académie Julien was quite big enough for me. Also, I did not like the associations of Sickert's easel. I took it to Rowneys, and they bought it – for only a modest sum, but I felt the atmosphere lighter when it had gone.

The *Shelley* proofs came from Cape. I wished Mother could have seen them, for *Shelley* was the first of my books she had read. Although a voracious reader, she never read about the war. *The Magical Dilemma* she bypassed for different reasons; but she had just read a biography of Harriet, Shelley's first wife, and so was interested to read my biography of Shelley. She did so in typescript, making pertinent comments; which was the reason why I dedicated it to her. Like the moon landing, it came just too late for her.

On 6 December 1967 Michelle, Professor Jones's daughter, rang to tell me her father was dead. It was not a surprise; born on 12 September 1881 he was eighty-six and had expressed to me a presentiment he was nearing the end of his journey in the present body. For his next incarnation he would go back to China again. 'I don't want to, but I have to.'

'Unfinished business?'

'Yes.'

He reminded me that when I first saw him I had had the momentary illusion of seeing a Chinese with small beard that he had not in this life. He had queried, 'Chinese, not Korean?'

He had asked because whilst he was giving a lecture once at Malet Street someone had seen him with a wholly different face, bodily build and even dress – Korean of the Middle Ages. He had no doubt whatsoever that he had been the Korean phonetician Se Jong, who had given Korea its alphabet. They hadn't had one and had used the Chinese, which was not well adapted to them as the structure of Korean was different from that of Chinese and anyway it placed Koreans under too strong Chinese influence. So he had devised an alphabet phonetically to represent the sounds of the Korean language. It had been a life-work, in a wooden hut 'without the facilities we have here', but in 1448 he finished it and presented it to the King. It is still in use. A few modifications and simplifications had been made, 'But it's still Se Jong's alphabet.' Five hundred years since he gave it them. He was modestly pleased.

I asked him if he knew of any intermediate incarnation. He said he had wondered about the eighteenth-century Sanskrit scholar, Sir William Jones, but the coincidence of the name made the identification seem too facile. The entry in the *Dictionary of National Biography* was solely adulatory and gave no indication of his faults. 'I think it is in the faults one recognises oneself, don't you?' If he came across some reference to Sir William Jones as having faults he could see in himself, he would believe.

In the library of University College I came across one of his books, The *History and Meaning of the Term Phoneme*, and in it a footnote to Se Jong, 'believed to be quite a good phonetician'. A modest self-appraisal his colleagues would not have suspected.

But now, thinking back to that vision I had had of him, that was obviously not of Se Jong but of some Chinese, possibly scholar, but of what date before and after Se Jong? It was pertinent because he had now to go back there.

'Why?'

'The Chinese have not been being very nice to the Tibetans.'

'You feel that was your fault?'

'Yes.' He believed he had used his influence in supporting a policy that was invasive of Tibet. Seeing now the ill that had resulted he had to go back there and do all he could to reverse that policy. 'I have to try to gain a position of influence and persuade them to behave better.' That could only be done by reincarnating as a Chinese.

I remembered an earlier conversation, in the College. He had said he did not want to lie up seven or twelve thousand years in *devachan* (the heaven world) but to come straight back here and get on with his work; to which I had replied, 'Then I am sure you will.'

Michelle said on the phone he had died with all his faculties intact.

I did not doubt it, and I thought, 'He has gone to China.'

On 19 January 1968 I received the first advance copy of my *Shelley*, brought by hand, from Cape's.

When I told Chatto my next book would be about Bacon, Ian Parsons exclaimed, 'Why anybody should write a book on dry-as-dust old Bacon I can't imagine!' I decided nevertheless to go ahead and write it – the *Shelley* had after all been turned down by twenty-one publishers but, twenty-second time lucky, had found a home, and a good one too. Tim had got me a complete Spedding's edition of the works of Bacon in fourteen volumes for a modest £70, and I was steadily reading through these before going to Lambeth Palace to see his letters in his original hand.

When my five further advance copies of *Shelley* arrived I took the first of them to Tim at The Times Bookshop. He was able to give me in reciprocity one of his edition of *The Magus* which had just arrived from America. This work of Francis Barrett had, as he informed his readers, first been published in 1801. Tim's introduction displayed his close knowledge of the Qabalah and its numerical system. Exchange of dedications.

On 23 February I received a letter from Irene enclosing a copy of the *Third Report of the Parliamentary Commissioners* concerning conditions at Sachsenhausen concentration camp, so that I might see that on p. 32 there was mention of *The Starr Affair* by Jean Overton Fuller with a six-line quotation from it. Rather a change from the way in which the Foreign Office had reacted to that book when it first appeared, so many years ago. I was now, it appeared, a respectworthy authority.

I was a good deal taken up with poetry. My mother's death had poured into a series of poems, and I entered them under the title *African Violets*, for *Manifold*'s first big competition, which was to be judged by the votes of the subscribers to *Manifold*. There was a tie. *African Violets* tied with a submission by a man for first place, and as the creators of *Manifold* had only money enough to pay for one publication, it was *African Violets* that they printed.

I had also been for some time working on a long narrative poem, 'Darun and Pitar'. People have tried in vain to find these characters in books on mythology. The names are my invention; nevertheless, Pitar has perhaps something perceptible in common with the Pitris in the *Secret Doctrine* of H. P. Blavatsky, and Darun with Narada in the same.

I was pleased with the review of *Shelley* in *The Times Literary Supplement* of 4 April. I appreciated the recognition that

Miss Fuller has made what appears to be a discovery, by straightforward literary research. Among Mary Shelley's reading lists is the title *Le Vieux de la Montagne*. The book (available in the British Museum) was translated by an anonymous Frenchman from an Arabic original. On it, apparently, Shelley based his fragmentary story, *The Assassins*. Unfortunately he broke off too soon to develop its part-hero, a spiritual-minded youth called Ariel, who is, we are told, a kind of Cupid of sublime, non-sexual love, but is constantly exposed to women's embraces. In this Ariel, rather than Shakespeare's (which of course inspired 'Ariel to Miranda') Shelley may frequently have seen his prototype.

[285]

This bit was also picked out in three other reviews but in general the papers went just for his love affairs. Mysteriously, *Shelley* obtained a notice in a Russian paper, but my Russian is so rusty I have never got down to it with a dictionary in hand so do not know what it says.

On 31 July Tim suggested over dinner at my place that we not only became antiquarian booksellers but publishers of small luxury editions starting with the poems of Corvo. I said if we did new work, there was a young poet in Poets' Workship (it had changed the Writers' to Poets'), Martin Booth, recently returned to England from an upbringing mainly in Hong Kong, who might be considered. One could hardly hope for the luck of finding a Dylan Thomas, but I thought Martin Booth's writing had a future.

On 1 August Irene came to dinner with me. I was half turned into the kitchen to make us coffee when she said, 'Dreadful about that school!'

This was a change of subject so unexpected that I wondered if I had heard correctly. 'What?'

'Court Lees. You must have seen the pictures in the *Sunday Times*. On the last day of last year. Boys' buttocks, black and blue.' From the canings administered by the headmaster to the boys at an approved school for juvenile delinquents. One of the junior masters, Ivor Cook, had been so shocked that he had taken photographs of their behinds showing their injuries and given them to the press. Roy Jenkins, as Home Secretary, had commissioned an inquiry and after reading its findings closed the school.

There had been questions asked in both the Commons and the Lords, and Ivor Cook had been attacked for his disloyalty to the headmaster, who did the caning, and to the managers.

'Like every MP, I was bombarded with imitation typescript circular papers of a most tendentious nature.' She believed they had gone to every member of the House. She found them so unpleasing that she gave up reading them and just consigned them to the waste-paper basket.

In favour of which side, I asked?

'The managers. All about how wonderfully they had managed. Probably written *by* the managers.' And filled with tendentious hints and insinuations concerning Mr Cook.

Of what sort?

'Political. I know nothing about this man. If he is very far to the left, many people are.' If in fact he was or ever had been a member of the Communist Party of Great Britain, that was not a crime, and not a sin.

The fact was, that if he had not done what he had, those children would be being beaten black and blue *still*. Nobody else lifted a finger.

On the whole, her party backed the managers, Labour Mr Cook. But her feelings were with the children. So she had not spoken in the Chamber. At the end, she had voted with her party in the Censure Motion on the Home Secretary, because it did seem to her that it might not have been necessary to close the school if the head and his deputy were removed and replacements brought in from other schools. But – and this was what was worrying her – Roy Jenkins was an intelligent man and must have thought of that for himself. Why was it that he did not think of doing that? Had Roy Jenkins reason to suspect something of which he was not telling the House – that other schools might be as bad and masters brought in from them no better than those got rid of? 'If only he could have taken us a little more into his confidence, that Censure Motion might have been avoided.'

She wished she could speak with Roy Jenkins about this, but being of different parties made it too awkward. It was a case where the two party system prevented what might be proper discussion. She felt sure Roy Jenkins was a most 'responsible individual' and thought his concern, like hers, was for the children. It was of a very practical concern for because, when sitting on the bench, she had had juvenile delinquents arraigned before her and directed them to be sent to approved schools. 'To be reformed. Not beaten black and blue.'

I had been so used to thinking of her as an MP it had slipped my mind she was also a justice of the peace and must often have had juvenile delinquents brought up before her.

'What were the inspectors doing?' she asked. There are inspectors who go round these schools. Didn't they inspect?' And again, 'Why didn't the children scream to high heaven, take their clothes off and show the inspectors what had been done to them?'

Perhaps they didn't dare, I suggested. They probably thought the inspector would be on the same side as the head and the managers and they would get worse punished if they complained.

Irene said, 'We have not heard the last of Court Lees ... Court Lees will come up again.'

The axe fell. The Times Bookshop was no more. On 2 December Tim phoned me to say they would let us have the existing stock at well below the market value, so we could start with stock instead of having immediately to buy stock from outside.

We were now looking for premises and, on 13 December, I found, at 76 Gloucester Place – only a few doors from the Theosophical Society – the best that I had seen. Tim came and looked at it too, and this was the one we settled on. I bought an armchair. The Times were letting us have eight imposing bookcases and eight cupboards with sliding doors for nothing.

On 17 December I took Tim to Mr Franklin. We told him we wanted to have equal shares and equal division of everything. The Articles of Association were drawn and Fuller d'Arch Smith Ltd came into being.

An early request for the valuation of a library up north took Tim away for a few days. When he came back, he said only a few of the books were valuable, but the poor man wanted mainly space in his house, 'and I hadn't the heart to take his few good things and leave him with his rubbish'. So he had brought back with him the few books we would sell from Fuller d'Arch Smith and would arrange for a lorry to collect the rest, which he would job off at low price on to second-hand booksellers.

Almost our first customer was Jimmy Page. Visualised by most people with his guitar, a rock musician, the star of Led Zeppelin, he was, Tim told me, a serious antiquarian book collector – and he knew who I was, had a copy of *The Magical Dilemma* and sent his regards.

In reviewing my *Swinburne* in *The Daily Telegraph* (9 January 1969) Anthony Powell congratulated me on a rather specialised achievement:

Miss Fuller's detective work reached an apex when she discovered three letters from Mary Leith written when both she and Swinburne were in their early fifties which unequivocally refer – though without modern psychological sophistication – to flagellation.

The Times, however, carried a column under the heading FAMILY PROTEST. Mary Leith's granddaughter, the Hon. Mildred K. Leith, referred to the cipher letters as just 'childish jokes'; but her grandmother liked the birch. I quote a few lines from the first:

Cy merest dozem,
    This little delay had given me more time to devote to your most interesting Eton book … it is exceptionally amusing to your mind though I could dish that it wealt with a pater leriod … Long may it be said of the birch as of the school, 'Florebit'.

On a small point I can meet her: the granddaughter says that a short poem 'Rocket' by her grandmother refers not to Swinburne but to a horse. Though it seemed to be about riding, I took the 'hand and heel' to be those of the rider, and the rider to be the 'comrade' of her youth hymned; if, however, the rider is the writer, there is no 'comrade' left save the horse.

This, however, is a one-off piece and has no connection with the cipher letters of flagellation.

I said in the book that I thought the Eton book referred to in the first 'Cy merest dozen' letters to be 'The Flogging Block' (or just possibly some familiar flagellant work). Tim, however, came across a commercially published, wholly innocuous book of Eton reminiscences by an old boy, covered all over with flagellatory comments in Swinburne's hand. The owner had no idea of this. Not liking to exploit the man's ignorance, Tim had warned him, 'Do you know whose hand this is? It's Swinburne's.' He expected the man would either want to keep the book or ask an impossibly high price, but he didn't turn a hair. Having given him his chance, Tim made an offer, which was instantly accepted and sold it for a healthy profit.

He put it to me that this copy of a printed work bearing marginal writings in Swinburne's hand rather than the manuscript 'Flogging Block' was the 'Eton book' to which Mary Leith referred. In that case, the 'pater leriod' (later period) she could wish it had dealt with would be the period during which Swinburne had been at the school, the innocuous printed work belonging to an earlier period. That can be so.

Again, however, the second of the cipher letters addresses Swinburne as 'My dear Clavering.' Clavering is the name given to one of the characters in 'The Flogging Block'. Perhaps she had seen that as well.

On 1 February we moved into our new Fuller d'Arch Smith office, at 76 Gloucester Place. The carpets were not down yet but I hung the curtains I had made and hung two of Mother's paintings to hide the wallpaper, which we did not like. It was in our office that I had my first meeting with Tim's mother. Any anxiety I may have felt as to whether she would like me was dispelled as she came through the door, put her arms round my neck and said 'Our Saviour!'

It was Tim who did all the work. He sat all day making and taking telephone calls. Except, that is, when the business took him out, as to value a library or bid at Sotheby's. Sometimes a far away customer would instruct him to go to Sotheby's and bid for a particular item up to so much. It was through his having to be there that he noticed when, unexpectedly, a number of 'Cy Merest Dozen' letters came up for auction. I must come and see, he said. Items for auction were spread out beforehand so that prospective buyers would have a prevous inspection. They more than proved everything that I had said on the basis of those I had seen in the British Museum.

I had been wanting to introduce Tim to Irene, and she suggested I should bring him to dinner with her at the House of Commons on 25 March. He was a bit apprehensive because he knew nothing about politics. I assured him she would not want to talk about politics; she would find it much more amusing and relaxing to hear about antiquarian bookselling. In fact it went off very well.

Eighteen

In *The Times* of 7 December 1969 one of the Letters to the Editor caught my eye: it was signed by Ivor Cook and it was about Shakespeare and the 'dark lady' of the *Sonnets*. It referred back to an article he had written, for *Shakespeare Survey*. He had found that the Sir William Harvey who became the third husband of the Countess of Southampton, was not the elderly man supposed but a younger one of the same name and title, which at once brought him into consideration as the Mr W. H. of the *Sonnets*, not a physician but a ship's master. He had found and photographed a document upon which this young man, on his return to England, had to cancel the certification of his own death, 'supposed drowned at sea', with the explanation that he had been held a prisoner in Spain. This called to mind the plot of *Twelfth Night*, wherein Sebastian is supposed drowned at sea but returns to marry the Countess Olivia, of whom Ivor Cook supposed the Countess of Southampton to the the original.

I talked with Tim about this over Christmas 1969, saying it seemed to me important. He concurred. Tim was acquainted with A. L. Rowse, received the odd Christmas card from him and had heard him espouse his theory that it was Henry Wriotheseley, Earl of Southampton, who was the Mr W. H. I said, this was up against three hurdles, his initials were the wrong way round, H. W. instead of W. H., it was not usual to address an Earl as Mr and the 'dark lady' whom Rowse paired with him was younger than the poet whereas the text of the sonnets made plain she was older than he. There were points I would like clarified, and I said to Tim, 'I think I'll write to Mr Cook.'

'Why not?' he said.

I wrote to him c/o *The Times*, asking whether he was the man in the Court Lees affair. He said he was; and he came to tea with me early in January (1970).

His mouth was set in grim lines, yet he bubbled over with eagerness to talk. The 'Mr' in the dedication he understood to refer to ship's master; he could have been known as 'Master'. The 'setting forth' would be on a voyage. He took the first seventeen sonnets, however, as addressed not to the Friend, Mr W. H. They all exhorted a young man to marry and start a family. It was customary to take them as addressed by a homosexual poet to his boy-friend, but marry and have a son was the last thing a homosexual man would want his beloved boy to do. He took them to be addressed to the young Earl of Southampton at the request of the mother. He was refusing to go through with his planned marriage to Burghley's granddaughter and Burghley was demanding punitive damages. Actually, the reason for the young Southampton's refusal was not what his mother feared; on the contrary, he was married already. When the penniless Elizabeth Vernon had told him she was with child by him he had married her, to legitimise the child, but not plucked up the courage to tell anybody. The poet knew only what the mother told him. She appealed to her poet friend to represent to him the delights of matrimony, and he served her. The Countess Olivia, be it remembered, was when first met mourning the death of a brother. The Countess of Southampton's brother had just died, 'and it may be presumed she mourned him.' I urged him to put all this down in the form of a book, before somebody else did. Tim and I were starting a small publishing side. Our first book would be of Martin Booth's poems and the next could be Ivor's book.

I had been studying the *Sonnets* to see if they shed any light on the Bacon-Shakespeare question, and in this connection had been interested by Leslie Hotson's book, *Mr W. H.* His candidate was William Hatcliffe because he was a student at Gray's Inn and there appeared a connection between Gray's Inn and the plays. Both *Love's Labour's Lost* and *Twelfth Night* had their first performances not in the public theatre but in Gray's Inn. Actually, there is a stronger connection than that, which Hotson missed. Spedding, Bacon's biographer, tells us (vol. viii, p. 327) that in the year 1594 the fellows of Gray's Inn had invited those of the Inner Temple to come and give a performance on their stage on 28 December. Their stage, however, proved not large enough to accommodate the number of players required for the intended piece and so the project was abandoned and *A Comedy of Errors* substituted. Spedding never interests himself in the Bacon-Shakespeare question, but the information he gives us may suggest the author of this was sufficiently known to the fellows of Gray's Inn for them to ask him to write something to fill the gap at short notice. Hotson's contention, however, is that the actor-manager from Stratford must have been a friend of William Hatcliffe who must have told him they had nothing to present on 28 December and begged him to write something for them. This, however, is a long shot for which there is no evidence at all. There is simply no connection known of between Shakespeare and Hatcliffe or Gray's Inn. Francis Bacon, however was a bencher of Gray's Inn.

I took the opportunity to ask Ivor Cook about Court Lees.

The taking of the photographs had been for him an enormous step taken with reluctance. The consequences were likely to break into the time he had free for the Shakespeare researches that had been his private delight, and could spell the end of his career as a teacher (which he had been since his demobilisation from the Army in 1966). He was married, with four children dependent on his earnings. His wife, Jill, however, felt that the wretched Court Lees boys should come first. Ivor's one extravagance had been the purchase of an exceedingly good camera, for the photographing of Elizabethan documents, and now he decided to put it to much more contentious use. On the morning of 7 April 1967 he approached the first of the four boys caned that morning, and asked him to come and stand on a chair in a cupboard, face to the wall, and said, 'Drop your trousers.' Absolutely terrified of being spotted doing this and of the wrong conclusion being drawn, he took the first photograph, then another, another and another.' All right, you can go now.' He then waylaid the next boy, and the next and the last: four photographs of each of the four boys, at two and a half feet range. Then he put them, undeveloped, into an envelope and posted them. As they dropped into the postbox he felt he had done a momentous thing.

The envelope was addressed to *The Guardian* newspaper, which he normally took and to which he had sent letters signed 'Approved School Teacher'.

The Guardian did not print the photographs. It passed them to the *Daily Mail*. The *Daily Mail* did not print them either but on 5 May printed an article describing them. This brought two inspectors down from the Home Office. They went into every room in the school, looking at the boys and at everything.

In a drawer of the headmaster's desk (though Ivor Cook did not know this) they found the canes, which were not of the legal type approved and sold to schools by the Home Office, but heavier ones that must have been acquired privately. On 9 May Ivor Cook went to the Home Office and had a two-hour interview with a Mr Gwynne.

Roy Jenkins, Home Secretary, commissioned an Inquiry. Presided over by a Mr Gibbens, this sat from 26 to 30 June. Expert witnesses called included a photographic one who pronounced the photographs genuine, a senior police officer who said that had he seen those injuries in the course of his normal duty he would have considered their infliction a matter for prosecution, a medical one who said he had examined the four boys and none of them suffered from a condition such as to make him bruise more easily than normal. They questioned the four boys, other boys and most of the masters, including Mr Haydon, the head, and Ivor Cook. Mr Haydon said he had found the canes in the drawer of his predecessor's desk and so never doubted that they were the right ones. No, it had not struck him that they were heavier than they should be.

After the courtroom was cleared, exhibits, including two sets of canes, the ones used and the right ones, were left on the table and Ivor tried them, gingerly, on his own hand; he had no doubt that it was the thickness of the ones used that had created the areas of purple bruising that had puzzled him.

Roy Jenkins closed down the school; the boys were distributed through other schools and the staff thrown out on their ears, jobless.

This was what had roused the questions in the Lords (25 October), a Conservative Censure Motion on the Home Secretary in the Commons (16 November) and further questions in the Lords (2 April 1968).

Each time there were questions in the Lords, the Bishop of Southwark had risen, to attack Cook. The first time it was to mention the school's 'yellow forms', or as he called them 'yellow tickets', which put him (Ivor Cook) in mind of what they meant in Dostoevsky's *Crime and Punishment*. The Bishop alleged these to be demands for caning, and that Mr Cook had issued them for trifling offences. But the yellow forms were not recommendations for caning. They were used to report anything untoward in a boy's conduct; the punishment, if any, was decided by the headmaster. Ivor Cook had never issued any in Haydon's time and none that he had ever issued had resulted in punishment worse than loss of good conduct marks or a small fine. On the second occasion when the Bishop had risen, it had been to say he supposed the Home Office knew why Mr Cook had left the Army. There was nothing mysterious. He was demobilised with the honorary rank of captain and it was his colonel who wrote him a reference which got him his first teaching job. What puzzled him was that an attack on himself should have come from that side of the House, because Southwark was a Labour bishop and the Labour members generally had been for him, the Conservatives against.

Utterances in either House were privileged, but newspapers reporting them were only so long as they stuck to reporting. If they took
themselves to assume the truth of what had been uttered, they lost their
privilege and were liable for libel. He had issued a host of writs. He did
not know how long he had to wait for the cases to come up. In the
meantime he had, after a long period out of work, got a teaching post
at Tylehurst, a school for disabled and maladjusted children, and was
getting back to his Shakespeare.

We exchanged a number of letters during the spring but in the summer he seemed to be fading away. Tim and I both felt he was unhappy.

Ivor Cook apart, the first part of 1970 was mainly a period of office
and literary activity. Martin Booth was starting his own small publishing business with the Sceptre Press, and was producing from it my narrative poem *Tintagel*. A Dutch publisher, a Sufi, wanted to republish
Madeleine in a luxury edition, expanded to take in the whole story of
her descent from Tippu Sultan and background in the Sufi movement.
This meant restoring to my typescript cuts made in it by Sheila Hodges
of Gollancz in order to make of it a slimmer volume, *Madeleine, a
Story of the Resistance*. It had by now run through two paperbacks by
Pan Books under their title of *Born for Sacrifice* and Gollancz now
relinquished the rights to the Dutch publisher L. C. Carp to publish
from his East-West Publications as *Noor-un-Nisa Inayat Khan, G.C.*

In May I received a letter from the landlords' agents saying they
required 4 Guilford Place for their own purposes, and wanted me out.
The law obliged them to offer us alternative accommodation, but that
had to be acceptable. By chance, walking from St Pancras along the
Euston Road I noticed a flat in 101–3 Whitfield Street being offered on
a 999-year lease. It was very nice. The agents agreed to assist and on
11 November I moved in. Armistice Day. I still thought of it as that,
rather than the Remembrance Sunday now substituted.

Ivor Cook had helped me take down bookshelves I had had put up
in 4 Guilford Place, and now came to help me put them up again in the
room I had reserved for my study. Early in the New Year he made contact again. Could he come and see me. 'Of course,' I said.

When he came on 17 January, he followed me into the kitchen and
asked, 'Have you an egg-timer?' I showed him one given me by
Mother.

'May I turn that upside down?'

I watched while he did so.

'Now what do you see?' he asked.

'I see the sand falling through.'

'Does it fall flat or making a pyramid?'

Suddenly I realised what he was talking about: 'Tyme's pyramids build up with newer might' – Sonnet 123.

Hotson took the reference to four pyramids, i.e. columns, brought from Egypt and set up in Rome by Pope Sixtus and used this to date the composition of the *Sonnets*, or at any rate of this one.

'But that wasn't what you wanted to talk to me about?'

'No.' He seemed to have some difficulty in broaching the subject; then said he had just finished at the school and returned to have his tea when there was a knock on the door of their house and one of his boys said 'Can I have a word with you sir?'

The boy then said a person he named was buggering him.

He just wished the boy had gone to the police, not him. If he had to go to the police it would mean his being marked as a trouble-maker and, he felt sure, his dismissal. It would be the end of his teaching career, 'my utter destruction'. He had only his disability pension from the Ministry of Defence and would become dependent on Jill.

'It's a dreadful thing to say, but you have to go to the police.'

He talked around the subject a bit. 'Court Lees was an iron tyranny. Nobody was allowed to do anything. This was just the opposite.' Anything went, carrying laissez-faire to an extent he didn't think right. There was a policeman he knew personally: he would talk to him about the buggery charge.

Tim asked me to ask Ivor if he had been caned, and if so what was his reaction.

I did ask Ivor. He said once, it was by a man for whom he had had great admiration, and the pain was not so much the physical as the sense of betrayal. Betrayal of trust. He was never able to feel the same towards that master again.

Immediately following upon his report to the police of the boy's allegations, Ivor found an envelope through his door. It contained notice of dismissal, without reason given and, needless to say, without a reference enclosed.

We heard that there was a school in Brussels run on Krishnamurti lines. We also had a friend who would support his application with the school's proprietess. I thought this would be a Heaven-sent opening for Ivor and was disappointed when he raised objections. He had to be in England for his court cases, whenever they should come up.

If he didn't want to go out of England, there was another sugges-
tion: that he apply for a post at Krishnamurti's own school, at
Brockwood, in Hampshire, near Winchester. Easily in reach of
London, and the staff were very well paid.

But he did not apply for that, either.

I did not understand at all, and still do not. It still seems to me to
have been a mistake.

On the evening of 11 March 1973, Ivor Cook rang to tell me all his
cases were coming up. He had won the first, against *The Daily
Telegraph* and been awarded £1,000. He was now in the midst of one
against 'Evans'. On the following evening he rang to say he had won
again and had been awarded £1,500. Next, starting tomorrow, would
be one against The Schoolmaster Publishing Company and Ebert, in
respect of a letter by the latter in *The Teacher*. After the Inquiry two
boys, Arnold and Waterman, had been taken to the Home Office,
shown the photographs of the four pairs of buttocks and asked to
point to the worst caned. Surprisingly, they had both picked out the
second worst. But now Arnold had contacted Ivor and told him they
were both promised instant release from Court Lees if they picked out
the one shown them in the Head's room. He felt sure Waterman, who
was now in the Scrubs, would confirm. He hastened to Wormwood
Scrubs and saw Waterman, who indeed confirmed the story and was
due for release in time to be a witness in the High Court.

'What's he in the Scrubs for?' I asked.

'I never ask them what they're in for.' The implication of the bribed
picking out of the second worst instead of the worst, was that the
worst, Darling's, was a fake. Ivor was going to make the point that to
accuse a scholar of faking evidence was like shooting a footballer in
the foot. Would I come to court tomorrow and give evidence for him
that he was a Shakespeare scholar?

The affair was becoming more and more bizarre. 'Of course,' I said.

And would I like to write a book on this whole Court Lees affair?
He had tried to write it himself but did not like what he had done. He
had read my *Swinburne*. It seemed to him I was the obvious person to
do his Court Lees book.

I had already had to break in to my *Bacon* to do an update of
Double Webs for a new paperback edition, but I felt I couldn't refuse.

Perhaps, Ivor suggested, I would like to come to court for the first
day of the hearing, tomorrow, and get to know some of the boys. He

was very much hoping Michael Darling would be there, but he was in the Scrubs. Ivor had petitioned the prison to get him out just to come to court but did not know yet if this would be allowed.

Whom had he got to represent him?

No one. He had spent £30 on the purchase of a book on the law of libel and slander and was representing himself, appearing in person.

I knew that to appear in court one had to wear a hat, so went out and bought one first thing next morning, a navy blue one, to match a navy suit, the most sober I had, before going on to the High Court. They were already in session, Ivor addressing the court. All along the bench were what I took to be Court Lees boys.

In the luncheon adjournment, Ivor collected me and the Court Lees boys and took us over the road to a cafeteria on a corner of Essex Street, facing the High Court. He then moved off to join another group and a man came and took his vacated chair. As the boys appeared to know him I supposed him to have been one of the masters and asked him his name. 'Wright.' When we had eaten we all trouped back into the Gothic pile, following Ivor Cook through its passages like duck-lings following mother duck. When the jury had been recalled, Ivor called me. I had not realised I was to be the first of the afternoon's wit-nesses. I took the stand and was sworn.

Ivor asked me, 'I believe you have a degree of the University of London.'

I felt it was not the time for hiding my light under a bushel and said, 'An Honours degree.' I confirmed that I was the author of biographies of Shelley and Swinburne and had for some years been working on a biography of Bacon. As I saw he was taking something out of his case, I exclaimed, 'Oh I recognise it! At least I think I do. Can I see it closer?'

He handed it to me.

'Yes, it's what I thought it was.'

The judge asked, 'What is it?'

'It's a copy of *Shakespeare Survey*.' I told the court it was a learned periodical, devoted entirely to Shakespeare studies, and contributed to by A. L. Rowse and other scholars. Mr Cook had got an article by him-self printed in it. 'He's very proud of it.' I began to give an idea of what it was about: Mr Cook urged that the Dark Lady was the Countess of Southampton ...

The judge, smiling, said we could not go into that controversy.

Ivor asked me if in my researches I had come across forgeries. I said that I had looked at some of the Wise forgeries of Swinburne first editions. Wise was a scholar who had ruined the credit of a mainly genuine collection by introducing a few mock ups. The result was, nobody trusted anything that had been through his hands.

Ivor asked, what was the effect upon a scholar's reputation of any suspicion of forgery?

I said, 'It's death.'

Hoolahan, the opposing counsel, asked me if Rowse accepted Mr Cook's theory.

I said, 'They have different Dark Ladies.'

Laughter in court.

But, said Hoolahan, scholars were contentious people.

I said that was why Mr Cook did not want there to be anything that could, in any contention, be used as an arm against him.

Hoolahan said he had no further questions for me.

After that, the Court Lees boys, headed by the two bribery boys, Waterman and Arnold, filed through the box for the rest of the afternoon.

Afterwards, standing in a passage waiting for Ivor, I exchanged a few words with Arnold, then at greater length with one who gave me his name, David New. He said, 'At Court Lees, Mr Cook stood up for us. Now it's our turn to stick up for him. That's how I see it.' He had only one reservation: the newspapers had given the impression Court Lees was a uniquely bad school. Before coming to it, he had been in a remand home in Kent. There, the caning was ever so much worse. He talked to me about it.

Ivor took me back to the cafeteria for tea. I asked him about his background; were his parents literary people?

No. 'I'm a sport.' In the sense botanists used the term.

Before the war he had been a clerk in the Gas Company. And he had been a member of the Communist Party.

This was not exactly a surprise to me, remembering what Irene had told me of the circulars she had received. But I said, 'I'll have to put that in the book.'

'No!'

I said I could not write the book and keep that back. It would come out, anyway, and I would be blamed for keeping back something material.

He used to stand on a chair outside the tube station at Ealing Broadway, spouting Karl Marx at the people as they came out. In halls, also. But he found the governing of the Communist Party of Great

Britain dictatorial, and was disgusted by the Soviet Nazi pact of 1939. He resigned from it, volunteered for the army immediately war was declared and had had no contacts with Communists since.

When I returned to the court on Monday, Hoolahan was explaining to the jury. 'There are occasions when the law allows ...' He was explaining qualified privilege. *The Schoolmaster* had been defending the interests of schoolmasters, which had been damaged by Mr Cook's actions and the Gibbens Report.

In the lunch hour I deserted to join Tim in our office, where we had to receive our accountant, and when I got back to the court, Hoolahan was still speaking. This went on for three days. Ivor, I thought, stood up to it with admirable good humour, but by the Thursday afternoon was looking so tired that I was worried. I wrote to Tim:

March 22nd 1973

Dear Tim,
 ... Defence is trying to re-try over again, while the Court Lees Inquiry suggesting conclusions of Home Office false and impugning its procedures and judgement ... Gibbens cannot be called to defend his judgement as he is a civil servant. What it may come to is that Ivor has to call Roy Jenkins, to go into the box and say that the proceedings of the Home Office and those who conducted its court of Inquiry were above board. We were discussing over tea whether there was any form of red tape that could prevent an ex-Minister from being subpoenaed.

Ivor was having to defend the findings of the Inquiry without having its expert witnesses.

Hoolahan got on to yellow forms. We had a day of them.

The importance of yellow forms was reduced when Leslie Thompson, former third in command of the school, went into the box. He said he issued an average of one or two yellow forms a week, which was four times the number attributed by the Bishop of Southwark to Mr Cook. Mr Cook's classes were orderly. Particularly impressive was his music appreciation class. He would bring his own records of classical music to the school and when he (Thompson) happened to come in it amazed him to see 'Court Lees boys sitting quietly listening to Beethoven'.

Afterwards, Ivor introduced us and we had tea together. Thompson said I must come down and see the school, as it was now reopened under the new name of Hays Bridge. And Ivor must come too.

Draycon, the second in command, was in the box for a long time, mainly on trivial matters.

It was a big moment when Haydon, the old head, went into the box. Ivor asked him, 'Are you a tennis player?'

'Yes.'

'A champion tennis player?'

'Yes.'

'Have you played in the quarter-finals at Wimbledon?'

'Yes.'

'Doesn't that mean you have a very strong right arm?'

He had not used his full strength on the boys. There was nothing personal in it. He always shook hands with the boys afterwards.

Finally, Ebert, the author of the offending letter, went into the box. I cannot be sure now whether it was just before or just after Ebert went into the box that the judge dismissed the Schoolmaster Publishing Company, leaving Ebert to face the charge alone. This was puzzling, both to me and to Ivor, as normally the publisher is co-liable with the author, in the event of a libel action resulting. It was for that reason that publishers' contracts include a clause in which the author assures the publisher the work contains no libel. But now Ebert was left facing the charge alone. He said what he had been given to understand by those whose judgement he respected was that the photographs were genuine but not of Court Lees boys; Mr Cook had obtained them from Russia. (Thompson had heard this idea circulated, too, though it was never mentioned at the Inquiry.) Perhaps, said Ebert, if Cook could have had the boys turn their faces over their shoulders to make their identification possible ... Ivor, helpfully practical, said it would have been impossible, because to get the faces in he would have had to step backwards so far as to make the close up of the flesh impossible.

Then Ebert said it was not he who had composed much of the libel. This – DUBIOUS EVIDENCE – contained much of the libel. I was sure Ebert spoke the truth about its not being of his own composition as, in my experience, the heading above a letter I had sent to a newspaper was usually not of my composition. One did not know what heading it would appear under. Something slapped on by a sub-editor. So for that part of the libel, *The Schoolmaster* was responsible – and it had been dismissed from the case by the judge.

There was also, on 17 April, whilst the jury were out, a bomb alert. It was the period of the IRA bombings, and we were all turned out of the court room and out of the building, and found ourselves standing, all mixed up, in Red Lion Square. Eventually we were all allowed back, no bomb having been found. The jury were still out.

They had been out since the previous day, and it began to look as though this day too would pass without a verdict, but at 5 o'clock they came back. The verdict they gave was for the defendant. The foreman, a girl, turned to Ivor and said, 'I'm sorry, Mr Cook.'

As we left the building I asked Ivor, 'What's going to happen about the costs?'

'I don't know. I can't pay. And if I could, I wouldn't. I shall appeal.'

We parted unhappily at Chancery Lane Underground Station.

I would have to use the Easter break to re-visit another theatre of war.

I had been researching Déricourt's background, first with the idea of bringing any new edition of *Double Webs* up to date, then of perhaps writing a whole new book on him. George Mann was interested by this proposal.

I had written to the French Embassy in Laos, and received over the signature of Denis Nardin an unexpected wealth of information. He knew a certain amount about Déricourt's Chinese mistress, Janine (I had not previously known her name); she had a little boy by a previous lover, was no longer in Vientiane. It was believed after Déricourt's death she had left for a foreign country. He enclosed a copy of Déricourt's death certificate, which gave the actual place of his birth with greater accuracy than I had had before: Coulonges-en-Tardenois, near Château Thierry. Déricourt's effects in Laos had been dealt with by Rémy Clément (this I knew to be the real name of his assistant 'Marc' in SOE). I wrote to Clément.

From the mayor of Coulonges I had a reply giving me the address of a Madame Simard Henrie who might have known the Déricourt family.

She replied, confirming this. She still lived in Coulonges and would be happy to see me.

There was a little delay before I heard from Clément, but then he wrote, confirming that he had been 'Marc' and saying Henri had occupied a great place in his life during the formative years ... Henri had often spoken of me and he would like to meet me if I could come to Paris.

I was touched that Déricourt should have spoken of me, but nervous because, as a friend of Déricourt's, Clément might not have liked my book. Supposing he said Henri was completely innocent?

I need not have worried. Clément called for me at my hotel with his car. What he knew of my book was what Henri had told him – he was unable to read it as he knew no English. But, he said, one must never take Henri's word for gospel. Henri was mythomaniac. He lived in a world of fables, created from his imagination. Clément had known him most of his life. Before the war, when they were both flying for commercial lines, he had been Henri's chief. During the war Henri had recruited him as his assistant, to help him find fields suitable for clandestine British airfields for use by the British, under the code-name of 'Marc'. After the war, in the Far East, though he had been flying mainly between Vientiane and Vietnam, Henri had been flying mainly between Vientiane and places in northern Laos, though sometimes to Hong Kong, but he had again been Henri's chief. 'J'ai été son chef: il a été mon chef: j'ai été son chef.'

He had been called to the scene of the crash and had to identify the body. The face was too smashed really to see, but he was sure it was Henri.

He took me to the Falguère, a beautiful, old-fashioned candle-lit restaurant. I asked, where did Déricourt disappear to?'

He didn't disappear.

I said his secretary was supposed to be posting me the completed manuscript of a book he had written. This never arrived. Then he said he was going to have to disappear for a while, and that was the last I heard from him.

Clément asked me the date. But that was the date Air Laos closed down!

He had said it was closing down. What did he do afterwards?

He remained staying in the same hotel. Yet something did change. Had I ever heard of the Triangle d'Or?

No.

It was a district in the north-west of Laos where the opium poppy grew wild. It was practically the only crop and the villagers would ask the pilots to carry it. After Air Laos closed he had his own aeroplane. It was Janine's people who got it for him and really put him in business. That must have become known to the authorities and his correspondence would have been monitored. It would have done me no good to have my name noted as a correspondent of his. Clément was sure, now, that it was from respect for me he had severed the connection.

Something came back to me: in one of my letters I had enclosed a cutting from a paper saying opium was passing from Laos and airline pilots were suspected of carrying it, saying I hoped he did not get mixed up with this. His answering letter contained no assurances.

He had written that he always tried to do right, but he could not have thought smuggling opium right.

'He never touched the stuff himself,' Clément replied.

'But it was profiting from other people's weakness for it.'

The temptation was great. Henri had all his life dreamed of making a fortune.

'What did he want it for?'

'I never asked myself.'

'His tastes were not expensive.'

'No.'

Madame Déricourt was not demanding?

'A château! He wanted to be lord of a great château. To be a *grand seigneur*!'

This seemed to me most extraordinary, out of key with what I had known of him.

The next morning I took the train from the Gare de l'Est to Château Thierry. Going eastwards, some of the place names recalled battles of the Western Front ... I began to understand why Déricourt had so often referred to the bloodshed of the First World War. When I got out at Château Thierry a voice on the loudspeaker asked Miss Jean Overton Fuller to go to the desk.

A Monsieur Godbillon introduced himself to me. Madame Henrie had asked him to meet me with his car and drive me to Coulonges. On the way he told me that he had known Henri Déricourt's father, Alfred. Alfred had been the local postman. Thinking to improve their lot, they had moved to Celles, near Paris, but could only get labouring work, shifting timber. But then Alfred got a job in an iron foundry owned by a M. Fontaine, and his wife became the concierge of Monsieur Fontaine's house in Paris. But Monsieur Fontaine had also a château in the country, at Varenval, to which he then removed Henri's parents. His father looked after the grounds while his mother became house-keeper.

He said Coulonges had been briefly occupied by the Germans in October 1914, and a re-occupation was feared in 1918. This seemed to be of greater import to him than the total occupation of France in the Second World War.

At Coulonges he delivered me to Madame Henrie and she took me to see the house in which Déricourt had been born. It had a red roof and was just part of a terrace, and not picturesque, but I made a line-drawing of it.

It had been Déricourt's mother Madame Henrie knew best: Georgette. A very sweet and modest person. But very poor. She had dreamed of their having a little shop but could never scrape up enough money for that. But Henri was too little to remember Coulonges. Most of his childhood would have been spent at the Château de Varenval. It was too far from Coulonges for me to visit it now, but she gave me a photograph of it. It was most imposing.

When I got back to Paris I telephoned Rémy Clément to ask if he could come and see me. I showed him the photograph and said, 'There's the château for you. But his parents did not own it. They were servants.'

He was most affected. He had no idea. If he had known he would have been more understanding.

He had brought some papers to show me. He produced the stub of the registration of a package sent to me from Paris. The date on it coincided with my having been in Carthage. I had found a note saying an attempt had been made to deliver a registered parcel to me, but when I called at the Post Office, they had sent it back. To Laos? To Paris, where the secretary was. I did not know her name or address.

I flew back the next day, and was back in the High Court the day after that, when it reopened after Easter.

Ivor's case had been that the Bishop of Southwark's attack upon him in the Lords (25 October 1967) had not gone unanswered. Lord Leatherland (Liberal) had said, 'I dismiss what the right reverend prelate the Bishop of Southwark has said, that Mr Cook is a peculiar type of person ...' and Lord Longford (Lord Privy Seal and Leader of the House) had rebuked the Bishop for referring to Mr Cook as 'Cook' (unacceptable familiarity in the Lords) and went on to say 'I feel that the right reverend prelate the Bishop of Southwark was extraordinarily unfair to that gentleman.' In failing to report these words, the *Telegraph*'s reporting had been unfair.

Denning, however, ruled that a journalist, in a necessarily abridged account of the proceedings, had the right to pick out just those bits that interested him.

That this should be Denning's judgment was very surprising, to Ivor and to me, as it seemed to breach the principle that reporting of debates in the Chamber had, in order to enjoy qualified privilege, to be fair. Ivor believed Denning's judgment could be overthrown on appeal to the House of Lords, but to appeal to the Lords one had to pay £10,000 down and supply twelve copies of the entire proceedings.

He just hadn't got that sort of money. And he still had the bill for the long case, which he estimated would be about £18,000. He had only his unemployment benefit and disability benefit. As we parted at Chancery Lane tube station, he said, 'I have to think very realistically now.'

And he thought, to some point. It came back to him that *The Daily Telegraph* had published, also, a 'Parliamentary Sketch'. There was still time for him within the six-year limit to serve a writ on them for that. So he wrote to the *Telegraph*'s solicitors suggesting that if he dropped this new case against them and abstained from appealing to the House of Lords, they should pay the costs of the appeal they had just won.

They did.

Meanwhile the expected bill for £18,000 for the long case had still not come in. Ivor now wrote to the solicitors of the National Union of Schoolteachers, which was funding the expenses of all the actions in which the defendants were its members, suggesting that if he dropped his next case, against Haydon and Cohen (the latter was chairman of the Managers of Court Lees), they pay the bill, estimated at £18,000, for the case they had just won.

They, too, did. All they asked for was a delay until 8 January 1974 in paying the damages owed him for the case against him which he had won. This he granted.

Ivor's next case was against Ebert alone, in respect of a cyclostyled paper he had been circulating, perhaps one of those that had reached Irene. Ivor told me in the luncheon adjournment he was going to reverse his tactics, not go into the box as witness for himself and call no witnesses, thus depriving Hoolahan of the opportunity to use his cross-examining skill. When they went back, the judge, Mr Justice Milo, said, 'Carry on, Mr Cook.' and Ivor replied, 'And that concludes my case.'

Hoolahan's next witness was the headmaster of Tylehurst, who said that on receiving his dismissal Mr Cook became 'verbally violent'. This I could believe, he tended to be so.

Then came Haydon, who said he had never accepted the photographic evidence. Ivor reminded him that he had been asked at the Inquiry whether he wished to challenge it and had replied, 'Sir, I cannot do so.'

Haydon said he had been trying for a week to get his counsel to challenge it.

Mr Milmo reminded him that he and his counsel were 'one legal person'.

As we issued from the courtroom into the long gallery, Ivor, unable to contain the exuberance of his joy, leapt into the air crying, 'Yippee!'

He had just heard that Hoolahan had been made a QC, and when we went back after lunch congratulated him and asked, 'Is that on the strength of beating me?'

Mr Justice Milmo, summing up, said Mr Cook attached the greatest importance to Mr Haydon's failure to challenge the photographic evidence at the Inquiry, 'and on reflection you may agree with him'.

On 25 May 1973 the jury found for Ivor and awarded him £10,000.

Hoolahan rose and submitted his clients should not be liable for costs.

Mr Justice Milmo said simply, 'I find against you.'

As we were packing up, Hoolahan saluted Ivor with a reluctant, 'Well done.'

I had still to meet Jill Cook, and on 1 June Ivor brought her to my door to collect me and take me to the Volga, a small Indian restaurant round the corner in Grafton Street. With her hair scraped back into a tight bun, she looked at first sight schoolmistressy, yet was warm and confiding. She was just longing for this whole legal business to be over, because it took him away from his Shakespeare. She looked back to the golden years when he hardly seemed to be able to put out his hand without finding a new discovery. Timidly she suggested that if when this dreadful legal business was ended they had some money, would my partner and I publish Ivor's book on Shakespeare?

I said Tim and I had been talking over the possibility of our publishing some of Ivor's work on Shakespeare, but we would prefer it to be something short enough for us to do at our own expense. In fact it turned out that the book was 1,300 pages long. I did eventually see it, and it seemed not of the same value as the short piece we might have taken on.

The next day, 2 June 1973, it was in the papers that Irene who was retiring had been made a Companion of Honour. Elizabeth rang me in the evening, saying she had thought Irene would have had a peerage. She wondered how friendly Heath, now Prime Minister, really was to Irene. She was the oldest serving member and but for one period out during a Labour Government would be 'the father of the House'. But, 'Just those qualities we like in her might be annoying to Heath.' She had been a constant source of awkward questions for years.

On 31 July *The Times* carried an article written, by John Vader, from information supplied by a Mr Norman, headed 'Tortured Officer Did Not Crack'. Ostensibly a defence of Norman's son (who was not tortured), it put the blame 'for hundreds of deaths' on to Henri Déricourt, named in full. Déricourt's casualties were only four and Philby was not in SOE. I wrote:

31 July 1973

Sir,

I write to defend the memory of Henri Déricourt from blackening in your columns as the man who betrayed the 'Prosper' network. I probably know more about this man than anyone in the world having researched into the subject over twenty years. I, too, at one time thought he might have been the big traitor, but have long known this is not the case. He was a double agent, whose case was of infinite complexity; he gave some things away but saved more and was acquitted by court-martial.

JEAN OVERTON FULLER

The editor at first refused to print this, but I was insistent.

Coincidentally, 23 July had brought me a letter from Rémy Clément suggesting I come on 12 September, when the moon would be full, and have a look at the Lysander landing grounds.

I took an early plane, Clément met me at Orly and drove me through Chartres and Vendôme, left the main road near Amboise, and suddenly there was before me a signpost reading Pocé-sur-Cisse. One of Déricourt's fields was here. We got out. Clément showed me where they parked their bicycles, in a hedge. We would bypass Le Vieux Briollay and Pont-de-Braye and see them on the way back as he wanted me to be on the field at Soucelles by the time the moon rose.

We crossed the Loire more than once, and the birches gave way to poplars, always a sign of wetness, and passed weirs and locks and mills. The chief crop I saw was maize.

When we reached Angers, we booked rooms at a hotel and returned to the car, crossed a hump-backed bridge and suddenly Clément cried in excitement that the vast field before us was the one. He led me through thistles to the spot at which they had stood waiting for the plane. The full moon was already up; I made sketches, trying to get in some of the foliage, to make a picture of it later.

The next morning we saw Le Vieux Briollay, the small sloping field on which Noor had come down. He told me that when, at the railway station, they had split up so as not to attract attention as a party, it was with her that he had shared a carriage. She was very tensed up, and, he felt, very nervous.

He showed me the two little railway stations they had used to get the local stopping trains which would take them to the one from which they changed on to the express. All the way, he talked of the operations.

My letter to *The Times* about Déricourt, printed belatedly on 28 August, brought me a letter from William Kimber inviting me to write a book on SOE for publication by his firm. I had really enough on my plate, my work on Bacon having already been broken into by renewed work on Déricourt and by following Ivor Cook's cases in the High Court so as to be able to write a chapter on them in my book on the Court Lees affair, but I went down to Kimber's office and after a certain amount of discussion it was agreed between us my title should be *The German Penetration of S.O.E.* Actually it was the easiest and least time-taking of any of my books as I had most of the material in box-files under my desk.

Irene brought me a document she had obtained from Brigadier Nichols which I could use as an illustration. It showed, in three lines, diagrams of perfect Morse sending and the actual sending of two different senders. In the Dutch disaster the captured agents had played their own sets back to London but none of the captured French Section agents had done so. 'Even I can see the difference!' declared Irene. How it had failed to be noticed that the sets were no longer operated by the same operators beat us both.

The Foreign Office files remained closed to us, but Irene now obtained permission for me to put questions to Colonel Boxshall, who was in charge of them, which he would then endeavour to answer for me after inspecting them himself. This was a permission later granted to other writers, but in the beginning it was a privilege obtained by Irene just for me. The detailing was not all one-way. Concerning the operation of the night of 15/16 November, I had the number of passengers as five, following Foot: Rémy Clément had told me they were six, the one left out being Fille Lambie: would Boxshall confirm? No; according to his file, from which Foot had worked, there were only five, no Fille-Lambie among them. I insisted: Clément was positive about the existence of this person, recalled things he had done and said. Boxshall then consulted another file and found that a Captain Fille-Lambie had arrived in England on that date, by what means of transport being apparently unknown.

There was also some information he gave me about the field at Le Vieux Briollay which was wrong; I told him I had seen that field, walked about on it. He was quite chagrined and apologetic.

Nineteen

On 8 January 1974 Ivor arrived at my place having just come from the office of the NUT solicitors.

'You've got your cheque?' I asked.

'Yes.' And he had got something else. He was carrying two suitcases, which he now opened. They were all the papers which had been exhibits during the several court cases, and included a complete transcript of the proceedings of the Inquiry. 1,468 pages, and photocopies of all his yellow forms.

He left the lot with me, to digest and work from.

On 20 January 1974 I went down to Blindley Heath to see Ivor at 23 Featherstone. I found Jill in the garden, which she was trying to convert into a rose bower. I asked, 'How are you?'

'Just longing to retire.' She would like to have a farm again, 'with cows and pigs'. As for all this litigation, she was just 'longing for it to be over'.

It was on the following day that, still going through all the papers brought to me, I came to Ivor's yellow forms. None had resulted in a caning; only in a small fine or loss of good conduct marks. The one produced and quoted from in the House of Lords by the Bishop of Southwark, dated 1 February 1966, read:

Whitby, for wearing socks in bed, to be fined 1/–.

Not caned, as the Bishop told the Lords.

Although I had been told about this, it was still with a shock that I saw what I was holding in my hands. I rang Ivor, saying something must be done about it, though I did ask him why wearing socks in bed was an offence.

The practical, though slightly comic, explanation was that when a boy had been working on the farm attached to the school his socks acquired a certain amount of mire best not transferred to sheets.

He might have suffered from cold feet, I said. Couldn't he have been given bedsocks?

'I didn't think of it.'

I wrote that night to Irene, now retired.

January 21st, 1974

Dear Irene,

I would very much like to see you. I have just come across what appears to be absolute proof that during a Debate in the House of Lords a few years back one of the members misled the House. I have some documents in my study ... The misleading of the House resulted in an appalling injustice to an individual ...

Then, three days later, I wrote again:

I have been reflecting and I feel that the right Lord to deal with the matter ... would be Lord Longford.

He rose after the misleading speech and described it as 'monument of unfairness ... extraordinarily unfair'.

I have spoken with Mr Cook, the victim of the onslaught, and he agrees with me we should take Lord Longford into consultation and that he would be the best placed person to act, if he will.

Only, I do not know him. I do wish that I had an introduction. I am wondering whether you know him and could introduce us, or whether, even if you are not personally acquainted, a common membership of parliament if of different Houses would make it proper for you to write to him asking him to see me. You can show him this letter, if you like.

With love,

JEAN

A point I might have made was that Longford was Leader of the House at the time. Irene replied that what she was doing, as she had met Lord Longford, was to send my letter to him. As soon as she heard from him, she would get in touch.

In the evening of 5 February, my telephone rang. 'Lord Longford speaking.' Dame Irene Ward had sent him both my letters. 'She tells me you are a very great friend of hers.' Would I like to come and see him tomorrow morning?

'Would you like me to bring Mr Cook?'

'No.' He said this with such vehemence I wondered what lay behind it. The answer was of course that Ivor did not endear himself to people. Years later I was in correspondence with Roy Jenkins (by then Lord Jenkins of Hillhead) over whether I could quote from the transcript of the Court Lees Inquiry in my possession. Roy Jenkins wrote:

> For your private information, I formed the view that Ivor Cook was in a category of people who have figured in a whole series of exposures of malpractice, objectively performing a beneficial public service, but subjectively a horror to work with (even had the school been well run), awkward, disputatious, obsessive. The world needs such people, but not too many of them!

As we were about to hang up, he said, 'I suppose the member who misled the House was the Bishop of Southwark?'

'Yes.'

'I was afraid so. He's a great friend of mine.'

'How awful! It's the one thing I never thought of.'

'But justice will have to be done.'

I was in his office, above the publishers Sidgwick & Jackson, by ten o'clock, carrying two files of the exhibits. Longford began by saying Court Lees was in the diocese of the Bishop of Southwark and it would have been from that point of view the Bishop concerned himself with it.

I showed him, in the *Hansard* covering the debate, the passage reporting the Bishop's reference to 'the supreme penalty of corporal punishment' meted to the boy who 'wore his socks in bed'. And I showed him the yellow form, on which the actual punishment was written: 'To be fined 1/-.'

He looked at it. He looked at a number of the yellow forms. He asked the meaning of the word 'file' written on some of them.

'It means file for record. No other action to be taken.'

'Bishop Stockwood wouldn't know that.'

'It doesn't mean cane.'

'Bishop Stockwood can never have seen these.'

I pointed out the Bishop claimed to have them in his possession. Indeed, he appeared to have them in his hand, quoting from them.

Longford noted that the penalties were written in a smaller hand than Haydon's. Whose was it?

'Fidoe's.'

'Who's Fidoe?'

'The previous head. The predecessor of Haydon.'

He felt the Bishop simply had not read the words written in the smaller hand. He had all this from Haydon.

[313]

Ivor had always wondered whether it was from Haydon or from Judge Cohen that the Bishop had got the yellow forms. To be quite sure, I asked, 'Haydon, not Cohen?'

'Haydon.'

I thought he had probably telephoned to the Bishop the night before, to brief himself for the interview.

He said that at the Lords people were always putting things into one's hand and asking one to speak about them.

I said surely it was very unwise to get up and speak upon the basis of a document on which one had not read all the words because of some of them being in a small hand.

He said, 'You must accept that Bishop Stockwood is a Christian and everything he has done was as a Christian.' Then he asked, 'What do you want me to do? I'm not going to get up in the House ... I will write to him and ask him if he would like to alter anything he said.'

'He should withdraw his words publicly.'

All this had happened a long time ago, he said. Everybody had forgotten it.

'Mr Cook hasn't forgotten it.'

'If the Bishop were to retract this – I don't know if he would – it still wouldn't get Mr Cook another job.'

'That's not the point.' (Actually, Jill had told me Leslie Thompson had told her if Ivor liked to apply for his old job back there wouldn't be any difficulty now.) 'It's to clear his name.'

'Why has it come up after all this time?'

I told him about the lawsuits and that Hoolahan was quoting the Bishop out of *Hansard*.

He asked about the issue of the lawsuit, and said, 'I'm glad he's got something, at least.' He asked about Mr Cook's financial situation, damages apart, about his marriage. He suggested Mr Cook write him a letter which he could use as the basis of one he would write to the Bishop. 'That is, if he is able to write a letter.'

I looked at him in astonishment, and he said, 'I had been given to understand that he might not be, by this time.'

I told him Mr Cook had conducted his own cases and was a Shakespeare scholar.

He said, 'Tell him to write me a letter, of not more than two pages, the size of this.' Holding one up. 'With no abusive language in it. I will not copy out vulgar abuse.'

As he saw me to the door, he said, 'It's no use asking people to eat dirt. They won't do it. I think the Bishop might say something like, he is sorry Mr Cook's feelings have been hurt, or he is sorry Mr Cook has had a difficult time ...' I knew he was feeling for a formula which would allow the Bishop to use the word 'sorry' without admitting fault. But that would be of no use to Ivor, who needed abolition of an allegation. I said that as a Christian, the Bishop ought to want to put right the wrong he had done.

Longford drew himself up and said, 'He may or he may not.'

Ivor brought me his letter to the Bishop:

February 12th, 1974

Dear Dr Stockwood,

Xerox copies of the yellow forms you referred to have been supplied to me by the solicitors of Messrs Haydon and Ebert. Examination of these proves conclusively that there is no truth whatsoever in your attacks on me, and that, I regret to say, you lied ...

I shook my head. 'It contains phrases I do not think Lord Longford will copy out.' He had better let me do it.

Later in the day I telephoned when I thought he would have got home. Jill answered and I took the opportunity to say that in some of the letters that Ivor wrote, such as the one I had just stopped from going forward, he came over as violent and unruly. 'Can't you vet them before they go to the post?'

'No, I can't. He writes them in the evening when he comes back from the pub and carries them straight to the post. I don't see them.' They gave him, she said, such immense satisfaction and emotional relief.'

'But they do him harm,' I said, wondering now if he was drunk when he wrote them.

I wrote to Longford that I believed the best thing would be for me to see the Bishop. But then Ivor telephoned saying this case against *The Express* would probably come up at the beginning of the next session. He could not take the risk of the Bishop's words being quoted as factual and he ought to give the story to one of the other newspapers.

I said it seemed rude just after I had asked Longford to put me in touch with the Bishop.

It was a moment of supreme tension. Then he said 'You can tell Longford you have with great difficulty persuaded me to hold my hand.' He would be satisfied 'if the Bishop would withdraw his words,

[315]

either in the House of Lords, a letter to *The Times* or a statement to Associated Press'.

I wrote to Longford that night.

In the afternoon of 25 February my telephone rang.

'Frank Longford here.' At least this was an improvement on 'Lord Longford', the first time. He said, 'There has been a mis-statement.' He said it as though he had been thinking it over and come to a resolution.

I said the Bishop need not lose dignity if he made the announcement himself, as if unprompted. I said he could come over as a man who, having discovered himself to have made a mistake, was at pains to put it right. 'That could only add to his stature as a man of rectitude and scruple.'

'Yes! Yes!' Longford exclaimed, grasping at this.

He said he thought it would be best if I wrote a letter to the Bishop, which he could send on, enclosed in one of his own. '*You* – not Mr Cook – Mr Cook is given – that is, I have heard he is given – to the use of pungent phrases ...' I should remind the Bishop of what he had said, tell him what was wrong with it, 'and then make your recommendations'.

He would be leaving the office at 4.30 but would be back in the morning.

It was 3.15 now; Sidgwick & Jackson was so near to my flat I thought I could bring it to him before he left at 4.30.

I walked back to my flat and wrote:

February 25th, 1974

My Lord Bishop,

You may recall that in the course of a debate in the House of Lords, on the Court Lees affair on October 25th, 1967, you made some reference to Mr Ivor Cook.

The intention of your speech was to show him as a hypocrite, in posing as an opponent of corporal punishment citing 110 yellow forms, which you represented as virtual recommendations for caning made out for trifling matters, the one you held up for principle ridicule being that for a boy, Whitby, sent up for 'the supreme penalty of corporal punishment' for 'wearing his socks in bed'.

In fact, yellow forms were not recommendations for caning, and Mr Cook knew that none of his yellow forms resulted in a caning, only at the time of your speech he had not his yellow forms to refer to: you had them; you told the House you had them in your possession.

But recently Mr Cook obtained a complete set of copies from the solicitors for the other side in a law case, and sent them to me as I am writing a book on the affair, and I think you cannot have read all the words on them; in the one concerning the boy Whitby in respect of the socks is marked at the foot, 'to be fined 1/-', and of the other four cases you mentioned, two were 'to lose ten marks' and the remaining two are marked 'file' for record, in other words, no penalty imposed. They are all marked with tiny fines, loss of good conduct marks or mere 'file'. You have, therefore, terribly misrepresented Mr Cook.

Also, 100 yellow forms is not a great number. In the High Court recently Mr Leslie Thompson, third in command of the school at the time and now deputy head went into the box for Mr Cook and say he used to issue one or two a week, which is twice to four times the number attributed to Mr Cook; in fact Mr Cook issued rather few.

You can if you wish ask Mr Thompson to recapitulate the evidence which he gave in court. The school is now re-named Hays Bridge and is in South Godstone, Surrey.

The matter is very urgent for Mr Cook, because he has a further case coming up in the High Court, a libel action against *The Daily Express* in respect of your speech. This would be covered by privilege except that they have mis-quoted you, making the defamation even worse, that it is their worsening of it he is suing on. Nevertheless, as damages are assessed with relevance to the character a man is presumed to possess, if the jury does not understand that you represented the matter amiss, they are going to think he has no character anyway and may not give substantial damages in respect of the extent to which the *Express* has made the matter worse. He is, therefore, obliged to show your words were incorrect and has even toyed with the idea of making that plain through the medium of the press before the case starts. I do, however, think, and he agrees with me, that it would be from every point of view preferable if you would put the matter right yourself.

If you would either make a statement in the Lords or write a letter to *The Times* or make a statement to Associated Press explaining that yellow forms were not recommendations for caning and that none of Mr Cook's yellow forms resulted in caning, and that he did not issue a great number anyway relative to other members of the staff, then he would not need to assume the role of attacker the public would see in you a man who, having discovered himself to have made a dreadful mistake, hastened to proclaim the matter and put it right.

There is also one other matter. In a further debate in the House of Lords, you supposed the Home Office knew the history of Mr Cook, why he left the Army and why he left Devon County Authority, implying some discreditable but unspecified circumstance. Mr Cook joined up the day after the war was declared and after the war discharged with the honorary rank of Captain and draws a pension in respect of ill health sustained while on active service. The year he spent at Bidford Secondary Modern School was perhaps the happiest of his teaching career, and the headmaster Mr Green, wrote him a testimonial when he moved to Court Lees. So what did you mean? Would you withdraw these aspersions too? Mr Cook would give you his authority to apply to the Ministry of Defence for a certified copy of his record of service.

If you have heard some story to his discredit, would you at least be good enough to say what it is, so that he can answer it.

I would be more than willing to meet you and to show you the papers to which I have referred.

Only, time is short. Mr Cook's case against the *Express* was referred from the last session and so may come at the beginning of this one, which starts in the first week in March.

I am, my Lord,
yours faithfully,
JEAN OVERTON FULLER

I took this by taxi, handed it in at Longford's office and looked at my watch. It was 4.10.

I received a reply from Bishop's House:

Dear Miss Fuller,
   The Bishop of Southwark is in the Middle East. Your enquiry should be addressed to his Legal Secretary, Mr David Faull, of Lee, Bolton & Lee, 1 The Sanctuary, SW1.

Yours sincerely,
MARY CRYER,
Secretary

Young John Norton, Betty Grass's son – now seventeen – happened to call in. I told him about it. He asked, 'May I hold that in my hand?'

I handed it to him and he held it up to the light, then asked, 'What is the Bishop's name?'

'Mervyn Stockwood.'

'Interesting that he dictated it himself.'

He passed it back to me to hold up against the light, and then I saw, beneath the raised white blob of the fluid typists use to obliterate their errors, the initials MS/MC

Mervyn Stockwood / Mary Cryer!

Next, I received a letter from Faull on the paper of Lee, Bolton & Lee:

March 4th, 1974

Dear Miss Fuller,

Your letter of 25th February to the Bishop of Southwark has been passed to me as his Legal Secretary.

I think the Bishop has made it clear on several occasions that the speech he made in the House of Lords was priviledged [*sic*)]and he feels it would be improper for him to make any further comment on such a speech.

I think that the matter must rest there.

Yours sincerely,
D. W. FAULL

When I read that to Ivor on the phone he said 'Lord Longford may not have received a copy of that. As he took the trouble to send your letter to the Bishop enclosed in one of his own, he might be interested to see the manner in which it was received. The Bishop was snapping his fingers at Longford, who had been Leader of the House at the time.' With some asperity he added, 'The Bishop is not a Christian, or he would be afraid to meet his Maker with such a sin on his soul.'

I wrote to Longford:

March 12th, 1974

Dear Lord Longford,

I think you would wish to see the reply I have received from the Bishop's Legal Secretary, which I received yesterday.

I do find it disappointing. Parliamentary Privilege was never intended to protect mis-statements of fact for the destruction of the character of an individual.

I rang Mr Cook on the telephone and he is thinking what he can do now and I shall hear more about this when he comes this evening to dinner with a friend of mine. But I would like to thank you on his behalf for sending my letter to the Bishop in one of yours.

Yours very sincerely,
JEAN OVERTON FULLER

The friend I was dining with that evening was Tim, at his flat. He had said I must bring Ivor to dinner with him.

This became now a council of war. The next person to appeal to must be the Archbishop of Canterbury, and it was agreed between the three of us that I should write him a letter. It was while Tim was in the kitchen, having served us Greek food to start with – I did wish Ivor had not objected to the touch of garlic and so rudely kept on about it – that Ivor began totting up what he hoped to get from the *Express*, on this count and on that, arriving at more and more unrealistic (as it seemed to me) figures, finally arriving at a quarter of a million. I said nothing, as he needed to be full of confidence when presenting his case, but I felt he was losing touch with reality. This forecast, I remembered, had once been £10,000.

I wrote my letter:

March 14th, 1974

The Archbishop of Canterbury,
Lambeth Place, SE1

My Lord Archbishop,

I am sending you a copy of a letter I wrote to the Bishop of Southwark, Dr Mervyn Stockwood, which Lord Longford, after studying the papers referred to in it which I brought to show him, sent on to him enclosed in one of his own.

I send you also a copy of the reply sent me on his behalf by his legal secretary. I feel it does not meet the case at all. As I have written to Lord Longford, Parliamentary Privilege was never intended to protect mis-statements of fact for the destruction of the character of an individual.

In any case, the issue is not legal but moral. A person who has uttered a mis-statement of fact greatly to the detriment of another has a moral duty to put the record straight. Will you please speak to the Bishop of Southwark about this?

I would willingly show you the papers.

I am, my Lord, yours faithfully,

JEAN OVERTON FULLER

I received a reply from his secretary:

27 March, 1974

Dear Miss Fuller,

You wrote to the Archbishop of Canterbury about the Court Lees case and what the Bishop of Southwark said in the House of Lords some years ago.

The Archbishop does not intend to intervene.

Where now?

What was needed was somebody to stand up in the House of Lords. Ivor wrote to Lord Byers, a Liberal peer, who lived in the district, laying the whole situation before him. Lord Byers replied that he could do nothing as he was not a member of the Government. Ivor then wrote to Lord Garnsworthy, a Labour peer. Lord Garnsworthy replied that he could do nothing as he *was* a member of the Government.

But it was time I took Leslie Thompson up on his invitation to visit Court Lees – Hays Bridge as it was called now – and on 3 April 1974 I took the train. Thompson met me at the station with his car. 'Ivor doesn't want to come to the school,' he said. And as we entered it he said in his deputy head's room, 'I admire Ivor for what he's done. I couldn't have done it. I know I couldn't. Roy Jenkins had been closing the approved schools down and turning them into community homes, as fast as he could. 'You can tell Ivor it's what he's done. I never would have believed that *one man* could achieve the overthrow of the entire system.'

Three boys were brought in. They had been throwing stones at a horse. Thompson said, 'In Haydon's day, that would have meant six of the best. Now it just means loss of some privilege.'

He gave me a boy to take me round the various rooms. The boy asked me if there was anything in particular I would like to see?

'The cupboard in which Mr Cook took the photographs.'

'It has been destroyed.'

And then suddenly Ivor was driving up to the front door.

[321]

'You wouldn't like to come in?' asked Thompson 'Look around the old place again?'

Ivor answered only with a shuddering shake of the head. He had only come to collect me and take me to tea with Jill.

On 27 April I met Irene at her London club. She was seventy-nine now but looking very springlike in pink.

She looked at Faull's letter and said, 'This is nonsense. Privilege only means you can't be sued, not that you can't correct a mistake.' The usual procedure was to ask – the Speaker in the Commons or the Leader of the House in the Lords – for a minute or two in which to make a personal statement.

What puzzled her in the affair was that, 'This was a Labour Home Secretary facing a Conservative Censure Motion. And a Labour Bishop, if he got up, ought to have been trying to help him.' But this could only have been an annoyance to Roy Jenkins.

I showed her her the yellow forms.

She studied them; then she said, 'A dirty trick has been played on Mr Cook, and it is not in the interest of democracy the matter should rest.'

She would first write, herself, to the Archbishop of Canterbury and, if she got no better reply than I did, to the Archbishop of York, his probable successor – for Ramsey was on the point of retiring. If he couldn't do it, she knew Sir Marcus Worsley, Ecclesiastical Commissioner, and would put it up to him. If he failed she would lay it before the Privy Council. If still no joy, 'I shall appeal to the Queen.'

How had Mr Cook learned of the attack on him in the Lords?

From the newspapers.

Didn't the Bishop send him a draft, or warning? Or a Hansard?

No, to all three questions.

That seemed to her extraordinarily rude. If she was going to attack an individual in the House, she always sent him warning. This gave him the opportunity to explain the actions she held him responsible for.

I remembered that she had sent me, to send to Déricourt, the text of her motion critically concerning him.

We talked a little about her not having been given a peerage. Why hadn't Heath given her one?

'He thinks I'm so old I'll die soon and it isn't worth it. I'm only fit to be put out to grass.' She had had a letter from him which depressed her.

But Heath had just called and lost a General Election (on 28 February) so there was still the Dissolution Honours List to come. I understood that the new Prime Minister always invited his defeated rival to submit recommendations.

'Mr Wilson won't want to fill the Lords up with Tory peers. Ted will have to keep his list short.'

She had had a letter from Lord Hailsham saying he couldn't think why Ted hadn't given her a peerage.

Irene asked me to dine with her again at the Helena Club on 3 June and to ask Mr Cook to join us there at for coffee afterwards.

How would true blue and flaming red get on? Ivor said, 'I've always been a long way to the left of you, Dame Irene.' She did not appear to hear. He said, when she wrote to anybody at least she got a reply, even if not a satisfactory one, 'When I write, so often I don't get a reply at all.'

'That's not accidental,' she said. 'To acknowledge receipt of a letter incurs responsibility to do something about it. They hope if they don't reply, you'll just go away and die.'

Ivor asked suddenly, 'If you've spent your life being a nuisance to Ministries, is that why they haven't given you a peerage?'

She couldn't help laughing. 'Could be.'

She kept to her programme. The Archbishop of York replied that he had written about this matter to the Archbishop of Canterbury. 'At least he sounded concerned.'

Marcus Worsley was no longer Ecclesiastical Commissioner.

She asked me to write a statement of the whole case in a form she could simply hand to the Privy Council.

The Privy Council decided the matter was not within its remit, so she asked me to write it out again in a form she could take to Buckingham Palace.

This, too, failed. She had been received by Sir Martin Charteris, who came down to meet her and conducted her upstairs, to the Library, but said, 'The Queen has just stopped work.' He took the petition, that is, my summary of the case, with copy of Faull's letter attached, read carefully and said, 'The Queen can do nothing about this.' He reached down from the shelves a book, which he opened for her at a page whereon it was made quite clear that the Sovereign had no power to do anything about anything that had happened in either of the Houses of Parliament. The proper person to deal with this was the Archbishop of

Canterbury. As she did not want to go back to Canterbury he advised her to take it to the Home Secretary.

'It's the same Home Secretary,' I exclaimed. 'Roy Jenkins back in his old post!'

'That might work out quite well,' she said. She would write to him.

'But he can't do anything,' I reflected.

She knew that! But she had always had a feeling that a conversation between herself and Roy Jenkins might be useful.

Ivor's case against the *Express* opened on 17 June. I sat between Tim and Thompson. We lunched at the ABC and went back in the afternoon. When Ivor began to talk of his Shakespeare, the judge said to Hoolahan, 'I assure you we shall not spend a long time on Shakespeare exegesis.'

Thompson went into the box and said he would be happy to work with Mr Cook as a colleague again. So did another master, Newmark.

On the second morning, the judge allowed Ivor to call me to state 'very briefly' the quality of Mr Cook's Shakespeare scholarship.

I said, 'Very high indeed.'

The judge asked Hoolahan, 'Have you any questions for this witness?'

Hoolahan, smiling at me, very sweetly, said, 'No.'

On the 19th Ivor was saying, 'The Bishop of Southwark is a liar.'

The judge looked rather startled and said he didn't think we could try the Bishop here.

The judge, summing up, stressed that, in spite of all that had happened, two of the other masters had said they would be happy to work with Mr Cook again.

The jury found for Ivor; but only awarded him £500.

'Five hundred!' Because of his higher expectations, to him it was like a defeat. His only satisfaction was that he had managed to say 'The Bishop is a liar' in open court to which the press was admitted. (Not that it appeared in the papers.)

I thought he would have done better to have acted upon Thompson's suggestion he apply for his old job back. I did understand that place gave him the shudders, yet to be reinstated in it would be his triumphant vindication against all that had been uttered against him, far more impressive in most people's eyes than victories in court.

Then, more cheerfully, I had a letter from Irene:

I have had a letter from Roy Jenkins. There is nothing he can do, either, but at least he has written to me *himself*, not through his secretary. He has written very fully.

She enclosed his letter, for me to keep. In October Heath called and lost another election, which renewed Irene's chances of a peerage in the next honours list. She got it – Baroness Ward of North Tyneside.

Twenty

Shares on the London Stock Exchange were sinking and the news-papers were warning of possible hyper-inflation. Apart from my share capital I had only my Indian Army Officers' Family (daughter's) Fund that was reliable, royalties from my writings being far too erratic. I had not been able to find a publisher for my book on the Court Lees affair – principally, as was explained to me at a meeting at Jonathan Cape, because of the risk of libel.

On 25 September the FT index fell through the 200 barrier, I went to the office to talk to Tim, but he was out and so I typed a note saying I wondered if I should sell my flat and buy a house in the country. In the evening I telephoned Martin Booth, who had just sold his house in Rushden and bought one in the village of Knotting, and asked him if there were near him allotments in which I could grow vegetables. He said allotments were sold only to people who owned houses in the district, but why didn't I sell my flat and buy a house, where I would have Helen and himself for neighbours? They had seen one they thought very attractive, in a village called Wymington, oldish, no front garden but back garden large enough to grow all the vegetables I could want; downstairs, two reception rooms one large, upstairs four bedrooms, and two lavatories, one upstairs and one downstairs, in the bathroom. Price £12,000. He was free this Saturday and could me drive to to see it.

'I'm trying to meet a deadline for delivery of the book on SOE, Kimber commissioned from me.'

'This has priority. The publisher can wait. The house may not.'

Tim was worried about finance too. We had had to vacate our first premises but had found new ones off Oxford Street. It was there we had given a party for the launch of George Macbeth's book, *Lusus*. Since then we had given fortnightly at homes, but now the Westminster rates had risen so appallingly that Tim did not see how we could continue to pay them on our office. We could either look for an office where the rates were lower or, perhaps, manage to do without an office at all. We were not like shops, dependent on people coming in to look at what we had to sell. They bought from our catalogues, or rang to say they wanted a copy of something or other, 'Will you get it for me?' We could get an accommodation address. The most important thing was to get rid of the lease of our present premises, and that might not be too easy now that the rates payable on it were so steep.

As a limited company we had to have a registered address, and if I were to buy a freehold house in the country that could be the address of Fuller d'Arch Smith registered at Companies House, and perhaps we could divide up our office furniture, files and stock between our homes.

I went to see the house. Martin met me at Bedford and drove me to Wymington. The house was on the steepest part of a hill and faced the churchyard. I knew I wanted it.

'She doesn't need to get a mortgage,' Martin was telling the people trying to sell it, as though this were a perk.

But I was hoping to find a purchaser for my London flat so as not to have to eke the whole out of capital.

And so into 1975. Irene, writing to thank me for my congratulatory letter on her peerage, promised she would deal with the Bishop of Southwark as soon as she got settled in. She was considering tactics. This was not the fault of the Labour Party. It concerned only the Bishop as an individual. 'It'll have to be a non-party question, and they're always the most difficult.'

On reflection, she thought the Bishop's impugning of Ivor Cook's army record was more important than the business about the yellow forms. One would be addressing an assembly of people who did not know what yellow forms were and have to start explaining, and so lose attention. But everybody knew what an Army record was and why to impugn somebody's was a serious matter.

On 8 April I moved. Ivor drove me and the cats up, following my two furniture removal vans all the way to the house, where Tim, standing on the doorstep, welcomed me with my keys. He had gone ahead to collect them from the departing previous owners.

I had sent Turck the proofs of *The German Penetration of S.O.E.* and been to Paris to check that I had his story right. He suggested I should see his old chief, Brigadier Leslie Humphries, so I wrote to him and he invited me to lunch. We had hardly sat down when he said, 'Buckmaster was the worst colleague I ever had.'

The previous head of F was Marriot, who was in quarrels with the reigning powers, and talked of resignation. 'I said to him, "Marriot, if you resign meaning to go, well and good, but don't resign hoping to be called back." He resigned and Buckmaster was in there within hours.'

The publicity by which Odette had been surrounded he declared ridiculous. She was 'the only person to be awarded a George Cross on her own self-recommendation'. Where were her witnesses?

I remembered that Madame Fabius had posed the same question and told me that when she was put up for her Croix de Guerre she was visited by a French officer who put so many questions she could have felt she was suspected of a crime rather than recommended for a medal.

Gilbert Turck did not escape Humphries's criticism. He had told him not to get mixed up with Buckmaster's people. So why did he do that? His job was to help shot-down pilots escape from France, not get mixed up with secret agents arriving. So why was he renting that wretched Villa des Bois for usage as a safe-house by all those Buckmaster-men arriving by parachute? All his troubles stemmed from that first disobedience. How did he come to know the de Vomécourts at all? He deplored that Turck should have asked me to write a book about his story. The de Vomécourts were quiescent now. Why stir them up again? I could tell Turck from him, 'Let sleeping dogs lie.'

The only person for whom he expressed unstinted admiration was Vera Atkins. He had known her family, the Rosenbergs, and had been a guest at 'her coming out ball' in Bucharest. Her father had taken Romanian nationality. Had been in South Africa. When Vera came to England 'I vouched for her' on her entry to SOE. Also when she applied for British nationalisation. (This was the information Irene had been refused by the Home Office when she asked for it so long ago. Now, presumably, it was no longer secret since the sponsor had identified himself.)

After she entered the Buckmaster Section she ceased to tell him anything of her work, 'as it was quite proper she should'. The sections had their own secrets and she was loyal to Buckmaster. 'Very loyal.'

'Why does she cover up for him?'

The words were hardly out of my mouth when I knew that as soon as I had gone he would ring her up and she would tell him not to tell me any more.

In the *Hansard* entry for 16 July 1975 it was recorded that Irene had done her bit for Ivor. His Army record was cited, dispelling the previous assertions.

Then in November I received a letter from Ivor enclosing a cutting from *The Times* of the previous day (22 November) about a youth called Patric Mackay. As a child he had tried to strangle his mother, before being diagnosed a psychopath. Since growing up he had strangled a woman of 83, killed a Roman Catholic priest of 65 with an axe and was additionally charged with the murders of another woman, aged 76, and a man aged 82. What *The Times* did not mention was that Mackay was an old Court Lees boy. Ivor remembered he had arrived at the school with a psychiatrist's report saying he was 'a potential murderer of women'.

Also enclosed in the envelope was an article by Ivor himself which was published in the *Observer* on 30 November entitled 'The Mind of a Murderer'. It began 'I taught Patric Mackay ...' He wanted me to put this at the beginning of my book on his Court Lees affair. I did not want to do this as it was not the school that had made him into a murderer; it had merely failed to cure him of the murderous tendency the psychiatrist warned the school he came with. Also there seemed to me something opportunistic about using this case to try to sell the book to a publisher, which I found distasteful.

He also wrote:

> I want you to write at once to your local MP referring him to the *Observer* article and to the fact that I gave earlier warning about Mackay on 10/9/67. Point out that 10 people at least have died as a result of neglect, and ask him to press for a public inquiry in the widest terms of reference into the failure of the social service organisations (hospitals, probation and social services) to deal with this case.

I was not too happy about this. Perhaps I bridled at the marshalling tone. I had no knowledge of the case except through Ivor, who had told me in his letter that a woman in Mackay's home had thrown boiling water over him when he was a child. But what should have been done? One could not lock someone up for crimes he had not committed because somebody thought he might commit them.

I did not put the Mackay case at the head of my book. I did however write to my local MP, Sir Trevor Skeat, Conservative, North Bedfordshire. I gave Ivor Cook's name as the source of my information. He must have sent my letter on to Roy Jenkins, who must have passed it to David Owen for reply, copy of which was sent me by Skeat. Ivor had apparently written to two other MPs, Phillip Whitehead and Geoffrey

Howe. David Owen wrote: 'I share the concern of Miss Fuller and Mr. Cook, and the public in general, aroused by the tragic case of Patric Mackay but I do not think that any form of enquiry is necessary since the facts are known in their entirety.'

Ivor's response was that it wasn't clever of me to have given away that I had written on prompting from him.

Irene fared little better with Ivor. He had wanted to take her out as a thank you for her utterance in the Lords, and a date was fixed at a restaurant in Earls Court. But she did not come and as the hour passed, he began to say she 'must have been got at'. I knew this was absurd. There must have been some misunderstanding; but we became gloomier and gloomier.

The morning brought a telephone call from Irene asking what had happened. Ivor had asked her, long before, to dine and she had entered the date in her diary but he did not confirm, as she had expected him to do, nearer the date. She had sat by the telephone in the Lords until after seven, expecting him to ring. She did not know where she was supposed to go.

When we later that month had lunch together at the House of Lords, she said suddenly, 'I can't do anything more for Ivor Cook.' She had had a number of communications from him, ranging from a suggestion he should write her biography (long promised to me) to wanting her to ask a Parliamentary question based on his article in the *Observer* about the Mackay case, which she did not want to do. 'It was obvious I had done everything wrong and he was very cross with me.'

I was horrified. 'But you have done more than anybody for him!'

She brushed the matter aside: 'We meet these people.'

I told Ivor I was shocked by what I had heard from Irene. He took it ill. Nevertheless, the final breach came over a thing, a trifle in itself, the meaning of the word 'carneades' in the works of Thomas Nashe. Once, when he had been talking about Hervey, I had asked him, 'Do you think you *were* Hervey?' He had replied, 'No; if I was anybody in those days I was Thomas Nashe. Always in quarrels, always in trouble, that's me.' Well, it could have been. The word 'carneades' comes in his pamphlet 'Four Letters Refuted' (the four letters of Gabriel Harvey, with whom he was having a quarrel). It was Ivor's submission that the word meant something to do with meat, and therefore was a hit at Shakespeare and proof he really did write the plays that stand in his name. What else could it have meant? I was sure Ivor knew his Nashe better than I did but was not satisfied by this assertion. I didn't know what it meant, but I wasn't convinced Ivor did either. I suggested the matter be just left in abeyance. He wrote back asking if I wished to reduce our correspondence 'to the nullity of "Dear Jean, How are the cats?"' I did not write back.

On 23 November 1976 I took my first driving lesson. This was with some trepidation, given my age and my unfamiliarity with matters mechanical; and indeed it was destined to be a very extended saga. I started off in a Ford, which was perhaps too heavy for me. Anyway my first instructor finally lost patience with me after an unhappy incident with a lorry. So the next April I had my first driving lesson with Graham Inwood. It was suggested that I might find a Fiat easier to manage, so Graham gave his lessons in a Fiat. He was confident of getting me through.

On 9 November the following year I entered for the test for the fourth time and really thought I was almost 'home' when a black dog, a Labrador retriever, ran out in front of my wheels. I braked hard but I also swerved, hoping to divert any impact from his head to his tail-end. When we got back to base, the tester explained to Graham he had failed me because when the dog ran out I had both braked and swerved; I should not have swerved. I carried on with my lessons with Graham and intermittently retook the test. On one attempt, having completed all the manoeuvres without mishap, I thought I was through, and was puzzled to be failed, this time for 'failure to make sufficient progress'.

'What does it mean?' I asked Graham.

'Not going fast enough.'

Was that a crime?

Well, it could be annoying to other motorists who wanted to get along faster. I had been being so careful to execute all the manoeuvres precisely that perhaps I had been going so slowly as to be crawling.

On Tuesday 23 December 1980, at 2.15, I had another test. We ended at 3.15. 'Have I passed?' I asked the tester.

'Yes.'

Graham was so happy for me that he hugged me.

After two hundred and seventy-seven lessons. Four years.

We drove back to Palace Motors and I chose a red Fiat 128, and I paid the deposit on it, then we went together to the insurer's office where I paid for my insurance. Graham said he would drive the car to me on the Saturday after Christmas. This he duly did. Having nowhere else yet to put it, I parked it in my garden.

It was on 26 April 1980 that I had heard on the ITV evening news that Irene Ward had died. It had been no surprise. In January I had received a telephone call from a man introducing himself as her nephew, David Greenslade. He said that the previous September she had fallen over a fender in the Helena Club and broken her hip. She was now in Knaresborough Nursing Home, London SW6. 'I don't expect her to leave it.' He had found my address in my correspondence with her, and gained the impression I was a good friend of hers. 'Her memory is gone. She does not remember names, but if you go and see her she might recognise your face.'

On 13 January 1980 I went to London and found my way to the Knaresborough Nursing Home. She was in bed and so emaciated it was a shock to see her. She did recognise me when I got close to her, but no longer knew what SOE was. When I referred to Elizabeth she asked, 'Elizabeth who?' and when I spoke of Penelope she asked, 'Penelope who?' She did know I had bought a house in the country with a garden and was growing my own vegetables, and said she would have liked to have had a garden. She said, 'I can't remember how I got here. I don't understand how I came to be here.' I told her, 'You fell over a fender in the Helena Club and hurt yourself and were brought here.'

When I rose to go I asked if I might give her a kiss. She said, 'Yes,' and put up her face to receive it. Unhappily, I knew it was for the last time.

The newscast seemed to be trying to give her a working class image, which was misplaced. Her speech was very much of the upper classes and I wondered there had not been – as had happened before – a confusion with her near namesake, Ms Eireen Ward, Labour Member of Parliament. That some people pronounced Irene as though it were spelled Ireen, made the sound identical with that of the Labour Lady.

I took a few notes of what she told me when thinking I might write her biography. Her full name was Irene Mary Bewick Ward, she was born at a few minutes to midnight on 24 February 1894, in London. Her father was a London architect. But he died when she was only two and her widowed mother decided to rejoin her own family up north, and took Irene with her. As a child, she supplemented her ordinary schooling with lessons in singing, elocution and dancing. She also played tennis – as she said to me, she was inclined to do too many things to do any of them well. She would never come first in a competition, though sometimes second or third. She had a good singing voice and the most serious of her aspirations was to sing in grand opera. It was curious, looking back, to recall she was called 'the butterfly' for her tendency to settle on too many things, whereas she had become, as a parliamentarian, known for the doggedness with which she would pursue an issue.

Her entry into politics was accidental. She had been giving a recitation from the platform at some local do when afterwards a woman came up to her and said she represented the Conservative Party and that she liked Irene's quality of voice and clarity of speech. They were looking for a woman to put up against Labour's Margaret Bonfield, the first woman Cabinet minister. 'They wanted me to beat Margaret Bonfield.' She beat Margaret Bonfield at Wallsend in 1931.

As she lived in a coal mining area, she interested herself in the mines. There was new and expensive machinery which some mines had bought in other districts. She took it upon herself to visit a mine in which it had been installed, go down the shaft and creep along to join the men at the pit face and ask them how they found it. Was it really a help? Would they advise mines that had not got it yet to get it?

She never lost her interest in opera, was a Trustee of the Carl Rosa (she referred to its style and that of another company as 'robust' and 'anaemic' respectively), and received complimentary tickets for both Sadler's Wells and Covent Garden – which was why she sometimes took me.

She did not think herself as psychic but had had one odd experience. She and a woman friend with whom she at one time shared a flat in London went together on a motoring holiday. As Irene did not drive it must have been her friend who did so. They were nearing the Welsh border, going along a country lane that had a high bank with a hedge on top of it. They came to a place where there was a gap in the bank. With its back to a gate to a field, was parked a very old car with a starting handle in front. They were both so surprised that they decided to stop to have a better look at it. When they looked round it was no longer there. They were both bewildered. They had both been astonished to see such a car still on the road. Surely nobody could be driving one like that still; it must have dated before 1919. But it had certainly been there. Had they *both* had an optical illusion? They admitted to each other that they were frightened. Something had happened apparently contrary to the laws of nature. As the last thing either of them

[333]

wanted, in their walks of life, was a reputation for seeing things that weren't there, they decided not to say anything about it to anybody. The only thing that cheered them was that there was a book called *An Adventure* (in Versailles) by the Misses Moberly and Jourdain, who had apparently seen Versailles for a moment as it was in Marie Antoinette's time. There had just appeared a book by a woman destructively critical of their account and Irene wanted to know whether I had read either and if so which side I came down on. It was this that had led her to tell me of her and her friend's own adventure. The only thing that did perplex her in the account by Moberly and Jourdain was that they neither of them mentioned what they had seen to the other until some time after. 'We talked to each other about it at once.'

What did I think could be the explanation? If it had been a human being standing at the gate that was there one minute not the next she would have thought it had been the person's ghost, but a motor-car, something with no soul, could not come back as a ghost. She thought the car must have belonged to a man who was accustomed to park it there, and what had become visible to them was 'a photograph of the atmosphere' either of the car or of the owner's thought about it.

With this I inclined to agree.

I never talked about religion with Irene, but I remember her mentioning once that on some trip she attended service in a church of different denomination every day. 'It didn't worry me a bit – so long as one is within the fold.'

A friend of hers was Billy Graham, the American evangelist. He never came to London without calling for her and taking her out to lunch. She did not mention having heard him preach or talked about religion with him but spoke as though they were just pals. She thought him 'a very fine person'.

I had been busy writing. In mid 1981 my book on Francis Bacon came out. Its appearance was acknowledged by a real stinker from A. L. Rowse in the *The Sunday Telegraph*. That did not disturb me, as when one writes on a controversial subject which is irritating to many, one must expect a few stinkers; and *The Sunday Telegraph* printed my reply on 12 July. I did, however, wish that Ivor had acknowledged receipt of the advance copy I sent him. Perhaps he had not been able to bring himself to read it, but if he had he would have seen that I had paid generous tribute to his discoveries.

On 5 September there was a fête at Hinwick and people were invited to take joy-rides on an immense carthorse. I scrambled on to his back – and believed I could ride a horse again. I had thought I was too old. Now, suddenly, I thought why?

I called in at the Rectory Riding School, spoke to Mrs Warner and told her it was time for me to ride a horse. I had done a little riding as a child, though that was a long time ago. I was now sixty-six and a half.

On Tuesday 8 September I had my first lesson with Shirley Warner – on a horse called George, dark brown. I remembered how I had been taught to place my feet in the stirrups, pointing upwards, the whole foreleg forwards. No, one did not do it like that now. That was how people used to be taught. Now the position was different. I had to un-learn before I could learn. On her advice I took lessons of not more than half an hour, once a week. On the second I was rising to the trot, on a grey horse called Blue, on 1 October on a skewbald mare called Rose, cantering now. On 8 October, on Rose again, for the first time ever I jumped. This I had never been allowed to do as a child. I was all right. I came down the other side still on the horse.

I was by this time longing to have a horse of my own, that would get to know me, and wondered if I could buy Rose. Tim thought a horse of my own would be too much of a responsibility. Where would I put her? Would I have a stable made in my garden? In the way of the car? Could I face up to cleaning out the stable, as well as grooming the horse? Then I was told Rose had suffered an injury to one of her feet and could not be ridden. I still hankered for her. Eventually I was told she had been parted with, to breed from.

After a while I was promoted to membership of a group, 'Riding with Shirley'. We just rode around in the countryside, instead of round the enclosed area of the school.

I kept up my yoga. I did the headstand daily, followed always by the shoulderstand, ten minutes each, and a number of the big stretches. When I had energy enough, the handstand as well.

I was all this time working on a book on Saint-Germain – *The Comte de Saint-Germain: Last Scion of the House of Rákóczy*. It had occurred to me that whereas I would never write of a poet without having read his poetry, here I was writing about someone who (during an admit-tedly short period in his varied life) was writing music, without my having heard any of it. I found a student who played me one of the piano pieces I showed her, and a violin teacher who played me one of his solos for violin. But then I saw a card on a board in a shop advertis-ing piano lessons. I rang the number. 'Do you take adult beginners?'

[335]

'Yes.'

An appointment was made for 21 October. A Mr Wilkinson began to teach me the scale of C Major. I said, 'No.' When I was a child I was taught the scales of C, G and F and never got any further. 'I'm not going to start again on scales. This is what I want to play.' And I produced from my bag the photocopy I had got from the British Museum of one of Saint-Germain's shortest pieces, a song beginning 'O wouldst thou know what sacred charms ...'

'You can't play that! That's a complicated piece, in B Flat.' He took it from my hand, then recoiled exclaiming, 'Good God, it's figured bass! You see all those little numerals – those are not fingering. Only the bass note of each chord was shown – '3' meant three notes up from it, a '5' five notes above it, all three to be played together, in the bass.

'What's the first note shown?' I asked, pointing to the first in the treble.

'B Flat.

'Where is it on the piano?'

He showed me.

I put my finger on it.

'What's the next?'

'E Flat.'

'Where is it?'

And so to the next two, F and G, then back to B Flat.

'Well, I can do those,' I said, and did them.

'But there's a rhythm in them.' He showed me.

I did it with the rhythm.

Richard Wilkinson was warming up to this eccentric method of learning, intrigued. I learned during that first lesson to play the first two bars, and when I got home telephoned to Tim that at that rate I ought to be able to play the whole piece in about fifteen lessons. Compared to my driving instruction career, it was a blink of the eye.

Indeed, on 26 October I played the whole thing through, in the treble only. The bass was harder. I volunteered to transcribe the whole into modern notation.

The trouble was, I needed a piano to practise on. Between lessons his mother let me in to practise on his piano, but I needed my own.

I saw one advertised and on 21 November drove to Weston Favell to see it. I got it for only £50. This was because the soft pedal didn't work (which did not matter) and the lacquered veneer on part of the top had peeled off where a goldfish bowl had been stood on it and leaked. This reminded me of a dictum of Mother's, 'Never stand anything containing water on anything electrical or the piano.' Another dictum was, 'Never hang a picture over anyone's bed, in case it comes down in the night on the sleeper's head.' Mother was something of a decorative fatalist.

My piano was delivered to me on 25 November, which meant taking the Chinese whatnot upstairs to make room for it. It was very old, and Richard Wilkinson, coming to see it, much admired its tone. A few months later he left the district but I carried on with the piano and when Tim came on 20 August 1981 I played him the whole of 'O wouldst thou' ... plus another, 'Jove when he saw ...'

On 10 September I handed the publisher the completed typescript of *Saint-Germain*.

I next got to work on a book on Madame Blavatsky, the Theosophist. In the early part of 1983 several of my meetings with Tim were in the Students Room of the British Museum, where we had the Mahatma Letters out. The writing needed careful research, and it was not until the opening days of 1985 that I was able to send Tim the first drafts of my chapters on 'Cosmogenesis' and 'Anthropogenesis'. He was reassuringly complimentary.

Twenty-one

An American called Larry Collins had been in touch with me some while before. He was gathering material for a book that would have as its background SOE. He asked me a lot of questions about Déricourt and told me – which startled me – that Déricourt had been paid in diamonds and that these diamonds came openly from Buckmaster's office.

In due course Larry Collins sent me printouts of the tapes he had made of the interviews with me and with other people. Amongst them was one with Goetz. So it was that from Collins I obtained Goetz's address. I wrote to Goetz, explaining who I was and that I had always wanted to see him but had only just got his address. Would he come and see me if I paid his air fare? On 25 June 1985 I had a letter from him saying he would come. Then the following morning his wife telephoned to say he had heart trouble and couldn't come. Would he prefer me to come to Germany? No. He would come when he got better.

I had brought up to date a completely new handling of the Déricourt story and what Goetz would tell me would make a new chapter. I waited in suspense. On 5 July he telephoned to say his heart was much better and he hoped to come at the end of the month or the beginning of August.

He came on 21 July. I decided we should travel by taxi from Heathrow. I sent him a tiny photograph from which to recognise me and stood beside my taxi-man, who was holding up a card. A big white-haired man with brown eyes, informally dressed in a plum woolly pullover, came hesitatingly towards me. 'Goetz!'

As we settled into the taxi I asked him, 'Have you been to England before?'

In 1945. As a prisoner. He crossed his wrists to indicate handcuffs. Was he well treated?

All right. The food was 'abundant'. He was kept, together with some others, not in an ordinary prison but in a house somewhere near or beyond Kensington Gardens. After some days a man came in and asked them if they had any complaint to make about the conditions of their detention.

'No complaint, but a request.'

What was their request?

'To see Buckingham Palace.'

This appeared to cause the gentleman some surprise, but a few days later they were put into a car, the doors locked 'on both sides, from the outside, so that we could not disappear into the streets', and driven along the side of a park he heard called Kensington Gardens, turned into another street and suddenly Buckingham Palace was before them. The car now went very slowly, so that they could see the sentries in their red coats and bearskins. He made the bearskins tall shape with his hands.

'Do not tell Colonel Buckmaster I am here,' he said.

'I won't. He doesn't like me.'

'Do not tell Miss Atkins I am here.'

'I won't. She doesn't like me either.'

He had not seen Buckmaster. His interrogation was by Miss Atkins. 'She wanted to know *which* captured British agents had talked to the Germans, and I had not to tell her.'

I brought him into my house and he told me his background. He had been teaching French and Spanish at a school in Hamburg when he was conscripted and directed to an office in Toulouse where somebody knowing French and Spanish was needed. Then he was directed to go to Paris and to Kieffer's office, as interpreter. Kieffer had Vogt already but the work was too much for Vogt alone. In the beginning it was just helping Kieffer communicate with whomever he had to meet. When a British agent, Marcus Bloom, was arrested in April 1943 in Toulouse, Goetz was sent back there to question him. Bloom's French was so bad he should never have been sent to France. 'Never could he have been taken for a Frenchman.' It was over Bloom's circuit he made his first attempt at the radio-game but thought London rumbled it. Back in Paris, he was due for a fortnight's leave from 19 June, to visit his wife, who was having a baby, but after only ten days received a telegram from Kieffer requiring his immediate return. 'I would have liked the four remaining days with my wife and baby', but the imperative summons could not be ignored. When he arrived back at Avenue Foch everything was different. Prisoners were being marched about on the stairs and in the corridors. Kieffer told him he and Vogt had been interrogating newly captured British agents round the clock and must rest;

he wanted Goetz to take over the interrogation of one of them and was handing him the file, showing what he knew about him already and what we wanted to know from him. He went by the code-name of 'Archambaud'. Goetz composed a message to be sent to London in 'Archambaud's' name and had it transmitted by one of their very good German radio operators. This time London failed to detect the substitution and it was the first of the sets successfully played back.

As we talked, the light was beginning to go. I switched on the electric and he cried out, 'The window! The curtain! You have not drawn the curtain. We are all illuminated.' Did he suppose there was some hidden marksman waiting to pick him off? In Wymington? I drew the curtains to put him at ease.

By the time of the Normandy landings there were fifteen radio circuits that he was controlling. An order came from Berlin to send mocking messages over all of them at the same time, in identical words and all signed GESTAPO. It seemed to them a pity to 'blow' all of the circuits as there were some that could still be worked fruitfully. They controlled fifteen and it was decided to send the mocking messages over twelve, still keeping three to themselves And even after receiving the mocking messages on the twelve circuits, London had continued to treat as all right the three on which they had decided not to send them. I brought down for him the file of press reviews of *The Starr Affair*, and showed him THE COLONEL'S REPLY: 'She states that not one but several of our networks became German-controlled. I know that it was only one and consider I am in a better position to know the facts than she is.' Foot had, of course, made clear in the official history that there had indeed been several and had given the tonnage of arms and explosives dropped to German reception, but I had not managed to find in his pages the exact number. It was Goetz who had given me that.

He said, 'Reading this, I feel that I am in danger, being here.'

'You are not in danger.'

'Truly, nobody knows that I am here?'

'Truly.' (Except Tim, of course.)

What I most wanted to hear about was his contacts with Déricourt. (I was by now writing the book that was eventually published as *Déricourt: The Chequered Spy*.) When I had taken him up to show him his room on arrival, he had seen the photograph of Déricourt cut from a newspaper that I had put on the landing, and had instantly exclaimed, 'That's him!'

Kieffer told him he was to meet an agent of Boemelburg called

'Gilbert'. The first meeting was in a car, the subsequent ones in an empty flat. They lasted about half an hour. 'Gilbert' wold give him the expected time and place of arrival of British aircraft and of which type and number – 'two Lysanders' or whatever. Goetz would then telephone all the anti-aircraft batteries along the indicated route and say, 'British aircraft, number and type coming, do not attack.' So the aircraft had a protected passage, 'We might watch but not touch.' Because if they made arrests, the game was over. In return Déricourt would, when he came to know it, tell them the date and place of the invasion. The four arrests were accidents. Their French collaborators, Bony and Laffont, had orders to trail the incoming agents as far as Paris and thence until they went either into some building in Paris or into a railway station other than that by which they had arrived. Then report. Bonotaux had walked around Paris then returned to the station by which he had arrived. That perplexed the trailing gang and they arrested him, which was unfortunate. Then the case of the three arrested 'by the November moon'. When they got out at the station in Paris it was noticed that there were French police at the barrier requiring passengers to show their papers. Bony and Laffont had no way to refer back to their chief (Boemelburg), but supposed he would not want the incomers in French hands. So they arrested them, which was the worst thing they could have done. Boemelburg was furious, because it must make 'Gilbert' suspect in London, as indeed it did. 'Gilbert' was recalled. Kieffer told Goetz that he was invited to dinner with Boemelburg, at his villa. So Goetz changed into his best suit – and found that his fellow guest was 'Gilbert'. Apparently relaxed but not really. He said he still hoped to come back to them. Boemelburg asked if he would like any money and he said, 'No.' So they let him depart in peace and never saw or heard more of him. Goetz said he always thought Boemelburg unwise to pin such hopes on the deal; for they had no guarantee 'Gilbert' would learn the date and place of the invasion or if he learned it that he would tell them. 'But "Gilbert" was to make the glory of Boemelburg. Through "Gilbert" Germany was to win the war.'

He recognised also the photograph of Noor, but winced. 'She was very frightened of me. She felt, I believe, some confidence in Vogt.' He meant *confiance* in the French sense of trust. 'None in me. I could not get near her.' She should not have been sent. Too straight, too emotional, too vulnerable, too transparent. Every emotion showed on her face. He knew if he had touched a sensitive point by the way she started. (He could have been echoing Spooner's judgement.) She was the opposite of 'Gilbert'. His face bore never any expression. The perfect card-player's face. No thought or feeling ever showed on it.

In the morning, he told me he had been looking from the window of his room at the church and the infants' school. He had seen children playing. 'I can tell my wife I have seen an English school.'

He would so much have liked, now that everything was over and neither of them had anything to fear, to meet 'Gilbert' again, 'and ask him what he had in his mind'. Goetz hoped very much that the air crash in Laos might have been faked. He would like 'Gilbert' to walk in on us here. 'I think he is here.' Would he know how to find me at this address?

We walked out into the garden and he allowed me to take a photograph of him on my promise not to put it in the book.

He would like to see the inside of the church. I took him into St Lawrence's. It was very old, thirteen or fourteen something. 'You are a believer?'

'I try to believe.' Catholic religion. But interested in Buddhism also, as in all attempts to explain the mystery of life. 'I think atheism is not such an explanation.'

I took him for a stroll up the Green Lane. As we stood by the wheatfield we came to be talking about Kieffer's having been hanged by the British. 'That was murder!' he exclaimed. 'His poor family ...'

I had gathered from Starr that what he was executed for was having had three captured uniformed commandos shot in a wood. It had been on an order from higher up.

'Kieffer was very obedient,' Goetz said. He would never have disobeyed an order.

I had inquired, after my first conversation with Vogt, to obtain a transcript of Kieffer's trial but there had been some difficulty. But that was thirty-five years ago. It might be easier now and I would try again.

After lunch I took him for a drive in my car, through Knotting, where we looked into the old church, St Margaret's, and round about.

In the evening, as the shadows gathered and I drew the curtains, he asked suddenly, 'That lady to whom you waved, she will not tell anybody I am here?'

'What lady?' Then I remembered that as we passed along Green Lane I had given a wave to Shirley, who was on her side of the hedge. He must have been worrying about that all afternoon. It had been a woman's wave that had been the signal to arrest Narsac.

'She does not know who you are. She will not tell anybody.'

During the evening, and the next morning in the taxi, we continued talking about particular mysteries that puzzled us. He even seemed less generally apprehensive. He had told his wife, when she had seen him off, 'If I don't return you will know it was a revenge killing.' That was a joke, but as he sank into his seat aboard the aircraft it must have been with relief and great relaxation of tension.

I was still trying to think of a title for my new Déricourt book. *The Delphic Spy* didn't quite work. Tim suggested *Honour Bright* which I thought was clever. But Michael Russell, who was publishing it, suggested *Déricourt: The Chequered Spy*, which used the imagery of the chess-board. Chess was Déricourt's favourite game. It was Michael Russell's idea, also, to have Déricourt's photograph in alternate squares of positive and negative.

I had visited Déricourt's birthplace, but it was Varenval which was the seat of his childhood memories and I wanted to see that too. There was a coach that ran between London and Paris, so on 20 September 1985 I took a taxi from Wymington to Victoria Coach Station, and thence via Dover-Calais to Paris. There I caught the 8.35 am train for Compiègne from the Gare de l'Est. The carriage was so luxurious I thought I must have made a mistake – I was not travelling de luxe or even first class. French trains had certainly looked up since I first travelled in France.

I checked in at the Hôtel du Nord in Compiègne, where I had booked a room. Then I breakfasted and found a taxi rank. 'A Varenval.' The route lay first along the north bank of the River Oise, then diverged from it through a patchwork of small fields, mostly maize, until branches of oak from the woods practically brushed the windscreen; we were in the Forêt de Compiègne.

Monsieur Miroche, the present owner of the château, was in Paris, but the gates were open and we drove straight in. We were in a world of giant hogweed, beneath which the roses remembered by Madame Henrie must long ago have disappeared. The château itself rose from the mists dark and gaunt against the sun, its towers of unusual height and different design. This was what Déricourt had wanted all his life to own. M. Miroche had said in his reply to my letter that he was trying to sell it; did I know anyone who would like to buy? Price £20,000. Oh Déricourt, you should have been here now, your pockets bulging with ill-gotten funds. It seemed too cruel that the château should have come up for sale when he was no longer here to hazard an offer. In front, on what must have been the lawn, was an enormous pair of wheels, the wheels Madame Henrie had told me Déricourt had played on as a child, believing them to come from a cannon captured from the Germans in the Great War. To me, its long rake-like teeth suggested a harrow, but would a harrow have been given the place of honour on the lawn? Perhaps it really was something seized from the enemy.

Déricourt's father had been bailiff of Varenval, his mother the house-keeper. I asked the taxi-driver to take us to nearby Jonquières where they were buried, and found their grave, the tombstone inscribed:

Alfred Déricourt
1868–1944
Georgette Magny 1869–1945

In French law, a married woman retains her maiden surname.

Returned to Compiègne, I made the round of the places that figured in the story of Joan of Arc, climbed the tower, stood in the room in which she had been imprisoned and looked down for a long time from the window through which she had jumped in her attempt to escape.

Back in Paris the next day. I refreshed my memory of old scenes connected with the dramas of SOE agents, then walked up the rue Pergolese and found number 58. I had never done this while Madame Déricourt lived, as Déricourt did not wish me to make contact with her. Now, of course, everything was locked up. I pressed all the bells but nobody came to the door.

Continuing up the street I noticed a restaurant with the name IGNACE above the door. That was the name Déricourt had given to his smug-gling contact in the fictitious story he had told the magistrates at Croy-don. Anything behind that?

I walked on, to the Place des Ternes, and sat down at one of the outside tables of the Brasserie Lorraine, which had figured so dramati-cally in the stories of both Christmann and Déricourt. Before me stretched the flower-market, a sea of gladioli and chrysanthemums. Yes; I saw what Déricourt meant: it was a safe place to sit down for coffee or any critical meeting as anybody approaching must be seen from a long way off. If anybody who looked suspicious or possibly dangerous was seen approaching, it would be easy to go inside the brasserie, as if to visit the gents, and leave by its side door.

I caught the evening coach and was back in London in the early hours of 23 September and was thankful to see my taxi-man waiting at Victoria Coach Station.

On 27 January 1985 I received *A Fall from Grace*, by Larry Collins. It was nice of him to have sent me a complimentary copy, though I did not believe in the idea he was trying to put over in the novel that the Air Movements Officer (given a fictitious name but clearly identifiable as Déricourt) had been briefed by the British Intelligence Service to betray the agents, who had been briefed with false information concerning the date and place of the invasion, which, breaking down under torture, they would feed to the Germans. This to my mind was fantastic. And I knew Goetz would be upset. I warned him in a letter, 'You will not like it.' Indeed he did not. He, too, had received a complimentary copy and was furious. He had thought Collins came to see him in some official capacity or as a serious historian, not as a novelist. 'To think I received that man in my house!' And he referred to him in terms I had better not repeat. He reaffirmed what he had said earlier, at my house, that none of the prisoners appeared to have been told anything about the date and place of the invasion. For Collins's thesis to be viable, 'They should have been telling us Calais!'

Next I heard from a Mr Robert Marshall that he was writing a BBC programme on the theme and would like to see me. I thought better not to see him, as his programme would be transmitted before my book could be published and I did not want anything I had to say to be used by someone else, in a context I could not check, beforehand. Tim thought I was right to refuse. So did Martin Booth. Despite my letter to this effect, which Tim read in draft before I posted it, there followed a succession of telephone calls, but I hung up the moment I heard that voice that I now recognised. What Marshall most wanted from me, of course, was 'Déricourt's German contact'. From his reaction to Collins's book I did not think Goetz would appreciate my handing on his address.

On 4 November Collins telephoned and asked me to return the transcripts of his interviews which he had lent me, as he was 'getting phone calls'. I had photocopies made before I returned the papers he had sent me. I later learned it was to pass to Marshall that he wanted them.

14 February brought two letters from Goetz: he had received a letter from Marshall but had refused to see him. He sounded quite a bit worried. Then, on 26 February, he telephoned. He had told Marshall, as a way of putting him off, that he had given me a promise not to give an interview to anyone else. If Marshall contacted me and asked me to relieve him of that promise, would I please tell him I refused to do so. I set his mind at rest.

On 21 March Kieffer's trial papers arrived: 333 pages, in German and in English on facing pages. Kieffer had said in evidence that on 8 August he was summoned by telephone to the office of Dr Knochen, as also was Dr Schmidt, and they both were shown a teleprint order from Muller, head of the Reichssicherheitsamt in Berlin to have those uniformed commandos changed into civilian clothes and shot. Schmidt had organised the firing party. There was no dissension between the defence and prosecution as to the facts, only on the way in which they should be regarded. I told Goetz. He said Muller was so high up it would have been impossible for Kieffer to have disobeyed an order coming from him. I believed that in British military law a man had to obey any lawful command given him by his superior officer; if told to put poison in his mother-in-law's tea that obviously could not be a lawful command, but there could be cases where the legality or otherwise was less clear and I did not know how it stood in German law, or whatever exactly Kieffer belonged to. Goetz said if Kieffer had refused to obey that order he would have been shot. All one could really say was that, in that case, he would have died a martyr, whereas obeying, he was hanged by our people.

A Theosophical acquaintance of mine, Leslie Price, had floated the idea of a magazine devoted to Theosophical history and this had fruited in a quarterly of that title, *Theosophical History*. In July a Conference was arranged in connection with it and he invited me to be one of the speakers. My talk was on the Saturday, with Leslie in the chair. I gave a foretaste of my coming biography of Blavatsky, concentrating on some aspects of the Coulomb affair.

The publisher Carp had expressed himself delighted with the *Blavatsky*, but it was a bit long for the East-West's purse and he had invited the Theosophical Society to come in on it with him. The Theosophists then conceived the idea of doing it entirely by themselves, without Carp; Helen Gething, who would be in charge of the Theosophical publications side (and head of the Esoteric School), later came round to the idea of a partnership; but finally it was not the Theosophical Society but the Blavatsky Trust (Chairman Geoffrey Farthing) that invested some of its funds in the publication and had to sell some of its securities to do so.

Marshall's book *All the King's Men* appeared in January 1988. From the acknowledgements I gathered it was for him that Larry Collins had wanted the transcripts of his interviews. I was glad to see Foot's review of it in *The Sunday Times* of 24 January: 'Bad books on SOE abound.

Alas here is another.' This gave me the occasion to write a letter which appeared in the following week's issue. What chiefly annoyed me was that he had sourced one of his remarks 'Déricourt correspondence with Jean Overton Fuller'. This gave the impression I had granted him access to my papers, which was not the case. I wrote to him to complain about this. I also noticed that he appeared to have found in Madame Déricourt's flat a novel which Déricourt had asked me to translate into English but which had gone astray in the post. (I supposed that it had arrived whilst I was in Carthage, and had been returned to the address written by his secretary on the back, which must have been rue Pergolese, so that his wife, not he, would have received it.) Marshall replied that the quote he had given was from a fragment of correspondence Déricourt must have intended sending to me which was amongst the papers in Madame Déricourt's flat, of which the door was wide open when he called so that anything might be picked up; and that the novel was out of his hands as he had sent it to have it translated. I had indeed been told by someone that Marshall did not know French.

On 2 May 1988, I received a letter from Rémy Clément, thanking me for having sent him a copy of *Déricourt: The Chequered Spy* but lamenting that it was in English so he could not read it. Would I tell him what I had said in it?

The evidence in that book is rather complex to lend itself to simple summing up, but I managed over the telephone to give him an idea. And I told him one thing I knew would be important to him. When, in conversation with Goetz, I had mentioned the name of Rémy Clément, Goetz had asked, 'Who is that?'

'"Marc". Déricourt's assistant.'

Oh he knew Déricourt had an assistant called 'Marc' but never heard his real name.

I heard the sudden intake of breath over the phone, and I continued to assure him: Goetz had told me he was never given the civil identity of 'Marc'; he had no idea where he lived. He was never trailed. '*Vous n'avez jamais été suivi.*' I felt he would die happy.

Twenty-two

On 29 June I held my *Blavatsky and Her Teachers* in my hand, brought by the morning's post. Now that it was out, I had learned enough Tibetan to realise that there was on p. 289 a mistake. I had said, 'Tibetan is a tone language.' It isn't. Its affinities are not with Chinese but Sanskrit; even the grammar shows this in its preference for the passive over the active tense: not the dog bit the man but the man was bitten by the dog. Curiously enough, though the book has had its critics, not one of them has noticed this mistake. Helen Gething told me someone had told her there was a mistake she had failed to check – something about the speed at which a horse trots. But there, I had had the prudence to consult Shirley Warner, who had participated in a long-distance trotting-race in which all the participants finished in a bunch. She gave me the speed as seven miles an hour.

On 2 July, the first complimentary copy of the *Saint-Germain* reached me, though written so much earlier; looking very nice.

I was speaking again that year at the Theosophical History Conference. My talk was on the Saturday at 2. Erica Lauber warned me Bob Gilbert would be opposing me at 2.30. I said it didn't matter about Bob. She was surprised at my being so blithe. I had not meant to be dismissive only that Bob Gilbert, a fellow antiquarian bookseller, was a friend of Tim's, a good chap and everyone knew he was anti-Blavatsky.

As I knew he would say she could never have got into Tibet, I dealt with that in advance, saying I didn't know why people imagined her having to climb over the Himalayas. When Mother joined her father in Rawalpindi in 1911 they made a holiday trip to Kashmir by horse and houseboat: up the Indus on houseboat towed from the bank by horse, guided by the sayce; then, mounting the horses they crossed land to the River Jhelum, where they re-took the boat. It was at leisure on the boat that Mother made her paintings of the Indian lotus and of the solemnity of the high Himalayas reflected in the water with its fragile flowers (I think I took two or three of them). They had no intention of entering Tibet, but they reached Gilgit and the foot of Mount Haramuk, from which they looked up at its descending glacier, and it was her impression that had they just gone on and on, the same way, they must have crossed into Tibet unless there were guards at the frontier. More recently, the German Heinrich Harrer, escaping from the British internment camp during the Second World War, made his way into Tibet, on foot, along the river banks, by just that route. Erica Lauber, in the front row, was particularly impressed by this part of my talk and said, 'Now that I know there is a much easier way ...'

It was that year, 1988, England was host to the international conference of the Theosophical Society, to be held at Chalfont St Giles. Lilian Storey, the General Secretary, asked me to give one of the talks. I talked about the Coulomb affair. A woman who came up afterwards said what made my talks lively was, 'You act it.' I had never thought about it but perhaps I did. I never write out what I am going to say, as if one has to read from a paper it gets between one and one's audience and prevents direct, spontaneous communication. If I am talking about people, certainly I feel with the people I am talking about and so represent them.

I was by this time considering what my next book should be. I thought to follow the development of theosophical and kindred (and rival) trends from Blavatsky to the present day. I thought of a title: 'The Smoke and the Flame'. I would give most weight to Krishnamurti.

I wrote to Mary Lutyens. (The Huntington Library in San Marino, California, possesses what is known as the Rajagopal Collection. This consists mainly of letters from Krishnamurti to Mary's mother, Lady Emily Lutyens.) Mary invited me to come and have lunch with her in London. She was friendly, informal and easy to talk to. She asked what was the view within the Theosophical Society today of this and that – it was so long since she had been in touch. I told her there would be no official view; if she asked half a dozen members she would probably get as many shades of opinion. She said it was Wedgwood and Arundale who drove Krishna out of the Society; she did not think Arundale would have behaved so badly to him but for the influence of Wedgwood.

'You think Wedgwood was a worse man than Leadbeater?'

'Yes.'

'Was Leadbeater homosexual?'

She had no positive line on this. 'He disliked women in the way that many men who are not homosexual dislike them.'

'Chauvinist?'

'Very chauvinist!' He was very rude to a woman who had come to take a photograph of the group at the Manor. Quite unnecessarily rude. The poor woman was only trying to get all the figures into her viewfinder and asking people to keep their heads still – he was waving his head around looking at his cat as it walked around instead of into the camera – and was quite upset by the way he bellowed at her. Mary Lutyens did not feel with Leadbeater the sense of very positive goodness that she did in the presence of Annie Besant. 'One met her and one felt that she was *good*.'

She said what was needed was a biography of Krishnamurti. '*You* write it.' She had bought my *Blavatsky* and read it and felt I was the right person.

Now it was something I had long ago thought of. I remember that at the moment when my telephone rang to tell me my Mother had died I had been thinking of a biography of Krishnamurti as a thing I might one day do. But then I had seen in a paper that Mary Lutyens was going to do it.

I said, '*You* have written one, in three volumes.'

She said she felt what she had written had more the character of Lutyens family memoirs than a biography.

Perhaps, I said, but that was what gave it its value. It was packed with things that only she and her mother could know.

Yes, in that sense she had made a contribution. But there were areas she had left untouched. There was still a biography to be written and I was the person to do it.

Joe Links, Mary's husband, walked with me afterwards to my coach. 'Mary and I have both had strange lives,' he said, 'especially Mary. I don't understand the teaching but I got on with Krishnamurti well at a personal level.'

I kept in contact with them both, by letter and telephone.

Then there were lectures: one in a pub in Bloomsbury to some social, Leslie Price in the chair; one to the Northampton Lodge of the Theosophical Society, for which I was fetched by the President in her car. I called it 'The Youth of Madame Blavatsky' and told them I had found in the British Museum some short stories by her, which – dictionary in hand, for my Russian was very rusty now – I had managed to make out the gist. She had leaned out of a window with a fishing-rod and fished the toupee off the head of a man passing beneath, revealing his bald scalp. The President laughed and said it showed that as a child, at any rate, she was normal.

In April 1990 I opened a letter from Tim to find enclosed in it a newspaper cutting bearing an obituary of Ivor Cook. I wrote a note of condolence to Jill.

On 9 May I received a reply signed Pippa Carter. She was, she explained, Ivor's stepdaughter, daughter of Jill by her first marriage. Jill had predeceased Ivor, though not by very long. As her father had died when she was small, it was Ivor whom she felt as her father.

She told me of his early background. I thought again about that old book I had written on the Court Lees affair. Cape had declined it only because of fear of a libel action from the Bishop, but perhaps I could re-word some things in a way to avoid that.

Pippa returned to me the whole big box of papers which I had so many years ago returned to him, the transcript of the Inquiry, Ivor's transparencies of the boys' injuries. I set to work.

But Tim suggested I should write to *Private Eye* and ask if they could send me copies of the bits about 'Merve the perve' as they called him. I had always assumed that to be an allusion to his homosexuality, but Tim thought it might be to something else. He had always fancied Mervyn Stockwood was really flagellant – that he suffered from Swinburne's perversion, a liking for beating – at any rate Tim would be interested to see if the *Private Eye* allusions bore this idea out at all. I wrote to them and they sent me, for the mere price of the photostats, a pile of entries concerning him ... 'Merve the perve lives in the diocese of Southwark'. Then I came across a longer piece, 'THE BACON CUTS'. It was in their issue for 22 May 1981, and concerned a girls' school described by the *Eye* as 'a lively centre of caning'. There had been complaints from the parents of the girls who were regularly beaten even on the bottom – but 'nothing can be done because the governors, largely clergy, share the headmasters' pro-caning views ... one notable friend is the former Bishop of Southwark, Dr Mervyn Stockwood.'

How very odd. Tim's hunch appeared to have some foundation.

I had added a contribution to the rather wearied theory about Sickert and the Jack the Ripper crimes. This stemmed from Mother's friendship with Florence Humphrey Holland (*née* Pash), which I have touched on earlier and which also brought me into contact with Barry Humphries, the eminent 'Dame Edna Everage'.

A collector of rare books, Barry had been one of our earliest customers at Fuller d'Arch Smith. He told Tim he wanted anything about Charles Conder, the Australian painter on fans. Tim said there were references to Conder in Mother's unpublished 'Letters to Florence from Sickert, Conder and Moore'. He asked if he might see the text, so I made a photocopy of it and sent it to him.

Tim brought Barry to see me at home. He had read my Sickert book and he asked how Joseph, Sickert's son (now dead), had taken it. Remarkably well, I said. He said his mother told him as a child that Florence was a person whom he should hold in high regard. As for my book, he had rung up to say that it had brought him a visit from three Japanese, who offered him three million 'good English pounds' for his father's old red scarf. (It was a belief of the police that the Ripper killed his victims by strangulation with a scarf.) 'I refused it,' Joseph said. 'It is one of the very few things I have of my father's.'

Barry Humphries was incredulous. It seemed a stupendous amount of money to be refused by an illegitimate son whose father had left him unprovided for. 'Do you believe that story?' he asked. I said, 'Yes.'

Chris Morgan, my publisher at Mandrake, on the fly-leaf of *Sickert and the Ripper Crimes* listing earlier books by the same author, added beneath the list – in spite of our warnings over libel – FORTHCOMING, *In Camera, Ivor Cook and the Court Lees Affair* (Mandrake, 1991). So I looked at the material again, although it never saw the light of day.

First, as he had used the word 'private' I thought I ought to ask Roy Jenkins whether he would allow me to quote a letter from him in the book. He replied (13 May 1991) 'I did not write to you for publication, but on reflection I do not think that there is any compelling reason why you should not quote what I said about Ivor Cook. I shall look forward to your book.'

On the files Pippa Carter had sent me I found the addresses of some of the Court Lees boys, probably out of date by this time, but I wrote to all of them and had two replies. One was from the mother of Robert Downs, chiefly just to confirm the evidence for Mr Cook she had given in court and to say Robert was now 'as well as can be expected'.

The other was from Eric Cuff, who drove all the way to see me from somewhere south of the Thames. As I settled him into an armchair with coffee, he asked, 'Why was I not called to give evidence in court?'

I thought Mr Cook called on the four boys whose injuries he had photographed and the two 'perjury' boys; the others who turned up did so on their own initiative having seen in the papers that the case was coming to court.

He said he would have come if he had seen that it was going to come on. He had been beaten, but worse by Garlick than by Haydon. Garlick would run half the length of the room to get up momentum. 'The cruelties that went on in that place were unimaginable.'

I told him a friend of mine, Irene Ward – he probably wouldn't have heard of her but she was in Parliament at one time – said to me she 'couldn't think why you hadn't all stripped off your clothes and shown your injuries to the Inspectors when they came round'.

It wouldn't have been possible, he said. The Inspector came in with the headmaster, stood beside the headmaster, with them all assembled in front, and said, 'Everything all right?' They couldn't possibly have murmured, and silence was taken for acquiescence. On the subject of useless inspections, Gilby's voice came back into my memory. Whilst at Beckenham he had a retirement job as Inspector of Hospitals. Considering expected inspections to be useless, he never gave notice he was coming but just walked in, and sometimes this incurred the reproach, 'If only you had told us you were coming, Colonel!' But then everything would have been prettied up. He would not have seen anything amiss or untidy. In one place, seeing a row of plates of meat and two vegetables standing on a row of tables, he asked, 'What are those?' 'These are the patients' dinners.' 'But why are they standing unattended, getting cold?' The staff who brought them from the kitchen put them there for the staff who went into the wards to take up. But in the meantime, he pointed out, they were getting cold; and not only would they reach the patients less nice than they should be, but having been uncovered and unattended they could have been settled on by flies. A plate must always be carried by one and the same person from kitchen to patient's bedside, without putting it down anywhere on the way.

Eric Cuff was saying he didn't think this lady could have realised how cowed, how craven they were. 'And we thought they had perhaps the right to do this to us. The Inspector was part of the system.'

But one wonderful thing happened while he was at Court Lees, the Great Train Robbery. That really gave them all a lift!

'You were on the side of the robbers?'

'Oh yes! Even though they were caught in the end it was wonderful what they did. Holding up a train. It was batting against the system.'

But Mr Cook was different. 'The music class was always well attended. Using just one finger of each hand, I could pick out a tune on the piano. Mr Cook was trying to teach me chords.'

They felt Mr Cook was on their side. Reflectively, Cuff said, he felt Mr Cook was 'on our side. In his different way, Mr Cook was batting against the system.'

I wasn't sure that wasn't a bit true of Irene, too. At higher level.

Theosophical History, Leslie's creation, had proved very successful. I had been a contributor from the first issue, my last article for it being about a painting by Albrecht Dürer showing a theosophical symbol. But now the work connected with it had become too much for Leslie and he had parted with it to an American scholar, Dr James Santucci, of the Department of Comparative Religions in the University of San Francisco. Naturally I continued to be one of its contributors, and in 1992 it gave another Conference. This time it was at Point Loma, one-time seat of Katherine Tingley's dissident (i.e. anti-Besant) movement, near San Diego. I felt certain personal curiosity about this place as it was where my great-aunt Annie Dick had been taken by her husband. The date came rather close to a big university do (at which I was to be presented to the Princess Royal, the Chancellor of London University, as one of the graduates who had studied for our degree during the Blitz); but I could get back from the one in time for the other. I was the only person come from England, though several Australians had flown the Pacific to attend. I found myself sitting next to Gregory Tillett, author of the somewhat hostile biography of Leadbeater. My talk was kindly received. Indeed everybody was very kind.

When I came down at breakfast time one morning in 1992, the first thing I noticed was that the lights were on in the sitting-room. Then I saw that things which had been in the Japanese cabinet were lying in a trail over the floor to where the window on to the garden was broken. The silver cups inscribed to my father who had won them in competitions, arranged in a row on one shelf were gone. Gilby's medals! I looked at once in my cabinet, to find my worst fears confirmed. They were gone. My father's medals stolen at Runia's, now Gilby's. It seemed too cruel. A bead bag knitted by Mother, one bead on every stitch, in 1924, was also gone from the cabinet. She would have found it a wry compliment that anybody should have thought it good enough to steal. The worst loss lay in the disappearance of the brass table. I loved that thing, and the brass animals as I had sometimes been allowed to clean as a child. One or two of them I retrieved from the garden, where the thieves had dropped them on their way. The room would never be the same without it. It was part of my childhood. The Japanese cabinet was of course gone, with, incidentally, my christening certificate and other papers in the drawers within it. The beautiful silver spirit-kettle which used to stand on it was gone. A silver-backed mirror which had belonged to Mother's mother was gone, and a tiny vase awarded to Mother as winner of a small golf championship.

But Alexander, my ginger cat, came back. I picked him up into my arms with immense thankfulness.

My insurance company paid up without making difficulties; but it didn't compensate for the loss of things that had been part of my childhood. A social worker called, and asked me, 'How do you *feel*?' I said, 'I feel I would like my things back'. As a condition of renewing my insurance, they wanted me to have alarm bells fitted, not only to my front and back doors but even between different rooms in the house. Though I am grateful to them for having paid up promptly, this seemed to me an impossible condition as the constant ringing of the bell would drive my cats out of their senses, not to mention my neighbours and me. I consulted Stella. She said she would consult John.

John was the eldest son of Ken and Stella. He no longer lived at home, being married with children, but in a house not very far away, and I had met him, though only occasionally, when he called on his parents. He was a qualified electrician and had recently put in all the lighting for a new estate just built outside Bedford. He said an alarm system would be set off by my cats every time they passed through the cat-flap and, 'They can even be set off by a spider.' I should ask my insurance people if they would not accept a security *light*, or find an insurance company which would accept a security light. He would put it in for me, charging nothing for the labour and only what he had to pay for the lamp and wires etc. at the trade price.

Tim recommended an alternative firm of insurers. I wrote to them telling them the whole story and they accepted the installation of a security light. After all, the obvious valuables were gone. (Notwithstanding, I was later subjected to another burglary in which my precious Tibetan prayer-wheel was taken.)

John came, and I remember his looking down from the top of a ladder whilst Charles, the younger son, also an electrician, stood at its foot to give any help needed.

That was in the summer.

On 18 October, whilst I was steaming the coley for the cats, my bell rang. It was Stella. 'I've something to tell you,' she said. 'John is dead.'

I brought her from the hall into the sitting-room.

She said, 'Someone has shot him.'

John had breakfasted as usual with Alison (his wife) and their children Marcus and Holly. Then he went out, as was his regular practice, to take his two dogs for a walk before driving to work.

Somebody then knocked on the family's door and told Alison their two dogs were running about without their master. She knew something must be wrong. Marcus had jumped into his car and driven off in the direction his father would have taken. He turned into the quieter road where his father released the dogs from their leads, and there he found him, lying on the ground, with five bullets in his body.

Stella said, 'John was here yesterday, with Alison, laughing and joking.' None of them had had any premonition ...

Whilst I had known Stella for years, it had been mainly upon the plane to do with our gardens, our cats, and matters of household and local interest. But now she sat down on my sofa and told me a very long story. It suggested, shockingly, a line of inquiry. Then she was gone, leaving me amazed.

It hit not only the local but the national press. There were posters up in Rushden appealing for information. There were police everywhere. The murder was featured on BBC 'Crimewatch'. The two dogs – golden retrievers – shown in the programme were John's own, an actor playing the part of their master, the scene at the breakfast table re-enacted.

The man whose name Stella had mentioned to me had left the country and nobody knew where he had gone. A man suspected by some of having played the role of hit man was tried and acquitted. The police were not looking for anybody else.

None of this is part of my story. And yet it is part of my story because I was so close to those affected and felt the impact.

At the beginning of 1992 I was writing *The Bombed Years*, a sequence of poems recollecting my experience of the Blitz, the 'doodlebugs' and the V2, dedicated 'For my friends of those days and those who were not there in those days to tell them what it was like.' I had indeed started it much earlier, but thought it could suitably appear next year, which would be the fiftieth anniversary of the end of the war with Germany. It was published by Jim Vollmar, himself a poet, from his Greylag Press.

[356]

It was one day during the summer that, whilst walking in Rushden, I felt a sudden twinge in my neck and, in case it should signify anything serious, went to see Dr Lessell. He prescribed for the vein, but, in case I could have anything amiss with my heart referred me to a heart specialist. He saw me, made tests, and at a further consultation reported that my heart was sound. 'You have a strong heart muscle. But it does not always get enough blood come back through the veins.' He would write a report for Dr Lessell, who would doubtless give me something homeopathic (already had done) but in the meantime he gave me digitalis.

I took this for the first time before breakfast the next day, 28 July. On 30 July, driving towards Rushden, I felt a bit odd. But I arrived safely and did my shopping. Then I felt a bit odd as I was walking back to my car. Ought I to drive? To leave in the car park and take a taxi seemed silly. I got into it but I think I knew before I had left the car park I had made a mistake, for as I turned into a street I had what wasn't a blackout but more of a whiteout: everything seemed to have gone white, lost colour and shape. I knew I had hit something – fortunately nothing that mattered.

I don't want to go back to the events of that day. It was the end of driving, for me, as well as the end of taking digitalis.

Tim said he believed I was 'allergic to the whole of conventional medicine'.

Dr Lessell showed me the specialist's report, which suggested the slight occasional dizziness I had mentioned to him might have to do not with my heart but my ears. I remembered being told that ears and balance were connected. I had been using a hearing aid for some years now. Dr Lessell gave me a vitamin B12 injection, which he thought a vegetarian could do with anyway.

Tim and I were discussing Court Lees. He asked me where Fidoe got his unauthorised canes. It had emerged in evidence at the Inquiry that the canes used in Court Lees were not of the authorised type, issued free of charge by the Home Office, but thicker and heavier, which accounted for the broad areas of bruising. Haydon had explained that he did not order them but found them in use at the school when he arrived and therefore assumed them to be the right ones. Violet Thompson, secretary to his predecessor, Fidoe, gave evidence confirming this. Mr Fidoe had told her to order the ones he had marked in a catalogue.

I had suppressed the name in my typescript because I did not want to send it custom, but said, 'Wildman, I think.'

'That's it!'

As the name was meaningful to Tim, I got the transcript out, found the place and showed him. 'Yes. The Eric A. Wildman Tutelage Company.'

'That's it,' Tim said again, a firm that had been in trouble with the police over pornography catering for the flagellant interest.

Something came back to me now. If from Lamb's Conduit Street one turned east up Theobald's Road, then, just before one came to the public library I used when at Guilford Place, there was a newsagents with a board outside carrying advertisements on cards. Most of them were respectable, a second-hand typewriter for sale, kittens free to good homes, but there was always one most repellent one headed, so far as I could remember, 'Society for the Retention of Corporal Punishment'. 'That's Wildman,' said Tim. 'Ivor can't have known or he would have brought it up in his libel actions.'

It came back to me now that Quintin Hogg (later Lord Hailsham) had mentioned in his contribution to the House of Commons Censure Motion that the company supplying the canes had at one time been 'catering for more than one type of clientele'. Ivor had told me he had a vague memory of a case which had got into the newspapers about police having entered and made arrests in a house where there was a party going on in which guests caned one another as a form of entertainment, but as he could not remember either the date or the names of any of the persons concerned he had been unable to look it up in the *Times* index. I felt sure he did not know Wildman advertised on the newsagent's cards.

Tim was really rather staggered. He said, 'Wouldn't you have thought Fidoe would have said to Garlick or Garlick would have said to Fidoe, 'We *can't* order from a firm like that!'

He believed there were Wildman papers in the Private Case. (This is a department in the British Library to which are consigned books and papers the trustees deem indecent. An ordinary reader's ticket used not to give one access; to gain it there was a special paper to be signed.) He asked, 'Would you like me to consult it for you?'

'Yes.'

On his return to London he rang to say he had verified that one of the names Wildman operated under was The National Society for the Retention of Corporal Punishment in Schools and the Corpun Educational Association. The Private Case had six parcels of his papers. 'I'll indent for them.'

A few days later he rang again: 'I've been to the Museum and had out the material.' It was mainly Wildman's typescript magazine. There were instructions as to how to position the boy, how to remove parts of the boy's clothing in the most salacious language.

Most of the material was in the form of letters to Wildman from apparent purchasers of his goods signed with suspiciously pun-like names, such as Belton, for example:

Dear Mr Wildman,
The ten inch spanking tawse arrived yesterday ... We have had a girl of nearly ten and a boy of fourteen who have been getting thoroughly out of hand.

Lascivious enjoyment was transparent in the announcement:

... We have obtained a supply of freshly cut 'cherry' birch and are in a position to supply well manufactured birch-rods ... Rods may conveniently be preserved ... by immersion in brine.

Tim said, 'There were seven parcels of the stuff. I waded through two of them, then couldn't face any more.'

But then, he wondered aloud, how did Fidoe come to have its catalogue in his study? Was it supplied to Court Lees gratis? 'Or was Fidoe a subscriber?'

From David Harvey, President of the Bristol Lodge of the Theosophical Society, I had a letter in August 1996 saying he had been interested by my monograph on Joan Grant and would like to talk to me about it. When we met he asked if I had thought of writing something comparable on Cyril Scott.

I knew it was an open secret that the three *Initiate* books were by him, but no, I hadn't thought of writing about him.

He wished I would. From the reincarnationist point of view, there was interest. Scott believed he had been Chopin.

I rang Tim. He had always heard that Scott's wife, Rose, née Allatini, was an interesting person in herself, had written a controversial novel under a pseudonym ... yes, might be interesting to go into.

For the Theosophical History Conference of 1997 I was put down for a talk on Cyril Scott. Leslie Price was in the chair – a necessity for me as he 'translated' in his familiar clear voice the questions I could never hear coming from the back of the hall, even with my hearing aid.

Peter Michel had introduced himself by telephone call from Germany. He was writing a book on Leadbeater, showing him in a better light than had Tillett, and Radha Burnier (President of The Theosophical Society as a whole) had given him my number, saying if he had any difficulty with the English background he should ask help from me. He was very interested to hear that I was writing a piece on Cyril Scott, as he had read Scott's *Initiate* trilogy and some of his other works and would like to know what I made of him. He had read several of my books.

Santucci, however, expressed himself in some difficulty over the publication of my *Scott*; it was a good deal longer than my *Joan Grant*, the means at his disposal were restricted. Would I consider contributing to the cost of production? I felt it was one thing to give one's work for nothing to a prestigious publication but I did not expect to be asked to pay for it.

David Harvey at once offered to produce it for nothing from his and his wife's Ladybird Press, but Peter Michel felt that *Theosophical History* was the proper place for it; it should take its place amongst the *Theosophical History Occasional Supplements* and if the magazine could not stretch its finances so far, he, Peter Michel, would pay their printers' bill. And so it was that *Cyril Scott and a Hidden School* appeared from *Theosophical History* in 1998.

Peter Michel also expressed great interest in the news that I was writing a biography of Krishnamurti. He himself had written a book, *Krishnamurti Freiheit und Liebe*, which he had published from his own Aquamarin Verlag, Grafing. He sent me the English translation of it, *Krishnamurti, Live and Freed*, published by Blue Star, Woodside, California, and said he would like to see mine when sufficiently advanced. I began to wonder if he was thinking of making an offer for the German rights.

I reached the end of the first draft in October 1998. I would still have things to insert. Leslie Price, for instance, had told me he had stumbled on a long letter from Annie Besant to her lawyer about the Krishnamurti custody case, in what used to be the India Office Library, now in the British Library. He could tell me what floor it was on, and that it was indexed under David Graham Pole Papers and not under Besant, which was doubtless why Theosophists had missed it for so long. It would be quite a thing to be able to put in my book. I found it and copied it out.

On 6 April, the contract arrived from Peter Michel: not only for German translation rights but for world rights in my book *Krishnamurti and the Wind*. For rights in the English language original, application would therefore have to be made to him. If leasing it to an ordinary commercial publishing company it would be at the normal rates but if the application came from one of the Theosophical publishing houses, then he would be soft with them, regarding it as a service to the light.

It had been on 18 December 1998 that I had been called on by two people representing Carlton TV, initially 'just for a talk'. They would return with their camera crew. The subject was Déricourt. At once cautious, I asked from what point of view they intended showing him. 'Without bias' the one who appeared to be in charge assured me.

It was some time before I heard from them again. Then, on 27 July 1999, the same man called for me and drove me to the Holiday Inn outside Wellingborough, where his colleague was waiting for us with the camera crew. They had hired a room as a studio. It was his colleague who asked the questions but I could not see him as he sat behind a very bright light that was shone in my face. I was told his voice would be blotted out so that I would appear to be spontaneously reminiscing, but I was not told anything about the editing of what I had said. It lasted for perhaps two or three hours and was very tiring. They then took me to lunch with them at a hotel in Wellingborough. Since that time I had heard no more from them.

Then, on 30 January 2000, Stella brought me a copy of the *Sunday Express*. There was a trailer for the programme to which I had contributed, 'Churchill's Secret Army'. It was to be shown over three Sunday evenings. I appeared on screen in the second and third parts. My first shock was that I looked dreadful. Tim was sweet and said it was because I had been given harsh lighting. Much worse was that what I said had been so edited that only those things that could be used against Déricourt had been left in and everything I said in his favour left out. I had been a fool. I had forgotten my first rule, in dealing with the media, never say anything that, quoted out of context, could belie my meaning. I wrote to the people I had dealt with. The one who had asked the questions agreed with me the editing had been unfair but told me the un-edited text had been placed in the Imperial War Museum, where anybody could see it upon application. I was glad of this information, though, as I pointed out, few people, if any, would think of visiting the Imperial War Museum and filing an application to see the transcript, whereas large numbers would have watched what was shown on television, unsuspecting that what they were being shown was unfairly edited. There was no further reply. I wrote a letter to the *TV Times* but it was not printed.

Hugh Verity told me on the telephone that he wished he had not taken part in that programme, as his words, 'I remember that', meaning seeing Déricourt go through the hatch when dropped in May, had got misplaced before the mention of a controversial episode alleged to have taken place in the later summer of which he had no recollection. And Arthur Watt (Déricourt's radio operator) both wrote to me and rang me: he was distressed that the programme was 'very anti-Déricourt – and anti-Bodington, too'. On a more personal note, he regretted having given two hours of his time for two minutes on screen for no pay. My case differed from his in that I had been given considerably more than two minutes on screen, but wished I had not.

In the meantime, my film agent reported that she had secured me an option on *Madeleine*. A contract from Matrix Movies, belonging to Ellen Burstyn, arrived for my signature on 28 January 2000, and on 17 February 2000 Ms Burstyn, over on a brief visit from America, came to see me. Any fears I might have had concerning the ability of an American to understand Noor's Sufi background were dispelled by her telling me she was a pupil of Vilayat. I had not heard from Vilayat in many years, and she had seen him only days ago and told me about the teaching he was giving in California. She set up a video-tape apparatus so that her questions and my replies were recorded, and turned the machine to photograph all my paintings on my walls. Then her chauffeur took pictures of the two of us together. Afterwards there arrived a most enormous bouquet of flowers from her.

10 June 2000 brought a letter from France signed 'Josette Bossard'. She was the wife of Alain Bossard, son of Benjamin Bossard, an important member of the 'Prosper' network, whose home had been a 'letter-box' for the network. She had read my books, of course, and her letter was to prove the foundation-stone of a considerable correspondence. The most important of her discoveries was the date of 'Prosper's' 1943 return to the field. She noted that this was given by me (as it was given me by Madame Balachowsky) as 30 June, and by Foot as 12 June. In her submission, we were both wrong; it was 30 May. Having looked at the photocopied material she sent me, I realised she was right.

The importance lay in the fact that it put out of court a contention

[362]

of certain writers that between 'Prosper's' leaving France, for England on the night of 13/14 May 1943 and his return to France, he was received in London by Winston Churchill and deliberately misinformed by him of the time and place of the Invasion so that, on his coming arrest by the Germans, he would break down and pass them this misinformation. Churchill was out of England from 4 May till 6 June. It was a particularly shabby contention in any case, and now conclusively disproved.

Twelve years had elapsed since I first wrote to Robert Marshall about that typescript novel Déricourt had had his secretary post to me, which, arriving whilst I was in Carthage, had been returned by the post office to his Paris address. This time, Marshall said if I would post him the price of photocopying, he would send it. It arrived on 3 October 2000. I sat down that very day to begin the translating.

Déricourt had a dislike of slang and never used it, but some of the characters in his stories did – for the book he had written proved to be not so much a novel as a rather odd assemblage of loosely related stories. Tim sent me a dictionary of French slang, in which I found the most extraordinary expressions, but there was one that still beat me. A character put on his 'air de Jocrisse'. What was meant? On the morning of Christmas Day Tim telephoned a French publisher of his acquaintance and asked, who or what was Jocrisse? And the answer came immediately. A stock character of French farce. A person to whom any story can be told and he will believe it – a simpleton.

Michael Russell had published *Déricourt: The Chequered Spy*, so naturally it was to him I sent *Espionage as a Fine Art translated from the French of Henri Déricourt*. It was he who thought out the design for the dust jacket, rather echoing the positive and negative prints of the photographs which I thought so clever.

Since the days when I was first authorised, at the instance of Irene, to put questions to Colonel Boxshall to answer from his inspection of the papers at the Foreign Office, the SOE advisers – now the title of a succession of them – had been becoming steadily more cordial, the last of them Duncan Stuart. With his retirement, at the end of the year 2001, the office would end. There was to be no future incumbent, and Duncan Stuart was sorting out what could now be made public and throwing it over to the Public Record Office at Kew, where application for sight of it could be made in the normal way. On 28 December I received from him, as a parting gift, the whole file on Noor Inayat Khan, in photostat, also some pictures looked out for me by his kind secretary Valerie Collins. Duncan Stuart told me I would still be able to contact him at the Special Forces Club.

I had finished the translation of Déricourt's curious book of stories, *Espionage as a Fine Art*, supplied an introduction and extended commentary and sent it to Michael Russell. I had been in touch with Colyn Boyce, who had undertaken charge of the production of my *Krishnamurti*, including the typesetting, and the result was the new year 2002 found me correcting the first pages of the proofs of the *Krishnamurti* whilst still receiving those of Déricourt from Michael Russell. At the very same time, starting January 2002, Chris Morgan of Mandrake was sending proofs of his new edition of the paperback of *The Magical Dilemma of Victor Neuburg* – a more elegant edition than his 1990 paperback. Three very different sets of vibrations to tune into, Neuburg, Déricourt and Krishnamurti. We could hardly lift our eyes out of proofs. I was worried for Tim's; he was a much better proof-reader than I was but had had trouble with his eyes, and, to keep at bay an incipient glaucoma, was putting daily drops in them, prescribed by a London specialist.

A new book about Michael Ventris appeared, *The Man Who Deciphered Linear B*, by Andrew Robinson (Thames & Hudson, 2002). As Mother had written to the author of the earlier study *The Decipherment of Linear B*, John Chadwick (Cambridge, 1958), I now wrote to the author of the new work and he sent my letter on to the BBC, who were doing a programme based on it. On 21 May their Hannah Beekman and Michael Watts arrived with filming apparatus. I talked to them about Colonel Ventris and Dora, their having been pupil-patients of Carl Jung, and told them I actually met Michael though it was when he was only two and preoccupied with assembling toy bricks into the semblance of a house. (His formal adult qualification was not as a classics scholar but as an architect.) They were appalled when I told them Michael had never been touched. Never a hug or a cuddle. They seemed to think that could explain much. I got out for them one of Mother's old photograph albums and showed one of a group of officers, pointing out, 'That one is Colonel Ventris.' They took a close-up picture of it.

The programme on Michael Ventris, 'A Very English Genius', was to be transmitted on 22 July, on BBC 4. It was beautifully done. And to my relief, I looked all right this time. The film introduced Tessa, the daughter of Michael Ventris. She said, 'I admired my father. I did not like him.' That cast a chill and was not explained. I thought that strange upbringing, in a virtual vacuum, intended to allow him to be free of complexes, might have made it difficult for him, when he grew up, to respond to wife and child. I wrote to her; but had no reply.

Espionage as a Fine Art was published in November 2002. On Saturday 25 January 2003 Sarah Helm came to see me. She had come when she was thinking of writing a biography of Vera Leigh, one of the agents who had escaped the attention of other writers. But she had now changed her subject to that of a different Vera. She had a commission to write a biography of Vera Atkins, and had access to her family papers. I felt her work would be serious and was very interested by some of the things she had to tell me. These seemed to deepen both her Communist and her German connections. Sarah referred to a passage in *Espionage as a Fine Art*, p. 183, wherein I had spoken of Miss Atkins's disclosure to me of her Communist sympathies. She confirmed this. Vera went to Communist meetings and the like, and was perhaps more innerly involved. Then she flashed out with, 'I wonder you didn't think she might be a straight German agent.'

This took me by surprise. I said. 'She was Jewish. I can't imagine a Jewish person wanting the Nazis to win.'

'Not by conviction. By blackmail.'

I didn't know she had anything to be blackmailed about. Besides, I would have thought she would have been strong-minded enough to resist pressures. It was true Sarah Helm had just mentioned to me family connections of Miss Atkins who might be under German pressures, and I remembered that at the Censorship they did not like people to have relatives who could be in German hands in case threats to harm these relatives could create a compromising situation. But I certainly had no grounds to suspect Miss Atkins of any ambivalent loyalties.

On Tuesday 17 June I received a letter from Duncan Stuart, no longer on the paper of the Foreign Office. He had read *Espionage as a Fine Art*. Déricourt, he thought, 'is too much the *poseur* and this comes across as unsympathetic, and consequently as a poor apologist for himself. But who should know this better than you?'

> ... I cannot comment as comprehensively as I would like on your Introduction and Commentary, which are by far and away the most important part of the book. But I have a few observations.

First of all, the facts that you have gathered over the years about Déricourt and others elicited from whose who knew them, including the Germans, add enormously to what is available in official papers and are often uniquely valuable to any attempt to understand what happened. I believe that you are in touch with Francis Suttill junior, who is pursuing his own quest for truth with commendable energy and common sense, and will know that he has also dug up the odd new item. For example he has seen Churchill's appointments diary and thus usefully added to your very convincing demolition of the Marshall/Maloubier fantasy. But neither he nor anyone else, including Foot, can match your collection of evidence in the post-war period.

When Tim came up for my birthday, 2003, the *Krishnamurti* proofs now done, I said to him, 'What am I going to write now?'
'Your autobiography.'
'No.'
I had made, in days long past, one or two attempts, only to abandon them. More recently, Martin Booth had urged me to do it but I had said impossible.
'Too many things I would have to leave out.'
'Occult?' asked Tim.
'And other.'
Well, let's see.
After he had gone I typed out a few pages and wrote by hand over the top 'DRIVEN TO IT'.

Index

advances from Slaughter, resigns, 52;
Bragg-Liddell Shakespearean
Company, 52–6; Joseph Bloor's
company, 56–7; Maurice Hansard's
company, 57–8; Billy Lynn Repertory
Company, 58 **drawing and painting**: 3,
4, 11–12 (exhibited), 17, 18, 20, 21,
24–5, 46, 50, 69; and Académie Julien,
116–18; submits painting to Royal
Academy, 123; and Camberwell School
of Art, 123, 126; *faux naïf* style, 176;
fuchsia, 249; Iceland, 272 **occult**:
36–7, 62–3, supernatural experience,
89–90 **pets**: 4, 5, 14, 15, 19–20, 27–8,
30–1; dog Taffy, 35; Siamese kitten
Bast, 115, 123 **piano**: 336–7 **riding**:
14–15, 21–2, 56, 335 **Theosophy**: 88;
author's great-aunt a Theosophist, 91;
'kundalini', 97, 108, 111; Madame
Blavatsky, 97, 104, 107, 115, 127,
177, 350; Krishnamurti, 44–5, 110,
115, 128, 138, 270, 349–50; Lodge,
176; contact with 'Vivian' in Paris,
107–8, 109, 110, 111, 113, 115, 118,
177; Convention in Paris, 113; idea for
book, 349; Theosophical History
Conference, 348–9, 353–4; Cyril Scott
monograph in *Theosophical History*,
360 **writing and publications**: 59,
poems, 59–60; novel, 64; prize for
poem, 70; *African Violets*, poems, 285;
Blavatsky and Her Teachers, 127, 337,
346, 348, 350; *The Bombed Years*,
356; *The Comte de Saint-Germain*,
335, 348; *Cyril Scott and a Hidden
School* (monograph), 359–60; *Darun
and Pitar* 285; *Déricourt: The
Chequered Spy*, 215; research, 302ff,
340, 343–4; title and cover, 343; for
background *see also* Déricourt, Henri;
Double Webs, 215, 237, 238–9, 245;
French edition abandoned, 249;
paperback update, 297; *Espionage as a
Fine Art* (ed.), 364–5, 365–6; *The
German Penetration of S.O.E.*,
309–10, 327; *Horoscope for a Double
Agent*, 252; 'In Camera, Ivor Cook and
the Court Lees Affair', 326, 352;
further research for, 352–3; *Joan
Grant: Winged Pharaoh* (monograph),
359; *Krishnamurti and the Wind*,
360–1; *Madeleine*, contacts Vera
Atkins, 130–1; visits Yolande Lagrave,
132–3, 134; Starr, 135–7; Baroness van

Tuyll (Noor's illustrator), 137–8;
interview with Buckmaster, 138; meets
Noor's acquaintances in Paris, 139–40,
145ff, 153–4; meetings with Vogt,
155–72; further research, 173–6;
publication, 177; reviews and author's
response, 178–9; film option on, 362;
see also Inayat Khan, Noor; *The
Magical Dilemma of Victor Neuburg*,
proposes, 254–5; meetings relating to,
255–60; writing, 262; 266–7;
paperback, 364; *Shelley: A Biography*,
uncertainty over agent, 266, 268;
272–3; accepted, 279; proofs, 283;
finished copies, 284–5; *TLS* review,
285; *Sickert and the Ripper Crimes*,
351–2; *Sir Francis Bacon: A Biography*,
334; *The Starr Affair*, 183–5; quoted in
*Third Report of the Parliamentary
Commissioners*, 285; 340; *Swinburne:
A Biography*, proposed, 279; Anthony
Powell reviews, 288; flagellation
protest, 288–9; *Tintagel*, 295; *Venus
Protected*, 262

Fuller, Captain John Henry (author's
father), killed in East Africa, 1; sepoys
recall, 1–2; 'Dalai Lama' visits, 10–11;
39; medals stolen, 85; 281–2

Fuller, Violet Overton (*née* Smith,
author's mother), 1–2; move to
Beckenham, 2; as artist, 3; encourages
author's drawing and painting, 3–4,
11–12; piano, 6, 21; 7; questioned over
author's education, 8; and religion,
8–9, 10; and 'Dalai Lama', 10–11; and
Gilby's remarriage, 14; moves to
London hotel, 17; studio, 21; holidays,
22; takes author to *Treasure Island*,
25; moves to Brighton, 26; operations,
27, 30; Lugano and Paris, 32–5; and
Lady Northey, 39; and author's fever,
40; moves back to London, 42; makes
dresses for author's stage appearances,
46; appears on stage, 50; and Gilby's
illness and death, 51–2; recalls author
to London, 56; friend Tom, 56, 71, 72,
77; and author's twenty-first birthday,
71; meets Neuburg, 72; returns to
London, 76; and bombing hazards,
81–2; 85, 91; finds author new flat,
96–7; and liberation of Paris, 102; and
VE Day, 103–4; 115; and Florence
Humphrey Holland, 117, 351; relates
Jack the Ripper theories, 118–22; 151,